NEW ENGLAND INSTITUTE
OF TECHNOLOGY
LEARNING RESOURCES CENTER

AUTOBIOGRAPHY &
POSTMODERNISM

E D I T E D   B Y

K A T H L E E N   A S H L E Y

L E I G H   G I L M O R E

G E R A L D   P E T E R S

The University of Massachusetts Press   *Amherst*

This book is published with the support and cooperation
of the University of Massachusetts at Boston.
Copyright © 1994 by
The University of Massachusetts Press
All rights reserved
Printed in the United States of America
LC 93–32437
ISBN 0–87023–899–x (cloth); 900–7 (pbk.)
Designed by Mary Mendell
Set in Adobe Caslon by Keystone Typesetting, Inc.
Printed and bound by Thomson-Shore, Inc.

Library of Congress Cataloging-in-Publication Data
Autobiography and postmodernism / edited by Kathleen Ashley,
    Leigh Gilmore, Gerald Peters.
        p.   cm.
    Includes bibliographical references.
    ISBN 0–87023–899–x (alk. paper) — ISBN 0–87023–900–7 (pbk.; alk. paper)
    1. American prose literature—20th century—History and criticism.
2. English prose literature—History and criticism.
3. Postmodernism (Literature).   4. Autobiography.
I. Ashley, Kathleen M., 1944–   .   II. Gilmore, Leigh, 1959–   .
III. Peters, Gerald, 1952–   .
PS366.A88A92   1994
828'.910809492—dc20   93–32437
                                    CIP

British Library Cataloguing in Publication data are available.

Contents

∎

PART IV **"I am truly becoming a specter"**

Preface

∎

This collection of essays grew out of a conference on the Subject of Autobiography held in Portland, Maine, during the fall of 1989. A majority of the essays were given as short papers and then substantially expanded and revised for the book. The other essays not given at the conference were solicited for the volume. Only Andrei Codrescu's banquet speech appears here in its original form.

We acknowledge a generous grant from the Maine Humanities Council in support of the Autobiography Conference. University of Southern Maine's English Department and Dave Davis, dean of the College of Arts and Sciences, also contributed to the original project, and the organizational abilities of Willard Rusch were invaluable. We are also grateful to the following English majors who assisted in running the conference: Mark Bishop, Jim Jellison, Marlene Kenney, Kathy Polhemus, Glen Powell, Jessica Reisman, and Tim Stover.

In keeping up with contributors and in assembling this volume, Michael Mulhall's assistance has been much appreciated. A special word of thanks must go to Paul Wright, editor at the University of Massachusetts Press, who has been with the book since the beginning. After attending the conference, he solicited the collection of essays we planned and has been persistent and patient throughout the long process of bringing this book to publication.

Finally, this volume and the conference that preceded it testify to the value of collaborative work. Our joint efforts over the past four years on various autobiography projects have proved that collaboration can bring both profit and pleasure.

Acknowledgments

Leigh Gilmore's "Policing Truth: Confession, Gender, and Autobiographical Authority" appeared in different form in her *Autobiographics,*

PART I

Introduction

The Mark of Autobiography: Postmodernism, Autobiography, and Genre

LEIGH GILMORE

■

Every text participates in one or several genres, there is no genreless text; there is always a genre and genres: yet such participation never amounts to belonging. And not because of an abundant overflowing or a free, anarchic, and unclassifiable productivity, but because of the trait of participation itself.—Jacques Derrida, "The Law of Genre"

It is indispensable to develop a theory of the subject as a decentered, detotalized agent, a subject constructed at the point of the intersection of a multiplicity of subject positions between which there exists no a priori or necessary relation and whose articulation is the result of hegemonic practices.—Chantal Mouffe, "Radical Democracy: Modern or Postmodern"

The essays in this volume respond to the following questions: What do the theories, methods, and insights of postmodernism allow us to know about autobiography? What do the techniques, practices, and cultures of autobiography reveal about postmodernism? Autobiography, as a self-representational practice that is complexly situated within cultures, and autobiography studies, as an increasingly transdisciplinary critical practice, have incorporated postmodernist techniques and critiques with a variety of results. It seems appropriate, therefore, to consider the mutual historicization of autobiography and postmodernism, especially in the context of their shared interest in theorizing the subject. Rather than articulating a shared vision of postmodernism's possibilities and liabilities, the essays in this volume expose how postmodernism's performance of questioning not only intersects with but powerfully structures contemporary interest in autobiography.[1]

The critical potential of postmodernism is explored in this volume through an emphasis on the subject as an agent in discourse, where the subject itself is understood as necessarily discursive.[2] These essays take up Chantal Mouffe's call for a theorization of the subject, for they view autobiography and other forms of self-representation through the lens of postmodernism, as a site of identity production; as texts that both resist and produce cultural identities. The concern throughout is less with what postmodernism *is*, in any ultimate sense, than in what it *does,* and what can be done with it.[3] Projects that seek to define postmodernism's internal properties, its own identity, presume, if only provisionally, that postmodernism is a stable and grounded entity, that it is an antifoundational practice that nonetheless possesses a foundation.[4] The essays here put forward the collective argument that postmodernism's potential as a critical method is on the historical move, its relation to autobiography reciprocal and contested. Moreover, postmodernism is most useful to the study of self-representation when an ensemble of cultural, historical, and textual practices are viewed in their specific performances.

While postmodernism's effects have been felt throughout many institutions at the end of the twentieth century, we are still trying to say what hit us.[5] This has been no less the case in autobiography studies than it has been generally in the practice of literary and cultural studies. A glance at the history of autobiography studies reveals that at the end of the 1970s, just as the challenges to traditional modes of scholarly practice posed by more explicitly political forms of criticism and theory were affecting the academy, the study of autobiography was being remade. Two collections of essays published in 1980 inaugurated a new wave of interest: *Women's Autobiography: Essays in Criticism,* edited by Estelle C. Jelinek, and *Autobiography: Essays Theoretical and Critical,* edited by James Olney, were characterized by the vital conjunction of autobiography and emerging forms of criticism.[6] Jelinek's collection situated feminist criticism in relation to autobiography, and Olney's collection examined autobiography through a range of emerging poststructuralisms. Together, they demonstrated the impact of contemporary theory on the field; moreover, in both volumes there was evidence of an emerging critical focus on the mechanisms of value by which some autobiographers and autobiographical practices had been marginalized.

The essays in this volume, too, represent a historical moment in autobiography studies, one that is characterized by disciplinary experimentation, an interest in the politics of writing in the first person, and a reconceptualization of the relations between ethnicity, gender, race, sexuality, and differing forms of representation.[7] Certainly, postmodernism calls all categorical thinking into question along with the modes by which categories are consolidated and maintained. In terms of autobiography and autobiography studies, the categories under scrutiny are not only those by which genre is constituted, but critical interest itself. Even more specifically, literary and cultural studies in postmodernism have focused on the analytical and experiential category of "the self" and the limits of its representation. The essays in this volume turn their attention to the "self," as it has been constructed in and by autobiography, by questioning the methodologies that produce and reproduce its cultural identity. By situating self-representation in relation to a range of critical and disciplinary texts, a context of inquiry emerges that challenges autobiography's previous generic definition. The conjunction of postmodernism and autobiography seems particularly salient when many are questioning *what* autobiography represents at the same time they are wondering what postmodernism *is*. The foundations upon which inquiries into ontology and identity build are "answered" through the constructed references between "literary text" and "critical context," which, in turn, creates the referential effect of identity categories: is postmodernism an identity? can one *be* postmodern or be a postmodernist? is it a name one calls oneself, or is it designated by? is it a collectivity? an orientation? a discipline itself, even if it crosses disciplinary boundaries?[8]

The rumblings of postmodernist debate have also shaken the constructed foundations of autobiography studies. In traditional studies of autobiography the terms that are likely to shift within postmodernism—particularly history and subjectivity—are taken as the stable elements in the story of one's life. Texts that affirm this stability, or that can be construed as affirming it, form the "tradition" of autobiography. Clearly, the time has come to consider the implications of genre for autobiography. Postmodernism's skepticism about generic typology, as the critics in this volume show, offers useful conceptual leverage for the task. The insights of some postmodernisms into the functioning of ideology and representation offer an occasion to rethink the relation between autobiography and its tradition, as well as the status of autobiography as a genre. Currently, the study of autobiography flourishes and is concerned with texts that would previously have been barred from consideration as "autobiography." The Augustinian lineage drawn by traditional studies of autobiography has naturalized the self-representation of (mainly) white, presumably heterosexual, elite men. Efforts to establish a genre of autobiography based on the works of Augustine, Rousseau, Henry Adams, and so on, must be seen as participating in the cultural production of a politics of identity, a politics that maintains identity hierarchies through its reproduction of class, sexuality, race, and gender as terms of "difference" in a social field of power.

A postmodernist critique already skeptical of genre finds the non-classical and only-recently-shored-up "genre" of autobiography an apt focus. While on the one hand, most traditional critics of autobiography have sought to argue for autobiography's generic coherence and historical continuity in order to win some space in the tightly contested arena of literary studies, many postmodern explorations, on the other hand, seek to do without or do away with the definitional heft and limits provided by genre theory.[9] What one can know about a text and what a writer can be seen as representing in a text are, obviously, generically (over)determined. And it is precisely this limit of representability defined by genre's line in the textual sand that is crossed in this volume.

When we shift away from the effort to define autobiography as a genre, the debates about autobiography's status reveal much about genre theory itself. For example, autobiography has often been seen as insufficiently objective because the eyewitness may be simultaneously the most sought after and most suspect interpreter of events. At the same time, autobiography has been spurned as insufficiently subjective (or imaginative) because it relies too much on the constraints of the real to be taken as art. Thus autobiography has fallen outside both fiction and history. Despite its defenders' efforts to win it some space in the hierarchy of genre, the form of the problem is more to the point here because such critical maneuvers avoid autobiography's contradictory nature. Construing autobiography as a genre has depended, at least in part, on domesticating its specific weirdness. Its doubled nature confounds definition through preexisting generic categories, even as the judgment of its duplicity follows from those categories. What we can call autobiography's resistance to genre can now be taken as a crisis in genre itself, rather than the cause of autobiography's dismissal or rehabilitation.

In "The Mark of Gender," Monique Wittig analyzes the grammatical category of gender and the ideological implications of this mark.[10] Following her in this line, I would claim that there is also a mark of autobiography, a mark that can be located provisionally in the always problematical deployment of the **I**. As we know from Jakobson, Benveniste, and others, the **I** does not properly refer.[11] To the extent that definitions of autobiography derive from the reference between the person who says **I** and the **I** that is not a person but a function of language, these definitions can always be destabilized through reference to this dissonance. But this problematic should also be contextualized in terms of self-representation: what readings of autobiography are possible when the linguistic element upon which one would most wish to depend for some sense of stability, some sense of being at home in a word, offers both collectivity and individuality? What writings of autobiography are possible when the autonomous self is not the privileged speaker, when the mark of autobiography—the I—may designate a place from which to speak, an authority in some discourses and not others, the signature of self-representation wherever it appears?

Although much criticism of autobiography returns to the questions of reference just raised, the point for the critics and autobiographers represented here lies in the potential for reconfigurations of autobiographical identity in relation to a variety of discourses rather than in further inspecting autobiography's relation to the "real."[12] I would claim further, that the mark of autobiography, figured by the I, attaches to other more stable genres, as in the catachrestical "autobiographical novel." Thus while the mark of autobiography might first be specified in terms of a linguistic function, its implications for the politics of genre are more in line with the interests in this volume. Specifically, the mark of autobiography disrupts the simpler designation of Cindy Sherman as photographer, Julian of Norwich as mystic, Carmen Martín Gaite as novelist. It calls into question those generic frames and their classic hierarchies. The mark of autobiography indicates a disruption in genre, an eruption or interruption of self-representation in genres in which it has not been previously legitimated.

Furthermore, although many writers indicate the genres in which they are operating, their own designation may be called into question by critics who use the mark of autobiography to authorize or deauthorize the work. The mark of autobiography may delegitimate (as in, "this is not a novel, but an 'autobiographical' novel") or elevate ("this is not merely an autobiography, but an epic," or lyric, etc.). The crisis that structures autobiographical form as a crisis in genre is an evaluative one. The mark of autobiography is a discursive effect, an effect of reading in relation to certain discourses, defined through the simultaneous assembling and disassembling of other discourses and genres. Thus, the mark of autobiography creates an enlivening instability in both text and context. But it is also, to be sure, a crisis in the hierarchy of autobiographical identities, for it is the autobiographer who becomes the site of meaning in this activity as producer of meaning and organizer of knowledge. The critics here, then, are more likely to recognize how a variety of self-representational texts, many of which have not previously been called autobiographies, have failed at being assimilated into pure generic classifications, and have thus resisted being coopted into the service of autobiography's post-Enlightenment project of saving autobiography for the politics of individualism.

The Essays

The essays are grouped under two headings: "The thing that's most exciting is contradictory versions" and "I am truly becoming a specter." These headings are drawn from texts discussed in the first essay of each section and are meant to suggest the general theoretical focus of the section as well as the self-representational practices described. Preceding the scholarly treatments of autobiography is an essay by Andrei Codrescu, Romanian expatriate, autobiographer, and National Public Radio correspondent, that enacts the boundary-blurring between Art and Life on the grounds of self-representation central to postmodernism's inquiry into categories. As if in a dream, or nightmare, of increasing self-reflexivity, Codrescu explores autobiography as a performance played before others who witness (and may judge) how writing itself is one way of "Adding to My Life." It is an autobiographical mise en scène focused on the always-complicated position of the ones who represent themselves.

The first section explores the politics of genre through contradictions in the discourses of self-representation. In contrast to those critics of postmodernism who fear for the human subject and human agency, the critics here offer critiques of dominant constructions and representations of the subject and the political and social forms of agency, but in an important sense they demonstrate that autobiography gives postmodernism a text and a discourse through which to theorize human agency. The lamentably decentered human agent of so many postmodernisms does not emerge here as *the* subject of autobiography; rather, we see human agents as producers of discourse who tend to heighten the contradictions in the discourses of self-representation and let those form the explanation for disruption or discontinuity. The subjects of these essays record the effects of fragmentation and generate further contradiction by claiming to do two things simultaneously; hence, the subtitle of the first grouping of essays, drawn from Christopher Ortiz's essay on Carmen Martín Gaite's *Back Room:* "the most exciting thing is contradictory versions."

Arguing for the disruptive effects of contradictory self-representation, Christopher Ortiz explores the link between genre and gender in "The Politics of Genre in Carmen Martín Gaite's *Back Room*." Ortiz argues that both genre and gender have been naturalized; that is, their functions and forms have grown so familiar that we no longer perceive the processes by which this has happened, nor the ideological work such naturalization performs. Ortiz presses the argument about familiarity to question the generic "strangeness" of autobiography and how its refusal to obey the "laws of genre and gender" has been viewed in the case of *The Back Room* as a failure in the text rather than as an interrogation and disruption of genre itself. His analysis focuses on how "woman" is a "genre" and on how specific women have resisted their genericization.

The critique of genre is further enjoined in "Policing Truth: Confession, Gender, and Autobiographical Authority," in which I describe confession as a discursive practice that produces and polices "truth," "gender," and "identity." I argue that autobiography recuperates the technologies of self-representation present in the confession and deploys them to authorize and deauthorize certain "identities." Indeed, as I demonstrate, autobiography draws its social authority from its relation to culturally dominant discourses of truth-telling and not, as has previously been asserted, from autobiography's privileged relation to real life. The extent to which the discourses of "truth" and "lying" underwrite aesthetic production and judgment is further explored through an analysis of how critical language participates in policing truth by criminalizing certain autobiographers.

Michael Fischer's essay describes the uses of autobiography in the development of a postmodern anthropology. According to Fischer, autobiography and ethnography have overlapping interests in first-person accounts; autobiography offers a "native point of view" that is otherwise only accessible through the "in-depth interview." For Fischer, autobiography offers a way of overcoming the limits of traditional social theory that would require the autobiographer to construct a life account according to the researcher's limited self-representational models. Yet multicultural identities that are not identical to that form of self-representation are nonetheless represented through its constraints. Ultimately, then, autobiography can be looked to as a site where clues for new social theory can be found, clues that exceed the limits of autobiography or social theory as they are traditionally understood.

In "Postmodernism and the Autobiographical Subject: Reconstructing the 'Other'," Betty Bergland draws on a range of theories in order to move the subject of autobiography into the field of postmodern theory. In a strategy meant to recontextualize the subject, she asks, "do we read at the center of the autobiography a 'self,' an *essentialist individual*, imagined to be coherent and unified, the originator of her own meaning; or do we read a *postmodern subject*—a dynamic subject that changes over time, is situated historically in the world and positioned in multiple discourses?" This displacement, from what we could call a traditional humanist notion of the subject to a postmodern view, is crucial to Bergland's interpretation of ethnic autobiography. As Bergland argues, the assimilationist politics that entrap the immigrant and ethnic autobiographer are replicated in criticism that would make a select group of autobiographers into "representative voices." Bergland cautions that "we need to question any easy relationship between discourse and the speaking subject, particularly the notion that *experience* produces a *voice*—that, for example, *being a woman* means speaking in *a woman's voice.*"

Like Bergland, Kirsten Wasson argues that autobiography's own marginality to other discourses, as well as its internal contradictions, offers the ethnic and immigrant autobiographer and critic room to maneuver. Wasson emphasizes the contradictory discourses by which the immigrant subject is interpellated and is concerned with the simultaneous inscription of and resistance to American ideology in her essay, "A Geography of Conversion: Dialogical Boundaries of Self in Antin's *Promised Land.*" Wasson locates Mary Antin as speaking from "the 'melting pot,' the immigrant's prescribed location for transformation, where identities of the past are dissolved and replaced by generic masks of faithfulness in America's democracy and hierarchies." Despite the relative lack of power granted one who speaks from Antin's position, Wasson argues that Antin's "'conversion' reveals a distinct ambivalence toward adopting the word of the American fathers in order to be, in turn, adopted into the privileges of the dominant discourse." Wasson reads Antin dialogically and thereby traces Antin's changing relation to the "American code of transformation."

The destabilizations effected in the theory of genre in the first section move us a long way toward reexamining autobiography as discourse*s* of self-representation rather than as *a* genre defined in its post-Augustinian lineage. Indeed, there is something decidedly multiple and extratextual in the autobiographies read here, from Cindy Sherman's photographs (her "still-lifes") to the naming practices of Plains Indians to identity's body as an autobiographical text. Rather than reading this "otherness" as the autobiographer's unsuccessful attempt at appropriating the forms and techniques of many discourses—without fully assimilating them to a single form or canonical model—the essays explore autobiography's estrangement from an identification with a Western, bourgeois, white, male self and broaden it to include other autobiographers as well as more multicultural modes of self-representation.

The second section of essays begins with Paul Jay's discussion of posing and takes its title from Roland Barthes's response to the constraints of posing for a photograph: "I am truly becoming a specter." By focusing on photography and the broader implications for self-representation of posing, Jay's essay questions the limits of autobiographical representation that shape the essays in this section: To what extent have conventional definitions of autobiography prohibited us from understanding the implications of self-representation? What is off-limits in autobiography? What does not figure as "identity" therein? The postmodern interest in the self provides a different way to ask the questions central to both traditional autobiography studies and more contemporary discourses of and on self-representation: what is the subject of this discourse? how do I take myself as a subject of representation? These questions differ for postmodern critics and traditional humanists, to be sure, but the evidence of an epistemic rupture in the discourses of identity does not constitute the erasure or negation of the question's historical antecedents. Indeed, they may go quite far in revealing their structural legacy.

Taking Barthes's anxiety about "posing,"—the endpoint of which is the ironic though still anguished utterance, "I am truly becoming a specter"—Jay describes the underinspected role of visual memory in autobiography and self-identity and thereby challenges the sufficiency of a single medium to the project of self-representation. The visual language provided by the culture offers the autobiographer a dense realm of images through which to represent identity. Jay explores Cindy Sherman's photographic "objectification" of herself through her self-portraits based on public images of women, as well as Mayme Scott's construction of an Indian identity for herself staged in photographs of herself in feather headdress, in order to contextualize how self-representation is controlled by the images from popular culture *and* simultaneously offers the self-portrayer a medium for experiment and critique and thus a kind of agency.

In "Plains Indian Names and 'the Autobiographical Act'," Hertha Wong explores how the discourses and materials through which one may represent identity are culturally marked. The self-representational aspects of Plains Indian naming practices have not previously been considered autobiography; nor have their producers been considered authors. The implications of falling outside a cultural elite's definition of authorship has serious implications in a form that claims to depict identity, to render an eyewitness account of history. The autobiographer, bound by the law of genre through interpretive practices, is judged in more than literary ways.

David Haney returns to the issues of boundaries in genre and autobiography—a boundary broached playfully by Andrei Codrescu—by reading a poem that claims to be autobiographical, Wordsworth's "Farewell." It is precisely the boundary between literary genre and life that becomes, in Haney's analysis, a boundary between what can and cannot be represented. In his essay, "Nuptial Interruptions," largely influenced by deconstruction, Haney takes this boundary as the location for the most productive analysis and, of necessity, raises rather than resolves questions. Through careful elucidation of the figures of nook and garden, courtship and marriage, and gift-giving, Haney suggests that Wordsworth in 1802 was "struggling with the complex boundaries of three relationships that pose these issues of boundaries and legitimacy: the legitimate relationship to Mary, the illegitimate relation to Annette, and the most important relation to Dorothy, which confounds categories of legitimacy as it forms a kind of fulcrum for both the legitimate and the illegitimate relationships." Wordsworth's figural strategies simultaneously present the connection between inner and outer worlds and represent "a recognition of the skeptical distance placed between the poet and the object of knowledge." Haney emphasizes the contradictions in texts and critical contexts, forcing an acknowledgment of that which is not represented and, therefore, of the limits of representation in autobiographical writing.

In "Identity's Body" Sidonie Smith explores the complexity of embodiment for women and its implications for identity and self-representation. Smith argues that various discourses of identity work to fragment the body, to recognize its parts in order to give it a sexual or racial identity. Both the intimacy of the body and its potential for estrangement lead Smith to question, "What might skin have to do with autobiographical writing and autobiographical writing with skin?" The extent to which one is all wrapped up like a person in what Smith calls the "skins and skeins of meaning" implicates the gendered body, the body of the text, and the body politic in any notion of personhood. Following this inquiry into the relation between the body and identity in autobiography, Smith compares Virginia Woolf's representation of the gendered body as grotesque in *Sketch of the Past* to Cherríe Moraga's representation of the body as a site of exile and return in *Loving in the War Years*. Smith

claims that Woolf's representation is consistent with women's autobiographical practices up to the twentieth century in that "women had to
discursively consolidate themselves as subjects through pursuit of an
out-of-body experience precisely because their bodies were heavily and
inescapably gendered." Moraga's inscription of a Chicana, lesbian body
as "home" marks a break with previous autobiographical practices and
recodes autobiography as "a new way of interpreting the practices of
the body politic through the articulation of the material body and its
desires."

Connecting historical, generic, and cultural antecedents to their impact on autobiography, Shirley Neuman notes in her essay, "'An appearance walking in the forest the sexes burn': Autobiography and the
Construction of the Feminine Body": "The histories of autobiography
and of its criticism construe the self as individuated and coherent rather
than as the product of social construction and as a subject-in-process and
work consistently toward repression of the representation of bodies in
autobiography." What are the implications of "the absent body" for
autobiography? Neuman here links the repression of bodies to autobiography's traditional view of the individuated self as its subject in order
to explicate the consequences for women autobiographers. Yet Neuman
takes gender, as all the feminists in this volume do, as a "*social mapping* of
the body" and not as "something originally existent in human beings."
Neuman reads the ideological effects through which the female body is
produced and the psychic consequences of this (self-)production in Kate
Simon's *Bronx Primitive* and Violette Leduc's three-volume autobiography. Leduc's autobiographies record the arduous training in what
Simone de Beauvoir called "becoming a woman," especially in the simultaneous and compulsory heterosexualization and feminization of
women. Through Neuman's analysis, lesbianism's psychoanalytic encoding as a secondary attachment following from heterosexual disappointment is overturned in favor of Leduc's specific engagement with the
cultural script of femininity.

Future work in self-representation will undoubtedly further explore
the areas of ethnic, lesbian and gay, and African-American autobiography through a range of theoretical intersections. This future is already
emerging as new work appears, and the essays here on lesbian, Native
American, Chicana, Mexican, ethnic, and immigrant self-representation contribute to the contemporary rethinking of American identities.
Autobiography and Postmodernism seeks to demonstrate the radical alter-
ation it is possible to perform on genre and other strategies for organiz-

ing texts by mutually historicizing and reconfiguring modes previously thought to be discontinuous and even contradictory. The mark of auto-biography, then, is the discursive signature of the subject and signifies agency in self-representation.

Notes

1 Postmodernism is frequently described in relation to questioning: it seems to call the question in a general sense whenever it is invoked and to function as a question-ing mode within contemporary discourses. Thus its status as exterior (as a critical mode brought to bear upon a topic) or interior (as *always already* present) is always at issue. On the relationship between questioning and postmodernism, see Judith Butler's "Contingent Foundations: Feminism and the Question of 'Postmodern-ism'," in *Feminists Theorize the Political,* ed. Judith Butler and Joan W. Scott (New York: Routledge, 1992), 3–21.

2 Feminist criticism and theory have gone especially far in merging politics and postmodernism on the topic of self-representation and in developing a notion of the human agent as a producer of culture as well as its most complicated text. See especially Judith Butler, *Gender Trouble: Feminism and the Subversion of Identity* (London: Routledge, 1990); Jane Flax, *Thinking Fragments: Psychoanalysis, Femi-nism, and Postmodernism in the Contemporary West* (Berkeley: U of California P, 1990); Teresa de Lauretis, *The Technologies of Gender: Essays on Theory, Film, and Fiction* (Bloomington: U of Indiana P, 1987); and Denise Riley, *"Am I That Name?": Feminism and the Category of Women in History* (Minneapolis: U of Minnesota P, 1988).

3 Significantly, and despite the aims of many of its practitioners, the issue of human agency seems to be wielded against postmodernism. In part, this follows from understanding postmodernism as a monolithic and concrete entity, which it can never be. But it also derives from a series of polarizing emphases that turn on the presumed incompatibility of politics and poetics. The titles of Linda Hutcheon's two books on the subject illustrate this tension: *The Poetics of Postmodernism* (New York: Routledge, 1988) followed by the *Politics of Postmodernism* (New York: Rout-ledge, 1989). Following from this discrimination, critics of and in postmodernism tend either to embrace the freeplay bequeathed through Derridean deconstruction and Lacanian psychoanalysis or to reject it in favor of various political moves: locating the possibilities for human agency allowed by a postmodern emphasis on subject positions, inspecting the shifting discursive field of social life, and exploring the political interventions a subject-in-process may effect in a world of power relations.

4 Postmodernism is an umbrella term usually used to designate, broadly, postmodern culture as a situation rather than as a fact or discernible practice. This, of course, leads to confusion, the consequences of which can be seen as various critics, groups,

and institutions line up in postures of sympathy or antagonism to a variously defined "postmodernism." In our own era of constrained and increasingly politically regulated funding for the arts and humanities, terms worthy of debate in their own right, such positioning has legal and monetary consequences. Where artistic practices can be attached to a general term, such as "postmodernism" (used as a synonym for progressive, liberal, or radical politics), and thereby denigrated, these terms and the representations associated with them are mobilized in the service of political and ideological agendas. To neoconservatives, postmodernism appears as an apocalypse of civilized, literate (and literary), post-Enlightenment progress. An epithet of fragmentation, loss, and exile, it can be illustrated by such wide-ranging though allied effects as the loss of Great Books courses in the academy and the cultural hegemony of television. To some Marxists postmodernism is the typical culture of late capitalism (Fredric Jameson, "Postmodernism, or the Cultural Logic of Late Capitalism," in *The Anti-Aesthetic: Essays on Postmodern Culture*, ed. Hal Foster [Port Townsend, Wash.: Bay, 1983]). To some feminists the dissolution of profoundly patriarchal notions of identity and authority and the politics they everywhere erect are certainly welcome. To other feminists and to so many others located on the culturally constructed margins of power, the postmodernist glee associated with the dissolution of notions of the self is hardly a welcome prospect for those already all too familiar with the social reality of selflessness. Notice, for example, the simultaneity of positioning in relation to postmodernism: Many feminist artists positioned themselves against male-dominated practices in the New York and Boston art scenes that were being described as postmodern; while Craig Owens and other critics define the vitality of postmodern art through the contributions of feminist artists (Foster 1983).

Postmodernism lacks a disciplinary or scientific stability and derives much of its influence from its definitional instability; it may be attached to a number of phenomena though none are fully reducible to its name. Linda Hutcheon, one of postmodernism's most vigorous defenders, grapples with this instability (1988). In her introduction to *Poetics of Postmodernism* she claims that postmodernism is *here*, but also claims not to recognize it in critiques and caricatures by Terry Eagleton and others. She debates Eagleton point by point but never erases the issue installed by her own premise; namely, if postmodernism *is*, how can it be so thoroughly misrecognized and misrepresented? Indeed, the trope of (in)visibility reveals the problematic status of any production located in a political field of representation. Its unknowability requires defense and explanation, but this reveals the extent to which postmodernism is an interpretive and ideologically interested phenomenon as much as it is an artistic practice, and patient explication of the latter will not enlighten practitioners of the former.

5   Depending on how you look at it, postmodernism either benefits or suffers from its tremendous capacity as a descriptive term. The relative instability of "postmodern" as a descriptive term is further exaggerated by its differing uses in architecture, art, performance, and literature. In architecture, postmodernism designates the work of

Robert Venturi, Denise Scott Brown, Michael Graves, and the deconstructivists, and describes the practice of quoting past historical styles, signs, and signatures in contemporary architecture. Postmodernism in architecture also refers to a self-conscious staging of the play between deep structure and surface, and to the relation of the built environment to popular culture. See, for example, Venturi and Brown's *Learning from Las Vegas* (Cambridge: MIT P, 1972). This brief rehearsal of the differing meanings and emerging traditions named "postmodernism," quickly reveals the slippage that characterizes definitions of postmodernism. The contradictions that structure its definition turn on both ontological and epistemological axes. The question "what is postmodernism?" seems *always already* to have begged some other nagging question like "what is modernism?" Fredric Jameson, who is associated with one form of postmodernist critique, argues that postmodernism is positioned both ideologically and historically in relation to modernism (1983). See Jameson's *Political Unconscious* (Ithaca: Cornell UP, 1981); and "Postmodernism, or the Cultural Logic of Late Capitalism."

Perhaps what is most notable about the language of instability that structures debates about postmodernism is its relentless turn toward some affective dimension, some level at which the critic feels unsettled by or sympathetic to postmodernism, as if the main question must be: if we are in a postmodern condition, how do we feel about it? The characteristically doubled representation that produces postmodernism as contradiction itself reveals the binary mode of much evaluation, as well as the ways in which antipodal interpretive agendas can seize upon the same subject. When postmodernism's contradictions and instabilities are taken as a stalemate, rather than a potentially productive disregard for and disloyalty to tradition, then its implications for the human subject seem to presage some apocalypse, some end of history, and provoke the question: what possibilities for politics and human agency does postmodernism allow?

6   One critical precursor of the renewed interest in autobiography was Roy Pascal, *Design and Truth in Autobiography* (London: Routledge, 1960). A survey of important work contributing to the transformation of autobiography studies would include Elizabeth W. Bruss, *Autobiographical Acts: The Changing Situation of a Literary Genre* (Baltimore: Johns Hopkins UP, 1976) and William Spengemann, *The Forms of Autobiography: Episodes in the History of a Literary Genre* (New Haven: Yale UP, 1980) with a valuable bibliographical essay; as well as James Olney, ed., *Autobiography: Essays Theoretical and Critical* (Princeton: Princeton UP, 1980) and Estelle C. Jelinek, ed., *Women's Autobiography: Essays in Criticism* (Bloomington: Indiana UP, 1980).

7   Currently, the field of autobiography studies, in which the essays in this volume must also be contextualized, can be represented through this limited list of notable texts: William Andrews, *To Tell A Free Story: The First Century of African-American Autobiography, 1760–1865* (Urbana: U Illinois P, 1986); Shari Benstock, ed., *The Private Self* (Chapel Hill: U of North Carolina P, 1988); Bella Brodzki and Celeste Schenck, eds., *Life/Lines: Theorizing Women's Autobiography* (Ithaca: Cornell UP,

1988); Paul John Eakin, *Fictions in Autobiography: Studies in the Art of Self-Invention* (Princeton: Princeton UP, 1985); Paul Jay, *Being in the Text: Self-Representation from Wordsworth to Roland Barthes* (Ithaca: Cornell UP, 1984); Arnold Krupat, *For Those Who Come After: A Study of Native American Autobiography* (Berkeley: U of California P, 1985); Francoise Lionnet, *Autobiographical Voices: Race, Gender, Self-Portraiture* (Ithaca: Cornell UP, 1989); Nancy K. Miller, *Subject to Change: Reading Feminist Writing* (New York: Columbia UP, 1988); Felicity Nussbaum, *The Autobiographical Subject: Gender and Ideology in Eighteenth Century England* (Baltimore: Johns Hopkins UP, 1989); Ramón Saldívar, *Chicano Narratives: The Dialectics of Difference* (Madison: U of Wisconsin P, 1990); Sidonie Smith, *A Poetics of Women's Autobiography: Marginality and the Fictions of Self-Representation* (Bloomington: Indiana UP, 1987); Valerie Smith, *Self-Discovery and Authority in African-American Narratives* (Cambridge: Harvard UP, 1987); Domna Stanton, ed., *The Female Autograph* (1984; Chicago: U of Chicago P, 1987); Robert Steptoe, *From Behind the Veil: A Study of African-American Narrative* (Urbana: U of Illinois P, 1979); Hertha Dawn Wong, *Sending My Heart Back Across The Years: Tradition and Innovation in Native American Autobiography* (New York: Oxford UP, 1992).

8   The field designated by the name "postmodernism" is already far too large to map, but the following emphases are significant to this discussion. In literary studies postmodernism has a range of influential theorists, whose diversity is belied to some extent by a shared descriptive vocabulary. Jean-François Lyotard, for example, is illustrative of a postmodernism captivated by a language of surface and structural decompositions. His emphasis rests on dispersal; the fragment characterizes postmodern narrative and marks the end of allegiance to all metanarratives. For Jean Baudrillard, the mass culture of television and advertising creates a hyperreal space. Surface compositions and decompositions define the hyperreal as a simulacrum. Simulation is all; the real does not exist. In her introduction to *Postmodern Genres* (Norman: U of Oklahoma P, 1988), Marjorie Perloff enumerates the features associated with the postmodern text: violation, disruption, dislocation, decentering, contradiction. Surface fragmentation, once the sign of modernism, becomes for Perloff the sign of the postmodern. Her discussion reveals the extent to which postmodernism is indebted to and, perhaps, recycles interpretations of modernism.

9   One notable intersection of these aims can be found in two recent feminist anthologies where women's autobiography is stabilized, at least provisionally, to offer a counterdiscourse to autobiography studies written largely by and about men, as well as to interrogate the category of autobiography itself. See Brodzki and Schenck; Benstock. For an enlargement of the traditional form of autobiography, see especially Sommer ("'Not Just a Personal Story': Women's *Testimonios* and the Plural Self" 107–30) and Schenck ("All of a Piece: Women's Autobiography and Poetry" 281–305) in Brodzki and Schenck.

10 Monique Wittig, "The Mark of Gender," in *Poetics of Gender*, ed. Nancy K. Miller (New York: Columbia UP, 1986): 63–73.

11 See Emile Benveniste's *Problems in General Linguistics* (Coral Gables: U of Miami P, 1973). Brodzki and Schenck take up the implications of the "I" for autobiography at length in their introduction to *Life/Lines*, 1–15.

12 I have described autobiography's relation to a variety of realisms at length elsewhere; see my *Autobiographics: A Feminist Theory of Women's Self-Representation* (Ithaca: Cornell UP, 1994).

PART II

Adding to My Life

Adding to My Life

ANDREI CODRESCU

∎

I am delighted to stand before you exactly the way I will in the first
chapter of the third volume of my autobiography, in which the narrator—that is, myself—stands before the world's authorities on autobiography and is about to make a speech.

My previous two autobiographies were the result of accident, but each
one begins with the equivalent of standing before people trained in the
judging of lives. In the first one, titled modestly "The Life & Times of
an Involuntary Genius," it is my mother before whom the impending
story is about to make its cheeky and devastating appearance. "You're not
old enough to wipe your nose!" my mother exploded. "*I* should write my
autobiography! *I* lived!" That was doubtlessly true, but she would never
do it. She had not only had too much life but she had such an active
quarrel with it that she would have been hard put to find anyone to
address her story to. I was twenty-three years old: I had had as much life
as I cared to remember and my audience—beginning with my mother—
was vast. There were more potential witnesses to my life than there had
been people in my life so far—a heady feeling. I could add them all to my
life by writing my life. Which is not why I wrote the book, but it was a
thought. Furthermore, it was high time that I became the author of
something I could call "my life" in order to get on with it. Saying farewell
to my mother, leaving her story, as it were, was not simply a matter of
individuation. It was also a matter of sabotaging her story, a less than
benign thing.

Just before the book came out I asked my mother about a certain
incident I had labored hard to render accurately. It was about the time
she left me with my grandmother, the Baroness, in Alba Iulia. I was five,
and the Baroness kept chickens. There were chickens everywhere in the
formerly grand manse she now had the top floor in, and both my mother
and I were sternly warned to watch where we walked because there were

eggs everywhere. In fact, there were eggs in my bedroll when I went to sleep, and I woke up the next day holding in my hands two miraculously unbroken eggs. It seemed to me that over the years this story had become something of a legend among our kin. But my mother, when I asked her about it, said that the Baroness kept little pigs! That, furthermore, I was only three when I went to live with her, and that I was only there for one month. *I* remembered living there for one year. PIGS! I wasn't about to change anything so dear to me, so I let it slide. A year after the book came out, I was visiting my mother in Washington, D.C., and she said that she felt very sorry that she'd had to leave me with my crazy grandmother and her chickens when I was five years old. BUT MOTHER, I said. PIGS! WHATEVER HAPPENED TO THE PIGS? What pigs? She was annoyed. She denied ever having said anything about pigs. It had been chickens all along.

A strange power this, changing your mother's memory cassette. Her memory just crumbled before the printed page—which may explain in a small way why, in places where history has been falsified by the authorities, people are hard put to remember their true experiences. It's chickens for everybody whether they like it or not.

My friend Michael Stephens wrote a wonderful memoir called "Season at Coole." It is composed entirely of fights at the dinner table of his huge New York-Irish family. His father never spoke to him after the book was published and claimed to have never read it. He had been a New York customs official. After his father died, Michael married a Korean whose family gave them beautiful old furniture. Thinking to ease the duties on the antiques, Michael told the customs chief at the docks that he was old Mr. Stephens's son. The man looked him over carefully, then asked: "You're not the one who wrote the book, are you?" "No," said Michael, "that was my brother." "It's a good thing," the boss said, "because we're still looking for the SOB who wrote that book. When we find him we'll break all his bones!" Turns out that old man Stephens had come to the office every morning for the past ten years, read a page of Michael's novel, and made everyone's life miserable the rest of the day.

My own life didn't cause such widespread unhappiness only because my mother wasn't anybody's boss. But she expressed her displeasure emphatically by announcing that she could never share my accomplishment with her friends. "Oh, why," she lamented, "did you have to call it an autobiography? Couldn't you call it a 'novel'?"

It is curious how, in the face of disaster, people suddenly reach for form. At the edge of the abyss they begin to have these formal thoughts . . . if only the genre had been changed . . . this wouldn't have befallen me. It's like getting religion before dying: one is suddenly beset by alternatives.

Every book needs a proper address. My mother was the one I addressed my first book to because she had been my author until I became one myself. But that isn't why I wrote the book. George Braziller, who published a book of my poetry, glimpsed between the rarefied vistas of my verse certain hints of stories. He suggested I write an autobiography, a suggestion I found absolutely intoxicating. Here I was, twenty-three years old, the possessor of a wealth of experience that had spawned an equal if not greater quantity of mythicizing anecdotes. I had no ax to grind. I'd changed countries and languages at the age of nineteen, a neat break that could provide a thousand books with rudimentary structure. In addition, I had the numbers: born in 1946, became conscious with the Hungarian revolt in 1956, came to the United States in 1966. Initiatory structures in plain view, natural chapter breaks for the taking. I had already practiced all the anecdotes and revealed their cosmic import to my new American friends in the process of learning the language. I was learning to view my journey, if not *sub-speciae aeternitatis,* than at least as a quest. I was a tragic hero because, most likely, I could never go home again, but I was having a great time on the way. Since I did not speak any English before I came to the United States—with the exception of a single sentence I will tell you shortly—I used my life story to buy my way into my new world. I had no money either. When you're that broke—without language and without money—you are doomed to a kind of choreography, a language of gestures and primal sounds that promise the coming of a story, as soon as some of the details—things like words and food—take their place within the structure. The only thing I had was my story, which, I was convinced, was the price of admission to everything. Money, I believed, and still do, is most peoples' substitute for a personal story. The symbols it buys always tell the same story, namely the success story of the prevailing culture back to the culture that spawned it. Money is one's way out of autobiography into the collective myth. The currency of outsiders is their personal story: Here I am. Let me sit by the fire. In return, I'll tell you about these pigs. . . . Of course, not speaking the language intensified the story about to unfold by announcing that it was also a *first* story, a genesis myth. Here I am then, rising from the need to tell my story, gathering language around it as I go, *un pequeno dios* conscious of nothing but its coming into being. And your attention, of course!

The one sentence that I was mighty proud to have put together in English, with the help of my friend Julian in Rome, six months before I came to the United States, was WHY DON'T YOU KILL YOURSELF?

We tried it out on people around the train station in Rome. A bunch of hustlers and pimps were hanging around the fountain there. We walked up to them.

WHY DON'T YOU KILL YOURSELF? Julian asked.

They had a conference. After some deliberation, one of them pointed us in the direction of the self-service machines inside the station. He thought we'd meant by "self," those places where you could get soft drinks and sandwiches. Since then I've always associated "self" with those self-service machines, and I think of "self" as a coin-operated contraption.

This primal notion served me well when Mr. Braziller offered to pay the advance to my life story in monthly installments. I literally constructed my life story in increments spewed out every time he inserted $250.

The Life & Times of an Involuntary Genius was written in the third person (with one chapter, a letter, in the second person singular). I needed this particular distance to view the self under construction. I reserved the first person for oral versions of the story, particularly ones meant to elicit an immediate response: "Hi! I'm Hungarian. Can you spare a dime?"

Ten years after the writing of *Life & Times*, Lawrence Ferlinghetti of City Lights Books asked me to write a sequel. He'd read the first one and wondered what had happened afterwards. I was curious myself because what had happened is that, meanwhile, I'd become an American. The sequel, which is not really a sequel at all, is called *In America's Shoes*, and it begins with an address to the Immigration and Naturalization Bureau, an entity I fought a long battle with for citizenship. Instead of addressing myself to my mother I began this book by addressing myself to the state.

In the first chapter the agent in charge of my case is looking through my voluminous file. I see my life passing through the policeman's eyes, arranged in an order alien to me, alphabetized by offenses and suspicions, a life that resembles mine in all but the structure of the narrative. Of course, I tell myself, "file" is an anagram for "life"!

In order to leave the world "my story" rather than "their" story, I proceed to write my autobiography. This time the book is in the first person singular, an emphatic first person at that, because the *file* is the third person. The first person now sets up a new distance, not between self and self, but between self and the state. In fact, this book, *In America's Shoes,* is an elaborate identity card. One very late night, my friend Jeffrey Miller and I were lost on a country road near Mendocino, California. There was a full moon and a feeling that Jeffrey later described, "Fuego." A police cruiser came out of nowhere and stopped us. The cop wanted to see my ID as well as Jeffrey's. I didn't have any. I handed him a copy of *The Life & Times of an Involuntary Genius,* which has my picture on the cover. He took it back to his cruiser, put his feet out the moonlit window and proceeded to read. Eons passed, a time during which Jeffrey and I stood under the millions of stars listening to the Pacific Ocean invade our sleep. At long last, the cop came back. He tapped the picture on the cover: "Anyone can fake a pitcher like this!" he said. "And write a book to go with it?" I asked him. "It's OK. This time!" he said. Which is why I wrote the second volume; I'm not sure when that cop's coming back.

It was my great luck, coming into America in the late sixties, to encounter several wayward myths ready-made for me, Transylvania being but one of them. Transylvania—at the time of my arrival—was a growing myth, full of potential, and anybody who bought stock in Dracula then must feel like an investor in early McDonald's. In the past two decades I have seen Halloween overtake Christmas as the nation's greatest holiday, and Dracula become bigger than Jesus Christ, and even John Lennon. Queasy at first about this Hollywood fantasy, I later considered it a gift. The dark stranger who bites blond Anglosaxony in her semi-sleep is the outsider, par excellence, the exile who brings history to a halt with his story. His bite ends being in time, it jump starts eternity, overthrows daytime and the bourgeoisie, reinstates aristocracy and difference. And it is a great way to meet girls. I never abandoned the profoundly gloomy existentialist disposition of my rebellious Romanian generation within which I had been raised as a baby dissident destined for great things and prison. No, I just put on a cape to complete the picture. Ionesco, my previous totem, was only a literary Dracula. To be bitten by the absurd is every bit as liberating as being bitten by an immortal, but why not be bitten by both?

Exile, in Romania, is a precondition of greatness for a certain kind of writer. I belong to a country whose main export is geniuses. The most famous exile of antiquity, Ovid, was exiled among the ancient Romanians and founded their literature. Since then, in misguided reciprocity, Romanians have been exiling their poets with a single-minded devotion to their beginnings. In the university we whispered the names of our great exiles until they sent chills up our spines: Brancusi, Tristan Tzara, Ionesco, Mircea Eliade, Emil Cioran! For us, the meaning of their exile overshadowed by far the meaning of their creations with which, at the time, we had but a furtive acquaintance. In my mind, exile assumed the proportions of a *place*. I wasn't just leaving my country, I was going to a place called Exile. I imagined Exile as a vast territory, a psychological place of great dimensions, with distinct boundaries, laws, and tourist attractions. Geographically, this may have been Paris, Rome, New York, Buenos Aires, but in truth it began outside the Romanian borders. This archipelago was inhabited mainly by creative citizens. It was an international Idea-State, the only anarchist system in working order.

On this well-primed soil fell the fertile rains of America's own myths of exile in the late 1960s. Generations were in exile from each other, thousands of young people roamed the continent in deliberate religious abandon. Exile was part of the popular culture, and its meaning had been expanded to take in anything from an hour of alienation to a summer of bumming around Europe.

The advantages of being a literal exile in a culture obsessed by a myth of it are numerous. The most obvious one was that I was able to gain admittance to a community of my peers with the promise of a story that was, at least in the beginning, only a series of gestures and inarticulate groans. I was able to obtain credit at the bank of the future on the strength of my generic mythical assets.

My mother, who looked for security as well as acceptance, had no active myth to see her on her way. Her generation, in America, was a television-narcotized middle class that had been traumatized by the rebellious younger generation and was suspicious of foreigners, if not downright xenophobic. Her next-door neighbors in Washington never smiled, and her attempts at making friends had been rebuffed or perhaps simply lost in the cracks between manners where all the sad foreigners end up. Her story had no one she could properly address it to, which is why she couldn't write her autobiography, no matter how many momentous events had befallen her. She could have addressed it to me, but I'd heard it many times already, and I disagreed most strenuously. My chickens, unless printed, rarely won the day. Her story was by far more tragic, and more typical than mine. She struggled like all energetic immigrants to make a living, and possibly some money. The money was to show the people back home that she'd become rich and powerful. Most of all she wanted friends. She made a living. She didn't make any money. She didn't make many friends. People her own age eluded her because, by and large, they preferred the soap operas they could all enjoy together to the peculiar life story in broken English of a single person. They did not necessarily lack compassion, but the same myths that helped me, Dracula and exile, were enemies to them, the myths of their children, who caused them nothing but pain. Had my mother become a rich and powerful woman she might have written her autobiography. It would have been addressed to her mother back in the old country, a skeptical soul who never believed that things were different elsewhere. To prove it she lived with chickens—which don't fly far and can be easily caught and eaten (at autobiography conferences).

Having the assistance of a wayward myth is a special kind of luck, vouchsafed to certain Romanians by Logos Central. Without it, no story can be rightly heard. This is what breaks all those tens of thousands of hearts who imagine that simply because they have had an eventful life there is a reason for writing it down. At times all those cabdrivers who were once former prime ministers and those heroes of wars no one cares to remember achieve a kind of epiphany as regards the importance of their lives.

"I wrote this book as a warning: I have lived through terrible things and I have been saved only in order to tell the story. This is my mission: otherwise why did everyone have to die while I went on? And go on, driving this cab which is a vehicle of destiny and a cage for stories. I was neither stronger nor luckier than the rest. Something or Someone kept me here to write this book. But a terrible thing must have happened to this Someone, because no one wants to publish my book. I have no choice but to pay a vanity publisher to publish it: the world will hear my story this way if this is how it has to be. I am going to the bank tomorrow to borrow money against the house. Ah, happy day! The book is published! I will pay the bank back for the book with the money I will make: the world will cry and buy. Or rather buy and cry!"

Days pass, then years. The world isn't buying because the world never sees it. Vanity publishers do not distribute the thousand of sad lives that they publish. They bury them, and that's the final joke. Most people were kept alive not to tell their story but to have their story *buried*. They were kept alive to be made fun of. *Life is funny,* no doubt about it.

Of all the kinds of literature, autobiographies, no matter how humorous, are the least funny. After all, how much genuine irony can an autobiographer muster? At best he can apply the benign version known as "affectionate irony." Anything stronger would be too strong: one's life, after all, is something one is disinclined to knock, even—or especially—if one wove it out of whole cloth. After all, one has taken the trouble to write it and, if for no other reason, labor must be respected. If one's life seems funny to one the result is more likely to be silence or awkwardness. Life is funny all right, but not the way one was hoping for. Most likely, funny things happen in the course of one's life, and those things, through the insistent refinement of being told over and over become "funny stories" because they amuse listeners over and over, containing, as they do, endurable and instructive doses of pain. A collection of these "funny stories" is, in truth, a terrible thing taken all together because the life in question is nothing but a series of cover-ups, a horrific giggle stretched over an open wound spanning time. If a life is all "funny stories," the autobiography itself is the saddest book ever written. The novelist cab-driver who has just banned smoking in his cab finds out that his house is burning. He can add this to the list of instructive experiences for the sake of which he's being kept alive.

In the past two decades there have been a proliferation of life stories, both autobiographies and thinly disguised autobiographical fiction. The latter, however, for one of those reasons of publishing fashion that are completely mysterious in their transparency, are more in vogue at the moment. "I would like you to write another autobiography," a well-known publisher said to me, "but make it a novel." My mother would have been pleased.

"Whence the reluctance?" I asked him. "Well, to be perfectly frank, you're not famous enough," he said. "This is the time of the Iacoccas!" It was. At the American Booksellers' Association meeting that year, every book being pushed was an autobiography by someone who was not a writer. Writers, in other words, if they wanted to live in the same world as the Iacoccas, had to hide their lives in novels. Autobiography had suddenly become a form for the rich and famous. There was no call for the outside story. At some point during the time since my last auto-biography, time had started flowing backwards. When Andy Warhol said that in the future everyone will be famous for fifteen minutes it sounded funny because time was still flowing forward. Then fifteen minutes became five minutes, then nanoseconds, and now we can safely say that everyone *was* famous for fifteen minutes at one time or another. Time flows back from the future now, already full of the velocity of a superfluous past that is being divided by several Iacoccas. We are longing to become part of the picture we have already been put out of. The mirrors there, at the junction between past and present, make it appear that there are thousands of Iacoccas. But there are only a few. This is the reason, no doubt, why the retroactive evidence of presence that is the autobiography is such a fiercely awkward phenomenon these days. It is proof of those fifteen minutes, which are now wholly owned by Iacocca Trump.

The future of autobiography is both bright and dim—like a TV set. The bright part is that the wealthy dead can now have video screens installed in their tombstones. Push this button, ye stranger going by, and see a life-size Iacocca appear on screen speaking his life. A coin-operated contraption, this video display offers a choice: fifteen minutes of distilled wisdom from a long life, up to a full five hours of detailed anecdotes about exactly what it took to bury such a great man.

The dim part is that fewer and fewer people can imagine a life that doesn't look like television. Up to a point, an autobiography would seem to be the exact opposite of television, the stand of the insistently personal against the collectivized story, the small tenant-farmer's resistance to the Sovietization of life. But, in fact, we know television families better than our own because they show us everything, while ours, those lumpy shapes on the couch next to us, are completely hidden. How can those strangers be so *visible* while we can only watch our dear ones from the narrowing peephole of our own inattentive, inarticulate, amnesiac little selves.

Our own little selves weren't always as little as all that. "I contain multitudes," said Walt Whitman—anticipating television by a hundred years—and going on to speak from the platform of that "I" for the multitudes we never really hear except as a background roar, like the sea. Rimbaud's *je est un autre* has always been an autobiographer's true challenge, though in my own practice, the *je est* is most often *un jeu*.

I once conceived a truly monstrous idea, and went through with it. My third autobiography, covering the ritualistic interval of another ten years, was not going to be either in the first, second, or third person, singular or plural. I sent out a questionnaire to friends and acquaintances asking them to describe in their own words incidents we experienced together. I asked them to include the story of our meeting, the story of meeting others in our circle, as well as rumors, fantasies, and fabrications. There was a special section for composing from the point of view of the subject, "hosting" myself, as it were. I collected some three hundred pages of these testimonials, which range from the surreal to the minimal, and began collating them into a single narrative with a view to making a book from the point of view of everyone who has ever admitted knowing me. The "me" under construction here was Nadia Comanici, the gymnast, the third member of my mythical triumvirate along with Ionesco and Dracula. Nadia, the way I saw it, gracefully walked the tightropes of this life, which were actually the seams between the various stories. After being Ionesco and Dracula, I wanted to be Nadia. This, I thought, would be the last perspective on my narrative of "self" and, no doubt, my last autobiography. In my first such book I was my own affectionate subject. In the second, I stood up to bad guys and gave them a piece of my mind. In the third, I am no longer speaking. Call me Nadia. Or ABC.

It was a great idea. The only trouble with it was that other people's stories—even though they were about "me"—bored me. The stories I had forgotten had something about them that made me see *exactly* why I had forgotten them. The ones I remembered, I could tell better. It's true moreover, that whatever you forget, other people remember; it's a nice thing to know in case you need witnesses in court. But amnesia is more important to art than total recall. Amnesia shapes the few remembered or misremembered scenes into whatever you're going to make. The kind of remembering that interests me is anamnesis, which is an intense flashback. Such a flashback is generally devoid of facts because it has room only for feelings. Outfitting these feelings with facts like a grand-mother with chicken feathers is a job I like very much. The truth is that I am not all that interested in "myself"—I am only curious to see what kind of person is going to emerge from a certain arrangement of personal stories, which are themselves not facts but earlier arrangements, for certain practical uses.

Furthermore, I'm only an inn for the Logos.

My early life story was recently written into a movie script by two well-meaning people. When I went to Los Angeles last week, a pro-ducer asked me if I was working on another autobiography.

"As we speak," I told him.

Here is how it starts. I am standing before a distinguished gathering of scholars of autobiographies. I hold forth for various trembling minutes until I realize that I have absolutely no idea how to end. I ramble on and on. The hall empties. I am all alone, rambling on and on. It will be two hundred years before anyone will come back.

Informed of my failure, my mother says: "Didn't I tell you to make it a novel? Oh, why didn't you make it a novel?"

Why indeed?

Thank you very much.

PART III

**"The thing that's most exciting is
contradictory versions"**

The Politics of Genre in Carmen Martín Gaite's

Back Room

CHRISTOPHER ORTIZ

∎

he Back Room is a text that Carmen Martín Gaite has designated a
novel but that she has declared in interviews and other occasions is
her autobiography, a confusing state of affairs when attempting to
affix an identity to the text.[1] The importance of *The Back Room* to discussions on autobiography is its exploration, through its own generic
ambiguity, of the political and ideological effects of the very conception of genre. In other words *The Back Room* investigates the protocols
of reading that determine how identity is constructed and interpreted.
Speaking on these very questions, Derrida notes in his "Law of Genre"
that genre also means gender and is related in some way to the law of the
father, to a certain type of discursive practice that has often defined what
history consists of and whom it includes or excludes.[2]

Gender, then, as social and political construct is something that is at
issue in *The Back Room*, something that has always been dressed up as
natural and put into the front room. The problem of genre in *The Back
Room*—to which one it belongs, autobiography or fiction—cannot be
resolved by attempting to categorize or define the text as either/or or by
conflating the two. That an understanding of *The Back Room* can be
gained from looking to history is what Martín Gaite seems to suggest.
History for her is not monumental, but rather effective: she explores how
discursive systems form and shape subjectivity, thus determining wom-
en's material and social conditions.[3] As she says, "The thing that's most
exciting is contradictory versions. They're the very basis of literature. We
are not just one being, but many, exactly as real history is not what is
written by putting dates in their proper order and then presenting it to us
as a single whole. Each person who has seen us or spoken to us at a
certain time retains one piece of the puzzle that we will never be able to
see all put together" (166:167).[4]

The Back Room, published in 1978, takes place on a cold and stormy night in Madrid. Carmen, the narrator, suffers from insomnia. When she finally manages to get to sleep, she is awakened by a phone call from a mysterious man whose name, we learn later, is possibly Alejandro. Dressed in black, the man arrives at her apartment and in a night-long conversation Martín Gaite speaks with him about her life in relation to literature and to her own narrative production. The man in black, as he is referred to throughout the text, is a literary critic or journalist; his status is never made clear. Their conversation and her interior monologues touch upon many themes and genres: romance novels, film, popular music, Franco, politics, and her family, to name a few.

The text has no chronological order or denouement toward which it progresses, but the events recalled occur mainly from her childhood and young adult years, roughly 1938 through 1955. Some critics have termed the work fantastic because of its direct invocation of Todorov's *Fantastic: A Structural Approach to a Literary Genre* as a structuring guide. They have noted as fantastic elements its lack of closure, the way in which the narrator seems to confuse her present with her past, and a few other apparently unexplainable textual features. For example, *The Back Room* is being transcribed silently on the narrator's typewriter, which is in the same room where she and the man in black are conversing.[5]

In an effort to categorize the text so as to locate some type of definable referentiality, some critics have analyzed the text as a fantastic novel, have termed it a fantastic memoir, have looked at it simply as an auto-biography, or have conflated all categories into one.[6] The direct reference to Todorov is in itself a sort of reading game, a purposely false clue that Martín Gaite puts into play at the beginning of the text. She is asking us to question what the text says about itself on a literal level and to con-sider the fantastic nature, unbelievable or unreal, of women's material and symbolic condition in Francoist Spain. My task here is not to ad-dress the question of the fantastic, but to address the question of genre, which seems to have been obfuscated by issues such as the fantastic.

In *El cuento de nunca acabar,* a collection of essays on the nature of literature, Martín Gaite sees the activities of reading and writing as an escape. Taking her use of *fugar,* "to escape," at face value, especially because of the allusion to Todorov, some critics have viewed *The Back Room* as escapist literature.[7] However, as Martín Gaite suggests, reading and writing against the grain allow us to think in new ways and, thus, free us, or allow us to escape, from habitual modes of interpreting our social context. In most of her writing Martín Gaite explores women's subject position in Francoist Spain in its various configurations. In this exploration the text becomes an agonistic site, where her inherited and learned models of literary behavior clash with the insights gained from placing in question a certain subject position and all the generic categories and protocols of behavior attached to it. Martín Gaite engages in a constant critique of the genres that have shaped her subjectivity and that still influence her; she at once criticizes these discourses and implicates herself in them. As she says, "It is difficult to escape the literary stereotypes of one's earliest years, however hard one tries later to renounce them" (138:141).

One of the man in black's recurring criticisms of Martín Gaite's narrative production is that she has allowed her writing to be limited by the generic conventions she has inherited. He believes that her first novel, *El Balneario,* could have been a novel of mystery and intrigue, "'Yes, it could have been a good fantastic novel,' he says slowly. 'It had a very promising beginning, but then you allowed fear to overcome you, a fear you've never lost. What happened to you?'" (41–42: 48). He goes on to state that she allowed her sense of what was normal and acceptable to interfere with her writing, "And the reader feels that he can neither believe nor fail to believe what is going to happen from then on. That is the basis of fantastic literature. It's a question of rejecting everything there in that hotel that subsequently seems perversely bent on appearing to you to be altogether normal and obvious, isn't that so?" (43–44: 50). Genre, which establishes norms and categories in and for discourse, restricts Martín Gaite's writing and, thus, her possibilities of expression.

At another point in their conversation, Martín Gaite mentions her plans to write a book of historical essays on romantic customs of postwar Spain to be entitled *Usos amorosos de la postguerra española.* The man in black cites this proposed project as continuing the pattern of her writing commented upon earlier: "It smacks of all your historical research. If that's the title you have in mind, I can see you burying yourself in periodicals libraries again, determined to deal exhaustively with your subject, to make everything absolutely clear. The result would be an estimable piece of work, one strewn with little white pebbles that would be a substitute for the footprints that you yourself have left behind" (198–99: 198).[8] He then accuses her of having lived life without leaving the refuge of literature, an accusation that is related to the image of an earlier conversation on traditional history as *piedrecitas blancas,* white pebbles that attempt to lead us back to some origin. Piedrecitas blancas and literature as refuge are similar concepts for a type of history that provides meaning by ordering events into a rational system of progression and conclusion.[9] Literature as escape is to live in the illusion that people are autonomous beings and can separate themselves from a determined social context. White stones as history represent a mythology of a progressive and rational history as counter-text to a seemingly confusing present of lived experience.

In the essay "El Gato con Botas" (The Cat with Boots, 1983), Martín Gaite says that she did not admire the characters in Perrault's fairy tales because they all followed the same destiny, mapped out for them by the conventions of the genre. She admires Puss in Boots because he challenges the conventions of the fairy tale by questioning reality. Martín Gaite uses "reality" as a term for status quo, or a particular social context accepted as given, which we allow to define us:

> Puss in Boots establishes as a challenge for himself the rejection of reality. Why accept irreversibly the version imposed by destiny, that his master, who has received at the death of his father no more inheritance than a sorry cat, should be and should continue to be until the end of his days the third orphan of a poor miller? Why not put to use that inheritance, which is he himself, and make the most profit out of it? And in that matter, rebelling against the fatality of facts, he begins by narrating them to himself in a distinct form, composing a fiction that transforms and magnifies them. (translation mine: 170)

Perrault's other characters fail to interest her because they appear "similar and without a distinct profile to the child's eyes" (translation mine: 168). The conventions of genre influence how one relates to a social context. In "La Cenicienta" (Cinderella), another essay in the same book, Martín Gaite develops the theme of "El Gato con Botas" further by giving reasons why children could find seductive the generic routine of fairy tales. That is, children always encounter a perfect listener, who makes sense out of the hero's adventures and situation for them (124). The stories valorize and privilege certain themes and conventions as more worthy subjects and more interesting structures of narration than others. If the child, according to Martín Gaite, accepts the canons of narrative acceptability implicit in these texts, then the child becomes an adult indifferent to other stories, such as those of actual maids and beggars (126). Genre limits reading because it breeds, among other things, familiarity in the reader. Just as the child learns to expect a predictable gratification from fairy tales, the reader has similar expectations in the realm of other genres.[10] Just as, in the fairytale "Cinderella," one learns to distinguish between "real" poor people and "fictional" poor people.

In several places Martín Gaite refers to a quotation, "Eloquence rests not with the speaker but with the listener," taken from Father Sarmiento, an eighteenth-century Benedictine monk and member of the Spanish Enlightenment.[11] That is, readers must define the text for themselves in interaction with it. Martín Gaite suggests that we often allow how the text labels itself to affect our reading of it. Autobiography and fiction, then, may not be as different in terms of referentiality as genre theorists would traditionally contend. Rather than posing the traditional questions, "Was the person real or not?" and "Can we verify the information in the text?" Martín Gaite asks, "What are our expectations when we read?" and "What are we taught to expect from certain genres?"[12]

Some critics have said that the narrator of *The Back Room* is not worthy of confidence, that is, credibility, because confusion exists between "facts" and "fiction."[13] In the sense that the narrator is not reliable in providing consistent versions of herself or of historical data, these critics are partially correct. Traditionally in literary criticism, terms like "undecidability" and "contradiction" have been mobilized to dismiss the seriousness or relevance of a text. Serious is a code used to describe a text that "refers to reality," that "has a political and ideological message," that "deals with real life." For Martín Gaite, however, undecidability and contradiction are what make all narrative compelling and effective and potentially subversive or repressive (167).

The question of genre is one fraught with undecidability and ethicopolitical concerns. Martín Gaite mentions that her uncle Joaquín was shot for being a socialist after Franco's victory, "Lo fusilaron por socialista" (116), and describes the anxiety in her liberal household: "An uncle of mine had been executed by a firing squad and my father had not sent us to schools run by nuns and had refused to have Germans billeted in our house. Our parents kept warning us that we shouldn't talk about things like that in public, and sometimes my mother would tell about how it scared her to wake up in the night on hearing a truck braking abruptly to a stop in front of the house" (193: 193). In an autobiographical sketch included in Joan Lipman Brown's book, Martín Gaite says that the main reason her liberal father, friend of Unamuno and other intellectuals, was not imprisoned or executed was that he was not affiliated with any political party. As ruler and arbiter of norms, Franco was present in a variety of ways: "Franco was the first real ruler in my life that I was ever aware of as such, because from the beginning it was clear that he was the one and only, that his power was indisputable and omnipresent, that he had managed to insinuate himself into all the houses, schools, movie theaters, and cafés, do away with spontaneity and variety, arouse a religious, uniform fear, stifle conversations and laughter so that no one's voice rang out any louder than anyone else's" (Lane 129:132).

Franco's ability to dictate social norms and his omnipresent figure become metaphors for genre, which is not a means of simply classifying literary texts for Martín Gaite, but, even more powerfully and insidiously, a means by which people take and justify power. Hidden in genre is the possibility of violence. Uncle Joaquín was a victim of an ideological use of a particular genre, that is, political rhetoric of nationalism, that saw its program as the totalizing telos and principle for its society.

In *The Back Room* Martín Gaite is not speaking about a facile abolishing of genre; she is questioning the mechanisms by which the concept of genre, linked always to questions of gender, shapes and fashions political-ideological norms of subjectivity. The interplay between two modes of reading, autobiography and fiction, shifts the ground of critical inquiry from one of genre, in its traditional function, to a consideration of how subjectivity is being represented. Genre as a concept, if accepted without question in both its figurative and pragmatic functions, is able to conceal its own complicity in maintaining a particular discursive system of power relations by creating the illusion that this system is natural. To read *The Back Room* in either of the two modes above is to run the risk of accepting certain categories that have traditionally defined subjectivity in the West, such as autonomous individuality, the subject-object split, the spiritual and material, the universal, to name only a few. By putting autobiography and fiction in play against each other, Martín Gaite is asking readers to question their categories and presuppositions about literature and "reality."

In *The Back Room* Martín Gaite describes children's behavior in terms of protagonism in a role: "We children were obliged to figure out [interpret] the details of that ominous text from the gestures, but the general outlines were laid down in accordance with a dichotomy that was only too comprehensible: staying put, conforming, and making the best of things was good; skipping out, escaping, running away were bad" (121: 125). *The Back Room* posits subjectivity (in the double sense of the word), not in terms of an autonomous individual confronting the world, but in language and discourse shaping consciousness and behavior. It is also a text, again agonistic, in which Martín Gaite learns to gain the courage to place in question her own classifications and the social roles imposed upon her.

Martín Gaite is acutely aware that how she sees herself cannot be separated from the discourse that has shaped her. Discussing her first novel, she says the experience that led to its writing, a stay in a spa with her father, was inextricably interwoven with literary models. Upon her arrival at the spa, she remembers that she looked at herself in a small hand-mirror and did not recognize herself: "I pretended to be removing a speck of dirt from my eye, but the disturbing thought crossed my mind that I wasn't me. Just as that place wasn't that place. And I had a sort of premonition: 'This is literature. I am being possessed by literature'" (43: 49).

At that moment Martín Gaite has the feeling that she is a character in one of the many novels she has read. In her essay "Las mujeres noveleras" (1983) Martín Gaite says that she would find it difficult to answer the question, "What literature has influenced you?" because "the first great enigma to solve is where the frontier lies between that which we call life and that which we call literature. It would be so difficult to elucidate the existing relation between literary behavior and our own" (translation mine: 94). The relationship between literary and social conduct for Martín Gaite is intimately related to the act of reading. Reading does not simply involve a printed text, but is the activity in which every person is continuously engaged. The text that children and the young Martín Gaite of *The Back Room* are taught to read is a social text that covers a wide spectrum from Cervantes to boleros, from religion to politics.

In "Las veladas de la quinta" (1983) Martín Gaite discusses the types of questions that children ask when they read and the reaction of adults to their questions. In fact, she relates much of her theorizing on literature in *El cuento de nunca acabar*, where this essay appears, to the ways children read and react to their social context. She discusses how reading can become a form of socialization that extinguishes children's natural curiosity. Because children's questions often disrupt or challenge the conventions and behaviors upon which social exchange is based, adults use their power to discourage them. The result is that children often accept as unchallengable and ultimately desirable the discourse of their elders:

> And thus, sooner or later, although they may not comprehend it, children understand that the only way to live in peace with their elders is to accept in full inherited norms of behavior. Children

accept these norms without attempting to figure them out. The result is that the place of their initial enthusiasm for imaginative activity, which tinted in red with sparks of gold their passionate interruptions of stories told, is eventually taken over by a gray apathy, by a faint-hearted submission to the confusing but safe discourse of their elders. The children end up admiring and accepting it as the pillars of an established order they feel unworthy to undermine. (translation mine: 150)

Reading in this mode becomes a question of gender and is absolutely necessary to a political and ideological system vested in the denial of difference. *The Back Room* also comments on genres, some shared by both genders and others not, and their social uses. As Martín Gaite says, "Rhetoric in the postwar era was devoted to discrediting the feminist stirrings that had begun in the years of the Republic, and stressed once again the unselfish heroism of wives and mothers, the importance of their silent and obscure labor as pillars of the Christian home and family" (87: 93).

The models of behavior and desire that were dictated for her and other young girls in this period assumed form in the many genres—popular music, fashion, romance novels, and film—that Martín Gaite discusses in *The Back Room*. Often these genres, such as fashion, clashed with the official rhetoric of the period. By juxtaposing fashion and the official rhetoric governing women's social role, as well as other examples, Martín Gaite reveals through this official discourse's gaps and contradictions its inability to contain the play of difference. In fact, the rhetoric of sacrificial heroism preached by the government and the Women's Section of the fascist party outlives its usefulness as Spain begins to industrialize under a capitalist model of consumption, a shift investigated more systematically in *Usos amorosos de la postguerra española*. Whether the language of heroic fascism or capitalism, the government's rhetoric led to one ideological goal, the subordination of women to men: "our status as strong women, the complement and mirror of the male" (87: 94). Through the exploration of genre, Martín Gaite investigates how her identity was constructed by the discourses of the historical period she recounts.

For example, Martín Gaite has a telephone conversation with a woman named Carola who is possibly the lover of the man in black. The incident remains shrouded in mystery, for the reader never knows for certain whether the man in black is the Alejandro to whom Carola refers. The young woman describes her relationship to Alejandro in terms of deciphering the hidden past of a complex and tortured man. In the middle of the conversation, Martín Gaite remembers a scene from the film *Rebecca:* "I remember Joan Fontaine again, unable to get to sleep in that immense old mansion at Manderley, lying with her eyes wide open in the dark. I hear that voice off-camera that sounded even deeper and more solemn as it echoed off the vaulted ceiling, repeating bits of conversations that gave her clues about her mysterious predecessor: 'Her name was Rebecca de Winters, everyone says that she was very beautiful, that her husband adored her'" (159: 161). The young woman who converses with Martín Gaite has as her only goal the deciphering of Alejandro's behavior; that is, she valorizes her own social role by whether Alejandro loves her or not. At first Carola views the narrator as a rival for Alejandro's affections. Martín Gaite listens to the young woman tell her story, and the conversation ends inconclusively. The young woman's acceptance of a subordinate position to men seems so natural to her that she accepts Alejandro's violence toward her as part of the relationship, or rather as part of the complex she is trying to decipher and cure (157:159).

Within Mary Anne Doane's model of classic cinema, there are two modes of female spectatorship: to view the film as a male spectator, since the male gaze is what structures the film, or to view it as a masochist, that is to identify with the female protagonist's incorporation into or under the male gaze (16–20). Related to a scene from classic cinema, Martín Gaite's telephone conversation with the young woman and her discussion of film in *Usos amorosos de la postguerra española* and in *The Back Room* touch upon spectatorship, which is both another form of reading and a social role.

Doane points out that classic cinema wished to deny subjectivity to the female spectator and operated so that all female spectators should submit to the masculine gaze.[14] In relation to *Rebecca* and *Caught*, Doane says, "Each of these films contains a scene in which the camera almost literally enacts this repression of the feminine—the woman's relegation to the status of a signifier within the male discourse" (155). By offering this model of behavior to women, classic cinema implied that in whatever history women participated they had no subjectivity or gaze.

A key phrase in Martín Gaite's recollection of *Rebecca* as her first film is that of "trying in vain to get to the bottom of the mysterious history of her predecessor" (145: 147). In other words, Martín Gaite perceives that although Joan Fontaine's stated goal is to understand her mysterious predecessor, the true goal of knowing Rebecca's history is to better understand her new husband, to erase the memory of the other woman. Martín Gaite does not get to the bottom of the young woman's story; they hang up the telephone and neither really knows more about each other than at the beginning. The young woman disappears into an unknown, but perhaps predictable, text, and the narrator moves into one in which she is attempting to define some type of subjectivity or investigate a lack of one. Martín Gaite's mention of film relates to women's absence or lack in the social imaginary, which has determined how they do or do not represent themselves.[15]

Just as film was influential among young postwar women, the Women's Section of the fascist party played a prominent social-political role in their everyday lives. In *Usos amorosos de la postguerra española* Martín Gaite details the influence of the Women's Section. The Women's Section acted as a government organization and was headed by Pilar Primo de Rivera, sister of the slain founder of Spain's fascist party. All young women had to complete the training program, which lasted six months or five hundred hours (64). The required courses included religion, cuisine, family and social formation, national syndicalism, flower arranging (59). Unless she bypassed it by getting married, a young woman had to complete this training and could not attend a university or hold any type of job without the appropriate document of completion (59). In *The Back Room,* the narrator describes social service in this way:

> All the harangues that our instructors and female comrades subjected us to in those inhospitable buildings, reminiscent at once of airplane hangars and popular movie houses, where I grudgingly did my Social Service, sewing hems, doing gymnastics, and playing basketball, all turned out to have the same aim: to get us to accept, with pride and joy, with a steadfastness that nothing could discourage, as evidenced by sedate conduct that would never be clouded by the slightest shadow of slander, our status as strong women, the complement and mirror of the male. (87: 93–94)

Martín Gaite's descriptions of the Women's Section are linked to the versions of official history that it presented to the young women in obligatory domestic training. They were encouraged to imitate Isabel the Catholic and the values attributed to her by this official history: "We were placed beneath her advocacy, we were given talks about her iron will and her spirit of sacrifice, we were told how she had held the ambition and the despotism of the nobles in check, how she had created the Holy Office, expelled the traitorous Jews, given up her jewels to finance the most glorious undertaking in our history. Yet even so there had been those who had slandered her because of her fidelity to her ideals, those who called her abnegation cruelty" (89: 95). In *Usos amorosos de la postguerra española* Martín Gaite notes, however, that the biographies of figures such as Isabel, Saint Theresa of Avila, and others were read for religious edification and to make women stronger and more effective in their role of moral guides for the home: "But those histories, even if they were able to inspire the self to definitive propositions, never stopped posing themselves as exceptions in which it was not convenient for the ordinary woman to see herself reflected" (translation mine: 150).

Martín Gaite views this official and monumental history as a tool of propaganda. Upon describing the official interpretation of Isabel's reign, she observes that it is based on the repression of difference—the expulsion of the Jews, the conquest of the Moors, and the invasion of the American continent. The goal of this fascist state-controlled propaganda was to provide a model of social identity based on sexual difference and employed in service of the state's political-ideological program. "As a consequence of the brainwashing of that mawkish and optimistic propaganda of the forties, my mistrust of resolute and self-assured individuals became more marked than ever, my eagerness for freedom grew" (90: 96).

For Martín Gaite, then, a contradiction exists between a unified view of identity—"resolute and self-assured individuals"—and the need for freedom. In her view a resolute and self-assured individual is one whose identity is based on an unquestioning acceptance of given social conventions and their binary logic. For her, subjectivity is an open-ended, agonistic process of questioning one's social text, the only means to an always provisional freedom. Official history attempts, on the other hand, to present a unified and stable vision of the world, divided into neat binary oppositions—good and bad, civilized and uncivilized, etc.

Martín Gaite describes not only cinema and official history as influential genres, but also romance novels as a genre addressed to women and one that modeled desire and subjectivity as dependent on and only possible through men. As she notes, "The role that romantic novels played in shaping the sensibilities of [in the formation of] young girls growing up in the forties is very important" (135: 139). In *Usos amorosos de la postguerra española*, she says that genres such as the romance novel caused young girls, including herself, to live on illusions. Usually the illusion was that a man would fall in love with them, transform their lives, and they would live happily ever after. "If someday one were to compute the number of times the words dream and illusion appeared in the songs that were sung constantly then and in the titles of the most popular films and novels, it would be surprising" (translation mine: 159). By omitting women from representation or distorting the reality of their lived experience, official history asked women to read themselves as if they were absence or lack; film and romance novels asked them to read themselves as masochists. Illusion might be considered another word for the socially constructed desire to be put under the male gaze.

For Martín Gaite the ability to read critically is an important skill. In her view, one can either read to reinforce one's incorporation into an already familiar and accepted network of social discourse or one can read against the grain. Reading against the grain can be a subversive and liberating activity. In *The Back Room* Martín Gaite recalls that she read a romance novel, *El amor catedrático*, about a young woman who dares to undertake university studies despite social disapproval and then ends up marrying her Latin professor. Martín Gaite says,

> The ending disappointed me a little. I wasn't really convinced that that girl had done the right thing by marrying a man much older than herself and a monomaniac in the bargain, apart from which I also thought "she didn't need all those provisions for such a short trip," placing so many hopes in studying for a career and defying society that prevented a woman from realizing those hopes, and then having it all turn out that way, the usual happy ending. Who could tell if it would have been all that happy, since sooner or later that girl was bound to feel disillusioned. Moreover, why did all novels have to end when people got married. . . . Very few novels or films dared to go farther and tell us what that love turned out to be like after the bride and groom vowed at the altar to love each other for all eternity, and to tell the truth that roused my suspicions. (88: 92–93)

Martín Gaite's questioning of the romance novel put her on guard against viewing marriage "as a reward for my possible practical virtues" (90: 97). Reading against the grain allowed her to explore the other texts present in a seemingly innocent and innocuous novel. In her essay "Las mujeres noveleras" (1983) she says that this term was not applied to women with a fondness for literature, but rather to women who felt themselves dissatisfied within the social roles prescribed for them: "They did not recognize themselves as particularly satisfied in the haven of the routine arguments that formed the plot of their existence" (translation mine: 96).

Interestingly, Martín Gaite uses terms such as *plot* and *arguments* to describe these women. Their subjectivity is structured by a gendered social role created and transmitted through language. She adds, "Those young women of Salamanca fond of fiction, who disquieted right-thinking opinion, grew up under the menacing shadow of those other rebellious and mythical provincial women whose legacy they have unknowingly taken up" (translation mine: 97). In "The Virtues of Reading" (1989) she declares that "books turn out to be revolutionary: they lead to a problematic ground that has always been regarded with a certain glimmer of distrust" (350). Even though the most rebellious of these mythic figures dies, for the young women of Salamanca to read themselves in another way, against the grain, was a subversive and liberating activity.

Throughout *The Back Room* Martín Gaite engages in an agonistic relationship with the texts that shaped her youth and young adult years in postwar Francoist Spain. Franco is the first ruler she experienced as such because before the war, in the republic, "people talked about whatever they liked, played whatever game they liked, and that was all there was to it as far as I could see" (129: 132). For Martín Gaite the years of the republic promised some hope of being able to openly question imposed roles and norms. And then the Franco years began. Looking back on those years, she says, "the thought came to me that Franco had paralyzed time, and on the very day that they were about to bury him I woke up, with my mind focused on that one thought with a very special intensity" (130: 133).

Franco as the paralyzer of time is an image for a political and ideological system, perhaps for many such systems, that's power is based on the ability to give only one interpretation to the social text and the illusion that it has restricted movement within that discursive field. Literally, the law of genre was the law of death and violence. To be a member of the socialist or any other party was to be dead. To be politically suspect was to suffer possible hardship. Censorship was a political fact: "staying put, conforming, and making the best of things was good" (121: 125).

By exploring the genres that have shaped her own and other women's subjectivity, Martín Gaite links the question of subjectivity and gender, representation and genre, to a certain political-ideological system of discourse. Thus she demonstrates that gender and genre cannot be separated. Political and ideological discourses determine representational practices, and these in turn determine the way in which subject positions are constructed.

Reading against the grain and representing subjectivity in a different way offer spaces of resistance and provisional freedom in the dominant social text and are acts of solidarity with other women. Paradoxically, this momentary space of a resisting and provisionally free subjectivity is created through the proliferation of interpretation and the displacement of meaning. Martín Gaite comments that the type of activity that led to reading against the grain and representing subjectivity in a different way was discouraged: "The word isolation comes from the word island. It was a dangerous feeling, forbidden by the instructresses in the Women's Section" (115: 120). Isolation, or the imagining of a space of one's own, was to attempt to see one's socially constructed identity as different or set apart from that of others. In *Usos amorosos de la postguerra española*, Martín Gaite notes "the aloofness of the 'strange' girl, little inclined to share her emotional states with her girlfriends, was interpreted as a lack of solidarity, as a symptom of unfriendliness that was almost insulting. From the very start, the 'strange' girl was not left in peace. As we see in another place, one fought to redeem her from her 'abnormal' conditions and make her obey the laws of the pack" (Translation mine: 182). Because of the laws of genre and social pressure, Martín Gaite states in *The Back Room* that her only space of resistance could be a mental one created by critical reading and eventually taking form in writing: "I would never have dared flee [at the light of day] from the light of the sun, I knew that I would escape, rather, by way of the dark, secret twists and turns of imagination, by way of the spiral of dreams, by way of a path within, without creating scandal or breaking down walls. I knew that everyone was born to follow his path" (122: 126).

The phrase "everyone was born to follow his path" can be interpreted to mean that within a cultural system one's path is already determined by and represented in a social text by the fact of gender. Martín Gaite's theoretical and historical discussion of genre and gender in *The Back Room* cannot be separated from (and actually arises from) her own struggle to be able to represent her subjectivity, a struggle that brings to mind Virginia Woolf on the steps of the Oxford library in *A Room of One's Own*. The need to represent one's subjectivity is also a working through of other texts. At the same time, a back room or a room of one's own is a place of resistance and repression.

In her essay "Women and Fiction" Woolf reminds the reader that the ambiguity of her title "is intentional, for in dealing with women as writers, as much elasticity as possible is desirable; it is necessary to leave oneself room to deal with other things besides their work, so much has that work been influenced by conditions that have nothing whatever to do with it" (43). In other words, those conditions have everything to do with their work. In *The Back Room* anger and hardship appear at moments and then seem to disappear. The narrator is asking the reader to see both her experience and her act of narrating it—both almost indistinguishable—as a counter-text to the genres she describes. That is, as a young intellectual woman struggling to be independent, Martín Gaite's path was not the one she should have been treading.

The Back Room does not explicitly state Martín Gaite's anger at the hardship of being a woman in postwar Spain. Martín Gaite recalls one day when her mother defended her: "'A clever person learns even such a thing as how to sew a button on better than a stupid one,' she retorted one day when a lady, shaking her head in disapproval, had said of me, 'A woman who knows Latin can come to no good end,' and I looked at my mother in eternal gratitude" (87: 93). Martín Gaite explains that the saying was meant to warn against becoming a spinster, and she assumes that the reader will catch both its literal and subversive content. Her grandmother also worried about her intellectual bent. "'Almost anything keeps that one amused,' my mother was saying. 'She likes studying so much.' 'Too much,' my grandmother was saying. 'Heaven only knows why she spends so much of her time thinking'" (72: 78). In *Usos amorosos de la postguerra española*, Martín Gaite observes, "Even within her own house, the isolation of a girl aroused suspicions, and not even invoking a reason as noble as her fondness for books managed to put in good standing her tendency to solitude" (translation mine: 182).

Fortunately for Martín Gaite her mother was supportive of her intellectual aspirations, even a little envious (*Back Room* 87: 93). Her mother also had her own back room when she was young (88: 91) and was delighted "to read and to play children's games, and she would have liked to study at the university, like her two brothers, but it wasn't the custom in those days for girls to prepare for a career, so the thought never even crossed her mind to ask to do so" (86: 92). *The Back Room* is not only Martín Gaite's story but also that of her mother and many other women like her. In a sense, Martín Gaite's mother prepared the way for her. And even with her mother's support, it was still difficult to take a path not marked for her.

Martín Gaite's intellectual experience is characterized by her awareness of the need for another text, another way of representing her social identity. This is also an awareness that one can never be free from other texts, but can only take learned models and transform them. In what is possibly one of the most poignant moments in the text, Martín Gaite remembers her best friend from school. The two invented their own island, named Bergai, and wrote about it. The protagonist of one of their novels was Esmeralda, a young girl who disdained wealth and escaped from her home on a stormy night to have adventures (183). Martín Gaite says that for both of them "the island of Bergai began to take shape as a land far removed from our world. It was much more real than things we saw around us. It had the power and the logical consistency of dreams" (195: 195). Her friend, whose parents were in prison for being Communists, had taught her "the pleasure of escaping all by oneself, that ability to invent things that make us feel safe from death" (195–196: 195).

From her friend, Martín Gaite learns the importance of seeing herself in a different way. Interestingly enough, the island of Bergai transforms the model of the romance novel. Neither the young girls nor their heroine find husbands and live the happy end; Bergai is a place for them to encounter each other and attempt to alter in some way the image imposed upon them by society. "'Whenever you notice that people don't like you very much,' my girlfriend said to me, 'or when you don't understand something, come to Bergai. I'll be waiting there for you'" (179: 180).

Though the two girls managed to represent their social identities in another way, they still used the models that were imposed on them. Representation, then, cannot be separated from the models of discourse that have shaped desire and affected behavior. Speaking of Carmencita Franco, Martín Gaite says, "We've been the victims of the same manners and mores, we've read the same magazines and seen the same movies. Our children may be different, but our dreams have surely been much the same, I'm as certain of that as I am of all the other things that can never be proved" (133: 136–37). She and Carmencita Franco have been victims of a discourse that was not theirs and subject to a role that it dictated. Martín Gaite is watching Franco's funeral with her daughter and her daughter's friend and cannot explain to them her feeling for Carmencita Franco: "It seemed impossible to me to explain to them my sudden emotion at the sight of Carmencita Franco, bereaved of that sempereternal father, who sometimes was photographed with her by the press in inaccessible rooms, during brief respites from his dictatorial vigilance" (134: 137).

At Franco's death Martín Gaite recalls that she thought about her origins, or the events that marked her birth (135). She related them to the death of several politicians: "I remembered that the deaths of Antonio Maura and Pablo Iglesias had coincided with my birth, and it suddenly came to me that a cycle of fifty years was about to end, that my entire life had unfolded between those two funerals that I had not seen and the one that I was seeing. I felt as though I were framed by that circle revolving about me, with two sunny mornings as poles" (133: 136). Martín Gaite describes her life in terms of the republic and the death of Franco and again connects it to the ideological and political structures that have marked her existence; her life is not simply hers, but part of a larger system of discourse and power. Her "I" is (de)limited by the male gaze and patronym that are described in terms of absence and presence. Martín Gaite reveals that neither history nor its facts are neutral.

By investigating the ideological basis of the discourses that have shaped her subjectivity, Martín Gaite challenges the private-public split that our modes of reading (genres) would have us accept. In this split, a back room becomes a place of confinement and separation. The writer has the illusion that her space is autonomous, separate from what is happening in the street, something she has created; she then participates in the very structures that would keep her in a room, separate and apart. Martín Gaite says, "I would like to talk to the man in black about the narrative vehicle that is implicit in these pieces of furniture, present him with all the images that, during this interlude, have appeared to me between the sideboard and the mirror" (91: 97). *The Back Room*, then, is part of other texts—the sideboard and mirror are images of the domestic activities to which women have been confined. She knows, though, that the furniture contains other stories, some not pleasant—of laborers cutting wood, of sweat, of profit. Everything in the back room is connected to something else, originates somewhere else, cannot be separated from systems of production. The back room is never neutral or private. For Martín Gaite it can only be a provisional space where she finds a moment's rest from habitual modes of thought, and only thus can she begin to question her social text.

Although *The Back Room* is a space of resistance, it is at the same time a text that implicates itself in that which it criticizes. When she reacts as a character would in a romance novel, when she recognizes a pose or attitude from a film she is reproducing in her own social interaction, Martín Gaite implicates herself and explores how she is oppressing herself. This process of politicization comes to characterize her exploration of the back room. And her critique becomes more forceful and more insistent as she explores the many forms of victimization she as a woman in a particular historical period has experienced: victimization by the discourses that surround her, victimization by men, and victimization by those women who help maintain the structures of a masculinist society.

As a result of the public-private split, the social-material conditions of women's lives that have shaped their subjectivity have been deemed unimportant to the march of traditional history—treaties, wars, battles, diplomacy—and have been relegated to the "private." In this way women have been placed in back rooms that were only always imaginary; thus they have contributed unwittingly and out of no choice to their own oppression, believing that their actions and behavior had nothing to do with "out there," in the street, in the bank, in the legislature, as if their lives could really be separated from an "out there." And these imaginary back rooms have also caused women not to be able to see each other as sharing the same material and social conditions, because of issues of race, class, and sexual desire.

In *The Back Room* Martín Gaite suggests that the (hidden) voices of women and their (unread) texts can show in what ways questions of subjectivity and gender are political and ideological ones and play themselves out in concepts such as genre. For Martín Gaite these are not simply abstract or theoretical concerns; thus she can never separate herself from the autobiographical moment nor define it in her writing.

Notes

1   See Martín Gaite's autobiographical sketch in Brown's book (1987); Celia Fernández.

2   See Derrida (74). In Spanish *género* means both "gender" and "genre."

3   See Foucault (153–54) for a discussion of effective history.

4   Unless otherwise stated, translations are from Helen Lane's edition of *The Back Room*. Page numbers after the colon refer to the original Spanish of the works cited.

5   Debra Castillo points out that "theory of one kind is quite clearly expounded in the novel, and critics like Manuel Durán point out the significance of the narrator's many suggestive references to Todorov's structural analysis of the fantastic genre. Yet the fantastic form fails to account for the power of the novel—as Durán realizes in giving his essay the subtitle 'Todorov y algo más'" (815).

6   See Debra Castillo; Jean S. Chittenden; Linda Gould Levine; Joan Lipman Brown (1981, 1986, 1987); Julian Paley.

7   Brown and Smith state that "much of the novel involves escapism, both through direct avoidance of reality and through the use of unresolved ambiguity to effect an

indirect evasion" (68). They add that this is escapism "in various senses of the word" (69), but the clarification only seems to further strengthen that they mean escapism in a literal sense. The statement that the text is a "direct avoidance of reality" seems to imply that they have some clear definition of what "reality" consists.

8   *Usos amorosos de la postguerra española* was published in 1987.

9   Foucault says that traditional history is "a suprahistorical perspective: a history whose function is to compose the finally reduced diversity of time into a totality fully closed upon itself; a history that always encourages subjective recognitions and attributes a form of reconciliation to all the displacements of the past; a history whose perspective on all that precedes it implies the end of time, a completed development. The historian's history finds its support outside of time and pretends to base its judgments on an apocalyptic objectivity. This is only possible, however, because of its belief in eternal truth, the immortality of the soul, and the nature of consciousness as always identical to itself" (152). He also adds that "'Effective' history differs from traditional history in being without constants. Nothing in man— not even his body—is sufficiently stable to serve as the basis for self-recognition or for understanding other men" (153).

10 Phyllis McCord points out that despite the critical questioning of generic categories, "most critics and readers, as well as publishers and authors, preserve the conventional distinctions between novels and life, fiction and nonfiction, literary works and 'other' texts" (59).

11 *La búsqueda del interlocutor* (24–25); "The Virtues of Reading" (351); *El cuento de nunca acabar* (146). Translation is that of Marcia Welles, "The Virtues of Reading."

12 Martín Gaite says, "Desde la muerte de Franco habrá notado cómo proliferan los libros de memorias, ya es una peste, en el fondo, eso es lo que me ha venido desanimando, pensar que, si a mí me aburren las memorias de los demás, por qué no le[s] van a aburrir a los demás las mías" (128). She indicates that writing in conventional and predictable ways also results from people accepting and expecting the features that become associated with a genre, thus her critique of some early *apertura* literature.

13 Kathleen Glenn states that "theoretically, this narrator should be worthy of complete confidence, since she literally speaks in the name of the author. The relation between the extratextual author and the intratextual narrator-protagonist is, nonetheless, fraught with ambiguity" (152).

14 *El cuarto de atrás* begins with an epigraph by George Bataille. He is concerned in some of his texts (e.g., *Story of an Eye*) with the problematic of the male gaze and its relation to the construction of desire.

15 As Doane points out, "In many respects, the most disturbing images of the two films [*Caught* and *Rebecca*] are those which evoke the absence of the woman. In both films these images follow projection scenes which delineate the impossibility of female spectatorship. It is as though each film adhered to the logic which characterizes dreamwork—establishing the image of an absent woman as the delayed mirror image of a female spectator who herself is only virtual" (174–75).

References

Brown, Joan Lipman. "A Fantastic Memoir: Technique and History in *El cuarto de atrás*." *Anales de narrativa española contemporánea* 6 (1981): 13–20.

——. "One Autobiography, Twice Told: Martín Gaite's *Entre visillos* and *El cuarto de atrás*." *Hispanic Journal* 7.2 (1986): 37–47.

——. *Secrets from the Back Room: The Fiction of Carmen Martín Gaite.* University, Miss.: Romance Monographs, 1987.

Brown, Joan Lipman, and E. M. Smith. "*El cuarto de atrás:* Metafiction and the Actualization of Literary Theory." *Hispanófila* 90 (1987): 63–69.

Castillo, Debra. "Never-Ending Story: Carmen Martín Gaite's *The Back Room.*" *PMLA* 102.5 (1987): 814–28.

Chittenden, Jean S. "*El cuarto de atrás* as Autobiography." *Letras Femeninas* 12.1–2 (1986): 78–84.

Chown, Linda E. "*Fragmentos de interior:* Pieces and Patterns." *Hispanófila* 91 (1987): 1–12.

Derrida, Jacques. "The Law of Genre." Trans. Avital Ronell. *Critical Inquiry* 7 (1980): 55–81.

Doane, Mary Anne. *The Desire to Desire: The Woman's Film of the 1940s.* Bloomington: Indiana UP, 1987.

Durán, Manuel. "*El cuarto de atrás:* Imaginación, fantasía, misterio; Todorov y algo más." Servodidio and Welles 129–37.

Fernández, Celia. "Entrevista con Carmen Martín Gaite." *Anales de la narrativa española contemporánea* 4 (1979): 165–72.

Foucault, Michel. *Language, Counter-Memory, Practice.* Ithaca: Cornell UP, 1977.

Glenn, Kathleen M. "*El cuarto de atrás:* Literature as *juego* and the Self-Reflexive Text." Servodidio and Welles 149–59.

Lane, Helen, trans. *The Back Room.* New York: Columbia UP, 1983.

Levine, Linda Gould. "Carmen Martín Gaite's *El cuarto de atrás:* A Portrait of the Artist as Woman." Servodidio and Welles 161–72.

McCord, Phyllis Frus. "The Ideology of Form: The Nonfiction Novel." *Genre* 19.1 (Spring 1986): 59–79.

Martín Gaite, Carmen. *El cuarto de atrás.* Barcelona: Destino, 1978.

——. *El cuento de nunca acabar.* Madrid: Trieste, 1983.

——. *La búsqueda del interlocutor.* 1973. Barcelona: Destino, 1982.

——. *Usos amorosos de la postguerra española.* Barcelona: Anagrama, 1987.

——. "The Virtues of Reading." Trans. Marcia L. Welles. *PMLA* 104.3 (1989): 348–53.

Paley, Julian. "Dreams in Two Novels of Carmen Martín Gaite." Servodidio and Welles 107–16.

Servodidio, Mirella, and Marcia L. Welles, eds. *From Fiction to Metafiction: Essays in Honor of Carmen Martín Gaite.* Lincoln, Neb.: Soc. of Spanish-American Studies, 1983.

Woolf, Virginia. *Women and Writing.* Ed. Michele Barrett. New York: Harcourt, 1979.

Policing Truth: Confession, Gender, and Autobiographical Authority

LEIGH GILMORE

■

For the least glimmer of truth is conditioned by politics.
—Michel Foucault, The History of Sexuality

Lying So Near the Truth

As Madonna, that Rorschach test of our time, has shown, the game of truth or dare operates less as an innocent model of personal revelation than through the intricate structural dynamics of the confession in which, according to prescribed rules, one is authorized to question and the other is bound to confess. When I used to play the game "truth or dare," from which Madonna takes the title for her 1991 concert film, "truth" was not only the expected choice (thus revealing the false binary of truth *or* dare) but the easier choice. Certainly, a "dare" had its appeal; it involved movement, gesture, bodily risk. Functionally, however, it was an evasion, for it drew attention away from the conspiritoconfessional moment in which I could become the one who whispers intimacies. I could be dared to do almost anything, but I would be asked to tell the truth only about a single topic. In the absence of witnesses who could deny or corroborate my answer, "truth" was always the best place to lie. That self-representational moment, structured and experienced as an exercise in truth-production, reveals something crucial about autobiography. In that discursive setting, where truth is known at least partially through its proximity to risk, identity emerges not as a thing in itself patiently awaiting the moment of revelation but as the space from which confession issues. In this confessional space, there is a preferred topic already structured through another self-representational nexus. Sexuality as what is confessed, or the *topos* of truth, is represented through the nexus of gender, identity, and authority.[1]

When a writer is seen in relation to the dominant discourses of power s/he was simultaneously inscribing and resisting, the "innocence" of autobiography as a naive attempt to tell a universal truth is radically particularized by a specific culture's notion of what truth is, who may tell it, and who is authorized to judge it. What we have come to call truth or what a culture determines to be truth in autobiography, among other discourses, is largely the effect of a long and complex process of authorization. Thus the canonizing question "What is truth?" cannot be separated from the process of verifying that truth. These are not discrete moments in any history, including literary history, where authority is established, for the production and authorization of truth emerge jointly in the confession, as in other exercises in truth-telling. Some are positioned in closer proximity to "truth" depending on their relation to other terms of value: gender, class, race, and sexuality, among others. When autobiography criticism preserves truth telling as a major symbolic, thematic, and referential dimension of the text, the autobiographer's ability to write her/himself into some proximate relation to the terms of value determines how the text will be interpreted.

Although the problems that constitute interest in autobiography have undergone major epistemic shifts since the "first" autobiography in English (Margery Kempe's *Book*), little contemporary attention has focused on a relationship that surely underwrites the autobiographical project: the relationship between truth telling and agency.[2] Authority in autobiography springs from its proximity to the truth claim of the confession, a discourse that insists upon the possibility of telling the whole truth while paradoxically frustrating that goal through the structural demands placed on how one confesses. "Telling the truth" so totalizes the confession that it denotes the imperative to confess, the structure of that performance, and the grounds for its judgment. Telling the truth may be a form of punishment, as well as an effort to stave it off. In order to stand as an authoritative producer of "truth," one must successfully position oneself as a confessing subject whose account adequately fulfills enough of the requirements of confession. Insofar as truth telling is a cultural production that offers varying rewards, is both embraced and resisted, upheld and revised through its practice, and forms a site in the Middle Ages where power was contested, an examination of the influence of the confession upon autobiography can reveal the possibilities and limits of human agency in the production of truth. Thus, the relation of the confession to subsequent forms of self-representation in which "truth" is taken to be at stake, from this point of view, does not entail a narrative of genre formation. Rather, the legacy of the confession for autobiography can be introduced as a history of valuing and devaluing, of determining and misrecognizing the profoundly political dimension of all discourses of identity.

The confession's persistence in self-representation and the meaning attributed to that persistence largely structure authority in autobiography. As a mode of truth production the confession in both its oral and its written forms grants the autobiographer a kind of authority derived from the confessor's proximity to "truth." Inasmuch as the confession's cultural authority, then, necessarily exists in relation to other discursive and historical formations—religion, psychology, philosophy—the grounds of cultural and autobiographical authority are subject to change. These shifts enable the confession's authority to be recuperated by a variety of practices and discourses interested in controlling and structuring the confessing subject's speech. Psychoanalysis, for example, is available to twentieth-century autobiographers as one of these "self"-authorizing discourses. Yet, the access to self-authorization is regulated, as I have suggested, in a variety of ways, and this way of contextualizing autobiography reveals how intimately bound up in the cultural practices of policing and resistance is a kind of writing that is more frequently thought of as simply private. That is, the confession did not merely prohibit, restrict, and censor speech. Indeed, the evident "thematic of regulation" in spiritual confessions enables the one confessing to develop alternative and rewarded competencies in telling the truth.[3] I do not want to overemphasize the liberating possibilities of the confession, however, but only to insist, as Foucault does, that power does not only flow from the top down. For example, the pressure placed on the church/ state by women's visionary experience prompted a discursive crisis: the language of the (patriarchal) ecclesiastical authority clashed with the language of mysticism (defined largely by women mystics) and the function of the confession was to police these contradictions.[4] In order to regulate potentially threatening speech in the Middle Ages, the church/ state developed an elaborate vocabulary that controlled, through both the setting and the language of confession, what one could and must say. To be sure, one could always bring a competing agenda to the confession, but one still had to convince the confessor in *his* language.

Foucault links the confession to the discourse of sexuality, but I am concerned with a different history from the one he charts, and with women as subjects in and of history. He sees the confession as profoundly involved with the discourse of sexuality and the sexualization of discourse. He examines the Greek and Roman, eighteenth-century, and Victorian periods, charting the "deployment" of sexuality by the eighteenth-century sciences and gesturing toward its relation to the Christian tradition of confession. By contrast, I focus on the "beginning" and "end" of the confession, on how it has become embedded in self-representation, and on its meaning to and for women. More specifically, rather than trace the history of mysticism and confession in a particular region or within a limited historical frame, I want to let the challenge visionary experience posed to the church/state apparatus stand as an example of power relations as Foucault describes them. That is, power relations have a "strictly relational character. . . . Their existence depends on a multiplicity of points of resistance."[5] Within this context, I wish to examine how women, in particular, negotiated the discourses of truth, how their writing reveals the widespread and relatively long-lasting practice of mysticism as a resisting force, as well as the ability of the church/state to adapt to, if not always to contain, its presence.

Autobiography cannot in this context be seen to draw its social authority simply from a privileged relation to real life. Rather, authority is derived through autobiography's proximity to the rhetoric of truth telling: the confession. The legacy of the confession for women's self-representational writing persists in two ways. First, the confession imports not only the spiritual but also the legal constraints of truth telling and potential punishment for error into the genre. The story of the self is constructed as one that must be sworn to and will be subject to verification. Second, truth is marked as a cultural production entwined with our notions of gender so completely that even the structural underpinnings of truth production are masculinist; that is, the maintenance of patriarchal authority and male privilege follow from the formation of rules in confession to the installation of a man as judge (authorized through that massive tautology of male power legitimating males to power). The confession is a discourse that both requires and shapes "truth" according to the notions of heresy and orthodoxy in the religious confession and according to criminalized definitions of human activity in the legal confession. In both arenas one confesses in order to be judged by a standard of truth that, despite its evident solidity, is nonetheless part of a cultural process. When readers of autobiography become detectives or confessors, when they seek to verify the facts of an autobiography, when they are dubious of an eyewitness account, yet look to the eyewitness for truth, they indicate the extent of the confession's power.

Thus, it is not enough to examine the role of the confession in literary history. If the legacy of the confession for self-representation persists, it does so by virtue of the confession's still-effective history, the policing it

sic modifications in the person who articulates it: exonerates, re-
deems, and purifies him [*sic*]; it unburdens him of his wrongs,
liberates him, and promises salvation. (*History of Sexuality* 61–62)

The confession must be regarded, then, as relational: neither penitent nor confessor is the source of truth-production. Instead, their
relationship forms the locus from which confession is generated. In
this sense, confession can be thought of as "self"-policing. In the self-
representational texts with which I am concerned, the proximity of truth
and torture, of confession and skepticism, critically construct interest in
women's visionary experience and mystical writing. That is, the desire to
report one's mystical experience and one's transformed perspective on
identity is not simply *informed* by the consequences of error; the confession is *structured* through the penalties and payoffs already in place.
Mary Mason has noted the tremendous anxiety women autobiographers
exhibit "to get it right" and, by specifying the gendered production of
confessional truth, focuses on an aspect of the power relationship which
Foucault neglects. The confession, I would argue, installs the production
of gender as a truth effect; one tells the truth insofar as one also produces
gendered identity appropriately. In this sense the confession hyposta-
tizes gender, condenses the differences among women into an institutional whole, and enforces that construction. For this reason I would
locate what Mason has identified as the pressure "to get it right" in the
confession's simultaneous construction of truth and torture and of self-
representation and self-incrimination *in relation to gender*. For the purposes of this discussion, I explore how this construction operates as the
confession's constantly reformulated legacy.

Gender both defines and saturates the notions of truth and confession which circulated and were formalized during the late medieval
fourteenth and fifteenth centuries when women's mystical experiences
abounded. The visionary who wished to confess her mystical experience
was positioned differently from her male counterpart with respect to
truth because of her place in the signifying chain of sin, error, deception,
and femininity. One hears the dominoes that produce this judgment as
inevitable "truth" falling through a metonymic chain of associations in
which sex becomes gender becomes heterosexual desire becomes identity
and which leaves in place the metaphorical equation of sin and femininity, sex and identity. Within this gender logic, women and visionary experience were seen as forms susceptible to the devil's seductions; indeed,
negative values attached to women spill into definitions of mysticism

and are addressed in the progressively formalized regulations concerning "truth" in mystical experience. Such definitional discourses marked the limits of the confession by establishing what truth could be told and installing a confessor, specifically a theologian, who would police those limits. Yet despite the exclusion of medieval women mystics from the priesthood (a location so near the truth as to be virtually a metonym for it), the authority devolving from their charismatic and visionary experience was largely unassailable, and the presence of such complex regulations evidences the church/state's desire to gain control over this power. If visions were verified, mystics could claim the authority to address popes and kings, to speak for God and for all. If visions were deemed demonic, the penalties varied. Special advisorial codes were developed to aid clergy in verifying women's visionary experience: confessors were to be especially wary of speech and undue curiosity.

Writing at the end of the fourteenth century on a topic of public interest and debate, Jean Gerson, chancellor of the University of Paris, formally took up the issue of authorizing women's visionary experience. The challenge to church/state authority by these "others"—women, lay people—prompted great concern, and Gerson elaborated a set of definitions, cautionary remarks, and prohibitions to advise clergy about what to do when mystical practice cropped up. Specifically, these codes offered a way to intervene in mystical and, from the church/state's point of view, self-authorizing speech. The codes allow us to see how women's mysticism was "organized" in terms of truth production:

49. If the visionary is a woman, it is especially necessary to learn how she acts toward her confessors or instructors. Is she prone to continual conversations, either under the pretext of frequent confession or in relating lengthy accounts of her visions, or by any other kind of discussion? . . . There is scarcely any plague that is more harmful or incurable than this.

50. Also, you must realize that a woman . . . has an unhealthy curiosity which leads to gazing about and talking (not to mention touching). . . .

51. Moreover the abiding peace of God is in quiet. Consequently no one will be surprised if such people, having embraced false teachings, turn aside from truth. All the more is it true if these women, itching with curiosity, are the kind whom the Apostle describes: *Silly women who are sin-laden and led away by various lusts: ever learning yet never attaining knowledge of the truth* (2 Tim. 3:7).[8]

field of male ecclesiastics and scholars—but rather in the mystical experience of being "oned" with God. That is, Julian's theology of motherhood follows from the totalizing insight into her own identity depicted in the revelations, and in this move she manages, at least in her text, to shift the grounds of authority on which she could be judged.

The visionary's burden, then, lies not only in finding a language to correspond to the divine language she hears during an ecstatic experience, although it may be difficult indeed to bring into writing an experience that mystics frequently describe as indescribable. Tropes of ineffability and unrepresentability abound in documents that also detail, with tireless precision, the whole range of bodily and mental effects. The point is, mystics do describe the experiences. References to the unrepresentability of the rapture do not, I am arguing, derive from a mystic's inability to interpret an anomalous event. Rather, visionary experience, with its rhetoric of the ecstatic body, its enactment of a lover's discourse, its eroticization of the relationship with God, is difficult to represent in the terms the confession demands: it cannot be described as a sin or transgression; yet this is the formal demand made by the confession. Thus visionary experience must be coded as a potential sin and then defended. There are no commandments regarding visionary experience, although there is sufficient biblical attention to false prophecy and demonic possession to put any mystic on the defensive. We should not underestimate the threat posed by a phenomenon that was so widespread that it was unusual by the thirteenth century to hear of a convent without a mystic. Potentially heretical claims about God's direct communication with individual women created a crisis in ecclesiastical authority. Thus, the mystic's self-representation was pressured from two sides: first, from the policing mechanism of the confession and her own internalization of its demands and second, from the oft-repeated desire to represent God's intervention in her mundane world accurately.

Julian interprets and represents *The Revelations* within the context of the confession she would later make. Her representation of the experience documents this regulatory presence and the extent to which she has internalized the demands of such policing. This internalization is demonstrated throughout *The Revelations* as she forms a judgment about her experience. The more perfectly the illness fits Julian's desire for it, the more it appears visited upon her by a merciful and accommodating God rather than by indifferent nature or cunning Satan. The less it fits those requirements, the more she suspects herself of raving. To interpret this illness as a gift from God enables her to control its capacity to "hurt." In

The Body in Pain Elaine Scarry suggests that pain empties consciousness of purpose and progress; there is only the growing moment of agony released from all boundaries.[10] Pain forces the past and the future to recede to the edges of consciousness. As Scarry describes it, this breakdown is the method of torture: the body is assaulted through a variety of degrading practices, and the voice, or capacity to speak at all, let alone to speak in one's defense, is reduced to a preverbal howl of pain. The mystics are rarely out of control in precisely this way, though the visionary found to be a heretic could expect horrifying consequences. Significantly, it was possible for confessors to disagree about the source of visions.[11] Thus, it is important to distinguish an out-of-body experience and the mystic's rapturous language from the language of the confession with its potential punishment for heresy in order to understand the controlling power to interpret that confession exerted on rapturous language. Between these irreconcilable possibilities, between the ecstatic body and the tortured body, lies the discourse of confession: the very language of truth in which the mystic who would confess every experience of rapture was trained to the point of self-policing.

The interpretation of pain as blessing, of vision as gift, of mystic as chosen is held in check by the confession. The connections between women's experiences and Christ's life must be situated within the confessional frame because those are the grounds on which to verify the mystic as authentic or condemn her as a heretic or the victim of demonic possession. Yet once the authenticity of the experience could be confirmed, God's invisible presence could be read in the visible alterations of the body. The saint's ravaged or levitating body confers a kind of facticity on the unrepresentable deity: the body becomes evidentiary text. The tension between physical abasement (the body in extreme need) and spiritual salvation (the new body redeemed by and absorbed into the body of Christ) marks passion as the nexus of pain and ecstasy. When she confesses, her discourse derives meaning through a dialectical relation to the confession. Thus it would be misleading to read mystical discourse as an ahistorical version of "writing the body." This body was written and read as a text within a particular discursive network of power relations. Through their remapping of the body, mystics represented it as a network of possibilities and not simply a biological fact, insisting simultaneously on its undeniable materiality and fantastical possibility, making it the major figure for the acts, images, and promise of embodied mystical rapture.

Mysticism provided an interesting test for the possibility of a counterdiscourse, as it revealed the limits of the church/state's tolerance in authorizing women's speech as "truth." Although mysticism was busily assimilated into an orthodox agenda, it was a counterhegemonic form of worship and, most important, began to generate its own discourse. Significantly, it was practiced largely by women.[12] Although men's mystical experience was also challenged, the codes of verification were devised mainly to contain women's mysticism, and the codes specifically addressed this norm. Mysticism was not practiced at the altar or in other authorized sites of worship. Mystics would display their power publicly, would rush about to take communion; in short, they made spectacles of themselves. Their visibility was part of the significance of mysticism and describes an incipient alternative form of authorization. Paradoxically, the power and authority of priests devolved from unseen sources; the abstractness of their power compounded its authority. Conversely, the seeming mystery of ecstatic and visionary experience was widely demonstrated, registered through the acts of the mystic herself or employing the rhetoric of bodily display.

In this sense and others, gender polarity and spiritual authenticity are mutually embedded structures, both sources and symptoms of policing. As Peter Stallybrass and Allon White have demonstrated in *The Politics and Poetics of Transgression*, it is useful to grasp the conceptual binarisms that determine cultural value.[13] While the structuring aspect of the high/low concept shapes the interpretations negotiated within it, gender polarity in a culture still allows for subtle distinctions within the male/female, high/low binarisms. Further, the high/low binarisms structuring gender, class, and religious devotion are articulated simultaneously through a variety of discursive effects. Although the high/low poles designate the ends of meaning, cultural meaning itself consists in the circulation of the values represented and constantly recombined between those poles.

The "need" for policing becomes especially evident when there is apparent dissonance in the codes of gender, authority, and truth. For example, a woman mystic in fourteenth-century England could be seen simultaneously as a privileged communicant with God and an error-prone, sin-laden daughter of Eve. Significantly, this tension does not always render her unknowable. Such dissonance in fact reveals the power of the high/low distinction. The high of mysticism includes the low of femaleness. Women were seen as more susceptible than men to Satan's deception: it happened once in the Garden; it could happen again. The high/low distinction between men and women enforces the church/

state's greater skepticism about the veracity of women's visionary experience, even while it acknowledges its occurrence. The high includes the low symbolically through the figure of Eve as an interpretive device for women's ability to tell the truth and to speak with God. Thus women could be socially marginal and symbolically central in making the church/state case about God's grace: if he speaks to women, surely he could speak to us all.

The liberatory power of women's visions, then, is less likely to obliterate the edicts against women's speech and authority when both of those can be assimilated to an official position. To deny female visionary experience any authority at a time when the mystics themselves were widely believed and much sought after would not serve the interests of the church/state. Thus the church/state was able to regulate a force that was, potentially, socially transformative. And insofar as it succeeded, visionary experience remained mostly individually transformative. The church/state controlled how visions were verified in order to maintain order. Women's visionary experience was not, therefore, a priori a force for social change. Many who saw long-contemplated icons begin to ooze blood and to glow or who found themselves physically levitated during prayers never managed to naturalize the phenomenon and lived in a state of watchful "otherworldly" attention. Others viewed mystical experience as so sufficiently interpretable as to be no less normal than any other moment of daily life. Mysticism came to transform, for a time, the church/state's notion of who receives God's word and how, but the church/state maintained its hegemony by giving the last word to the confessor, as the one who would interpret and judge, rather than to the mystic alone.

Autobiography and Its Authorities

As an enlargement of the confession, autobiography retains many of its characteristics, though its historical transformations are critical. A contemporary example of the intertextualization of confession and its rhetorical apparatus of truth telling indicates the persistence as well as the historical contingency of the relationship between autobiographical authority and the forms of policing that regulate it. Mary McCarthy once rather dramatically (on the "Dick Cavett Show," no less) accused Lillian Hellman of lying, insisted, in fact, that "every word" Hellman wrote in her series of autobiographies was a lie. This is an interesting charge from McCarthy, who is something of an expert in fictionalizing the past in order to tell a better story. Her first autobiography, *Memories of a Catholic*

if you are in the habit of writing fiction; one does it almost automatically" (153).

McCarthy claims she lacks an authority against which to test her sense of the past because she was orphaned at a young age. And it is the loss of her beloved parents that in some way generates her need to confess her childhood. This wounding loss, wrapped in nostalgia and grief, suffuses the autobiography and makes it, in part, an act of re-creation. That it mainly succeeds in re-creating grief and loss reveals the extent to which those emotional and, indeed, narrative structures spur her writing. Although the parents are dead, writing about them inscribes their presence in something less private and potentially more sharable than memory; writing, however, cannot avoid also inscribing this para-doxically generative sense of loss. More germane to this discussion is the sense in which McCarthy presents the death of her parents as the lack of a delimiting authority. Truth, she writes, may not be verified because her parents cannot offer the factual information standing between specula-tion and certainty. The finality of their knowledge, their authority, is nevertheless repeatedly undercut by McCarthy's refusal to privilege any eyewitness accounts that compete with her own (see the tin butterfly episode in "Yonder Peasant," for example). The loss of parental author-ity is coded as something to be defended, a kind of transgression, or straying from proximity to the truth, which causes McCarthy to position herself in autobiography as a penitent. She attempts to pull her own account into line with the rhetoric of truth telling and the rewards it offers.

Bereft of a corroborating other, she creates one in the interchapters by textualizing the confessional space. These are the only sections of the book written contemporaneously; that is, written *as* her autobiography. In direct address to the reader she challenges her own account, finds it accurate, and thereby preserves the structure of confession, with the self of the interchapters playing confessor to the self of the sketches. The reader is compelled to witness the account, which, as early as the title of the preface, is clearly addressed to her or him. The rhythms of con-fession McCarthy creates make it possible for her to perform multiple roles while requiring her reader to fill in for ones she temporarily vacates in order to inhabit others. At one time skeptical and challenging (as in the interchapters when she admits to fictionalizing), at another fully convinced of her authenticity (as when she insists upon her accuracy), the reader and the autobiographer gaze into the unfathomability of memory and concede that the telling of lies is inextricable from the writing of memories.

In terms of how autobiography builds in authority, an analogy can be drawn here between the church/state as an informing context of self-representation in the Middle Ages and psychoanalysis in the twentieth century. For self-representation that takes truth production as its mode, as *Memories of a Catholic Girlhood* does, and deploys the language of memory and repression as both impediment to and constituent of "truth" is informed by the pervasive influence of that other confessional space—the analyst's office—and the language disseminated through it. The effect of this language emerges through the kind of competency in truth telling McCarthy develops, the episodes she chooses to narrate, and how they function in the autobiography. Her interest in memory and repression, especially powerful in the final chapter on her grandmother, and the apocalyptic force attributed to forgetting reveal the persistence in twentieth-century autobiography of a confessional practice in which the dominant discourse of truth telling, at least for prominent white intellectuals such as McCarthy, is psychoanalysis.[16] The power of confession persists primarily through the psychoanalytic interest in the "self," the construction of that self through a specific discourse, and the power relation between analyst and analysand which produces truth. One sees this persistence by historicizing the project of confession and crediting its ability to structure discourses of "truth." Foucault's general historicizing approach yields this insight and also enables us to discern the crucial feature of "authorization" which configures confessor/penitent, analyst/analysand, writer/reader, and, significantly, critic/autobiographer on the grounds of truth.

For both its writers and its critics, autobiography is driven by an authorization complex.[17] Its writers attempt to situate themselves in relation to discourses of "truth" and identity while recognizing, in various ways, the insufficiency of any single discourse to express the "subject" of their writing. In the absence of a single, unified model of "autobiography," they weave testimonial texts from disparate discourses. The effect of this positioning defines autobiography's characteristic weirdness and accounts for its problematical status as a genre. Somewhere between reporting and fiction writing, autobiography challenges the limits of generic definition through its *bricolage*-like bravado. Critics and scholars of autobiography attempt to authorize their texts with introductions that contextualize their arguments within a comprehensible and already authorized field of study.[18] Indeed, autobiography studies even reveal traces of "canon envy" as they attempt to establish autobiography's legitimacy and authority through a series of familiar moves: claiming an origin, invoking formal continuity, stabilizing a canon, constructing alternative traditions, and so on. But we should consider these moves more closely: Under what circumstances could a kind of writing such as autobiography, a practice as diffuse as self-representation, be seen to take on thematic continuity? From what project must autobiography be distinguished such that it can be said to begin? That is, how did autobiography become recognizable as such, to the point it could require a history, a narrative of its development? These questions indicate an issue in the study of autobiography which has largely been obscured; namely, that critical practices have organized and continue to organize autobiography and are bound up with and indeed generate "authority" in autobiography. How, then, has authority been gendered and how is the maintenance of gender hierarchy policed?

Autobiography is a form in which the self is authorized, although autobiography is not itself simply a self-authorizing form. Those who seek to interpret autobiography as a self-authorizing form place its roots in the Romantic concept of the self.[19] Paradoxically, the influence of confessional practices has been minimized by tracing autobiography's literary history and formal characteristics from Augustine (a necessary origin for this argument) and subsuming him into a discussion of autobiography as an Enlightenment project. Autobiography can then be seen as a literary discourse that develops in line with the emergent political discourses of individualism.[20]

Contemporary critics committed to upholding autobiography as a post-Enlightenment project in which an individual produces truth bring their concerns to women's autobiography. Insofar as writers systematically and historically excluded from the rewards of a thoroughly patriarchal and class-bound individualism produce texts that resist this ideology—even, as is sometimes the case, in the very act of trying to reproduce it—they are deauthorized through this "failure." Although it may seem rather paranoid, if not grandiose, to describe the liberal literary criticism practiced in the late twentieth century as a form of policing, I insist upon this description not only and most obviously to foreground its politics but also to underline its ironic position in relation to those politics. Liberal humanism values free speech and the subject who can utter it despite the fact that the consequence, and perhaps the aim, of certain forms of speech is necessarily a context in which some speech is marginalized and even criminalized.[21] The relationship that feminists have described between male speech and female silence is not a simple binary but rather a cultural context in which the enforced silence of women can be read as the norm even when women manage to write and publish, to speak and achieve influence. For example, women writers frequently describe writing an autobiography as an empowering process through which they reach an understanding, however provisional, of the relationships through which identity is produced. Yet, until very recently, they were excluded from virtually all studies of autobiography. I would like to suggest that their absence can be read as the critic's participation in policing the limits of female "truth" and enforcing the remnants of Gerson's powerful interdictions.

As a "policing" critic, Philippe Lejeune would be a rather obvious autobiography gendarme. But perhaps this is the wrong word. Lejeune's autobiography cops belong to a liberal state imaginary in which the police lack preventive and interdictive powers. Rather, Lejeune's policing of the autobiographical pact authorizes a mobile readership of detectives who concern themselves with verifying the facts. One imagines them running credit checks rather than knocking on doors and demanding documentation, gathering and generating more paper as they track the facts to the truth. What do these inquiring minds most want to know? What really happened. Although this caricature is intended to indicate the lingering and reduced effects of some of the confession's more brutal legacy—the Inquisition, most notably—it is also meant to sketch the critical context in which women autobiographers have been read. The question "What really happened?" has only infrequently been a plea for more information. Usually it contains a way of valuing the testimony in question. When Hannah Tillich wrote her autobiography, *From Time to Time,* she was widely criticized for missing the point.[22] According to many of her reviewers and much of her reading public, she *should* have written the biography of her husband, theologian Paul Tillich. With access to the thoughts of "a great man," the critique went, how could she cheat history of the opportunity to know more of him? Ironically, Tillich supplied her readers with a good deal more than many of them wished to know about Paul Tillich, including his penchant for hiding pornographic materials in theology books. Thus questions of how to read autobiography frequently support an agenda for how to value the autobiographer.

Further illustrations of this claim abound, but Karl Weintraub's *Value of the Individual: Self and Circumstance in Autobiography* is especially appropriate for this context.[23] Weintraub construes the generic emergence of autobiography as a corollary to the cultural hegemony of individualism. Without an "individual" who can be defined through "his" developing self-consciousness, there can be no autobiography. Weintraub defines the "proper form" of autobiography as the self-conscious search for individuality guided by the questions: "'Who am I?' and 'how did I become what I am?'" (1). The similarity of responses in men's writing indicates the extent to which the questions themselves also participate in the production of "autobiography" as we know it. That is, the responses are embedded in the question: both in the form of the question and in the answer it recognizes. "Who am I" assumes that the "I" is contained within a set of boundaries that distinguish it from everything else around it, and "how did I become what I am" assumes that the history of this distinctive "I" is the process of constructing those delimiting boundaries. Further, these two questions imply a third, which is perhaps the most important; namely, "What is the significance of this 'I' that has been thus distinguished?" When the self is construed as an autonomous and self-authorized figure, the agency of others is reduced to their participation in "how did I become what I am"; that is, they are extensions of the self rather than selves in their own right. If we pursue Weintraub's definition of autobiography, we see that the growth of nations, the temper of the times, the political and cultural zeitgeist, and the exemplary man form a mutually reinforcing network of identity. The man is the mirror of his times; history can be told as the story of this self. Indeed, it is frequently the autobiographer's task to place—in the sense of both find and put—"himself" at the center of history and interpret from this perspective.

Forming a canon of autobiography depends on agreeing with a particular narrative of history and choosing autobiographers who reproduce it. Such a construction is always a political retrospective with the following limitation: what were once rather more clearly ideological and political criteria get recoded as aesthetic criteria. This process also confers on the writer the frequently dehistoricizing status of artist and allows, even requires, one to view textual production in familiarly generic ways, even when this interpretation is at odds with the broader discursive practices within which the writer was working. Precisely these limitations would require that I reorient my argument here, for example, within a discussion of more traditional literary categories; that I sufficiently distinguish literary from oral confessions, and finally, that I delimit the office of the confession in its ecclesiastical setting rather than implicate it in a far wider set of discursive and historical formations that are everywhere bound up with the power one seizes, reproduces, or resists by writing "I." Instead, the wide and shifting influence of the confession participates in the production of the "I" who writes autobiography, as well as in the structures in which autobiography is evaluated.

This canonizing impulse determines Weintraub's evaluation of two autobiographies by women in a chapter on the lives of saints: Saint Teresa of Avila's *Life* and Mme Guyon's *Autobiography*. Weintraub does not emphasize Teresa's successful manipulation of the church/state's massive technologies of "policing." In fact, Teresa, who wrote at the instruction of her confessors from 1561, when she was forty-five, through revision and amplification in successive drafts to completion in 1565, was especially successful at enlisting sympathetic confessors who would edit sections of the autobiography which otherwise would have been judged heretical. Her establishment of this network was a necessary condition for authorizing and, finally, canonizing this *converso* (a Jew who became a Roman Catholic) whose "truth" was always already suspect. By omitting this information, Weintraub, in effect, decontextualizes Teresa's position and self-positioning within an elaborate network of power relations. Instead, he aestheticizes her text and judges her account appropriately devout, finding affecting grace in a simple and direct style. Teresa's subjectivism is always tempered by fidelity to one of the two models of self-representation he authorizes, *imitatio Christi* and *individuum ineffabile est:* "Her self-conception stayed within the tradition of the model life" (220).

A discussion of literary merit, however, always has ample room for gender politics. Whether female gender is coded as emotionalism, chattiness, or subjectivism is not as crucial here as the persistence of its coding as negativity, its presence authorizing the police to take notice. Mme Guyon, whose lengthy tome was written over the years 1686 to 1709, does not fare so well with Weintraub, for she strays egregiously from the models of selfhood that underlie autobiography's "proper form." Whereas Saint Teresa is easily incorporated into the tradition of mystical writing and her reputation therein is without challenge, Mme Guyon is a fugitive from the models Weintraub acknowledges. He is put off by her lack of taste and proper restraint, both in perception and in language; he disdains the "exuberance of her expressions" (233), her egotism, and finally, her maddening self-sufficiency. His major complaint focuses on Mme Guyon's erotic mysticism, which explicitly surfaces in her descriptions of dreams. In one such dream, she is taken to

Mount Lebanon, where her divine spouse shows her a room with two beds. Mme Guyon wonders, "For whom are these? [Christ] answered: One for my mother, and the other for thee, my spouse." "Surely," Weintraub sniffs, "God deserves the right to a more tasteful reporting of his inspirations" (225). Although Mme Guyon is inspired by the same Holy Spirit whose most celebrated activity was to cause the Virgin Mary to conceive, Weintraub denies this form of modeling and, in that gesture, Mme Guyon's authenticity as an autobiographer.

Mme Guyon's great failure, for Weintraub, is that she is generally unimpressed by the model of humanism he so affectingly sketches throughout the critique. It is her effective resistance to either mode of self-conception and self-representation, either *imitatio Christi* or *individuum ineffabile est,* which he finds dangerous. Thus, she falls outside the limits of what he defines as humanism and of the study of autobiography set by his scholarship: "Where mystic leanings overstepped the normative lines drawn to guard the existence of sinful mortals, a dangerous, uncontrolled and uncontrollable subjectivism opened up which should not be confused with the ideal of individuality" (227). "Mystic leanings" are seen as an unofficial, extrainstitutional, ex-static form of knowledge and, as such, threatening to the "normative lines" maintained by what Althusser described as the institutional state apparatus. For Weintraub, subjectivism describes all marginalized forms of self-conception and self-representation. His analysis does not discriminate between forms of subjectivism; that is not its intent. Yet the two-model grid, which was initially offered as heuristic, has, by the end of the book, taken the form of an interrogation. What does not conform is open to suspicion and censure. Weintraub stands in for Gerson's confessor and finds Mme Guyon, who has clearly not been as fortunate in her confessors as Saint Teresa, to be in error. Her version of truth strays from the powerful criteria concerning the production and judgment of truth and women's fallibility which still circulate. Subjectivism versus humanism, or the ideal of individuality: such is the conflict in the history of the self. And it is precisely the proximity of these competing discourses which Weintraub polices. The distance between the subjects of these discourses is transformed into a term of value: Teresa is closer to an authorized discourse of identity; Mme Guyon is an outlyer. According to this critical edict, an individual declines in value when s/he loses sight of the tradition shaping the self, when s/he represents identity outside the "normative lines" of appropriate self-conception, for self-knowledge can be gained, according to Weintraub, only through an authorized discourse of truth. Guyon's self-representation is, in effect, deauthorized through this policing of the truth.

Notes

1 I thank audiences at the International Association of Philosophy and Literature, Emory University, 1989, the Autobiography Conference, University of Southern Maine, 1989, and the University of Texas, Austin, 1990, who responded to earlier versions of this article. My thanks, also, to Joseph Allen, Kathleen Ashley, Susan Sage Heinzelman, Kurt Heinzelman, Francoise Lionnet, and Evan Watkins whose critical insights and comments I gratefully acknowledge here.

2 I accept Mary G. Mason's designation of Margery Kempe as the first auto-biographer in English. See her article "The Other Voice: Autobiographies of Women Writers," in *Autobiography: Essays Critical and Theoretical*, ed. James Olney (Princeton: Princeton UP, 1980): 207–34. Much feminist criticism of autobiography has depended on just such against-the-grain readings of literary history and has produced the excellent work in such recent anthologies as *Life/Lines: Theorizing Women's Autobiography*, ed. Bella Brodzki and Celeste Schenck (Ithaca: Cornell UPI, 1988) and *The Private Self*, ed. Shari Benstock (Chapel Hill: U of North Carolina P, 1988). For a discussion of Margery Kempe in the context of community, see David Aers's *Community, Gender, and Individual Identity* (London: Routledge, 1988): 73–116.

3 The phrase "thematic of regulation" is D. A. Miller's from *The Novel and the Police* (Berkeley: U of California P, 1988): 38.

4 I refer mainly to mysticism as it was practiced or experienced in cloistered settings. Although there were women who dashed about to take communion or who went on pilgrimages, the cloistered settings in which mysticism was expressed offer the grounds for examining the institutional emergence of mystical writing. Caroline Bynum indicates that cloistered mysticism was so widespread by the thirteenth century that it was unusual *not* to have a visionary or mystic in the convent. See her *Holy Feast and Holy Fast: The Religious Significance of Food to Medieval Woman* (Berkeley: U of California P, 1987).

5 Michel Foucault, *The History of Sexuality*, vol. 1: *Introduction*, trans. Robert Hurley (1978; New York: Vintage Books, 1980), 95.

6 Clifton Walters, Introduction to Julian of Norwich, *Revelations of Divine Love* (1966; London: Penguin, 1988).

7 Brodzki and Schenck develop the term "singularity in alterity" in their introduction to *Life/Lines*. For an excellent discussion of confession, see Jeremy Tambling, *Confession: Sexuality, Sin, the Subject* (New York: St. Martin's, 1990).

8 Jean Gerson wrote widely on topics ranging from ecclesiastical law to mysticism. See G.H.M. Posthumus Meyjes, *Jean Gerson et l'assemblée de Vincennes (1329): Ses conceptions de la juridiction temporelle de l'église.* (Leiden: E. J. Brill, 1978) and Catherine D. Brown, *Pastor and Laity in the Theology of Jean Gerson* (New York:

Cambridge UP, 1987). I thank Kathleen Ashley for bringing this document to my attention.

9   For more on the literacy debate concerning Julian, see Mary G. Mason and Jennifer P. Heimmel, *"God Is Our Mother": Julian of Norwich and the Medieval Image of Christian Feminine Divinity* (Salzburg, Austria: Salzburg Studies in English Literature, 1982).

10   Elaine Scarry, *The Body in Pain* (New York: Oxford UP, 1987).

11   Joan of Arc, for example, was found by some official confessors involved in her trial to be telling the truth.

12   For more on male mysticism, an interesting phenomenon in terms of the construction of gender and the representation of sexuality, see Bynum, *Holy Feast and Holy Fast.*

13   Peter Stallybrass and Allon White, *The Politics and Poetics of Transgression* (Ithaca: Cornell UP, 1986).

14   Mary McCarthy, *Memories of a Catholic Girlhood,* Berkeley Medallion Edition (New York: Harcourt, Brace and World, 1966).

15   For the connection between literary studies and law, see Susan Sage Heinzelman, "Women's Petty Treason: Feminism, Narrative, and the Law," *Journal of Narrative Technique* 20.2 (Spring 1990): 89–106.

16   Perhaps the connection to *Discipline and Punish* is too obvious to mention in this context, but Foucault's discussion of the emergence of psychiatry is significant here, as is the way in which this discussion generates his later interest in "the care of the self." See *Discipline and Punish: The Birth of the Prison,* trans. Alan Sheridan (New York: Random, 1977).

17   See Shari Benstock, "Authorizing the Autobiographical," in *The Private Self,* 10–33; and Nancy K. Miller, "Changing the Subject: Authorship, Writing, and Readership," in *Subject to Change* (New York: Columbia UP, 1991), 102–21.

18   For two tracings of this history with very different interests, see Sidonie Smith, *A Poetics of Women's Autobiography: Marginality and the Fictions of Self-Representation* (Bloomington: Indiana UP, 1987) and William C. Spengemann, *The Forms of Autobiography: Episodes in the History of a Literary Genre* (New Haven: Yale UP, 1980).

19   Much of the advanced work on Romanticism tends to show how the Romantics themselves deconstruct or complicate the very concept of the self with which they are credited and discredited. I am thinking here especially of Mary Jacobus's *Romanticism, Writing, and Sexual Difference: Essays on* The Prelude (Oxford: Clarendon, 1989) and her chapter on autobiography.

20   American autobiographers have been acutely aware of this. See, for example, Benjamin Franklin, Henry Adams, and even Donald Trump.

21   The feminist critique of liberal humanism is undertaken by Alison Jaggar in *Feminist Politics and Human Nature* (Brighton: Harvester, 1983).

22   Hannah Tillich, *From Time to Time* (New York: Stein and Day, 1975).

23   Karl Weintraub, *The Value of the Individual* (Chicago: U of Chicago P, 1978).

Autobiographical Voices (1, 2, 3) and Mosaic Memory:

Experimental Sondages in the (Post)modern World

MICHAEL M. J. FISCHER

■

Title Words in Play

The word's power does not consist in its explicit content—if generally speaking, there is such a thing—but in the diversion that is involved in it.—Chaim Nachman Bialik "Revealment and Concealment in Language"

Autobiographical voices: Avoiding having to define autobiography as a neatly typified genre, "autobiographical voices" call attention to subject positioning in autobiographies and memoirs, also in life histories, certain kinds of autobiographically figured fiction, the tracings of authorial perspective in the writing of biographies, and the human screenings of writing about scientific discovery.

1, 2, 3 voices, or compositions of identity, dialogic relations with alterities, and triangulations of post(modern) sensibilities: Autobiographical voices are often thought of as deeply singular attempts to inscribe individual identity (1st voice). They are, however, not only mosaic compositions but may often be structured through processes of mirroring and dialogic relations with cross-historical and cross-cultural others and thus may resonate with various sorts of double voicings (2d voice). In modern times mediation by collective rational and rationalizing endeavors such as the sciences, which themselves depend upon explicit triangulations among multiple perspectival positionings and understandings, is increasingly important (3d voice).

Sondage is the archeologists' Francophone term for "soundings," for the search techniques of an exploratory dig. The experimental sondages here are efforts to listen to the many kinds of voicings in autobiographical forms that might on the one hand expand the ways genres of autobiography are recognized (beyond for instance the fairly narrow master narrative of Western individualism, or universalizing theories of individuation-maturation, which studies of autobiography are so often used to celebrate, innocent of any effort at serious cross-cultural validation) and on the other hand provide clues for keeping social and cultural theory abreast of a rapidly changing, pluralizing, world.

Mosaic Memory: Memory is layered in differently structured strata, fragmented and collaged together like mosaics in consciousness and in unconscious maneuverings, all of which takes hermeneutical skills to hear and unpack, which in another sense might also be called Mosaic, as a figure of the hermeneutical traditions created in the interface between orality (face-to-face, relational, immediately monitored-adjustable communication) and literacy (distanced, ambiguously playing on the graphics of absence). These hermeneutical traditions are located in old scriptural-moral discourses (Judaism, Islam, Christianity, Buddhism, Jainism, Hinduism, Confucianism, etc.) but they also are the less-acknowledged tap roots of contemporary literary and philosophical explorations (Freud, Joyce, Gadamer, Levinas, Jabes, Derrida, et al.). The story is that the tablets of Moses had to be broken so they could become humanly usable. The Islamic version is that there are two sets of revelation: the sequence of the Qur'anic text, ordered by metrical length with the longest chapters first (this is the order of the primordial Qur'an in the seventh heaven) and the historical sequence of revelation in fragments over the twenty-three year period of the Prophet's autobiographical prophetic career. In other words, deconstruction is nothing new. As Joyce puts it: "In the bugining was the woid, in the muddle was the sounddance, and thereinafter you are in the unbewised again."

Autobiography, Anthropology, and the (Post)modern Condition

And if you want [auto]biographies, do not look for those with the legend "Mr. So-and-so and his times," but for one whose title page might be inscribed, "a fighter against his time."—Nietzsche, The Use and Abuse of History

For the anthropologist, autobiography is a challenging three-fold force field of desire. First, standing between the individual and the social, autobiography is a site of interplay between the modernist vision of autonomous bounded egos, and postmodernist decentered selves. On the one hand, autobiography can provide access to the "native point of view," claiming a subjectivity grounded in cultural specificity that is empirical and otherwise accessible only through in-depth interviewing.

On the other hand, anthropology as a social science is committed to the elucidation of how individual experience is socially and culturally constructed. In that frame, autobiographical accounts are fallible data that need to be interrogated for their cultural structures and for their culturally formed blindnesses and unconscious programming.

The second deep attraction for anthropology is the possibility that autobiographies can help sketch out cultural and social terrain where traditional social theory is blind or archaic. Nowhere is this more evident than in the rapidly changing environments of what is often referred to by the much-disputed term "postmodern."

Postmodern for me is a simple cover term for three interrelated ideas. (1) It is a marker for the late twentieth century, for what is sociologically different about the late twentieth century from the early twentieth century when almost all the social theory still being used by professional social scientists was formulated. Bentham, Malthus, Mill, Marx, Freud, Durkheim, Weber, Nietzsche—these are theorists who formed their ideas out of the experience of the nineteenth and early twentieth century. Whatever it is about the late twentieth century—the increased speed of transportation and communication, the electronic media and information society, the industrialization of science and technology, the globalized movements of mass populations—there is a widespread feeling that social relations, culture, and psychology are being structured in significantly new ways. And we need to reconstruct social theory to match our contemporary experience and prepare for future changes. (2) Postmodern does not mean "after" modernism or modernity. It refers rather to the cycles of renewal and decay of modernisms or modernities. Postmodern refers to those modernities and modernisms that are distinct from previous modernities and modernisms. The postmodern involves a historical consciousness about modernity. Hence the typographic (post)modern, to accommodate both those who prefer to still speak of the late twentieth century as modern, as well as those who differentiate modernisms and modernities. (3) Substantively, one of the things the postmodern is about is the juxtaposition of things, events, and experiences once separated by time and space. Global integration is increasing in pace and penetration. It is not uniform: there is a new global stratification. It is not only jet set elites who move across the world; there are also mass movements of guest workers, displaced persons from war or from destruction of previous agrarian and industrial production, who form new proletarianized cross-national strata: Koreans; Indians and Filipinos working in the Persian Gulf; Turkish and Moroccan workers in

Europe; Mexican and Central Americans in the United States. If jet set elites are increasingly subject to the weightlessness, commodification, and volitional life-style that have been the subject of high culture complaint since at least Nietzsche and Dostoyevsky, and if the proletarianized masses are subject to the belatedness and anxieties of political-economic inequality, still in both cases there is a cross-cultural awareness and constant comparison that is of an intensity and pervasiveness that is new and defining of the contemporary era.

This postmodern condition allows for a degree of serious cross-cultural critique that was utopian only fifty years ago. Compare the impact of the style of cross-cultural critique practiced by a Bronislaw Malinowski or a Margaret Mead, in which an exotic pattern of child-rearing could be held up as a foil to our own patterns of child-rearing to show that they were not "natural," but alterable cultural conventions. Contrast the degree of intellectual control necessary under contemporary conditions of multiple readerships, where what one writes is read by those one writes about as well as by one's colleagues or cultural fellows.

Moreover, in the contemporary world, people increasingly construct their sense of self out of pieces that come from many different cultural environments. Maxine Hong Kingston encapsulates the point when she says "to be Chinese-American is not the same as to be Chinese in America," and to be Chinese-American has no role model. It is a new construction. Life histories of various forms have been used in the past for a variety of purposes, very often in the social sciences as organizing devices for typical life cycle stages in relatively stable cultural environments. But perhaps the most important use of life histories, increasingly so in the contemporary world, is the strategic use of a life frame that straddles major social and cultural transformations. This is, for instance, one of the richest veins of contemporary writing in English, drawing on interlinguistic and intercultural differences to remake culturally fuller individuals and social actors. James Joyce was a pioneer of such writing, followed in the contemporary period by such writers as Salman Rushdie, Michelle Cliff, and others from South Asia, the Caribbean, Africa, the Middle East, Latin America, and elsewhere who gift to English linguistic and cultural resources.

The third attraction for anthropology is that autobiography is a privileged genre where the reflexivity of human storytelling is foregrounded. Autobiography is not only a good place to observe how art follows life and life art, but also a vehicle to reflect on the discovery and construction processes of anthropology itself, and of science and knowledge in general, including the human sciences and the cultural products studied under the rubric of the humanities.

In the following pages, I sketch out more fully these three areas where autobiography seems particularly useful as a vehicle of access for anthropological investigation (and perhaps at the same time expand the somewhat parochial traces into which the study of autobiographical genres has fallen, particularly by insisting upon the cross-cultural as a tool for checking the validity of generalizations and readings that claim to be contributions to theory): (1) identity processes in the late twentieth century coded under such labels as ethnicity (domestic and international); feminism; and regionalism, or localism—in this essay, I focus on ethnicity, drawing on a longer essay published previously (Fischer, "Ethnicity and the Postmodern Arts of Memory"); (2) cross-cultural comparison and critique—alternative frames for articulating emotion, self, and agency, focusing particularly on the way these articulations work in alternative moral traditions, and their critical apparatuses, as they are being reinvented for the (post)modern world; (3) science as a collective human and cultural social endeavor, which constitutes a major component of contemporary epistemology, world view, and basis for moral judgment.

Autobiographical Voice (1): Identity Processes

The story of the bi-langue *and the* pluri-langue *exorcised his obsessions. He also needed the other language—your language, foreign in me—to tell himself the tale of how unadapted he was to the world and tell it with the joyful enchantment of a living man who sees his life before him, a life which sees itself enter into him, marry him, and of a dying man who glimpses death over his shoulder, behind him. . . . When questioned, he hid himself in his fictions: the soul of a pidgin screenwriter.—Abedelkehir Khatibi,* Love in Two Languages

Identity processes are complex compositions, using noncognitive modes as often as cognitive ones. Recent autobiographies by talented and ethnically musical authors provide one tool for gathering clues about these processes that might be used for further exploration of identity processes and of sociocultural reorganization in the late twentieth century among certain strata or segments of society.

My attention was drawn to autobiography as a methodological tool in reconstructing theories of contemporary ethnicity in the context of a

course on American culture, when I became aware of a rich vein of autobiography and autobiographical fiction that takes ethnicity as a focal
puzzle, but seems poorly accommodated by the sociological literature on
ethnicity. Maxine Hong Kingston's *Woman Warrior,* Michael Arlen's
Passage to Ararat, Marita Golden's *Migrations of the Heart* were not
well encompassed by such sociological categories as group support (mobility, political mobilization), transition (assimilation), or transmission
from generation to generation (socialization). There is a literature that
does fit these sociological categories: older immigrant novels centered
on themes of rebellion against the family or intermarriage. In an essay
on the newer autobiographical literature (Fischer 1986), I compared
five ethnicities in the United States—Armenian-Americans, Mexican-
Americans, Chinese-Americans, African Americans, and Native Americans—giving attention in each case to both female and male writers. In
the margins of the introduction and conclusion I also brought into view
my own ethnicity. Methodologically, I stressed the need in comparative
work to use a minimum of three cases, to avoid the better-worse false
moralisms that dualistic comparison tends to fall into.

What these newer works communicate forcefully is the sense that
ethnicity (and similar identity processes) is (a) reinvented in each generation by each individual; (b) what is invented is something new (for
example, Kingston's observation that there is no role model for being
Chinese-American); (c) that this something new is achieved by an inner
listening to different components of the self, finding a voice or style that
does not violate those multiple components; and (d) that ethnicity is
often something puzzling to the individual, something that the person
does not feel in control of, something often transmitted through processes more akin to dream-translation (from visual into linear verbal-
ization) or transference than to cognitive language and learning. Five
strategies or modes of articulation (both of identity and of texts) were
explored: transference, dream-work, alternative selves and bifocality, interreference, and ironic humor.

Two quick illustrations. Kingston's talk-stories illustrate the dream-
translation analogy. Her talk-stories are fragments of stories, customs,
and events, told by parents but not explained. "No Name Woman," for
instance, is a story of a father's sister who had an illegitimate child and
was forced by the shame to commit suicide. It is a story told to young
girls as a warning ("Now that you've started to menstruate") at a particular point in their life cycle. It is also told to test American-born children's
ability to establish realities: to distinguish what is peculiar to one's fam-

ily, to poverty, or to Chineseness. The story gains force as Kingston considers alternative interpretations—was this father's sister coerced (is she a figure of female submissiveness) or was she an active temptress? Kingston uses these alternatives as allegories for adolescent struggles. The teenager wants to be attractive but selectively (how to make a Chinese, but not a Caucasian, fall in love with me). Kingston's text illustrates dream-translationlike processes in which fragmentary images must be turned into coherent narratives; Michael Arlen's text illustrates transferencelike processes. Arlen suffers an anxiety generated by the silence of a father who wishes to spare his son the pain of the past (the massacres of the Armenians in Ottoman Turkey). The father's silence about the past creates a void, an obsessive need to explore, and fill in. Arlen goes to Soviet Armenia. He does not only find missing information or narratives, but more important, he discovers that he acts out behavior patterns he recognizes in his father (and his text enacts this pattern as well).

To explore such subtle patterns as transference or dream-translation (and other complex modalities of negotiating ethnicity), one needs good informants/autobiographies. I found this recent set of ethnically accented autobiographical texts particularly facilitating in thinking through the move anthropology (and the social sciences and humanities generally) is making from behaviorist and symbolist models of communication to structuralist and poststructuralist ones. Behaviorist models take words and symbols to be unproblematic tokens, combined and rearranged in meaningful chains of sentences or utterances, done in turn-taking, stimulus-response sequences. Thus analysts can build up models of culture based on sets of belief statements made by actors. Symbolist models recognize that symbols are not univocal simple tokens, but have fans of meanings, and that more is exchanged in any speech act than either speaker or receiver comprehends. Nonetheless, in symbolist models, symbols still are but more complex sign tokens—like overly full bouquets or pockets of fertile sediment—richly polysemic yet discrete. Indeed the richest symbols are like black holes: the entire culture is said to be condensed there. Symbolist analysts organize their models of culture around key symbols, symbol clusters, and nodes of semantic networks, somewhat like a crystal structure. There is a reassuring sense of relative stasis or stability in the symbolic system.

Structuralist, and particularly poststructuralist, models decompose symbols and metaphors into chains of metonymns or associations that play out into disseminating, ramifying, transmuting dynamics, attempting to model, in the structuralist case, the semantic-symbolic parameters of variation and transformation, and in the poststructuralist case, the transmuting ambivalences of meaning that keep texts and communication labile (unless forcibly controlled, in which case poststructuralist deconstructive sensibilities highlight the tensions and pressures of alternative meanings subversive to those intended and authorized by the controls). Thus, for instance, we have the multiple alternatives that Kingston explores in the "No Name Woman" fragment of her mother's narrative and the quite unexpected behavioral and psychological understandings Arlen finds in his interactions in Armenia.

These ethnic autobiographies are useful in three ways. Substantively they show up places where reduction to sociological function is inadequate, thereby highlighting the cultural. My tag for this is "cultural intereference," a pun taken from Michel Serres, meaning both cultural interference and cultural interreference of two or more traditions: this is one of the key tasks that ethnicity performs. Parallel social and cultural processes work across ethnic groups in America, but they produce only families of resemblance, because ethnicity is a construction from two or more particular, historical, cultural traditions. For example, Abelardo Delgado's poem "Stupid America" exposes the inability of Anglo-America to recognize in Chicanos their rich antiquity, creative modernity, and synthetic fertility. Chicano knives can be put to use in creative sculpture, as in the past santeros carved religious figures; Hispanic modernity in painting (Picasso) outpaced Anglo, and barrio graffiti could be much more; literature, too, can be powerfully synthesized out of a bicultural situation:

> stupid america, see that chicano
> with the big knife
> in his steady hand
> he doesn't want to knife you
> he wants to sit on a bench
> and carve christfigures
> but you won't let him . . .
>
> he is the picasso
> of your western states
> but he will die
> with one thousand masterpieces
> hanging only from his mind

Second, to methodologically explore these cultural intereferences, poststructuralist notions of nomadic meaning are helpful because cultural intereferences are embedded historically through fragments of language, sedimented metaphors, and linguistic disseminations. Consider, for example, Diana der Havanessian's poem "Learning an Ancestral Language":

> My ancesters talk
> to me in dangling
> myths.
>
> Each word a riddle
> each dream
> heirless
>
> On sunny days
> I bury
> words.
>
> They put out roots
> and coil around
> forgotten syntax.
>
> Next spring a full
> blown anecdote
> will sprout.

Once verbalized, articulated, worked out, these sedimented and embedded linguistic roots open into cross-readings of different cultural traditions with historical depth. This is the work that the often uncomfortable position of being ethnic generates, often expressed most powerfully in ironic humor. Thus, Gerald Vizenor's down and out Amerindian character Bart IV, "who failed as a trickster and settled for the role of a fool. Evil was too much for him to balance. As a fool he was a brilliant success, talking hilarious nonsense to get his case dismissed in court" or to weasel money out of his social worker. He's not a trickster in the mythic sense of one who can play the cosmic forces of evil and good against each other, overturning one with the other to show how they work; but in his role as ordinary human fool, he is able to play upon cultural expectations, stereotypes, and condescensions of white folks toward Indians to get things he wants—and to show the reader not only the falsity of assumptions on which social relations are so often built, but also the microcultural cues that are powerful structuring features of knowledge and power for underdog and mainstream, majority and minority actors.

Third, the figure of the ethnic (often called marginal, stranger, or insider-outsider) is not a figure of partial assimilation (child-learner), but a figure of learning, of access to further realms of meaning (teacher). This is a key to questions of depth/weightlessness in modern culture and of ethical individualism.

Since Nietzsche, at least, modernity has been called weightless (see T. J. Jackson Lears's *No Place of Grace,* for a vivid account of this mood in 1890s America), and things have only gotten worse as the pace of life, travel, and communication has increased. The grounds of moral certainty, and thus the sense of human actions and beliefs having true gravity, have become more ambiguous as life has shifted from small communities to globally interacting cosmopolitan urban societies: The numinous power of ritual, for instance, has been undercut by other people's different rites, values, interests, and perspectives; alternative life-styles can be simply chosen; and civic rituals have become ironic, entrepreneurial, and performed with a sense of playacting. To many over the past century, all meaning has seemed to come unrooted: all seems increasingly like semiotic play, with a purely hedonistic ability to chose alternative life styles (generating resentment by those who feel locked into traditional life styles), and with civic rituals no longer secure in a sense of purpose (generating resentment by those who feel traditional patriotism is being undercut by hedonistic others).

One of the contributions of anthropology in overcoming this sense of unease about the modern world is a wider comparative understanding of cultural, social, moral, and psychological processes, and of multiple identities held simultaneously by individuals and groups. The search into forgotten languages, histories, and traditions is one way depth—and gravitas, a sense of rootedness without implying single or exclusive roots—may be sought, not for simple appropriation, but for the strength that comes from comparative perspective and from thinking through the ethical implications of one choice versus another. Exortations to Progress, History, or Reason, for instance, are often slogans of the powerful who feel themselves in charge of a linear history or in a vanguard legitimized by the direction of "progress"; these words and their sloganeering power do not look the same to the small nations, to subaltern groups, or to ethnics, for whom such slogans often mean destruction of their ways, their interests, their values. (See for instance the writings of Milan Kundera for the notion of small societies of Central Europe for whom "Progress, Reason, History" meant the victory of other groups over them; or the writings of the Subaltern Group of historians for a somewhat similar perspective on the part of the colonized in India; or Gilles Deleuze and Felix Guattari's elaboration of "minor[ity] literatures"; as well as notions of hegemonic and counter hegemonic discourses proferred by Karl Marx, Walter Benjamin, Mikhail Bakhtin, Gershom Scholem, and Antonio Gramsci.)

Ethnicity can be a crucible for pluralism, for the coordination of diversity, for a new grounding and gravitas in multiple cultural resources, for understanding the arenas in which the creation of (post)modern society and psyches must be negotiated. Internationally, two obvious recent autobiographical texts illustrate some of these processes, as well as the new (postmodern) media through which modern ethnicities are disseminated and may be ethnographically presented. Edward Said's *After the Last Sky*, produced in collaboration with the photographer Jean Mohr, attempts to be a postmodern text materially as well as conceptually. Materially they try to use photographs and texts not to caption or illustrate each other, but as two voices mutually calling attention to the limitations of the other, thereby keeping the reader's critical skills awake. And indeed, the pictures often show up the contradictions in the assertions of the text. The text constantly invents stories to con-text the pictures, stories about loss and expropriations, saying for instance:

> Sometimes the poignancy of resettlement stands out . . . the fit between new body and setting is not good. The angles are wrong. Lines supposed to decorate a wall instead form an imperfectly assembled box in which we have been put. . . . Exile is a series of portraits without names, without contexts. Images that are largely unexplained, nameless, mute. I look at them without precise anecdotal knowledge, but their realistic exactness nevertheless makes a deeper impression than mere information. (Said 12)

But of course these portraits are posed by Jean Mohr who chose the angles and the walls against which to take the photo. Edward Said could ask Mohr the names, the contexts, the precise anecdotal knowledge. To chose to ignore the easily obtainable "mere information" in favor of invention is to engage in explicit artifice, which at times works with wonderful poetic insight, as in the commentary on the photos of young men body building: "The cult of physical strength, of fascination with body-building, karate, and boxing which has been a striking fact of life among Palestinean youth for quite a while, is obviously the response of the weak to a strong, visibly dominating other. But it is also an eye-catching, almost decorative pattern . . . an assertion of self, an insistence on details beyond any rational purpose" (Said 54).

At other times—as in the attempts to invest the photographer's choice of pose with laments of loss that we are invited to see in the posed subjects—the artifice draws attention to itself, undermining its seduction; advocacy and persuasion turn to simple propaganda, and the photograph mocks the text. The lament imposed on a little girl looking at the camera with attentive curiosity waxes so romantic that it moves the Garden of Eden (Paradise) from its traditional locus in Mesopotamia to what is now proclaimed its locus classicus: Palestine (Said 36). The book attempts to counter the negative imagery of Palestineans in the mass media, with counterimages and with a text that chronicles the creation of a new identity, Palestinean, out of both the fragmentation of old, small cultural worlds and a dialogue (often violent and agonistic) with, and modeling itself after, contemporary cultural others, particularly Jews and Israelis. Although the text tends not to be as helpful in dissecting the artifice of the photographs as the photographs are in undermining the pretentions of the text, still the possibility of this mutually critical double voicing is suggested as a valuable tool in cross-cultural texts. Above all, and in this lies the true charm of the text and the book as a whole, the text is personal, autobiographical, and disarmingly open about the difficulties of creating a modern identity:

> We have no dominant theory of Palestine culture, history, society; we cannot rely on one central image (exodus, holocaust, long march); there is no completely coherent discourse adequate to us (129). You can easily construct the plot of a logically unfolding conspiracy against us. Like all paranoid constructions. Perhaps I am only describing my inability to order things (130). All across the Arab world there is a mixture of cultural styles. . . . The commonest symbol of this process is to be found in the typical photographs of an old city across which is laid a grid of radio and television antennae (147). He too says that he is much more in contact with Palestineans today than when he was in Palestine. . . . "Thanks to modern technological progress. . . . But . . . I constantly experience the sense that something is missing for me. . . . Plane travel and phone conversation nourish and connect the fortunate; the symbols of a universal pop culture enshroud the vulnerable" (23).

Despite the rhetoric of a specific expropriation, there is also a recognition of a multiplicity of forces and contradictions that go into the making of modern identities.

Salman Rushdie's *Satanic Verses* is an even more controversial text that describes the interiority of a certain kind of urban Muslim immigrant in London constructed out of a struggle between film and traditional religion. Rushdie's entire corpus has been centrally concerned not only with the hybridizing processes of modern history and migration (partition of the Indian Subcontinent with its population transfers; migrants to Britain), but also with the role of the modern media and their interaction with traditional genres, media, and forms of storytelling and identity construction (see Fischer 1990). These processes are also being described and enacted by a series of other talented South Asian writers such as Amitav Ghosh, Bharati Mukherjee, Rustam Mistry, Hanif Kureishi, Farokh Dundy, Sara Suleri, Bapsy Sidwa, and Adam Zameenzad.

Other identity processes in the (post)modern world work analogously—albeit perhaps each with some distinctive differences—to the new ethnic processes. Among the elements of this newness is the stress on diversity and multiplicity by important, if by no means all, social fractions of those involved in defining new identities. Feminism, for instance, is perhaps the most potent contemporary reference point in academia both for thinking through identity/personhood issues as well as for many other areas of reconstructing social theory. Mary Dearborn's *Pocahontas's Daughters* explicitly uses an ethnicity model for analyzing women's writing tactics, and to some degree the parallel is a useful one. But more powerful is Alicia Ostriker's *Stealing the Language*, a reading of women poets over the last twenty-five years, such as H.D.'s reworking of the Helen of Troy story and Anne Sexton's reworking of the Brothers Grimm. These are strong poets, in Harold Bloom's sense: once they have retold these old stories, one can never think of them again in their unaltered form. The poets call attention to biases in older tellings, highlight possible readings and interpretations subversive to traditional understandings, and release new models and justifications for action. The tactic of telling strong alternative stories is a potent device, a far more powerful one than mere complaints against injustice or orthodoxy. (It is a tactic only partially recognized by the Said text cited above, and one used more fully by Rushdie, generating strong counter-reactions from those who would define modern identities in less pluralistic ways.) Feminist identity searches and ethnic ones have similarities and differences.

One advantage feminism has is that there is no tendency toward nostalgia, no illusion of a golden age in the past (a constant romanticizing danger in ethnicity searches). But as with ethnicity, what starts as an individual quest becomes, first, discovery of (partially) shared experiences and traditions (allowing common cause), and then recognition of multiple perspectives. An alliance of multiple interests and perspectives is often a stronger political and social force than attempts to enforce a unitary movement.

I've attempted to suggest ways in which the interrogation of autobiographical texts are useful in the analysis of processes of identity formation (autobiographical 1st voice) in the (post)modern world. I've suggested, albeit briefly, some of the ways in which identity processes seem to be new in the late twentieth century; but the point is less the adequacy or inadequacy of these formulations than the methodological promise or suggestion: because there is a widespread feeling that social changes in the late twentieth century are outrunning the adequacy of social theories largely formulated at the beginning of the twentieth century, autobiographies, carefully interrogated, can provide *one* important data base for reconstructing social theory "from the bottom up"; they provide fine-grained experiential loci of the interaction of changing social forces. Reading a few autobiographies is not a systematic source for verification of new theory, but it is an invaluable source for generating ideas on which to base new formulations: sites for seeing new connections, new articulations of how cultural, social, psychological forces are interacting in the consciousness of writers situated in various strategic social and cultural loci. Identity quests do not all fit liberal ideals of cosmopolitan celebration of diversity and multiple identity; some new identities of the modern world are reductionistic and "fundamentalist," nonetheless, redefining moral personae from what existed in previous generations. For instance, neither Muslim Brothers in Egypt nor those who burned Rushdie's novel in Bradford, England, are the kinds of Muslims that their grandparents in the villages and provincial towns of Egypt or Kashmir were. "Fundamentalist" here, despite the rhetoric against the materialism and moral anarchism of the West, often, does not include a rejection of modern technology or science.

Identity quests are focal points for the cultural creation of a new ethos for the postmodern world. The individual is one locus for the intersection of wider historical processes. The frame of a life history or an autobiography is one experiential field for identifying the ways these intersections articulate. The mosaic composition of an autobiographical voice is one access, and it needs to be read for the indirections and complexity that the mosaic texture provides.

Alter-Egos and (Auto)biographical Voices (2): Reinventing Moral Traditions

When she listened to me speaking Arabic, she felt left out, rejected from any absolute understanding. . . . It was a kind of linguistic frigidity, clothed in a scene of permanent seduction. I liked the fact that she maintained this distance, that she always spoke to me formally. When she used vous, *she did so with a sovereign charm. However, the day she spoke Arabic in a familiar manner to a maid, it sounded so fierce that I felt my dialect had been humbled. She was face-to-face with that which had so humiliated me when I was a child. . . . that which I desired in her was reversed in me: love's mirror so they say. Something had shattered there. I try to reassemble the fragments.* —*Abdelkebir Khatibi,* Love in Two Languages

Autobiography is often pursued through dual-tracking processes I will call mirroring, dialogic storytelling, and cross-cultural critique. Some of these have already been implicated in the ethnic autobiographies discussed above through the strategies or modes I called cultural inter-reference, bifocality, and alternative selves. A second set of texts elaborate these processes even more centrally and perhaps throw light upon the ways in which religious and moral traditions are being reconstructed in the (post)modern world. Although ostensibly biographies, this second set of texts relies centrally on a dual-tracking between the life of the author (autobiography) and that of his ostensible subject (biography).

Just as I was struck by the recent florescence of autobiographies that seem to explore ethnicity in a way helpful for thinking about identity processes in the late twentieth century, so too there seems to be, suddenly—providing a second ethnographic data set of the late twentieth century—a stream of superb biographies of religious leaders, which are quite different from traditional biographies and which take a large part of their meaning from a mirroring relation between the author and the subject of his biography. In other words, to use the rough conceit of my title, if the ethnic autobiographies at least superficially are written with the appearance of a single voice, these texts are written in two dominant voices. Two voices, two lives are involved in the construction of coherence. In the ethnic autobiographies there was a listening to an inner voice, a finding of a style that synthesized different facets of oneself, and the creation out of cultural intereferences a bifocal comparative perspective. In these biographical texts there is an even more explicit dual-tracking.

Insofar as the late twentieth century is seeing a pluralization of cultures on a global scale, the juxtaposition of life histories (autobiography, biography, life histories of various literary formats) taken from different traditions can serve as a tool of cross-cultural comparison and critique. Anthropology, of course, is uniquely charged with testing our own taken-for-granted assumptions and categories of thought against those of other cultures, including such categories as the individual, or autobiography. One of the ways in which anthropology has pursued this task is to explore alternative cultural frames for expressing emotion, psychology, personhood, and agency, and, at a more aggregated level, alternative moral traditions that work through their own "critical apparatuses," that is, that have their own hermeneutical, epistemological, and philosophical tools.

I will not say much here about alternative cultural frames for expressing emotion, psychology, personhood, and agency (I have written about it at some length in *Anthropology as Cultural Critique*, written with George Marcus), except to illustrate the issue with two brief examples. Lila Abu-Lughod's *Veiled Sentiments* describes the way in which emotion is expressed in slight alterations of a word or an intonation of otherwise stereotyped couplets of poetry among the Awlad Ali bedouin of Egypt's western desert. Ordinary public language, for women as well as for men, is an arena in which vulnerability is not expressed; one must always put on a front of stoicism, autonomy, and invulnerability. In the 1950s Arab researchers from the American University of Beirut attempted to use survey questionnaires to learn about Arab psychology. Given the linguistic usages described by Abu-Lughod, one can understand why so much of what these researchers collected was trivial, wrong, and silly. (What would an autobiographical or life history text of such a woman look like were it to be constructed with explicit attention to the ways in which interiority is in fact expressed in such a society?) A more broad-ranging example, also from the Middle East: Miriam Cooke in *War's Other Voices* describes how the poetry written by women in Beirut during the long civil war is quite different from the writings, both prose and poetry, of men; how instead of becoming enmeshed in the now-repetitive cliches of ideological-political discourse, these "Decentrist" poets encode in everyday events a richness of emotional and moral complexity that provides a unique access to the experience of women, and probably also of men. The experiential, the emotional, the cognitive all take on a different gestalt when explored in this way. These two examples may be sufficient to illustrate the fact that cross-cultural comparison can be epistemologically rewarding, but requires serious attention to local modes of thought, communication, and expression.

Among such modes, I want to highlight alternative moral traditions and their critical apparatuses by mentioning two projects that attempt to deal with autobiographical tools, that approach cultural critique by juxtaposing moral traditions in elaborated or extensive ways, and that explore how these traditions are being reinvented for the late twentieth century. In contrast, again, to the simple collection of an exotic way of doing something to use as a foil for our own ways of doing things, the challenge here is to explore moral traditions that have hermeneutical, epistemological, and philosophical tools of their own, and that moreover are aware (in varying degrees of sophistication) of alternatives to their own methods.

The first of these projects is a comparative essay on religious biographies, tentatively entitled, "Torn Religions: From Gandhi to Rajneesh, al-Hallaj to Khomeini, Shabbatai Zvi to R. Nahman and After." There is something about the contemporary world that militates against good biographies being written, as traditional ones were, as didactic models for emulation. All these biographies are deeply problematic texts, problematic in the relationship between author and subject, in the relation between biographical figure and social and psychological forces, and (most importantly) in the shifting moral grounds from small-scale communities to international networks of migrants and social strata. I am working with three moral traditions: Jainism, Islam, Judaism. The texts include the following: for Islam, the magisterial four-volume reconstruction of the life of Mansur al-Hallaj by Henri Massignon (a case where Massignon as a mystically oriented Roman Catholic finds a more enriching home in mystical Islam than in a Roman Catholic world grown alienating to him); the account of Musa Sadr by Fuad Ajami (a case of a rediscovery of Shi'ite roots by a secular author, in which the personal exploration leads to a rich account of sociological and political currents of Lebanon that allowed the charisma of Musa Sadr to flourish); the account of Khomeini by Amir Taheri (in which the author enacts the ignorance of elite Iranians about Shi'ism that was itself one of the most dramatic features of the revolution); and the account of a moderate mulla, now teaching in the United States, by Roy Motahhedeh (which enacts the nostalgia of so many Iranians for a past glory of culture that cannot explain the present). For Judaism: the extraordinary

account of Rabbi Nahman of Bratislav by Arthur Green (which reconstructs the powerful, manic-depressive personality who Ri Nahman at
the end of his life attempted to engage secularized Jews in a way many of
his followers did not understand; told by the leader of a group of modern
young Jews who attempted to invent an orthodox but fully modern
Judaism first in Somerville, Massachusetts, and later in New York City
and the account of Shabbatai Zvi by Gershom Scholem, which did so
much to reconstruct the whole course of modern Jewish historiography.
For Jainism: a tour de force memoir of the Gandhian Jain Stanakvasi
monk, Santabalji, by the Gandhian social worker and former Gujurat
State Minister for Education, Navalbhai Shah, in which the life of the
latter mirrors in uncanny ways the life of his mentor, for whom he
worked and with whom he parted ways over political differences (just as
Santabalji earlier had broken with his own mentor); and a set of ethnographic accounts of the ways in which the lives of those who take the
vows of monkhood or nunhood mirror their prior lives and alter the lives
of their former families. One of these, for example, is about a young
college-educated woman from a family that had lived in East Africa, a
girl who herself had been "a fancy girl" tooling about on her scooter in
designer jeans, whose decision to become a nun caused her businessman
father to reevaluate his own life and go into an increasingly ascetic
lifestyle himself.

All of these texts have four critical features: (1) they all are narratives
that in modernist fashion bring together several interlaced plots from
different, but mutually determined perspectives, and locate their composite coherence in the biography of individuals because the larger
myths of sacred history are no longer easily sustained in a pluralist world;
(2) they can all be situated as indices of larger cultural transitions: these
are all figures who crystallize generational or epochal shifts of cultural
perspective, and it is this that makes them of interest beyond their
own communities (Green, for example, describes Nahman as a first-
generation modern man, displaying in elaborate form the anxieties and
conflicts of that transition); (3) they all develop at least one side of what
Steven Toulmin calls the two radical sources of cosmological specula-
tion: the heavens (physics, astronomy, natural science) and ethics (moral
life, but especially the social psychology of changes in the moral life);
they all display rich psychic struggles; (4) they all draw attention to
global interconnections of worlds once more separate, foregrounding the
differences between religion as the focus of modernist anxiety versus
religion as postmodernist play: between a Gandhi and a Rajneesh, be-

tween a Khomeini and Aquarian age Sufis, between religiously affluent Jain or Hassidic diamond merchants and suburban ennui, between proletarian nativism (Hindhu revivalism, Islamic fundamentalism) and communal mutual support (mosques, temples in America).

The juxtaposing of these three traditions uses the methodological injunction that comparison must involve at least three. But it is also an opportunity to read social theory through alternative cultural eyes, to read for instance Weberian theories of the "protestant ethic" through the entrepreneurial Jains, to explore the interesting fact that at the same time as the rise of Freudian theory in the West, there was also an interest among Westerners to explore alternative imagistic and practice traditional Eastern modes for dealing with the psyche. Meditation, and experimental techniques for gaining control over the bodily processes, are not the only elements in, say, Jain and Buddhist traditions: confession is also a major technique, one that is manipulated to exacerbate, vent, and thereby relieve anxieties and obsessions, pride and other inhibitions to spiritual and social development. (Again, what do, or what would autobiographical texts constructed through these alternative symbologies, practices, hermeneutics, projections look like? For some hints, see Obeysekere's and Roland's efforts to present detailed "case histories" from South Asia; contrast them to the overly generalized psychoanalytic accounts of Sudhir Kakar. Would such texts "work out" differently than autobiographies constructed in Europe and America? See Obeysekere's suggestion that, for Buddhists, "depression" is realism and does not lead to disabling dis-ease as it does in the West.)

In these dual-voiced biographies, I am fascinated by the mirroring relationships between the life history of the author and the life history of the subject (mirrors can be set at varying angles; the reflections are not simple repetitions) and the ways in which the life histories of sometimes long-dead individuals provoke reflections on clarification and self-reconstruction in contemporary lives and reinterpretations of moral traditions. I am also interested in the fluidity of the line between autobiography and biography, or life history as narrative procedures.

Debating Muslims: Cultural Dialogues in Postmodernity and Tradition (written with Mehdi Abedi) explores this fluidity a bit further and is partly structured around seven life histories of people standing in different relations to the Islamic revolution in Iran, a revolution that claims to draw on the deep hermeneutical and moral traditions of a world religion to which one-fifth of the world's population belongs, at least nominally. The longest of these life histories is an autobiography that the

two of us constructed out of stories from Mehdi Abedi's life. Shorter life
histories of two provincial religious leaders are constructed similarly out
of stories from participants in their lives; life histories of two national
religious leaders are constructed out of orally circulating parabolic stories
about them, written biographical notes about them, and their own writings. Stories, oral narrative forms, are also the stuff out of which the
Qur'an is composed and with which (*hadith*) the Qur'an is interpreted.
The stories we select in the life histories often are attuned to the theo-
logical and hermeneutical issues of the Islamic tradition, resonating with
the chapter on how Muslims read, interpret, and evaluate (what is symbolic, what is historical, what is allegorical, what is plain sense) the
Qur'an, which in turn should reflect on the rhythm of attribution and
evaluation of information characteristic of oral cultures, and the stories
out of which the local life histories are composed. A key feature of
storytelling (and of learning) in this tradition is oral dialogue both in
the sense of being composed by an exchange between two persons, and
in the sense of arguments clarified by a play across counterarguments
(dia-logue).

The use of multiple life histories and autobiographical accounts is
intended as a technique of juxtaposition, or dia-logue, similar to the
juxtaposition of five ethnicities described above. Juxtaposition is a technique of triangulation, using a number of different (sociologically contextualized) perspectival positions to explore the social changes of Iran
and Shi'ism over the past several decades. The interpretive resources of
Shi'ite Islam are juxtaposed further with those of Judaism, Christianity,
and posttheological Western philosophy (Joyce, Derrida, Jabes). The
effort is to use autobiography and life histories as an access to hermeneutical and moral traditions, and in turn to interrogate those traditions to
show their possibilities and their historical "arrests" in frozen limitations. One wants not only to break up Western classificatory and monological stereotypes about legalistic or arbitrary qadi justice alleged to be
definitive of Islam and to block fundamentalist (equally monological)
claims to speak exclusively for Islam, but also to show how contemporary hermeneutics has historical roots and is not just a passing fad from
Paris; to invite Muslims as interlocutors in contemporary debates rather
than marginalizing them as archaic, and thus to expand the resources for
contemporary hermeneutics as well as create an arena for cross-cultural
negotiation and dialogue. Muslims are now increasingly members of
Western societies, and the cultural resources they bring can be valuable,
including the experiences of immigration itself and the hybridization it

encourages. They also offer reflections on pluralisms of old empires, different from the pluralism rapidly being created in the postmodern world, but which may yet have some things to teach us.

(Dual) autobiographical voices (2): cross cultural and cross-historical self-reconstruction. Studies of autobiography are still too often romantically focused on self and individual within an uncritical celebratory master narrative of the rise of individualism in the West. The purpose of this second voicing section was to draw attention to the ways in which individuals construct themselves through mirrorings with others and are constructed through systematic traditions of narration and dialogue that draw on culturally different principles and that need to be unpacked at various levels from alternative cultural frames for expressing emotion, psychology, personhood, and agency, to more aggregated levels of narrative, dialogic and moral traditions that have their own hermeneutical, epistemological, and philosophical tools. Not only are cross-cultural and cross-historical comparisons becoming part of everyday consciousness in the (post)modern world, but only through serious cross-cultural and cross-historical comparison can purchase be gained on the validity of commentaries and analyses of autobiography as a genre or a set of genre forms.

Autobiographical Screenings of Science and the Triangulating (3+) Voices of Rationality

What are we to think of such a civilization which has not been able to talk of the prospect of killing everyone except in prudential game theoretic terms.—Robert Oppenheimer

Visvanathan argues that the life histories of the major nuclear physicists in this century have been a movement from innocence, freedom and conviviality—from play, discovery and communitas—to the tyranny of secrecy, control and in some cases, elatory nihilism. The biographies reflect . . . the prototypical relationships between nuclear science and the scientists' self-defined social responsibility, which in turn reflects the culturally defined relationship between knowledge and power in the modern west.

[India] because it straddles two cultures has the capacity to reverse the usual one-way procedure of enriching modern science by integrating within it significant elements from all other sciences—premodern, modern and postmodern—as a further proof of the universality and syncretism of modern science. Instead of using an edited

version of modern science for Indian purposes, India can use an edited version of its traditional sciences for contemporary purposes.—Ashis Nandy, "Science as a Reason of State"

Let me complete the conceit of number of voices, a conceit like Wittgenstein's ladder that, once having served its purpose, should be thrown away: if autobiographies have the (false) appearance of being dominated by one voice, and the biographical texts just described by two voices, then autobiographies of scientists ought to foreground the third (or multiple), for science is a collective product composed of cumulative empirical and theoretical contributions. Again we are interested here in autobiographical texts to provide access to a substantive cultural field (the anthropology of science) and, at the same time, to interrogate the uses and constitutive forms of autobiographical writing.

Science is a collective social and cultural system we all share: we all have tacit faith in science; we certainly all depend on the goods produced through its use; and we also share the risks and dangers from its misuse. Scientists' autobiographies, then, might be seen as a set of texts in which the construction of an autonomous heroic ego, the "genius," can be placed in tension with the collective expansion of the aesthetics of rationality, which is often the outcome of fallible cooperation and competition, playing games (including at times deceit) as well as often becoming captive of state-, market-, or corporation-driven rationales that impersonally institutionalize violence. James Watson's *Double Helix* was one of the first autobiographical accounts of science that helped demystify the actual process of scientific discovery in the popular imagination. Rita Levi-Montalcini—Nobel laureate in medicine for 1986 for the discovery with Stanley Cohen of nerve growth factor—entitles her more recent autobiography, *In Praise of Imperfection,* in the quite serious belief that imperfection and making educative mistakes (rather than perfection and immaculate knowledge) lead to evolutionary progress. Putting it this way immediately problematizes, for instance, the genius trope, heroic mastery of the universe, which structures and mystifies so much popular writing about science. It is interesting to ask if there is patterning in the use of such tropes by country, ethnicity, class, generation, gender, or in-group student-teacher lineages. Do European women scientists write about their careers differently than do Americans? Do upper-class women scientists have experiences different from women scientists from lower-class backgrounds? (Why the insistence, for instance, by young American feminists that pioneering European women scientists rewrite their experiences to stress the slights and injuries that the former but not the latter feel?) Do certain fields of science encourage myths of individualism more than other fields? Are there patterns of social recruitment to particular fields? My colleague, Sharon Traweek, has been exploring some of these issues with respect to physicists and women scientists.

The troublesome issue of the relation between science and "reasons of state," which legitimate various forms of institutionalized violence, has been the subject of a series of studies, such as the provocative volume from the Center for the Study of Developing Societies in New Delhi, and the United Nations University's Programme on Peace and Global Transformation, *Science, Hegemony and Violence,* edited by Ashis Nandy. In one of the liveliest essays of this volume, Shiv Visvanathan (relying in turn on the Viennese science writer Robert Jungk) uses an analysis of the lives of different scientists to construct a matrix of competing positions on the relation between political democracy and big science: "Jungk is a master of what anthropologists call thick description. The multitude of anecdotes he provides coalesce into a choreography of positions available to science in relation to the violence of the atom bomb as a social fact. Within such a perspective, scientists like Einstein, Szilard, Teller, Bohr, and Oppenheimer appear not as idiosyncratic figures but as permutations within a scientific code. Names become role tags listing various possibilities as the table shows" ("Atomic Physics" 116). Thus Enrico Fermi stands for an "apartheid science—aloof from politics" ("Don't bother me about your conscientious scruples. After all, the thing is beautiful physics"). Niels Bohr stands for "the social organization of science itself as a model of communitas" ("Pure science had managed to avoid the violence of war by sublimating it into agonal play. The scientific paper was a precious gift, and it circulated in joyous exchanges. . . . Every conference was a kind of potlatch, each scientist showering the others with knowledge in exchange for eponymous recognition. The internationalization of science withstood the pressures of war"). Edward Teller "embodies the scientist as a political lobbyist playing on military and political fears to obtain larger financial sanctions for research." Szilard and Franck "urged greater public understanding and control of science" (all citations from "Atomic Physics," 116–18). The most compelling and disturbing portraits are the contradictory lives of such men as Karl Fuchs (who like Prometheus stole the gifts of nuclear fire and gave them to the Russians that a monopoly of terror might be broken), Hans Bethe (who opposed armaments research after Hiroshima, but by 1951 was seduced back into H-bomb research), and "the most fascinating figure in this danse macabre," Robert Oppenheimer, "a humanist Hamlet struggling against a scientific Prometheus" (126). Sociologically, Jungk and Visvanathan argue, all these different lives were caught in a three-fold shift in the nature of science: "the degeneration of science as a play form; the shift within science from epistemic uncertainty to vivisectionist hegemony; and the displacement of science from the university to the company town" (130). All three, Visvanatham continues,

> are symptomatic of the transformation of Western liberalism into occidental despotism, heralding the coming of the atom Staat. . . . For liberalism, the private was sacred and the public was open and accessible. In a bizarre inversion, vivisectionist science has opened up the privacy of body and soul to the public scrutiny of the clinical gaze, while science as public knowledge has become increasingly secret and forced into the most monstrous of total institutions—the research cities of the twentieth century. . . . As a mode of production, [the nuclear energy regime] demands a fail-safe system of security . . . and superhuman precision. . . . However the human body is a reluctant machine. (130, 146, 148)

What is important about Visvanathan and his colleagues in New Delhi is that they are not antiscience Luddites. Science to them is not evil, but must be controlled, redeemed through spiritually, ecologically, and democratically sound values.

One of the ways suggested, if not fully explored, in their contributions is the idea of alternative sciences, updated traditional sciences, and bicultural perspectives. Ashis Nandy:

> Contemporary India, by virtue of its bicultural experience, manages to epitomize the global problem of knowledge and power in our times. There is a continuity between the Indian experience of an increasingly violent modern science, encroaching upon other traditions of knowledge and social life [e.g., the rising debate over large-scale dams that displace thousands, can erode the landscape and cause long-term ecological damage, and transform the nature of agrarian relations], and the Western experience with modern science as the dominant cultural principle resisting the emergence of new cultures of knowledge [e.g., the resistance to investing in exploration and production of alternative forms of energy]. (Nandy 1988: 11)

And as Visvanathan illustrates, the use of lives containing the principled contradictions in the transformations of modern science can be a valuable tool both of explorations of the institutions and social organizations of science, and also of the narrative devices by which scientists make sense of their own activities.

As with ethnic autobiographies and modernist religious biographies, there are criteria that distinguish more-useful from less-useful texts. Autobiographies of scientists could help us explore a series of things: the sociology of science, the sensibilities of the scientific mind set, the aesthetics of science, the human history of the creation of the material conditions of modern life, the contradictions and bridges between pure and applied science, and the facilitators and blocks to such hybrid modern organizational forms as research institutes in the first and third worlds, perhaps even the heuristics of discovery procedures in science. For instance, feminist research on gender and science, using biographical information, has become a growth field (Keller; Haraway). Among its payoffs is a working sense of patterns of sociability, exclusion, ethnic and gender patterning, ways of foreclosing some lines of inquiry and speeding others.

The aesthetics of science is another area that is slowly being explored, both in texts that attempt to popularize science and, more impressively, in books like Thomas Pynchon's *Gravity's Rainbow,* and the Friedman and Donley book, *Einstein: Man and Myth* (written by a physicist and a literary critic) that explores the ways in which science has been seriously taken up and explored in contemporary fiction, as a way of talking about the changes in modern consciousness as well as the continuing misunderstandings of laymen about what scientists say. But little yet has been done in reverse fashion to use well-crafted autobiographies (and perhaps other literary genres used seriously by scientists to explain their sciences) to explore this aesthetics. Another potential of good autobiographies in science is a contribution to the heuristics of science. Philosophers of science such as Karl Popper have long argued that although confirmation and falsification procedures can be formalized, discovery processes are serendipitous. But recently there has been a counter line of thought, primarily by European historians and philosophers of science, that the historical circumstances of discovery can in fact be plotted and mapped, and perhaps, thereby, some insight may be gained into reasoning processes and heuristics. Perhaps the most intriguing of these efforts is by the inconstant student of Popper, Imre Lakatos, who in the footnotes to the dissertation submitted to Popper, developed a counterargument about the historical dialectics of the evolution of mathematical ideas. It reminds one of the dialectical ideas of two of the well-known students and colleagues of the Japanese Nobel laureate for physics, Hideki Yukawa, summarized briefly in the introduction to his autobiography.

In the following pages, I look at several science autobiographies and in a very preliminary way probe some of the ways they are structured. I also suggest that some of the reasons for their structuring have to do with the science fields in which their authors participate: that their form as well as their content may have something to tell us. But further, I explore whether these autobiographies can tell us anything about the nature of the wider (post)modern world in which we all live. I do this by looking first at autobiographical openings and then at a couple of middle passages.

One way to get a feel for the range of autobiographical style is to read the openings of a range of texts. Beginnings are wonderful places to examine notions of coherence, the degree to which autobiographers feel themselves to have coherent selves or narratives, the ways in which other autobiographers who acknowledge decentered, conflicted, contradictory, fallible selves position their multiple parts vis-a-vis linguistic, libidinal, social, historical, familial, generational, ethnic, gendered, technological, intercultural, or other processes; the ways in which attention is given to the media or vehicles of memory and forgetting, desire and information, documentation and impression. Some autobiographies enact, are performatives, in ways their authors perhaps do not realize. That too is interesting and is often signaled in beginnings.

Let us take a quick, unsystematic sample of the openings of six recent autobiographies (of five scientists and one philosopher of science): Hideki Yukawa, Philip Morse, Irene Fischer, Karl Popper, Norbert Wiener, S. E. Luria. Two of these begin with visual tableaux, or set piece dramatic scenes, that work as emblems of the text to come; two begin with meditations on the cliché that only when a life is nearly over can one hope to find a pattern because human life stories are recursive, hermeneutic, ever changing; and two begin with meditations on the problems and problematics of writing for nonscientific audiences autobiographies of lives rooted in scientific careers. Of these six, two come across as self-centered in inappropriate ways, cautioning the reader that the narrator is not to be fully trusted, yet enacting the grounds on which trust and distrust might be evaluated.

Sir Karl Popper is one of those wonderful characters whose philosophy is rational and democratic in ways that he himself fails to live up to: one is amused by his posturing, offended at times by his authoritarianism and eccentricities, and yet reassured by the explicitness of the arguments he makes. Norbert Wiener, on the other hand, while also arrogant, is more aware of the fact, constantly calling attention to it himself. Wiener is one of the two who meditates on the difficulties of writing a scientist's autobiography: the difficulty for him centers on writing science nontechnically, and there are repeated, explicit put-downs of laymen and an unconscious insistence that only males are scientists. By contrast, Luria's meditation on the difficulties of writing a scientist's autobiography focuses on the challenges of presenting personalities from multiple perspectives: Pasteur's religious faith, Darwin's neurasthenia, and Newton's mental illness are keys to understanding these powerful personalities at work "To examine Pasteur without his roots in French provincial bourgeois life, or Einstein without his relation to Judaism is to diminish them" (3). "Personality should emerge as a landscape composed of many vistas like . . . a Breughel panorama of peasant life" (3). Luria has formulated here a neat criterion that distinguishes uninteresting autobiographies from those that are in fact illuminating about the processes of life that go into the making of science. (Compare the autobiography of Rita Levi-Montalcini also from Turin, discussed below.)

One can also distinguish between the two autobiographies that use opening tableaux, or dramatic scenes, as emblems: Karl Popper's is the story of how he apprenticed himself to a carpenter and how this craftsman taught him everything; it is a nose-thumbing gesture repeated in the autobiography itself, where one of the main themes is to insist that Popper is very, very different from the logical positivists of the Vienna Circle, when in fact much of what he claims as his personal discovery was also their perspective. Irene Fischer's tableau is of her retirement party, of the flood of memories that came to her at that moment, of the stories she began to share with the many people who had been her longtime colleagues, which were commented on by them in the following days and weeks, and in turn stimulated the writing of her scientific memoirs. Here there is an interesting generative process: storytelling and shared experience are the markers of traditional solidarity, and this scientist, almost uniquely in these autobiographies, grounds the string of stories by faithful consultation with diaries, work logs, correspondence files, and published papers. Reference to these punctuate the text, with a rhythm of collegiality at once narrative and documentary.

Of the two scientific biographies that begin with meditations on looking back at a life as it comes to some sort of point of retrospective, Morris explicitly alludes to a theme that arises less explicitly in several of the others: that is, a key motive for writing and understanding the lives of scientists is the increasingly imperative need for governments, industrialists, and citizens to understand the workings of science in a world where the links coupling basic research and final application are becoming closer and everyday life is becoming more dependent on those linkages, including the possibilities of gross disaster if the linkages are misused.

Hideki Yukawa is the other meditator on the retrospective point of life, but his is a much more hermeneutic, scientific account of multiple perspectives. I find this, too, fascinating: the demonstration that the distance between scientific and humanistic perspectives are not opposed as so commonly is assumed. It is an exquisite text with multiple openings, each containing multiple frames, seeming to parallel the multiple alternative explanations and perspectival, partial models in physics. There are four openings: a foreword, a chronology, an introduction by the translator, and the opening chapter.

The foreword, only two pages, is an extraordinary collage of shifting perspectives, Rashamon done in cubist style, not just four points of view. It begins with the line about now that he is fifty years old, he can review half a century. The expectation of a coherent narrative thereby set up is disrupted in the next sentences which meditate on his two lives, which are one—the easy middle-class life of the son of a geology professor, easy enough, that is, to narrate; and the academic life, which is not so easy to analyze. The life of physics is further refracted: on the one hand, one could describe it easily enough as a life that was just carried along on the tide of a science that was rapidly changing in this century (a sweetly modest metaphor for someone who later admits that he helped shape the course of that science); on the other hand, this neat metaphor is dispelled in the observation that holds true for physics and for narrating a life: "today's truths may tomorrow be disproved, and that is why, from time to time, we must look backwards in order to find the path we must take tomorrow." This recursiveness is like the stream into which one can never step twice; one looks backwards not to achieve closure, but to track a course into the future; it is like the hermeneutical circle that never achieves closure because each new reading generates awareness of further horizons.

The pace of the text does not pause: it notes (again softly) that this particular life has already had multiple accounts of it written, both by Yukawa himself and by biographers. The author suggests that the public has an image, and he wants to offer more information so that that image can be judged. Note the imagery: this is not the normal public mask or private interior dichotomy, nor is it the correcting of a false public impression (the binary logic of public/private, right/wrong); instead it is a modern scientific sensibility of triangulation amidst more and more kinds of data, an image of increasing approximation, increasing comprehension of complexity.

Next the interior/public, subjectivity/objectivity trope is muddied. The Nobel laureate claims to have trouble expressing himself, to tend to view matters subjectively, and to know that if he tries to view things "objectively" he may "betray" himself. Objectivity and subjectivity, here, of course, are not the popular body/mind, reality/emotion, hard/soft binarisms, but something more like simplistic reification versus perspectival truth. "In any case," the text hastens on, "not even I can perceive clearly what is about to take shape." Note: here he is talking not of the future, but of the nature of the text that the reader is about to commence.

(By this point, I hope all Heideggerians are withering in their chairs fried by the false dogmas of technologism levied at all science and scientists; and Derrideans are dancing with Nietzschian joy. But we are not quite done in this Derridean delight: the falsity of proper names is next.)

Names are not what they seem, especially in Japan: we learn that Hideki Yukawa is Hideki Ogawa. Ogawa is his father's family name: upon marriage, he took his wife's family name, Yukawa. Moreover eventually we learn that his father had done the same, and that name in turn was also such a name. A lovely regression of ever receding uxorlineal nominations.

The foreword ends with a lyrical sentence that brings temporary closure to the opening sentence: Hideki Ogawa was born in 1907 at old Tokyo's Ichibei-cho Azabu. The house smelled of plum blossoms each spring. In chapter 1 we learn, of course, that this is a reported description, elicited from his mother, about a birth house of which he had no memory, certainly no olfactory one, a birth house moreover that no longer existed, having been burned in World War II. (Derridean traces of the ineffable.)

I won't go on with the description of the text, except to say that it continues in this fashion, insisting on the multiplicity of truth, perspective, and modeling. And to suggest that this is not a function of writing style, or of simple Derridean poststructuralist reading on my part, but a fundamental modern scientific perspective on reality. And finally to suggest that the result of multiplicity is not (as Alan Bloom fears) the undermining of knowledge, but the increase of purchase on truth and knowledge, by identifying the sources of uncertainty, the limits of particular angles of vision, and by triangulating them together.

Sciences are diverse in their procedures, methods, aesthetics, and organizational structures. Let us look at middle passages of two scientists' autobiographies, one from geodesy, a science that is closer to the applied mathematics end of the continuum, and one from neurobiology, a science that is closer to the life and human sciences end. Such juxtapositioning of different sciences may help pose questions about the varieties of models and practices of knowledge production we call science. Geodesy is a particularly clear example of procedures of modeling, mapping, indirect measurement, and increasing degrees of approximation or accuracy. Neurobiology is closer to that other image of science as almost anarchistically experimental, trial and error, inductive empiricism, leavened, of course, in this case with analytical biochemical detection of molecular weight and other physiochemical properties. The notions of multiplicity and triangulation, invoked by Hideki Yukawa, apply also in these two sciences in interesting variants: triangulation is a literal mapping procedure in geodesy, whereas the complementarity of neurobiological experiments and biochemical analysis was the sine qua non for isolating and beginning to explore the still mysterious hormonal mechanisms of the nerve growth factor for which Rita Levi-Montalcini and Stanley Cohen received in 1986 Nobel Prize in medicine.

These two autobiographies (of Rita Levi-Montalcini, the neurobiologist, and of Irene Fischer, the geodesist) might also be usefully juxtaposed to accounts in the emerging field of science and technology studies, to have other frames of reference with which to critically interrogate the autobiographies and to provide a reality check to the theorizing by nonscientists (often scientifically trained persons who, voluntarily or involuntarily, left the science career fast track) about what drives scientists to discovery and accomplishment. (No serious anthropology or even journalism takes native accounts at face value, yet no anthropological or journalistic account can be credible without building upon native perspectives). A useful preliminary foil, for instance, is provided by Donna Haraway's survey of the four temptations in studies of science—four tempting perspectives on science, each valid up to a point, but dangerous if allowed to silence the other perspectives.

The first temptation—useful to read against Rita Levi-Montalcini's quite different perspective—is the social constructivist view of science, which inquires into the power relations that affect the progress of particular lines of inquiry, particular careers, and, in its strongest form, affect the ways in which scientific knowledge polices its own boundaries against new ideas or new information it cannot easily incorporate. In its strongest versions, such as that elaborated by Bruno Latour and Steven Woolgar in *Laboratory Life,* the social constructivist view rejects ordinary notions of realism, ordinary separations of what is technical from what is social, and regards the criteria of pragmatic feedback from success in the world to scientific models as fundamentally underestimating the ways in which science can protect itself from falsification. Latour and Woolgar see science as a tactic of reducing conflicting interpretations of messy reality into unambiguous facts through various methods of transcription, translating into equations, and machine outputs. Over time, say Latour and Woolgar, what begin as probabilities, tentative generalizations, or approximations are incorporated into later stages of model building as undisputed facts. In the competition for success, scientists become invested in power struggles, defined in part as raising the cost of destabilizing reigning accounts so high that the effort is not worth pursuing. Haraway rightly calls such a description of science both attractive and dangerous: it draws attention to the constructedness and contingent nature of reigning scientific ideas, but is wildly overstated if treated as a complete account.

I will put Rita Levi-Montalcini's observations in fuller context; I want to simply observe here that she—like many scientists—foregrounds and revels in the contingency of scientific knowledge. Latour and Woolgar's "demystifying" account is only demystifying to popular accounts of genius and absolute truth, not to working scientists. But Levi-Montalcini places a different set of implications on this contingency: it is part of a larger picture of both science and life as an evolutionary process created through a capricious game of mutations and selection. She notes the necessity in both life and science of repressing knowledge that cannot be incorporated and that can be self-destructive: thus immersing herself in her experiments as the Nazis raged around her was a form of healthy repression. She also cites Russian neuropsychologist Alexander Luria's "law of disregard of negative information" in being able to repress negative experimental results that she would not be able to explain until years later, and that had she focused on might have derailed her work. Furthermore, retrospective histories of science often include, as Levi-Montalcini's does, explanations of powerful ideas that provided false confirmation for what were thought at particular points in time to be scientific results. She cites, for example, the sway of gestalt theories providing support to Karl Lashley's experiments, which seemed to suggest that the capacity to learn and memorize was not localizable in particular parts of the cortex. From a scientist's point of view, then, the social constructivist account is largely true but trivial, not very interesting (not adding systematic new information).

Social constructivism is Haraway's first temptation. Her second is a political mediationist view of science that inquires into the ways in which language, laboratory hierarchies, industrial or governmental patronage, etc., structure the perspectives through which truth is recognized. This could be taken as a variant of the social constructivist inquiries; it differs primarily in its concern to expose the systematic political, state- and money-generated patternings of what otherwise might seem to be more individualistic, contingent outcomes of strong personalities and organizations, or effects of measuring and inscribing devices. Haraway derives her version of the political mediationist questions from Marxist, feminist, and minority observations that the conflictual and inegalitarian relations of society are often opaque to those in positions of systematic domination and power; what seems to be true from one perspective may conceal problems that are visible from other positions. Weak and relatively trivial versions of the mediationist accounts of science are descriptions, for instance, of how popularizing accounts of science draw upon sexist imagery. Emily Martin's work on medical textbooks' metaphors for the biology of human reproduction is an example that foregrounds important ways in which the laity and the poor may be disempowered in their own thinking about reproduction or in their interactions with physicians, social workers, and others by the circulation of such metaphors; but this points up more about the poverty of scientific literacy in America, or of translation languages, than about the trajectory of scientific models. Haraway herself has a field day with the metaphors that have structured research programs in primatology from the days of "Man the Hunter (of Science)"—individualistic tests of manhood by such science explorers as Carl Akeley who went into the wilds to shoot great apes with gun and camera (with gun for specimens, with camera to preserve without destroying nature)—to the 1970s when *National Geographic* popularized Jane Goodall, Shirley, Strum, Birute Galdikas, and Diane Fossey as "Woman the Nurturer (of Science)"—for example, adopting orphaned apes, females being "closer to nature" and thus able to provide the conditions for animals to approach human beings and for human beings to reapproach the secret garden of nature. (Meanwhile, says Haraway, the cameras recording these women and apes were held by their [male] husbands and consorts in good, traditional gender-divided roles.)

A more serious part of Haraway's *Primate Visions* is the correlation of research paradigms in primatology with more general cultural anxieties: the concern from 1890 to 1930 with fear of decadence, stressing preservation and conservation of pure nature (including eugenics and racial purity); the concern in the 1940s with obsolence and stress in an increasingly technologized age, emphasizing molecular biology, systems engineering, the recognition that human beings are parts of human-non-human cyborg systems, and management systems of social control (focusing on food, sex, dominance-subordination, hormones) involving a movement from laboratory experimental settings with chimpanzees (conditioning, learning, behavior modification) to watching free-ranging animals in created colonies, in nature, and in nature preserves; the concern in the post–World War II period with antiracism and decolonization, and a biological anthropology that supported the unity and equality of all human beings, centering itself on population biology and adaptive complexes of functional anatomy and culture (upright bipedalism and tool-using); and finally in the 1970s and 1980s a sociobiology (genetic calculus, strategic rationality) that paralleled the rise of yuppie stress on competitive individualism.

But most importantly, Haraway acknowledges that in the course of the development of primatology, biological anthropology, genetics, and related fields, there has been a real positivist increase in knowledge base and sophistication that is not contained by either the popularizing metaphors or the correlations with encompassing cultural anxieties of the age. Hence her recognition that while political-mediationalist accounts of science have a degree of validity (especially in a field that is so prone to be a projective screen for thinking about human culture, psychology, physiology, and sociability—and hence her critical focus in the last third of the book on four women primatologists who have helped reorient the field and its generalizing implications), they are dangerous if allowed to silence other accounts of science.

Again, it is perhaps interesting to juxtapose Rita Levi-Montalcini's account, as a reminder that even when scientists write popular accounts they often eschew the kinds of metaphors Martin and Haraway foreground, insisting on simplified yet technically precise language, but, more importantly, to note the enactment of the separation between ordinary life full of metaphors, emotions, and chaotic forces, and a sphere of inquiry where inferences and implications are more narrowly interrogated and controlled. Indeed, Levi-Montalcini goes so far as to concentrate her account of her scientific career in the third part of her autobiography, with only occasional references to the scientific developments themselves in other more familial, organizational, or historical sections. Irene Fischer's account does not engage in this sort of segregation; it does insist on simplified yet technically precise language, pointing out the ways in which metaphors introduced for popularizing fun (as in the case of the "pear-shaped earth") are or are not analogically apt. Haraway's field of observation, primatology, is, as noted, one particularly subject to popularizing projections, and the recent subfield of sociobiology has had a spate of practitioners who have been particularly promiscuous and deliberately provocative in their use of popularizations that shift ambiguously between technical and inappropriate connotative meanings (for example, in the use of the word *altruism*).

More strictly political economy inquiries might also pursue Chandra Mukerji's suggestion that scientists at work on big science projects (oceanography, the supercollider, the genome project) are a reserve labor force of experts available to government, which can, by selective funding, ensure access to the expertise it needs and reduce the threat from expertise that might undermine its own policies. Scientists can remain autonomous in the details of their work while being simultaneously dependent in the major guidelines of their work; science in this sense is politics writ in a larger sense than the politics of labs and individuals fighting for the prizes of recognition, or in the various strategies that individual scientists use to extract resources for their own projects in the interstices of large science and bureaucracy. (Levi-Montalcini comments on the loss of interest in Italy in neurobiology, yet its continuation; she also comments on the differences in individualism—greater in Italy than in the United States—and the publishing demands in Italy that affect the course of risks and innovations scientists attempt).

The accounts of science by scientists themselves, which Haraway describes as usually realist and positivist, are the third of Haraway's four temptations. These accounts claim for science a degree of autonomy from the realities of their institutional and political settings, which are freely acknowledged to affect the progress of science. These accounts also frequently remind us that the metaphors of popular science are but very rough approximations of relationships that can often only be accurately rendered in the technical language of mathematical functions, that the two kinds of language do not translate very well, and that, therefore, to critique science by critiquing only the popular metaphors by which it is approximated is not tenable. Scientists distinguish between discovery (which may be serendipitous) and confirmation/falsification, between the sociology of science and the content of science, between theoretical models that are simplified approximations of reality and reality itself, between levels of precision and pragmatic feedback provided by the ability to predict or control outcomes, between probablistic truth and particularistic knowledge, etc. Science is heuristic, pragmatic, partial, approximate, evidence-relational, and modeling; all of which may involve reductionism, deterministic causality, mechanical as well as statistical models, but less as totalizing accounts than as components within larger modeling intentions. Internal scientists' accounts are "temptations" (insufficient by themselves) insofar as they ignore or downplay the sociological and political environments that enable them, or insofar as they tell the story of science discovery self-servingly from a particular individual's or group's point of view.

Finally, the fourth temptation is to consider science as a species of storytelling, which immediately opens the possibility that the same science may be narrated in multiple ways. The attraction of trying to tell multiple narrations of science is it provides a sense of how coherence is created, while drawing attention to perspectival and approximative tactics, or as Haraway puts it, individually having no power to claim unique or closed readings. To problematize and describe science in terms of the various stories (such as the four temptations) that can be told about the histories of discovery, the relation between science and nonscience parts of cultural understanding, the uses and abuses of scientific knowledge, unintended consequences and implications, and so on, is a relativizing move quite popular for cultural critique. To cast the first and second temptations as stories is in part to relieve them of their arrogance or sense of claiming to be the whole truth, rather than important aspects of the truth. But the temptation of turning all accounts of science into the status of mere storytelling must be resisted: the chemical effects of drugs, or the geometry of the earth, or the physics of atmosphere are not just stories.

One of the compelling characteristics of good science autobiographies is that they involve several, if not all, of the four temptations (or perspectives or stories), as well as others such as the historical and personal resonances between scientific activities and other parts of scientists' lives,

including such well-crafted allegories of methodology and meaning as ·
cited above from Hideki Yukawa. Resonances between scientific activities and other parts of scientists' lives are a part of the social and
cultural constructedness of science that is often screened out by social
science accounts such as the Latour and Woolgar study, but which can
contribute not only to an understanding of the psychology, or motivation, of scientists, but also to the larger aesthetics that informs and
encompasses their work. Let me turn then briefly to the autobiographies
of Rita Levi-Montalcini and Irene Fischer. Both are written by women
with European backgrounds and might be read against those mono-
chromatic feminist critiques of the science establishments that emphasize the difficulties for women in pursuing scientific careers: not
to dismiss those difficulties, but to emphasize Rita Levi-Montalcini's
philosophical observation that more important to success in scientific
research than either special intelligence or ability to be precise or thor-
ough are the qualities of dedication and optimistic underestimation of
difficulties.

The beginning of Rita Levi-Montalcini's autobiography is, like other
openings already cited, emblematic of the account to follow. It is a
three-fold meditation on the object of her science (nerve cells and nerve
growth factors), on science and technology, and on the relation between
rationality and life—each of these an analogue of the other two, all fitting
a model of "capricious games" of mutation and selection, an evolutionary
process in which advantages are built upon so that *retrospectively* there is
a line of irreversible progress. This is a facilitating frame for an account
of the development of neurobiology involving the interplay between the
availability of techniques (chrome-silver impregnation so that nerve cells
stand out), technology (the electron microscope, which allowed one to
see synapses; cathode-ray oscilloscope; and camera), the complementarity between biochemistry (to analyze the nature of snake venom and
mouse salivary gland serum and to purify fractions of these, which were
important steps in identifying nerve growth factor) and neurobiology (to
explore experimentally the spectrum of action of these protein molecules
by injecting them in developing organisms and in differentiated organisms), and a number of false leads. There is place here for the expansion
of knowledge and rationality, a sense of historical horizons (what was
possible or conceivable at different points in time), and for the chaos of
reality. Levi-Montalcini sees progress as stemming from imperfection—
in technology she contrasts the efficiency of the bicycle, which has not
evolved much from its introduction, with propulsion mechanisms that

have evolved in speed and efficiency; she says of herself that she lacked strong powers of logical thought, lacked aptitude for math and physics, and so on, but thanks to such characteristics as determination and underestimating difficulties she was able to make major contributions. Indeed her account in the third part of the book, where she chronicles both her own career and the advances in neurobiology that led to the explorations of nerve growth factor, is one of trial and error, of complementarity of competences between investigators, of putting aside intractable problems and results that could not be solved until further advances had been made. And in an unintentional feature of the book, she enacts dialectics of fallibilities and contradiction as well, first denying emotional complexes, then proceeding immediately to enumerate childhood anxieties (tendencies to solitude, neurotic fears of wind-up toys and mustaches) and complex emotional relations with parents, siblings, and mentors. More importantly in the present context, she perceives diaries and journals (and life histories?) as vanities, yet at the same time is thankful for the return of letters that allowed her to relive intense periods of her life and to construct key portions of her autobiography:

> I never developed the habit—nor do I regret not having done so—of keeping any kind of record, still less a diary, because I believe that, if memory has not taken the indelible imprint of a given event, then it could not and should not be brought back to life by mere written witness. I believe, in fact, that the very act of recording an event causes, if only unconsciously, a distortion resulting from the blatant desire of the diarist to make use of it as an account to be exhibited to third parties, as a way of reliving in old age a particular moment, and of making one's descendants partake in it or even, if one is especially vain, for its value to posterity. (170)

> Having never kept a diary, I was very pleased when, in June 1980, Viktor Hamburger sent me a large envelope containing all the letters—carefully preserved for so many years—that he had received from me during the period I spent in Rio, from September 1952 to the end of January 1953. . . . In reading them, I have relived one of the most intense periods of my life in which moments of enthusiasm and despair alternated with the regularity of a biological cycle. (154)

The philosophy, and the picture of knowledge and science, here is one of chaos, and often adversity (lack of funds, bureaucratic opposition, war), against which the drive to creativity leads to lasting results. She ends with a tribute to Primo Levi, and his citation, in the midst of concentration camp adversity, of Dante's Ulysses, "You were not born to live as brutes": a motto that serves also for the promise that neurobiology and the nerve growth factor studies may eventually bring cures for nervous system disorders. There is, to be sure, a certain kind of heroic trope here, but it is a markedly humble one, neither the macho version critiqued by Haraway, nor one that sees the scientist as a lone genius. The scientists described are all fallible creatures creating a collective understanding that itself is historically situated and contingent, if no less remarkable and promising for all that.

Levi-Montalcini's book is one in a series sponsored by the Alfred P. Sloan Foundation; they are largely popular accounts rather than systematic inquiries into the sciences themselves or their histories, though one does get capsule histories as in Levi-Montalcini. Irene Fischer's "*Geodesy? What's That? My Personal Involvement in the Age-Old Quest for the Size and Shape of the Earth, With a Running Commentary on Life in a Government Research Office*" is a more concentrated and sustained account of the development of a scientific field and career over a twenty-five year period. Unlike Levi-Montalcini's book, which tends to segregate the account of the science in one section, Fischer's text is characterized by an interlacing rhythm of personal life, technical scientific problems, collegial relations (both complementary and competitive), publications, bureaucratic difficulties, accomplishments, and rewards. Although at first sight the text may seem a forest of names—of people, articles, and groups—as one reads it takes on an almost mimetic rhythm of the social networks and step-by-step solution of the large puzzles posed by measuring the earth, aided by hints in the literature, personal interactions, technological breakthroughs, patient data accumulation, and recalculations and reconceptualizations as new thresholds of descriptive competence are achieved.

Unlike Levi-Montalcini's ambivalence toward diaries, this text is built on rich documentation of diaries, correspondence, and publications, allowing a textured interlacing of stories like Haraway's "temptations" (particularly the first and third), as well as personal and world-historical stories. Each chapter is constructed around an advance in terms of the scientific puzzle of being able to measure or model the earth's size and shape: the advance of surveys along the earth's surface; the different results that one obtains from different astrogeodetic, gravimetric, and oceanographic measuring techniques; the efforts to find a best-fitting ellipsoid to the irregularities measured on the actual earth; the efforts to piece together geoid maps for different parts of the earth into a unified world datum (of which the Fischer North American Geoid Chart was the first to cover the North American continent; the Mercury Datum, or Fischer 1960 Ellipsoid, became the official NASA and DOD world datum; and the Fischer South American Datum was the first to bring the various efforts of Latin American countries together); and the revolution introduced by satellite technology. This strand of the account works from chapter to chapter as an incremental series of historical snapshots or a progressional history of the creation of more complete, more secure, and reconceptualized knowledge.

Each chapter interlaces such scientific advances with accounts of the competitions and cooperation among different government agencies, scientists and support staff, different countries, and individuals (the "third voice," the sociological and social constructivist narrations). There is a trajectory to this narration from the esprit de corps of a tiny pioneering group within a larger social setting of gender, race, and nationality consciousness, to, toward the end of the autobiography, assessments of the effects of changing government management policies on the conduct of science. Each chapter also plays off the family and immigrant consciousness not only of the author, but of a scientific world in the United States after World War II invigorated by the inflow of European scientists and of closer international cooperation and competition. (Levi-Montalcini's book also contributes to this story—her medical school classes included Salvador Luria, Renato Dulbecco, and Rudolfo Amprino, and her own career benefited from cooperation between St. Louis, Rio, and Rome—but she focuses on this primarily with regard to the reestablishment of science in Italy after the war, not in the sea change transformation of American science and academia.)

These were still the days when the author could be told by a fellow female employee not to work so hard because women would never advance beyond a given level; when a military air transport steward refused to believe that the GS-12 Fischer, listed on his flight roster to be boarded first, could be a woman; when her 1957 Meritorious Civilian Award pin was designed to be worn only in a male jacket lapel button hole (subsequent awards corrected this oversight). These are remembered as only amusing markers of breaking through barriers. More serious were the time a paper had her name as author removed because the bureaucrats thought it unseemly or unlikely that a woman should be the author (much to the embarrassment of her superiors), and the earlier loss of a

job at Harvard as an assistant to Vassily Leontieff when students found
out and protested that a woman was grading their papers. (MIT students
of Norbert Wiener did not similarly object when she graded for him.
Working for John Rule at MIT developing stereoscopic slides, she excit-
edly tried to show them to Norbert Wiener only to learn that he had
only one functioning eye and, without depth perception, could not appreciate these three-dimensional figures.) More poignant still are memories of trying to break segregation patterns—women ate lunch together
to celebrate promotions, but blacks were usually not invited; this was
morally unacceptable to a Jewish refugee from racist persecution, and on
her first promotion she invited all her coworkers to a party at her home
only to have one black woman not show on a particularly flimsy excuse.

The immigrant sensibility provides a useful bifocal vision, a constant
sense of alternative perspectives, a reality check and stabilizing force. A
charismatic mentor, Dr. John O'Keefe, initiated and taught her what she
needed to know of geodesy and surveying, but in an environment of the
esprit of a small elite group where she proved herself by deriving for-
mulas during a placement quiz and by passing a series of covert informal
tests of knowledge. The group of five or so included a German-speaker
who knew of the Vienna Circle, of which she had been a junior follower,
which made her feel at home. It also included another refugee, the
former head of a geodesy organization in Yugoslavia saved from a dead-
end bureaucratic job by O'Keefe. That she could read the basic Jordan-
Eggert geodesy text in the original German helped (there was only a
partial in-house translation in English available at the time, done by
another German refugee), and her Viennese training proved superior in
many ways. The philosophy of Austrian physicist Ludwig Bolzman also
stood her in good stead both against show-off methodology for methodology's sake that got others into unnecessary trouble, and against lack
of interest in issues that she felt important, and that she was willing to
doggedly pursue until others realized the relevance: "Propose what is
true. Write so that it is clear, and fight for it to the death." (Bring vor was
wahr ist. Schreib so dass es klar ist. Und verficht's bis es mit dir gar ist)
(43).

For example, surveyors never thought the curvature of the earth important enough for their purposes, and this simplification was carried
over into early geodetic models, an absurdity that Fischer refused to let
lie. Eventually, as the field progressed, the fact became important and
required explicit incorporation. (Contrast the foreshortened time frame
and unduly pessimistic thoughts of Latour and Woolgar, above, about

the freezing of "facts," and compare Levi-Montalcini's similar perspective to Fischer's.) Amused by a colleague whose fancy math allowed him to set up 199 simultaneous equations with just as many unknowns—in contrast to her own step-by-step compilation for the same task using 300 equations but with only three, four, or five unknowns, which could be solved with a simple desk calculator—she quoted a friend, "An American scientist would rather bite off his own tongue before he permits his technial work to appear in easy detailed steps" (106). When their results disagreed, it took him months to find his error. Another friendly saying in German, by Einstein, also helped her keep her equanimity between conflicting geodetic and astronomic methods based on different unexamined apriori assumptions: "Der Herrgott ist mutwillig, aber nicht boeswillig." (The Almighty God is mischievous, but not malicious.) (55).

In Fischer's account, in other words, scientific life was not just a wonderful puzzle-solving delight; it was a network of intellectual lineages, historically created assumptions that could not be taken for granted, personalities, protocols, and bureaucracies: ranging from the genial Brig. Gen. Guy Bomford who used his outsize belly to teach students about the equatorial bulge to the indirection needed to get answers from the Russians. In one case, she asked which of two methods the Russians had used in a 1939 paper: the Russian geodesists at the international meetings claimed not to know, so she presented calculations based on two possibilities. Then a few months later she read their report on the meetings, in which they gave only one of her calculations: the one based on the correct method!

Indirection and competition, of course, were not only across international and Cold War lines. The computation division within her own agency finally agreed, under much pressure, to teach the researchers how to program the new UNIVAC computer; when the researchers tried to run some actual computations they discovered that the computer people, anxious to protect their own expertise, had taught them a program that was no longer operational. And there was the case of the rival agency in the U.S. government that had their work classified so it could not circulate, and another agency that plagarized their work. More amusing is the case of Charlie Brown: in 1958 the Vanguard satellite went up, and O'Keefe explained at a news conference that the new calculations of the shape of the earth showed it to be more pear-shaped than round. This appeared in a Charles Schultz cartoon of Charlie Brown, happy with a new globe until Linus told him the earth was not round but pear-shaped.

When Fischer wanted to use this cartoon in a publication, Schultz and his syndicator refused permission except in oral presentations, claiming it as their own intellectual property. This, of course, did not prevent Fischer from using a series of vegetable metaphors in training manuals and in speeches (such as the one to the American Philosophical Society delivered at the Cosmos Club where women at the time were not officially allowed). On a more cooperative note, Fischer was able to locate materials from the famous 1927–35 Sven Hedin expedition that were secreted away in Washington; she returned them to Erik Norin of Sweden, who was putting the final touches decades later on a book to accompany the Hedin atlas. And in 1965 she won a vote of applause from the Organization of American States by breaking the logjam, which had prevailed since 1944, on exchanging data. By demonstrating how a unified South American Datum could be constructed, Fischer generated the enthusiasm necessary for all to contribute their information. Even more impressive, perhaps, given nationalist sensitivities, was her skill in getting Argentinian cooperation: acknowledging their wariness of allowing their work to be appropriated by others, she invited the Argentinians to come to Washington for training and to use computer facilities; they in turn were willing to share their data, not with Fischer's agency (a part of the U.S. Defense Department) but with "me personally for the scientific purposes of the Figure of the Earth and the South American Datum" (193).

Again, only this initial taste of the text will have to suffice here. It is enough to illustrate the historical richness of the presentation of the evolution of a basic field of research needed, among other things, for all satellite and space technology; the analogical utility of this model of science (both in constructing this text and as one of several models of science involving mapping, degrees of approximation, modeling, triangulation, collation of multiple perspectives, indirect measurement, and constructivist-pragmatic approaches to knowledge); the human dramas (comic and serious, fallible yet cumulatively producing results, historically situated in world-historical terms as well as sociologically and culturally, and individualistic persons in a collective enterprise); and the joyful optimism of so much scientific endeavor (which all too often contrasts with the dour, suspicious, even angry, affect of much social science critique of science). The capsule accounts of changing methods and problems, from actual measurements on land, in the sea, and from space to creating models and measuring irregular reality as deviations from theoretical surfaces (be they geoidal equipotential surfaces or oceanographic theoretical levels) to collation and compromise, temporary solutions among competing methods, provide a fascinating conceptual education as well as a history: the early heroic achievement by surveyors of long triangulation arcs from Scandinavia to Cape Town, from Europe to Japan, from Canada to Tierra del Fuego; the calculation of deflections of the vertical (variations in gravity forces of the earth from place to place, which can affect rocket or missile trajectories) either by dense gravity surveys or by calculating the difference between astronomic and geodetic positions; the introduction of marine geodesy (stationing three transponders in an equilateral triangle on the ocean's bottom with a ship above sending acoustical signals, as a basic unit of triangulation; utilization of bathymetry to help estimate differences of deflection of the vertical from terrestrial measurements); the introduction of satellite geodesy (geometric satellite techniques—analogous to terrestrial triangulation—photographing a moving satellite against a star background from two stations, one of known position and one to be determined; dynamic satellite techniques—analogous to terrestrial gravimetry—measuring distances, not angles, by electronic, not optical, means); the disputes between oceanographers and geodesists about calculating equipotential surfaces of the earth and over the slope of mean sea level; the measuring of the irregularities of the earth against locally best-fitting ellipsoids and finding a global datum; and bureaucratic solutions of taking discrepant scientific results by differing methods and dividing the difference to produce a compromise datum for widespread use. Along the way are wonderful side studies into historical issues, illuminated by new scientific understandings: applying the world datum to the ice age; reevaluating the classic lunar parallax determinations; refiguring Eratosthenes's and Posidonius's calculations of the circumference of the earth and showing how errors have crept into the literature about those calculations; and, more generally, applying Vienna Circle pragmatic language philosophy to a retranslation of a famous, but often misunderstood, dictum of Rabbi Akiba about free will. Also along the way are astute analyses of attempts at management of science in the government—not jeremiads, but observations on how a new commanding officer was able to rekindle morale among researchers by separating status- and control-seeking administrators from scientists and dismantling stovepipe organization, as well as observations on the triviality, inappropriateness, and self-defeating philosophies of management courses, and an analysis of civil service reforms. And there are anecdotes rich in psychological, historical, and cultural resonance.

These historical soundings bring us back to the Voices and Mosaic of our title, the layerings of memory that are powerful anchors for the present. These are personal: the inner voice of Fischer's father who gives her support at various moments of significance; in the banter of O'Keefe and Fischer over fear of flying in her first overseas flight in 1955: Catholics have it easier joked O'Keefe, they know there's an upstairs, causing Fischer to reflect on Shaw's vision of the boring hymn-singing upstairs and on the Jewish version of sages debating, "but I did not think they admitted women there, and even if they did, I was not interested" (57), followed by a lyrical description of the world seen from the air, resonating with psalm, Beethoven, Isaiah, and a traditional blessing upon touching down safely—culture and religion. They are also historical, the connections and hesitancies of the last half century: at a symposium in Vienna—the first visit in more than thirty-five years—the convener addressed her in an inimitable Viennese idiom, "Gnaediger Frau, ich habe ein Huenchen mit lhen zu rupten" mixing polite and colloquial language, (approximately, *Dear Lady, I have a bone to pick with you*) (227), admonishing her for forcing him to speak in English for decades, not realizing she spoke German; poignantly remarking about her childhood city, "There seemed to be two towns on the same spot: the lively town of the Symposium, a beautiful town strangely suggesting we may have visited here before; and another personal town that was crying with silence, a ghost town" (226). And sometime later, in the course of giving thanks for an honor, finding it easy enough to speak the thanks in German, but, as she tried to turn to geodesy, needing to speak in English.

The third level of such Mosaic memory is the sounding in much deeper histories, Eratosthenes and the ice age, but also Petronius Arbiter (A.D. 66) on management: "We trained hard—but it seemed that every time we were beginning to form up into teams, we would be reorganized. I was to learn that later in life we tend to meet any new situation by reorganizing, and the wonderful method it can be for creating the illusion of progress while producing confusion, inefficiency, and demoralization" (319). This she posted on her file cabinet to provide a "long view [which] had a soothing philosophical effect," together with a pinup of Galileo Galilei: "He had a pensive look into the far distance. . . . His presence reinforced awareness of a clear distinction between real work and busy work in a researcher's value system, and helped allocate precious time and energies accordingly" (324). She had to fight repeatedly to protect his freedom on the wall against the government's inspectorate, and she hid away in her desk drawer, as a reminder to herself as an administrator, Lord Acton's "Power corrupts, and absolute power corrupts absolutely."

These Mosaic features are not just ornaments; they are repositories of philosophical perspective, of will, of motivation, of sense of proportion, things that help foster that determination and discounting of obstacles that Levi-Montalcini also spoke of.

Two features of these scientists' autobiographical texts are most important in the present context: the utility of autobiographical forms as exploratory access into the systematic features of science as a human endeavor and the well-craftedness of the best of these scientific autobiographies, well-crafted not only in the sense of being a pleasure to read, but in the sense of using their literary forms themselves to provide access. With regard to the three texts of Yukawa, Levi-Montalcini, and Fischer, I have suggested that the form of their life history narratives and the form of their scientific endeavors are formal analogues of one another, consciously, deliberately so, and in their variety they provide access to the diversity of science, its procedures, methods, and models. One of the interesting effects, I think, is the demonstration that the distance between scientific perspectives and humanistic ones are not necessarily as opposed as is commonly assumed and that the multiplicity some people fear as destructive of traditional pieties is not a pandering to irrationalities of postmodern irresponsibility; on the contrary it is ever more a feature of the contemporary condition, of rationality, and of grounded positions of critique that allow understanding (and perhaps social reconstruction) to advance.

Soundings and Si(gh)tings: Triangulations in (Post)modern Sensings/Sensibilities

Who will reassemble these pieces, continued Plato, and restore to us the robe of Socrates?—Denis Diderot, Les Bijous indiscrets

At the beginning of *Modern Times*, Denis Diderot satirizes the new empirical sciences in a ribald allegorical tale about an inquisitive Sultan Mangogul whose dreams and hundred diverse forms of experiment seemed only to deconstruct the foundations of deductive, rationalist philosophy: on the basis of empirical science, no new eternal synthesis was possible to replace systematic philosophy, only tentative, provisional constructions requiring constant further testing and securing in the physical properties of nature. The constant further testing is allegorized as a continuation of the Thousand and One Nights, Scheherazade's multiple substitutions and diversions that keep her tale and life viable and responsive to the changeable world. The structure of perception is voyeuristic, panoptic, third-person listening, caught in the paradox; as James Creech puts it, "No conclusion is possible then until the whole is metaphorically repossessed. But all metaphor for the whole is undermined by the synecdochal (metonymic) concatenation of the private parts that propel the sultan's quest" (cited in Pucci 161). It is an obsessive quest of desire, which Diderot literalizes through a tale of a magic ring that allows the sultan to stage and hear the desires of his harem women, ambiguously playing upon whether his presence otherwise would or would not be any more distorting than this magical instrument of inquiry: sexual desire and *libido sciendi* (the desire to know), as Suzanne Pucci puts it (157), are allegorizations of one another. The sultan (the Subject, the Knower, the Wielder of the Instruments of Power and Surveillance, the Self) in these tales (both Diderot's and the Thousand and One Nights), Pucci points out, is "a perceptual subject [who] is reacted upon by the properties of the physical world and in conjunction with his own physiological processes" (his dreams) (159); he is, in relation to his experiments, a third party (Scheherezade's tales are told to her sister Dinarzade while the sultan Shahriyar listens) who explores worlds, unknowable directly, through sounding and projecting instruments:

> To the aged philosophers described as garbed in the tattered pieces of Socrates' sacred mantle Mangogul's dream juxtaposes an allegorical figure, an unintimidating infant who nevertheless as he approaches the temple of philosophy grows to giant proportions, becoming the colossus of "Experiment/Experience." "In the progress of his subsequent growth, he appeared to me in a hundred different forms; I saw him direct a long telescope toward the sky, estimate with the aid of a pendulum the fall of bodies, ascertain by a tube filled with mercury the weight of air; and with a prism in his hand, decompose light." (Diderot, quoted in Pucci 158.)

If there is a parallel between the eighteenth-century sensibilities—a feeling of transition from stable knowledge that is no longer viable as a worldly guide into an insecure world knowable only through multiple probes and perspectives—and those of the twentieth century, it does not help to collapse the differences, to succumb to the mechanical Orientalist industry of Edward Saidian imitator-manques of imposing Us-Them, Self-Other, omnipotent-subaltern essentialisms. As Pucci nicely asks (albeit then herself succumbing partly to the masculine-feminine, voyeur-puppet industry):

> From whence comes the necessity at the present moment of rele-gating the varied cultures of the East to the non-specific, mono-lithic term of exteriority, of an "outside" ("exo[tic]")? At the time of a newly emerging economic, political and even cultural context, in which the exigencies of global interdependence appear to be, at the least, challenging Western hegemony, what critical value obtains in analyzing, perhaps even in fetishising the discourse of the exotic?
>
> The eighteenth century fascination with foreign lands and in particular with the Orient remains closely tied to the discrete entities that constitute a perspective still formally and textually separable into self and other, as yet unblurred by the notion of an otherness within, characteristic of the Romantic period. In effect, "exoticism" is defined (*Larousse Encyclopedique*) with respect to nineteenth century interest in the new world of America in contra-distinction to modes of the exotic linked to the Orient and to the rare object of the collector. (145, 146–47)

The late twentieth century is different from the eighteenth century, the Romantic period, and the nineteenth century, in part, through the actual cultural interreferences and pluralized perspectives that are no longer one-sided fantasies or projections but internal realities on increasingly large demographic scales, with effects that play themselves out not only in refined cosmopolitanisms of liberal desire, but also in devastating conflicts generated by political reorganizations, disruption through de-velopment schemes and wars, and economic competition.

One way to probe these changes of the contemporary world is to use autobiographical and life history frames to examine the ways the social processes of identity, moral understanding, and scientific world view are being reproduced and transformed. Autobiographical frames themselves are not given genres: if we wish to use them to extend social theory, to understand the changes of the contemporary world (rather than re-affirming the pieties of the past), we need to be attentive to the variant, culturally diverse formats they may inhabit.

I have raised many more questions than I can answer, from what is an autobiography to what do autobiographies signify? As an anthropologist, I have been trying to ask beyond-the-text questions: How do real selves in the world assemble themselves, and can autobiographies help analogize or investigate this? How do genres of self-portraiture change under different social conditions? Is it true that autobiography is a relatively new form? What does that mean? How different is Augustine's *Confessions* from Jain monkly ones (Fischer, *Mirroring and Construction*) or from those of the hunter-gatherer Okiek people of west-central Kenya (Kratz)? And what are we doing when repeatedly, again and again, over and over, we analyze only the first? How do social enterprises, such as science, refract themselves through the lives of their practitioners, and can individual-focused accounts provide larger than individual-limited knowledge? Beyond the text, beyond the single self, beyond the ego.

I have been making a plea for the cross-cultural, the comparative, the critique of the categories we use, and for cross-disciplinary conversation on uses of life histories to rebuild social theory, to rebuild the technological polity, to rebuild theories of psychology, and to refashion the world we live in. That seems to me to be a not unambitious project for the study of autobiography to undertake.

References

Abu-Lughod, Lila. *Veiled Sentiments: Honor and Poetry in a Bedouin Society.* Berkeley: U of California P, 1986.

Ajami, Fuad. *The Vanished Imam: Musa al-Sadr and the Shi'a of Lebanon.* Ithaca: Cornell UP, 1986.

Arlen, Michael. *Passage to Ararat.* New York: Farrar, 1975.

Bialik, Chaim Nachman. "Revealment and Concealment in Language." *Modern Hebrew Literature.* Ed. Robert Alter. W. Orange, NJ: Behrman, 1975.

Cliff, Michelle. *No Telephone to Heaven.* New York: Dutton, 1987.

Cooke, Miriam. *War's Other Voices: Women Writers on the Lebanese Civil War.* New York: Cambridge UP, 1987.

Dearborn, Mary. *Pocahontas's Daughters: Gender and Ethnicity in American Culture.* New York: Oxford UP, 1986.

Delgado, Abelardo. "Stupid America." *Chicano Poetry.* Ed. Juan Bruce-Nova. Austin: U of Texas P, 1982.

Fischer, Irene K. "Geodesy? What's That? My Personal Involvement in the Age-Old Quest for the Size and Shape of the Earth, with a Running Commentary on Life in a Government Research Office." Unpublished ms., n.d. Schlesinger Library, Radcliffe, Cambridge, Mass.; Institute of Physics Library, New York.

Fischer, Michael. "Ethnicity and the Postmodern Arts of Memory." *Writing Culture: The Poetics and Politics of Ethnography.* Ed. J. Clifford and G. Marcus. Berkeley: U of California P, 1986.

——. "Imam Khomeini: Four Levels of Understanding." *Voices of Resurgent Islam.* Ed. J. Esposito. New York: Oxford UP, 1983.

——. "Mirroring and the Construction of Indian Bourgeois Selves: (Auto)biographical Explorations among Modern Jains." Unpublished ms., 1990.

——. "Portrait of a Mullah: The Autobiography and Bildüngsroman of Aqa Najafi-Quchani." *Persica* 10 (1982): 223–57.

——. "Torn Religions from Gandhi to Rajneesh: (Auto)biographical Call and Response in the Postmodern Age." Unpublished ms., n.d.

Fischer, M.M.J., and Mehdi Abedi. *Debating Muslims: Cultural Dialogues in Postmodernity and Tradition.* Madison: U of Wisconsin P, 1990.

Fischer, M.M.J., and George Marcus. *Anthropology as Cultural Critique: An Experimental Moment in the Human Sciences.* Chicago: U of Chicago P, 1986.

Friedman, Alan J., and Carol C. Donley. *Einstein: Man and Myth.* New York: Cambridge UP, 1985.

Golden, Marita. *Migrations of the Heart.* New York: Doubleday, 1983.

Green, Arthur. *Tormented Master: A Life of Rabbi Nahman of Bratislav.* Tuscaloosa: U of Alabama P, 1979.

Guha, Ramachandra. *The Unquiet Woods: Ecological Change and Peasant Resistance in the Himalayas.* Delhi: Oxford UP, 1989.

Guha, Ranajit, and Gayatri Chakravorty Spivak, eds. *Selected Subaltern Studies.* Delhi: Oxford UP, 1988.

Haraway, Donna. *Primate Visions: Gender, Race, and Nature in the World of Modern Science.* New York: Routledge, 1989.

Kakar, Sudhir. *The Inner World: A Psychoanalytic Study of Childhood and Society in India.* 2d ed. New Delhi: Oxford UP, 1981.

Keller, Evelyn Fox. *Reflections on Gender and Science.* New Haven: Yale UP, 1985.

Kingston, Maxine Hong. *The Woman Warrior: Memoirs of a Girlhood among Ghosts.* New York: Knopf, 1981.

Kratz, Corinne A. "Amusement and Absolution: Transforming Narratives During Confession of Social Debts." Unpublished ms., 1990.

Lakatos, Imre. *Philosophical Papers: Mathematics, Science, and Epistemology.* Cambridge: Cambridge UP, 1980.

Latour, Bruno, and Steven Woolgar. *Laboratory Life: The Social Construction of Scientific Facts.* London: Sage, 1979.

Lears, T. J. Jackson. *No Place of Grace: Antimodernism and the Transformation of American Culture 1880–1920.* New York: Pantheon, 1981.

Levi-Montalcini, Rita. *In Praise of Imperfection: My Life and Work.* New York: Basic, 1988.

Luria, S. E. *A Slot Machine, A Broken Test Tube—An Autobiography.* New York: Harper, 1984.

Martin, Emily. *The Woman in the Body: A Cultural Analysis of Reproduction.* Boston: Beacon, 1987.

Massignon, Louis. *The Passion of al-Hallaj.* Trans. Herbert Mason. Princeton: Princeton UP, 1975.

Morse, Philip. *In at the Beginnings: A Physicist's Life.* Cambridge: MIT, 1977.

Mottahedeh, Roy. *The Mantle of the Prophet.* New York: Random, 1985.

Mukerjee, Chandra. *A Fragile Power, Scientists and the State.* Princeton: Princeton UP, 1990.

Nandy, Ashis. "Science as a Reason of State." In Nandy.

——, ed. *Science, Hegemony, and Violence.* New Delhi: Oxford UP, 1988.

Obeysekere, Gananath. "Buddhism, Depression, and the Work of Culture." *Culture and Depression.* Ed. Arthur Kleinman and Byron Good. Berkeley: U of California P, 1985.

——. *Medusa's Hair: An Essay on Personal Symbols and Religious Experience.* Chicago: U of Chicago P, 1981.

Ostrikker, Alicia. *Stealing the Language: The Emergence of Women's Poetry in America.* Boston: Beacon, 1986.

Popper, Karl. *Unended Quest: An Intellectual Autobiography.* London: Open Court, 1985.

Pucci, Suzanne Rodin. "The Discrete Charm of the Exotic: Fictions of the Harem in Eighteenth-Century France." *Exoticism in the Enlightenment.* Ed. G. S. Rousseau and Roy Porter. Manchester: Manchester UP, 1990.

Pynchon, Thomas. *Gravity's Rainbow.* New York: Viking, 1973.

Roland, Alan. *In Search of Self in India and Japan: Toward a Cross-Cultural Psychology.* Princeton: Princeton UP, 1988.

Rushdie, Salman. *Satanic Verses.* London: Viking, 1988.

Said, Edward. *After the Last Sky.* New York: Pantheon, 1986.

Scholem, Gershom. *Shabbatai Sevi.* Trans. Zvi Werblovski. Princeton: Princeton UP, 1956.

Shah, Navalbhai. *Santabalji: Satupani Sagdandi* (Santabalji: perapetetic path to saintliness). Ahmedabad: Gujurat, 1975.

Taheri, Amir. *The Spirit of Allah: Khomeini and the Islamic Revolution.* Bethesda, Md.: Adler, 1986.

Traweek, Sharon. *Beamtimes and Lifetimes.* Cambridge: Harvard UP, 1988.

Visvanathan, Shiv. "Atomic Physics: The Career of an Imagination." In Nandy.

——. "On the Annals of the Laboratory State." In Nandy.

——. *Organizing for Science: the Making of an Industrial Research Laboratory.* New Delhi: Oxford UP, 1985.

Wiener, Norbert. *I Am a Mathematician: The Later Life of a Prodigy.* New York: Doubleday, 1956.

Yukawa, Hideki. *Tabibto* (The traveller). Trans. L. Brown and Y. Yashida. Singapore: World Scientific, 1982.

Postmodernism and the Autobiographical Subject:

Reconstructing the "Other"

BETTY BERGLAND

■

etween 1945 and 1980 more than five thousand autobiographies were published in the United States. Autobiographies and autobiographical studies focused on ethnic groups and women have especially proliferated in the last two decades in the wake of feminist scholarship and the burgeoning field of ethnic studies. Thus, despite pronouncements about the end of autobiography and postmodern challenges to traditional notions of the self, autobiographical narratives proliferate and scholarly studies on them abound.[1] Tensions between the postmodern theorists, on the one hand, and the emerging narratives of marginalized groups, on the other, however, surface in readings of ethnic autobiography. Institutionalized efforts to incorporate literatures of the cultural other, and efforts to expand the canon, have meant that autobiographies of women and ethnics receive particular attention in the academy, as scholars become more receptive to cultural diversity and complexity. In this spirit, ethnic autobiographies often serve representative functions, evoking so-called minority literatures, cultures, and subjectivities. Maxine Hong Kingston's *Woman Warrior,* for example, may be seen to represent a Chinese-American voice, whereas Richard Rodriquez's *Hunger of Memory* may signify a Chicano voice. Because of such representative status, the burden of these texts becomes enormous, and how we read these texts raises profound questions; therefore it becomes imperative to develop a theory of autobiography that acknowledges the importance of marginalized voices, but avoids essentializing individuals and groups; that takes into account complex relationships between cultures and discourses that produce the speaking subject, but avoids viewing language as a transparent representation of the imagined real. Given the complexities of our postmodern world, the multiplicity of struggles, and the growing economic and social disparities revolving around differences based on race, class, gender, and ethnicity, and granting the assertion that autobiography presents readers with an image of the human, how we read and comprehend cultural difference raises critical questions with significant consequences. If understanding diverse cultures and multiply positioned persons remains an ultimate goal of cultural knowledge, helping us to live together cooperatively and harmoniously, then we must radically rethink how we read, understand, and teach autobiography, especially ethnic autobiography.

Autobiography, Postmodernism, and the Cultural Other

I begin with three propositions critical to autobiography, which situate this essay in three discourses—postmodernism, feminism, and ethnic studies. First, autobiography serves important ideological functions in the culture. Addressing a central issue in postmodern debates, Paul Smith, in his recent book *Discerning the Subject,* argues that autobiography "cannot be underestimated as a privileged form of ideological text wherein the demand that we should consist as coherent and recognizable 'subjects' in relation to a particular knowledge appears to be rationalized." Further, he asserts that the form has acquired generic power "to construct and legitimate a 'subject' which will guarantee juridical social relations" (105–6). The proliferation of life stories and the scholarly attention given to autobiography appear to corroborate these assertions. Since the autobiographical narrative makes its presentation of the human seem natural, autobiography remains a literary category, or popular form, and a genre possessing ideological power—in short, it serves a political function. In a culture that values individualism and empirical knowledge, the speaking "I" tends to validate prevailing knowledge, and so the form is privileged. Because of this function, scholars of autobiography can learn from postmodern theories that examine ideologies embedded in discourse. In addition, drawing on structuralist and poststructuralist thinking, Smith affirms that language cannot transparently *reveal* an essential and unified historical subject; rather, the speaking subject, historically situated and positioned in multiple and contradictory discourses, places the "I" in the world in positions conceptually possible in language.

The nature of the speaking subject, then, remains a critical arena for autobiographical and feminist discussions, which leads to the second proposition: the autobiographical self must be understood as socially and historically constructed and multiply positioned in complex worlds and discourses. Sidonie Smith, in *A Poetics of Woman's Autobiography*, writes that the autobiographical form is "androcentric and has reproduced the patrolineage for the last 500 years" (26); further, she argues, "autobiography has assumed a central position in the personal and literary life of the West precisely because it serves as one of those generic contracts that reproduces the patrilineage and its ideologies of gender" (44). If Smith is correct (and I believe she is) that the form is androcentric—and elevates the Renaissance male human being—the question becomes, how does the not-male human being, perceived in the culture as the Other, represent the self? By cultural Other, we generally consider those persons negatively constructed in the dominant symbolic order: not-male, not-white, not-American, etc. Sidonie Smith argues that until the twentieth century women could only represent themselves in scripts male discourse had constructed for them—as nun, witch, wife, or queen. Alternatives to these scripts remained linguistically and culturally unimaginable; thus, when cultural others would represent themselves in print, they were forced to use the prevailing symbolic order or remain silent.

Henry Louis Gates, Jr., described this dilemma for the not-white in African-American writing. He claimed writers used a "double voiced" discourse, "making the (white) written text 'speak' with a (black) voice."[2] The *not-white,* writer thus, faced an analogous problem of writing the self into being through the language of the oppressor as the *not-male,* writer and the analogy informs us about women's predicament historically in writing autobiography. The metaphor clearly problematizes the speech of the cultural Other, raising the central question of how we understand the speaking subject positioned outside the dominant symbolic order. The metaphor of a "double-voiced discourse" distinguishes between white speech and black voice—and by analogy, we could argue, male speech and female voice. Nevertheless, risks seem present here for the metaphor tends to essentialize the categories of *voice* and *experience* by *naturalizing* a black voice, a female voice, or a black experience, a female experience, and by ignoring the complex forces that produce voices and experiences. Do not the language communities we occupy shape perception of experiences? And why should we emphasize dualities? Does not the cultural Other reside in multiple linguistic—or discursive communities—not unlike Mikhail Bakhtin's illiterate peasants in *The Dialogic Imagination* who discovered that they lived in several languages: the religious community of prayer; the folk community of song; the official state language of petitions; the language of daily life— and that these language systems, indissoluably linked to different ideological approaches to the world, contradicted each other (295–96). As scholars focused on autobiography we need to acknowledge the (white) androcentric scripts dominating Western culture and establishing the realms of the possible. Nevertheless, how we speak about contradictions emerging from the speech of the cultural Other remains critical.

These observations lead me to the third and last proposition about autobiography, focusing attention on ethnic studies: we need to explore alternative strategies for reading and understanding autobiographies, and ethnic autobiography offers a rich site for this exploration. Michael M. J. Fischer argues in his essay "Ethnicity and the Post-Modern Arts of Memory," that "ethnic autobiography and autobiographical fiction can perhaps serve as a key form for exploration of pluralist, late industrialist, late twentieth century society." He offers three reasons for this: first, ethnicity is constantly reconstructed with each generation—in other words it is not static; second, there are no role models for hyphenated Americans, the Chinese-American, the Mexican-American, etc; and third, ethnic autobiographies are forced to find a voice or style that incorporates the several components of identity. Fischer insists, therefore, we must develop a concept of the self that is pluralist, multidimensional, multifaceted—and one which might be a "crucible for a wider social ethos of pluralism."[3] Fischer's strategy for exploring ethnic autobiographies includes noncognitive mappings of consciousness present in the autobiographical narrative, such as psychoanalysis, dreamwork, metaphor, and transference. While these noncognitive tracings represent *linguistic* markings and are thus linked to prevailing discursive practices embedded with ideologies, the value of using noncognitive strategies suggests a way of examining the cultural Other in autobiographical writings and avoids the risks of the double-voiced discourse. I argue in this essay that the chronotype—literally time/space—provides a meaningful noncognitive *and* nonlinguistic strategy for examining the subject of autobiography, a concept that serves as a framework for Bakhtin's discussion of Western literature in *The Dialogic Imagination.* I intend to illustrate its value in this essay; however, first, I return to a summary of the issues these propositions raise about autobiography.

These three propositions all share assumptions about the importance of autobiography in the culture, suggesting that the kind of subject represented in autobiography serves a cultural purpose, and they all presuppose a relationship between the speaking subject and the uttered discourse. Nevertheless, tensions emerge at the intersection of these propositions, raising at least three critical issues that resonate with larger cultural debates. The first issue revolves around the uses and purposes of autobiography. Does the form function only to guarantee juridical social relations, as Paul Smith argues, or can the form also serve to challenge dominant ideologies and prevailing social relations? The second issue focuses on the meaning of the speaking subject in autobiography: in short, do we read at the center of the autobiography a self, an essential individual, imagined to be coherent and unified, the originator of her own meaning, or do we read a postmodern subject—a dynamic subject that changes over time, is situated historically in the world and positioned in multiple discourses? Intimately connected to these issues is the third: how we theorize the relationship between the subject and the language the writer uses to represent the "I" of the speaking subject. Do we assume a transparent language implying that a speaking subject automatically conveys in language an intended meaning that is immediately apprehended, or do we understand that the discursive practices in which the speaking subject is situated and positioned shape possible utterances, which remain fragmented and partial, inadequate to represent the "I" who speaks? The implications here are profound because how we answer affects how we understand and read those marginalized in the culture.

I argue that in the pluralistic American society we must challenge the notion of the humanist and essentialist self at the center of the autobiography and recognize the multiply situated subject in autobiography, socially and historically shaped. In such a context ethnic autobiographies provide a meaningful site for exploring multiple subjectivities with implications for the larger culture, as Fischer argues. However, I propose a more critical reading of ethnic autobiography than Fischer's strategies, which rely on linguistic markers; since ideologies are also embedded in metaphors and dreamwork, ethnics may also articulate prevailing ideologies in these terms.[4] Thus I suggest we need to question any easy relationship between discourse and the speaking subject, particularly the assumption that *experience* produces a *voice*—that, for example, *being woman* means speaking in *a woman's voice*. The metaphor of the double-voiced discourse, implying a language and experience of the oppressor and the oppressed, risks naturalizing these categories. The metaphor problematizes neither language nor experience and denies their links and ambiguities, masking the postmodern claim that discourses shape the very way in which we experience the world. Roland Barthes's assertion that the subject can be defined as "an effect of language" suggests the complex relationship between the subject and language. If we acknowledge that human beings are positioned in multiple and contradictory discourses, then the effect of that multiplicity shapes the subject. Barthes also argues that "all those outside power are obliged to steal language"—as the poor have had to steal bread.[5] The metaphor invites us to ask how persons write their subjectivities in stolen language and at what point, if at all, does the stolen language speak differently for the one who must steal it? In other words, Fischer's call for a more invisible way of examining the subject of autobiography becomes particularly valuable for examining the subjectivities of those constructed as the Other in the culture. Using noncognitive approaches to read autobiography, specifically a chronotopic analysis, we can visualize the consequences of discursive practices on the speaking subjects and explore the implications of these effects both individually and culturally. The chronotypic analysis permits us to examine the subjectivities in autobiographies—both those elevated in the culture to guarantee certain juridical social relations and those that may provide resistant subject positions—and to unmask cultural ideologies embedded there.[6] With such a reading, I suggest that autobiographies might also provide a site for challenging prevailing social relations.

In *The Dialogic Imagination* M. M. Bakhtin argues that our image of what is human is always concrete—temporally and spatially positioned in the universe. Bakhtin's term for this time-space dimension, chronotope, borrowed from mathematics, expresses "the inseparability of space and time." Bakhtin argues that our image of the human being is "intrinsically chronotopic." In the literary context, he claims, the "chronotope makes narrative events concrete, makes them take on flesh, causes blood to flow in their veins. . . ." Further, the abstract elements in fiction and "the philosophical and social generalizations, ideas, analyses of cause and effect gravitate toward the chronotope and through it take on flesh and blood, permitting the imaging power of art to do its work. Such is the representational significance of the chronotope" (250). He also argues that this category functions to situate historical figures in time and space to make that place in the world seem natural. Certainly one could argue from Bakhtin's observations that it is through the flesh and blood power of the chronotope that ideology operates, making a certain social order seem natural because it is seen to reside in the flesh and blood. We might argue that this is the hidden effect of language.

The work of the linguist Emile Benveniste also supports a chronotopic analysis of autobiography. In *Problems in General Linguistics* Benveniste argued that within any system of signification personal pronouns are never missing, yet unlike other designators "they do not refer to a concept or to an individual"; the personal pronouns belong to a class of words that "escape the status of all other signs of language"—they remain indeterminate until an individual uses the word "I," addressing, and distinguishing itself from, a "you." The reality to which the "I" then refers is to the reality of discourse: "it is in the instance of discourse in which I designates the speaker that the speaker proclaims himself [sic] as the 'subject.'" Benveniste writes that when language is so organized "it permits each speaker to *appropriate to himself* [sic] the entire language by designating *I*" (226). The other class of pronouns that share the same in-determinate status as personal pronouns (I/you) are those words that "organize the spatial and temporal relationships around the 'subject' . . . 'this,' 'here,' 'now'" (226). These time and space indicators are always determined by the "I" that is proclaimed in discourses. Thus the "I" who speaks in discourse determines the spatial and temporal "here" and "now," "there" and "then." These linked pairs of linguistic indeterminacy are precisely the terms of autobiographical chronotopes: I/you; here/ there; now/then. As the autobiographical subject speaks, the "I" con-structs a here and now and thus defines the time-space of utterance, of being, also defining imaginatively the "you" (the reader). The there and then posit the opposite of the here and now, and thus we find through the chronotopic analysis of the autobiography the critical indeterminacy of language within culture. But it is precisely in these paired terms we also encounter the discursive power of language to shape the imaginative universe of what is human. They define the here and now of the speaker and provide the time-space through which we imagine the speaker, an image of the human. Autobiography is intimately linked to chronotopes. Because autobiography possesses power to shape an image of the hu-man, as the reader imagines the speaker in the here and now of the speaking "I," the chronotopic placement provides a powerful means of situating the speaker in the universe, because the chronotopic image is an effect of language, but generally invisible.

A chronotopic analysis becomes especially valuable for reading the autobiographies of the marginalized Other because in such an analysis the reader can see the effect of language. In other words, we can imag-ine where discourse positions the subject in the universe. If we accept Barthes's assertion, that "the subject is an effect of language," focusing on the chronotope permits us to examine concretely that effect. Implicit in that examination would be such questions as, what ideological forces led the subject to these chronotopes? What kinds of identities and social relations are possible within those chronotopes and what are not pos-sible? What cultural meanings do we associate with those times and spaces? What ideological significance can be attached to the historical subject's chronotopic positioning? A chronotopic analysis of three autobiographies serves to illustrate the possibilities in the approach.

Chronotopic Analysis of Three Ethnic Women's Autobiographies

Three Russian-Jewish immigrant women who came to North America at the turn of the century—Mary Antin, Anzia Yezierska, and Emma Goldman—situate themselves chronotopically in their autobiographies very differently. Their historical lives, however, invite comparisons. Born in late nineteenth-century Eastern Europe into Jewish families affected by official anti-Semitic policies, they all immigrated to the United States between 1885 and 1895 (part of the mass immigration during this period) and settled in immigrant communities of Boston, New York City, and Rochester, New York. Acquiring fluency in English, they all developed active public lives as writers and speakers; they all married and, with the exception of Goldman, bore and raised children. All remained in the United States, with the exception of Goldman (involuntarily deported), and all lived relatively long lives. They all addressed, directly and indirectly, attitudes toward America and their positions as women; all spoke ambiguously about family and ethnic identity, sometimes associated nationally (with Russia or Poland), sometimes religiously (with Judaism); all confronted Americanizing social institutions with their undercurrent of xenophobia and latent anti-Semitism; and all were affected by poverty and by political, economic, and social struggles. The chronotopic positioning in their autobiographies, however, remains vastly different for each immigrant woman: America-identified autobiographical Antin is situated primarily in the American school as an adolescent; dislocated autobiographical Yezierska, seeking an American home that she never finds, boards a train at the beginning and end of the autobiography, signifying that absence; and autobiographical Goldman, occupying multiple times and spaces generally forbidden to women, to mainstream Americans, and middle-class readers, challenges the naturalized images associated with prevailing views of Americans, women, and human beings. (In discussing these autobiographies, to avoid implications that we know a coherent self contained in pronoun references, I will distinguish (minimally) between the historical subject, referring to the biological life; the autobiographical narrator, the "I" who writes the narrative; and the autobiographical subject the speaking "I" in the narrative).[6]

Mary Antin's autobiography, *The Promised Land,* was published in

with America centers in the schoolroom, that site also signifies Americanization discourses. *Americanization,* understood generally as a process of assimilation to Anglo-Saxon culture, is attached historically to a specific movement at the turn of the century when mass immigration of thousands of non-Anglo, non-Protestant, non-English-speaking populations alarmed American gatekeepers sufficiently so that many feared civilization and the supposed natural order of things were threatened. While xenophobes sought immigration restriction, more reform-minded agents sought to halt the collapse of the moral order through education: the English language, Anglo-Saxon culture, Protestant virtues, and middle-class cultural values could redeem civilization and humanity, reformers thought. American schools played a key role in this transformation of the alien into the American, and language, namely linguistic competence, often served as the critical sign of patriotism, morality—and humanity.

Autobiographical Antin narrates the initiation into the discourses of the school, and especially of the teacher. George Washington served as a primary signifier of the Americanization discourse for autobiographical Antin: because he was a "king in greatness" and he and Antin were "fellow citizens," autobiographical Antin felt "nobly related." The autobiographical Antin occupies the space of the schoolroom for much of the remainder of the autobiography, along with spaces related to the school by virtue of the knowledges they represent—namely, the Boston Public Library; the private library of Dr. Hale, the "grand old man of Boston"; and, by extension, the Hale House Settlement, where Antin is introduced to the Natural History Club and nature.

Like the school, both in the knowledge it contains and in the architectural order it signifies, the Boston Public Library represents ideologies of Americanization and Western rationality. Although the Boston Public Library became known as the "People's Palace" after Oliver Wendell Holmes's dedicatory poem, the library's beaux arts architecture, associated with the classical ideals of ancient Greece and Rome, and its lavish construction (which made Holmes's label partially ironic) signify a democratic—that is, the people's—topos. But that label is ironic for the library also signifies an elite culture. The kind of knowledge elevated in the library becomes clear when the autobiographical Antin visits her sister Frieda and reads in Frieda's tenement kitchen not what might be called the people's stories (not Russian, Yiddish, Hebrew, or even American literature) but what the authorities at the school and library said should be read and valued: the classics, specifically, Cicero, Ovid, and

Virgil. (The sisters especially liked to read the *Aeneid.*) The elite nature of this knowledge is reinforced when juxtaposed with Dr. Hale's library on Highland Street. Going to Hale's library before school and the Boston Public Library after school, autobiographical Antin was able to endure the slum: "Who would feel cramped in a tenement with such royal privileges as these," she proclaimed. "One could be happy a year on Dover Street [the slum] after spending a half hour on Highland Street [location of Hale's upper-class home]" (345–46). The contradictions residing in this topos signifying American cultural assimilation become explicit when we consider that these spaces—the school and library— offer no meaningful residence in any sense; the knowledges they represent denied Antin, as woman, the franchise (legitimacy) as she wrote; and the economic insecurity of Dover Street, contrasted with Highland Street, contradict the alleged American Promises the autobiographical subject affirms.

In the final chronotope of the autobiography, the reader finds the Antin autobiographical subject in front of the Boston Public Library, an adolescent who has just returned from a Natural History Club outing to the sea, having been left on the steps of the library. Autobiographical Antin holds a specimen jar from her nature collection and reflects on being the "youngest of America's children." The final topos of the auto- biography aligns the Antin subject with two dominant epistomologies of Western culture—elite cultural knowledge housed in the Boston Public Library, before which she stands, and scientific rationalism, which col- lects, labels, and controls nature, signified by the day's catch in the specimen jar. The school and library, the primary chronotopes of the autobiography, and the sites of her narrative rebirth, merge in this final image. And by aligning the speaking subject with these knowledges, the narrator would secure the autobiographical Antin as an American. However, the reader cannot imagine her beyond the steps of the Boston Library. Although the historical Antin was "nearly 30" when the auto- biography was written (and she had studied at Barnard, married, borne a child, and moved to New York), the life of the autobiographical subject ends with the adolescent on the steps of the Boston Public Library. The Antin subject the reader meets in this autobiography is an adolescent who reached neither adulthood nor maturity; she is neither a sexual nor social being. The Antin subject is rooted in no specific place or commu- nity. Female sexuality (along with marriage and parenthood) dissolve in the final chronotope, along with ethnicity. The assertion of American- ness erases both gendered and ethnic difference as well as embodiment.

Consequently, the meaning of rebirth as an American remains an abstract utterance, contradictory and without real meaning. We might argue that this explains why the work is frequently cited as a "classic immigrant autobiography."[7] In 1918, a few years after the publication of *The Promised Land*, the historical Antin suffered from what was diagnosed as neuresthenia, from which she never really recovered. Surely the psychic struggle of the historical Antin is not unrelated to the enormous contradictions between the idealized American represented by the autobiographical subject, for whom adulthood, sexuality, and difference remained unimagined and unimaginable, and the actual conditions of the historical Antin—woman, wife (separated), mother, Russian-Jewish immigrant, author. For historical Antin, dominant cultural discourses provided no language for these positions, rendering them unimaginable; consequently, narrator Antin lacked a language for articulating the contradictory positions of the historical Antin. To suggest that the America-identified autobiographical Antin represents the so-called real Mary Antin denies the historical Antin the contradictions and complexities of that life, while it renders the notion of classic immigrant autobiography abstract and provides the reader no glimpse of what it means to be an adult American, female and ethnic.

Anzia Yezierska also immigrated with her family in the early 1890s as a preadolescent, but she published her autobiography, *Red Ribbon on a White Horse*, in 1950, nearly a half-century after Mary Antin's publication. The book was initially applauded by critics, but Louise Levitas Henriksen, Yezierska's daughter, asserts it "died almost immediately" (273). A critique of American culture embedded in the narrative may explain its sudden death in the wake of McCarthyism of the early 1950s; however, today, in the context of ethnic studies and feminist scholarship, publishers have reprinted and anthologized her autobiography and her fiction, and several biographies of her have appeared. As feminists rediscover writings of foremothers and ethnic studies scholars recover immigrant writers, Yezierska's works have been interpreted generally in the context of either literary studies or social history, "as an interpreter of the Jewish immigrant experience" (Kessler-Harris v). Within these traditional frameworks, scholars often assemble fragments from fiction, the autobiography, or historical records in order to grasp a presumed essential Yezierska. The search invariably disappoints. In *American Literature*, Eric Sundquist claims that *Red Ribbon* "portrayed less *the true Yezierska* than an author still sometimes acting the part of the 'sweatshop Cinderella'" (121; emphasis mine). The expectation that the reader might

find a true Yezierska, and the subsequent disappointment of not finding
it, means the Yezierska herself is critiqued not only for avoiding truth
but also for hiding behind a mask. Mary Dearborn argues in "Anzia
Yezierska and the Making of an Ethnic American Self" that though the
writer "was in fact 'made' by others, by the nascent public relations
industry, it is important to keep in mind her conscious participation in
the process" (117). Dearborn's concept of self-invention implies that although Yezierska had help, she originated her own meaning; further, the
association of this self with public relations implies a deception that
hides the alleged true self. Thus pursuit of an essential, or true, Yezierska, like pursuit of a real Mary Antin, fails because language cannot
represent the totality of the being. However, the expectation of finding a
coherent self not only masks the discursive practices and cultural ideologies shaping the possible and the desirable, but also devalues the
historical subject for failure to represent an unrepresentable totality, or
for failure to represent that impossibility truthfully. If readers abandon
notions of an essential Yezierska, it is possible to explore cultural tensions and meanings surrounding gender and ethnicity in American discourses; unlike Antin, the autobiographical Yezierska occupies American spaces as an adult.

In *Red Ribbon on a White Horse,* the Yezierska narrator, like narrator
Antin, addresses the difficulty of being foreign-born in America and the
struggle to become a person. Also like Antin, the Yezierska narrator
erases gendered positions in the autobiography—as a wife, mother, and
teacher in female-dominated fields such as domestic science—although
these were positions the historical Yezierska occupied. However, unlike
Antin, autobiographical Yezierska reaches adulthood and occupies that
temporality through most of the autobiography. Further, while narrator
Antin moves chronologically and spatially from the Old to the New
World, narrator Yezierska juxtaposes the Old and the New so that the
autobiographical subject occupies both simultaneously. The New World
basically provides the topos for the autobiography; however, the Lower
East Side of New York City (geographically in the New), signifies the
Old generally through imaginary figures whose voices intrude in the
New World (American) spaces.

The autobiography's three divisions signify three ideological spaces
where autobiographical Yezierska sought residence, or a metaphoric
home, away from the Lower East Side and its evocations of the Old
World: Hollywood, signifying material well being, but also the decadence of the consumer culture; the uptown literary world of New York

City, signifying artistic achievement, but also a cultural elitism; and, in the third section, the Writer's Hall of the Federal Writer's Project (momentarily a utopia) and a rural New England community, signifying a national past, but also a provincial and xenophobic historical memory. In the midst of the American spaces memory of another world surfaces as the narrator inserts the voice of imaginary characters signifying the discourse of the father, Jewish ethnicity, and a spiritual world. This oppositional voice of the father is embodied in several Jewish men (imaginary, the biographers tell us): Boroch Mayer, whose fan letter requesting a ship ticket to die in Poland impels her to leave Hollywood; Zalmon Shlomoh, the hunchbacked fish peddler who draws her to Hester Street and bequeaths to her his lodge money; and Jeremiah Kintzler, the Spinoza scholar in the Federal Writer's Project who spoke of utopian longings.

Collectively, these ideological spaces signify tensions between American and ethnic discourses, primarily in the 1920ss and 1930s. By juxtaposing two temporal arenas—the historical present and the memory of a past, Old World, ethnic culture—autobiographical Yezierska dramatizes the struggle to find a meaningful space to reside in the universe. Initially, autobiographical Yezierska is drawn to the American spaces—Hollywood, uptown literary world, rural New England—to escape the poverty and struggle of the Lower East Side; she eventually rejects and is rejected in each space. On the other hand, autobiographical Yezierska does not simply embrace an ethnic past that offers her no strategies for living in the present world: recalling her dead father's spiritual life at the end of the autobiography, the narrator writes, "he ignored the world I had to live in and compromise with. Centuries yawned between us" (218). No place provided sanctuary. Consequently, in the beginning and end of the narrative, autobiographical Yezierska occupies a train, signifying her inability to find a place in the universe: in the first chapter she has boarded a train for Hollywood; in the last, she sits aboard a train, leaving New England for unknown destinations.

Autobiographical Yezierska first appears in part one looking out of a Lower East Side basement tenement and cooking "stale tea leaves" when she receives news that Goldwyn has offered $10,000 to develop a film script for her award-winning collection of short stories, *Hungry Hearts*. Within pages the autobiographical Yezierska emerges from a train in Hollywood and is driven by a limousine to the Miramar Hotel, where her room contains "criminal luxury," including extra towels, two faucets, and canary toilet paper. The opulence attracts and repulses: "I had earned all this . . . proof that I was really a writer" (42). Later, as a dinner guest at Rupert Hughes's home, the narrator reflects: "Where have I seen this visionary space before . . . when I was in the dark hold of the steerage . . . when I was sewing buttons in a factory . . . when I walked the streets" (58). Fascinated by the material comfort that seemed to confer personhood, autobiographical Yezierska exclaims: "For once in my life I was where I wanted to be. For once I was part of everything. . . . I've arrived! I'm in with Hollywood royalty! Pushcart clothes and all—I am the guest of honor at the feast . . . that's America!" (61). However, while occupying the luxury palaces, autobiographical Yezierska articulates its opposite and evokes the father's critique: "Not me [was] invited to this dinner, but the sweatshop Cinderella" (55). And so there is confusion: "On Hester Street, I knew my way," writes the narrator. "Black was black; white was white. Right was right; wrong was wrong. Now Black, white, right wrong—nothing was real anymore" (41). Denied a complexity that includes that past, the narrator asserts that in Hollywood, "I stood empty, homeless—outside of life. Not a woman—not a writer" (87). The two competing ideologies hail the autobiographical Yezierska—Hollywood (signifying material success, mobility, and consumerism) and the Lower East Side (signifying piety, godliness, community, but also poverty); and both discursive communities disturb her. Thus, although Boroch Mayer's letter requesting money serves to pull autobiographical Yezierska away from Hollywood and back to New York City, once there, she finds the fictionalized Mayer dead, and she cannot bear the poverty of the Lower East Side. She moves to the Grosvenor Hotel on Fifth Avenue.

In part two, living on Fifth Avenue during the early 1920s, autobiographical Yezierska has achieved material and literary recognition, but after three years the "high-towered luxury" of the Grosvenor "still did not feel at home" (101). Thus she visits and recalls the Lower East Side through memory, but she resides uptown and occupies the spaces of the New York literary establishment. Both cultural arenas generate tensions for autobiographical Yezierska. Dining at the Algonquin Club, author Yezierska finds herself surrounded by literary agents who consider her a "prize" and the object of debate: Who discovered her? Who first published her? Who made her visible? Recognizing their "possessive solicitude" (which she likened to the Hollywood moguls), author Yezierska feels objectified and exploited; on the other hand, despite "an overwhelming nostalgia" that takes the autobiographical Yezierska back to the ghetto on the East Side, to the "pandemonoium of familiar strains," to "this home that had never been a home" (101–2), she cannot reside there. These two geographic spaces signify the tensions of the competing ideologies that autobiographical Yezierska can neither wholly accept or reject. Two men in this middle section embody these ideological tensions: John Morrow, a fictionalized representation of John Dewey, with whom historical Yezierska had a brief romance, and Zalmon Schlomoh, the poor fish peddler and friend from the East Side. Morrow "recognized [me] as a person," the narrator writes, "he saw me, knew me, reassured me that I existed" (107). Together they visit the Lower East Side: "What I had found coarse and commonplace was to him exotic" (109). Through his eyes the autobiographical Yezierska rediscovers that space, but this "real American" sees her cultural world as exotic. She and this world become objectified by Hollywood and the literary agents, because exoticism both celebrates and objectifies. But Shlomoh cannot hold her either: autobiographical Yezierska appreciates his humor (if she asked him about his luck, he would say, "except for health and a living, I'm perfectly fine"), and she shares his joy of romantic escapes from "unlived lives" (through Beethoven's "Moonlight Sonata" and Caruso's *Pagliacci*), but seeing Schlomoh's hunchback and poverty make the autobiographical Yezierska also feel a "cripple," and his fish smells affront her—perspectives learned in American discourses. Neither of these ideological spaces (the high-towered luxury and the streets of the Lower East Side, along with the men who embody these) provide a home where autobiographical Yezierska could take up residence, signifying the struggle with and against dominant and ethnic discourses.

Temporally, the final section of the autobiography occurs during the depression years of the early 1930s and is situated, first, in the living and working spaces of those employed with the Federal Writer's Project (FWP) and, second, in Fair Oaks, an imaginary New England village. The narrative portion devoted to the FWP represents about fifty pages (one-fourth of the autobiography), suggesting a temporal moment when autobiographical Yezierska found a meaningful home. The narrator emphasizes the shared experience of poverty and unemployment during the depression, dwelling especially on the sense of community that develops among poor writers of all races, classes, and ethnic backgrounds: held together by a "strange fellowship of necessity" and a common purpose of writing, the group laboring in the Writer's Hall evokes a microcosm of utopian America. In this world Jeremiah Kintzler, the Spinoza scholar from Warsaw, emerges as a spokesperson for the utopian potential embodied there, speaking for justice, equality, and the idealism of artist and scholar; he also signifies the father's discourse. The utopian moment of equality in a shared struggle is short lived, however; as the project becomes bureaucratized, the writers function as "wordage machines," and Kintzler, their inspiration, dies, exposing the empty contents of his briefcase. Autobiographical Yezierska leaves the project and travels to New England; her search for a home operates as the central metaphor in the last two chapters. Responding to a newspaper ad, the autobiographical Yezierska takes up residence in a farmhouse, where for a moment she finds "the peace and quiet of home." In time, however, the narrator discovers her aloneness, signified in visual objects: "prim, New England things . . . belong. They spoke of stability, security, a homeplace for generations" (213); and in the New England hills where she sees her own homelessness. The narrator dramatizes this isolation and separation in a high school pageant centered on the *Mayflower*, which provokes discussion between autobiographical Yezierska and a neighbor about cultural histories. Autobiographical Yezierska points out parallels between Plymouth Rock and Ellis Island, and she views "the Pilgrims as immigrants and dissenters—like me." The New England neighbor, however, reading the meaning of the historical narratives differently, sees autobiographical Yezierska as a Jewish immigrant, an "outsider." The sting of once again being the alien provokes the autobiographical Yezierska to board a train leaving New England—for a destination unknown. On the train, the narrator reflects that she carries the past with her: "The ghetto was with me wherever I went—the nothingness, the fear of my nothingness" (219).

The train serves as a critical topos for the adult autobiographical Yezierska seeking a place to reside, a home, in the universe—not as an object but as a person. Seeking personhood, autobiographical Yezierska enters the ideological spaces of Hollywood, the Algonquin, Writer's Hall, and rural New England—signifying America; but she both rejects and is rejected—signified by the metaphor of the train. The reader, therefore, meets an autobiographical subject, framed by trains, in search of a literal and metaphoric home, a subject who has achieved literary and financial recognition by "writing herself into personhood," yet a person who cannot find a meaningful residence in the historical and material world. The Yezierska subject shares spaces with the wealthy in Hollywood homes, with literary elites in the Algonquin Club, and with *Mayflower* descendants in New England farmhouses; but in each of these spaces the memory and fish smells of poverty inscribed in consciousness represent a history and complexity not permitted, while everywhere femaleness is erased. Yet the tenements of the Lower East Side signify a medieval world view, economic exploitation, and poverty, where meaning lies buried and unimaginable. Although the Yezierska subject, unlike the Antin subject, occupies the temporal arena of adulthood, the metaphor of the train serves to signify alienation from a world in which the adult—woman and ethnic—finds no meaningful space in which to reside, for in all those spaces the multiplicity of the subject positions she occupies must be denied or ignored.

Unlike autobiographical Antin, autobiographical Yezierska does not experience rebirth in the New World; nor does she simply reject the New World by embracing an ethnic past. If the Antin autobiographical subject utters the hope of a young adolescent immigrant girl on the steps of the Boston Public Library in the discourse of dominant American ideology, the Yezierska autobiographical subject, situated as an adult, articulates the problematic ideology embedded in that discourse for those positioned as Other. In short, the Americanizing discourses that defined personhood in patriarchal and Anglo-Saxon terms demanded denial of female positions (wife/mother) and alien positions (Polish/Jewish immigrant) except in so far as foreignness represented a place that one abandons. (Although the historical Yezierska had married, divorced, and raised a daughter during the temporal periods of the narrative, these positions are notably absent in the autobiography.)

If autobiographical Yezierska's search for a home in America ultimately fails, historical Goldman struggled to make the universe a home for all peoples. Consequently, autobiographical Goldman occupied multiple geographic places—forbidden spaces—signifying subjectivities radically different from those autobiographical Antin or Yezierska occupy, thus offering a chronotopic image of the American, female, ethnic, and—indeed—human being, that is radically altered and embedded with possibility.

Emma Goldman's two-volume autobiography, *Living My Life,* begun in 1928, was first published in October 1931 while she lived in exile in Saint-Tropez, France. Encouraged by friends to write, and eventually receiving an advance from Alred Knopf, historical Goldman hoped the book would provide financial security for her remaining years and gain her reentry to America when the injustice of her exile became evident (Wexler, *EG in Exile* 132). Neither of these purposes was realized, however, but the reception to the autobiography was primarily favorable: Alice Wexler cites one critic who described it as "the most extraordinary document ever penned by a woman," one that "certainly ranks with the great autobiographies of the world" (154). Nearly sixty years later, the two-volume publication is still in print and critical discussion of the work continues. Wexler argues that the autobiography "mythologized Goldman's life, creating a larger-than-life female hero with little of the depression, anxiety, bitterness, jealousy, or loneliness so evident in her letters. It was this figure who increasingly preempted the historical woman in the popular imagination, for *Living My Life* would become the main source of information about Goldman, and for a long time, about anarchism in America" (156). Thus the historical and the autobiographical Goldman collapse in the imagination of most readers in the twentieth century. Scholarly attention to Goldman's autobiography has persisted up to the fiftieth anniversary of her death in 1940, though it is strikingly absent in discourses where one might imagine it, particularly in studies of ethnicity and women's autobiography. Werner Sollors and Mary Dearborn, who have written extensively about American culture and ethnicity, virtually ignore Goldman, and although feminist scholarship has generated significant biographical studies, namely those by Alice Wexler and Candace Falk, Goldman is also strikingly absent in studies of women's autobiographies—Estelle Jelineck accords her a few lines within "Exotic Autobiographies Intellectualized" in *The Tradition of Women's Autobiographies*. It is within traditional academic disciplines that Goldman has received the most attention—especially literary and historical studies; however, relying on prevailing standards of aesthetic taste and historical veracity, traditional approaches to Goldman's autobiography often lead to harsh and misleading judgments and, I suggest, diminish the effect of the autobiographical subject for the contemporary reader.

Critics, Wexler notes, have pointed out "incongruity between her [Goldman's] ideological aspirations and the imaginative forms in which she expressed them" (147). Attacking her for relying on "stock figures" and "cliches of American popular romance," critics use terms such as *sentimental, popular, conservative aesthetic tastes,* and *romantic* to disparage narrator Goldman for not putting her radical ideas in radical forms. A recent example of this critical perspective is found in Peter Conn's essay on Emma Goldman, "A Glimpse Into the 21st Century: Emma Goldman." Overall Conn's approach aims to be sympathetic to Goldman; demonstrating Goldman's commonality with Henry James and other Americans of the period who possessed a "divided mind," Conn seeks to reveal her "American family resemblance" (315) and thus make her less alien. The argument, however, rests primarily on Goldman's language—what Conn seems to consider jarring religious metaphors for a Jewish anarchist (New York City as a "baptism" and Berkman's imprisonment as "a Calvary") and descriptions of her love affairs, which draw on the "tradition of romantic love" and "Harlequin love songs." He concludes that Goldman's "vision of the future was entangled in the debris of the past" (313). By identifying Goldman with her language (and, one might argue, reducing her to it) and emphasizing disembodied ideas, Conn links her with Henry James (an Anglophile from an upper-class, patrician family, who became a British citizen in 1915). In the process, he not only depoliticizes Goldman's life and ideas, he also ignores the discursive possibilities available to Goldman. How did *anyone* write about female sexuality, human intimacy, and love in 1928? As Michel Foucault has so persuasively demonstrated, discourses on human sexuality in Western culture, dominated by the medical profession and religious institutions, revolve around constructions of health and morality and in the last century by Freudian psychoanalysis—all undesirable frameworks for describing intimate human relationships. Popular romance remained an alternative. That autobiographical Antin and Yezierska virtually excluded expressions of love underscores the problem as cultural. Further, that radical aesthetic forms do not automatically produce radical ideas is evident in Gertrude Stein's *Autobiography of Alice B. Toklas*, which virtually ignores sexuality and eroticism. What remains remarkable about Goldman is that, chronotopically, she takes readers into forbidden spaces, such as her bedroom, when neither autobiographical Antin, autobiographical Yezierska, nor Gertrude Stein, could. Yet, unlike writers of erotica, autobiographical Goldman also takes the reader out again, also claiming other spaces for women, namely public spaces—lecture halls, union halls, the streets—as she occupies them herself.

Clearly, literary approaches that focus primarily on linguistic patterns, metaphoric allusions, and traditional aesthetic standards remain inadequate for reading those positioned as the Other, who must steal language. On the other hand, assumptions about the transparency of historical veracity lead some critics of the autobiography, reports Wexler, to charge that narrator Goldman distorted the truth and that portraits, particularly of Alexander Berkman, Ben Reitman, and Johann Most, were motivated by "an act of revenge" (149). Wexler cites two particular limitations of the autobiography noted by historical critics: that she wrote of the anarchist movement as though she were the center and that she avoided discussing the ideas of anarchism. Chronotopically, however, the autobiographical subject occupies all the spaces the dominant culture forbade her—female embodiment of these spaces becomes itself an anarchist statement. Further, the attribution of personal motivations, such as revenge, seems to mask the larger critique of patriarchy embedded in the autobiography. From the framework of postmodern feminism and cultural theories, contemporary readers can appreciate Goldman's struggle against patriarchal power and control. Though lacking contemporary language for that critique, narrator Goldman used her positions as anarchist *and* feminist to resist patriarchal oppression both within dominant institutions and among male anarchist friends with whom she shared a larger political agenda, but who were often blind to their own formations in oppressive patriarchal ideology. Ed Brady, anarchist leader and mentor, wanted Goldman to marry him, to abandon her public life, and to assume woman's natural position as mother. Goldman's refusal to be possessed in marriage or to assume a subordinate position in a heterosexual relationship evokes a contemporary feminist position, which she could assume at the turn of the century because of her multiple subject positions—particularly those of anarchist and feminist. Examination of chronotopic positions of autobiographical subjects permit us to see more clearly the effect of radical discourses, and such an analysis helps contemporary readers appreciate the power of those positions and thus of the autobiography.

In the opening of *Living My Life* the narrator positions autobiographical Goldman at the moment of arrival in New York City from Rochester, New York, not the Old World: "It was the 15th of August 1889, the day of my arrival in New York City. I was twenty years old. All that had happened in my life until that time was now left behind me, cast off like a worn-out garment" (3). Although historical Goldman had been in the United States for four years, had married, and worked in Rochester, what provokes the rebirth is the imprisonment and execution, 11 November 1887 in Chicago, of anarchists charged with murder in the Haymarket Riot. Unlike autobiographical Antin's rebirth as American, which leaves her in adolescence, autobiographical Goldman's rebirth as a political radical positions her as an adult—chronotopically, in New York City at twenty—prepared to struggle against injustice in America. Narrator Goldman closes the autobiography in 1928 (the time of her writing) reflecting on efforts to release Sacco and Vanzetti, Italian anarchists also charged with murder, imprisoned (1921–27), and executed (22 August 1927). Although the Goldman narrator covers the period from her birth in 1869 to the time she began to write the autobiography, she frames the life story with these two events that dramatize American injustice—the Haymarket Affair and the execution of Sacco and Vanzetti. The strategy of framing the autobiographical narrative with these events, rather than immigration to or deportation from the New World, aligns the autobiographical subject with a communal history, particularly of the anarchists in the United States and struggles against injustice, rather than an individual history. This stimulates the reader to reflect on the injustices historical Goldman spent a lifetime fighting and serves to focus on the cause of justice rather than a personal story.

The framework also contains Goldman's deportation from the United States in 1919 and self-exile with Alexander Berkman in 1921 from postrevolutionary Russia after the Kronstadt revolt and massacre. By situating these events in the middle of the narrative, the autobiographical Goldman occupies the centers of Western capitalism (America and western Europe) and Marxism (the Soviet Union), signifying what Jean-Francois Lyotard calls "the grand narratives," whose credibility and value have been questioned in the postmodern era. But historical and autobiographical Goldman also leaves these sites, in effect diminishing their authority. Historical Goldman was exiled from both these geographic and political arenas (involuntarily from the United States in 1919, voluntarily from the Soviet Union in 1921); however, by foregrounding neither event in the autobiography, the Goldman narrator calls attention to the struggle against injustice within both grand narratives and delegitimizes the power and authority of both systems. The effect is to align the autobiographical subject with postmodern critiques of these grand narratives. Although the bulk of the autobiography is set in America, where historical Goldman spent half her life (1885–1919), by framing the narrative with the Haymarket tragedy and the memory of Sacco and Vanzetti (evoked on the last page), narrator Goldman foregrounds the injustices and the struggles against these. The primary chronotopes signify that critique.

The autobiographical subject, primarily an adult, occupied spaces unimaginable to autobiographical Antin or Yezierska—spaces theoretically closed to women. In late nineteenth-century American discourses addressing gender, the ideology of separate spheres prescribed appropriate spaces for males and females: males occupied public arenas, females the private arenas, namely the home. Autobiographical Goldman's presence in the proscribed public spaces, particularly on the streets, challenges those ideologies. One moment early in the autobiography illustrates this pattern, which is repeated throughout the narrative. In 1891 radical German, Jewish, and Russian socialist groups in New York City decided to mark International Labor Day on 1 May, secured Union

Square for the celebration, and promised anarchists a platform to speak. When the platform was denied the anarchists, Emma Goldman was lifted onto a socialist truck. The narrator writes, "I began to speak. The chairman left, but in a few minutes he returned with the owner of the wagon. I continued to speak. The man hitched his horse to the truck and started off at a trot. I still continued to speak. The crowd, failing to take in the situation, followed us out of the square for a couple of blocks while I was speaking" (I:80). The image of historical Goldman speaking from the back of a wagon, pulled down the street away from Union Square, and followed by a receptive audience signifies not only a woman occupying male/public spaces, but a radical female claiming the right to speak amidst radicals who would silence her. The image evokes the way in which autobiographical Goldman throughout the autobiography occupies forbidden spaces. Perhaps the one site that most signifies the forbidden spaces she occupies, and the anarchist critique, were the prisons. "For people with ideals," writes the Goldman narrator, "prison is the best school" (I:116), alluding to Alexander Berkman and inverting autobiographical Antin's celebration of the schools. Historical Goldman's formal schooling, three years in a Realschule in Konigsberg, consisted of cruelty, as well as sexual and physical abuse (I:116–17), an experience surely contributing to her critique of the schools as another oppressive state institution (and anticipating Althusser's analysis of the School (replacing the Church) as a primary Ideological State Apparatus, functioning with the Family in late capitalism as the dominant ideological institutions).

Indicted on three counts for a speech at Union Square "inciting to riot," although all witnesses agreed there was no riot at Union Square, historical Goldman was sentenced on 18 October 1893 to one year's imprisonment at Blackwell's Island Penitentiary. Though the exchange at the trial suggests she was tried for her beliefs, especially for rejecting a Supreme Being, the judge pronounced sentence and called her a "dangerous woman" (Drinnon 60–61). In Blackwell's, fellow inmates initially shunned the incomprehensible anarchist, who refused to attend required church services; however, narrator Goldman writes that by defying prison authority (refusing to oversee workers in the sewing room and refusing the matron's request to translate a letter to an inmate written in Russian) historical Goldman won their hearts. The narrator concludes the chapter on imprisonment with reflections on its meaning in her life. Admitting she owed her development to many, autobiographical Goldman says, and yet, more than all else, it was the prison that had proved the best school. A more painful, but a more vital, school. Here I had been brought close to the depths and complexities of the human soul; here I had found ugliness and beauty, meanness and generosity. Here, too, I had learned to see life through my own eyes and not through those of Sasha [Alexander Berkman], Most[Johann] Ed[Brady]. The prison had been the crucible that tested my faith. It had helped me to discover strength in my own being, the strength to stand alone, the strength to live my life and fight for my ideals, against the whole world if need be. The State of New York could have rendered me no greater service than by sending me to Blackwell's Island Penitentiary. (I:148)

By occupying this forbidden space she not only inverts the prevailing ideology and allies herself with victims of injustice, but she gives dignity to those who share that space, not only in Blackwell's but in other prisons where she empathizes with victims of injustice; there, her conviction was reinforced that crime is a result of poverty and the endless chain of injustice and inequality. Historical Emma Goldman, one might argue, was deported precisely because she occupied forbidden spaces, ideologically and politically, but also spatially, for women as well as for Americans. And by occupying forbidden spaces the autobiographical Goldman challenges prevailing images of Americans, women—and human beings.

If prisons signify the forbidden spaces autobiographical Goldman occupied, the spaces she did *not* occupy also signify her multiple and contradictory subjectivities. The place prescribed for women in the culture remained the home (that elusive place autobiographical Yezierska never found), a place to contain female subjectivity, to keep women economically dependent on men, to control sexuality in bonds of marriage—an institution Goldman equates with prostitution. Historical Goldman took up residence where she could find it and continued her work; so, too, perpetual motion marks the autobiographical subject but, unlike autobiographical Yezierska's quest for home, autobiographical Goldman assumes a home wherever the struggle for justice takes her. Thus she finds residence in apartments, hotels, offices of *Mother Earth*, a brothel, prisons, with friends or family, on the Museum of the Revolution—in travels across the United States, Europe, the Soviet Union, and Canada.

Traditionally, the ideological space of the home also signified the site of motherhood. Diagnosed with an inverted uterus and unable to bear children, historical Goldman never took steps that might have reversed that condition, although Wexler argues she may have suffered from endometriosis. Nevertheless, reflections on motherhood appear in the autobiography:

> My starved motherhood—was that the main reason for my idealism? He [Ed Brady] had roused the old yearning for a child. But I had silenced the voice of the child for the sake of the universal, the all-absorbing passion of my life. Men were consecrated to ideals and yet were fathers of children. But man's physical share in the child is only a moment's; women's part is for years—years of absorption in one human being to the exclusion of the rest of humanity. I would never give up the one for the other. But I would give him my love and devotion. Surely it must be possible for a man and a woman to have a beautiful love-life and yet be devoted to a great cause. We must try. (I:153–54)

Although not occupying the sacred space of the idealized American home (a privately owned, detached, single-family dwelling) and not taking up her supposedly natural female position of mother, autobiographical Goldman assumed alternative positions outside the home, dignifying the not-mother/female and legitimating the spaces outside the prescribed home. On the other hand, in her position as midwife she empathized with the struggles of poor women, asserting that "women and children carried the heaviest burden of our ruthless economic system" (I:187). Further, because Goldman resisted patriarchal ideologies that devalue spaces designated for women, she could take up those spaces joyfully and defiantly. Unlike autobiographical Yezierska, who erases positions held in female-dominated professions, autobiographical Goldman speaks of being a "proud holder of two diplomas, one for midwifery and one for nursing" (I:174) and she worked for years in these professions. Goldman occupies forbidden spaces and refuses to occupy prescribed places, but in the process she dignifies delegitimated spaces and the people residing there, while she redefines prescribed spaces.

Within the range of forbidden and prescribed, autobiographical Goldman assumes multiple spaces throughout the narrative, evoking multiple subjectivities: as woman, Russian-born immigrant, radical, Jew, anarchist, feminist, agitator, lecturer, writer, daughter, sister, aunt, friend, fellow-prisoner, lover. The narrator writes, "I was not hewn of one piece, like Sasha or other heroic figures. I had long realized that I was woven of many skeins, conflicting in shade and texture" (I:153). The multiplicity of subject positions are reflected in the multiple chronotopic positions autobiographical Goldman occupied, those that speak of a radical public life—delivering speeches at Union Square, lecturing on anarchism and drama at American universities, addressing an anarchist congress in Amsterdam, nursing the poor, defending herself and others before judges, or riding the Museum of the Revolution across Russia to collect materials of the revolution. And those spaces that speak of a personal life—exchanging ideas in private homes with friends, viewing dramatic productions in theaters, celebrating victories in restaurants, and lovemaking in her bedrooms. The multiple chronotopes evoke the various subjectivities that challenge patriarchal and Americanizing discourses, suggesting a range of social relations and ideological positions foreclosed in prescribed spaces by dominant cultural narratives. Autobiographical Goldman evokes for contemporary readers alternative subject positions to those of the dominant discourses by occupying forbidden spaces; she consequently challenges prevailing ideologies surrounding an image of the presumed cultural Other, especially the female, and points to alternative chronotopic images for all human beings.

If Bakhtin is right that our image of the human being is always spatial and temporal—that is, concrete—then the value of a chronotopic analysis for exploring autobiography seems manifest, particularly if we look for less visible and noncognitive ways of reading the speaking subject and the cultural Other. The chronotopes are not natural or self-evident categories, but culturally prescribed, and embedded with cultural meanings. Autobiographical Antin, allied with signifiers of American discourses, situated in the schools as an adolescent, assumes her place in a prescribed space, meaning adulthood for the ethnic woman becomes unimaginable. Autobiographical Yezierska, seeking home in dominant American spaces, while drawn to an ethnic past ill-equipped for a contemporary world, finds no place of residence for the multiply positioned ethnic woman. Autobiographical Goldman, however, occupies multiple and contradictory spaces, transgressing the prescriptions of patriarchy and nationalism. Thus she posits alternative subjectivities for a postmodern, feminist cultural vision. Reading autobiographies chronotopically, especially those of the cultural Other, permits us to read differently—to apprehend the effect of discourses in which the autobiographer is situated by examining the subject's temporal and spatial placement in the world. Further, such an approach also permits a cultural critique of prevailing ideologies.

Postmodernism, Autobiography, and Subjectivity Reconsidered

Postmodernism, Chantal Mouffe argues in her essay "Radical Democracy," need not imply an outright rejection of modernity, but we must reject the "Enlightenment project of self-foundation" (meaning the autonomous, unitary, meaning-making self). Nor, she argues, need we abandon the political project of modernity—equality and freedom for all. Rather, she asserts, "we must ensure that the democratic project takes account of the full breadth and specificity of the democratic struggles in our times. It is here that the contribution of the so-called postmodern critique comes into its own." She continues her argument:

> How, in effect, can we hope to understand the nature of these new antagonisms if we hold on to an image of the unitary subject as the ultimate source of intelligibility of its actions? How can we grasp the multiplicity of relations of subordination that can affect an individual if we envisage social agents as homogeneous and unified entities? What characterizes the struggles of these new social movements is precisely the multiplicity of subject-positions, which constitute a single agent and the possibility for this multiplicity to become the site of an antagonism and thereby politicized. (34)

For contemporary readers who wish to understand the multiplicity of subject-positions that constitute a single agent, ethnic autobiographies provide a site for developing that perspective; they enable us to see the concrete effects of multiple discourses in the culture, and thus permit a better understanding of cultural construction of difference. Mouffe writes of this importance:

> To be capable of thinking politics today, and understanding the nature of these new struggles and the diversity of social relations that the democratic revolution has yet to encompass, it is indispensable to develop a theory of the subject as a decentered, detotalized agent, a subject constructed at the point of intersection of a multiplicity of subject-positions between which there exists no a priori or necessary relation and whose articulation is the result of hegemonic practices. Consequently, no identity is ever definitely established, there always being a certain degree of openness and ambiguity in the way the different subject-positions are articulated. What emerges are entirely new perspectives for political action, which neither liberalism—with its idea of the individual who only

pursues his or her own interest—nor Marxism—with its reduction of all subject-positions to that of class—can sanction, let alone imagine. (34–35)

Clearly, in order to appreciate the multiple ethnic groups and struggles that characterize our postmodern world, we must develop new theories of the subject and new ways of reading narrative texts. Postmodern theories begin to provide us with a vehicle for understanding the multiplicity of subjectivities. Applying postmodern theories—and a chronotopic analysis—to autobiography can help us to appreciate and understand the multiple struggles and diverse social relations emerging on a global terrain by tracing the effects of discourse on a subject. Furthermore, postmodern theories enable us to reread our own cultural stories differently—a chronotopic analysis, especially, permits us see the effect of discursive practices on subjectivities, both in canonical and marginalized literatures, so we can consider whether as a culture we wish to cultivate these subjectivities or critique them.

A chronotopic analysis of so-called classics in American autobiography demonstrates the spatial and temporal limitations of our cultural and autobiographical traditions. The speaking subject, particularly those frequently cited as representative Americans—such as Benjamin Franklin, Henry David Thoreau, and Henry Adams, often the center around which other American autobiographies are perceived to revolve—represent the temporal and spatial arenas in which readers are asked to imagine the so-called American self. Positions of power in revolutionary America and France, isolation at Walden Pond, and Boston's Beacon Hill or Harvard, sites of "representative" American autobiographies, do not signify chronotopes in which women, blacks, and the poor can imagine themselves; yet the time-space dimensions of these representative American selves serve as an invisible effect of their self-representation, the plane on which the reader is asked to imagine those persons, thus aligning those temporal and spatial arenas with Americanness, and humanness. The issue is not only that cultural standards have prevailed over aesthetic ones in shaping canonical American literature—an argument that Nina Baym has effectively made—but also that the notions of cultural essences that have ruled naturalize particular temporal and spatial arenas in which the racial, ethnic, and gendered Other has been denied access. Yet these have stood as images of the human and remained idealized in the name of a common cultural heritage and canonical integrity. Consequently, the pattern for imaging of the human being in American literature and autobiography—intrinsically chrono-topic—excludes the Other. A chronotopic analysis, especially in the context of cultural discourses on race, class, gender, and ethnicity, suggests ways to interrogate subject positions elevated in the culture that ensure certain social and juridical relations.

One contemporary ethnic autobiography illustrates the value of this approach. Richard Rodriquez's *Hunger of Memory: The Education of Richard Rodriquez*, first published in 1982 and frequently reprinted, is often read by Anglo-Americans as a representative Chicano autobiography, while it generates deep controversy within the Chicano community. Richard Rodriquez, a second-generation Mexican-American immigrant, begins the autobiography as he enters school in Sacramento, California; he ends it thirty years later while writing the narrative, after completing a dissertation on Renaissance literature (doing research at the British Museum). In a sense, however, the autobiographical subject never leaves the schoolroom, the space that confers legitimation as American. Like the Antin subject in *The Promised Land*, autobiographical Rodriquez identifies with the dominant cultural ideologies, making the chronotopic parallels striking: both narratives isolate the "I" from the ethnic community in a rather solitary struggle; both subjectivities reside primarily in the schools; both close the autobiographies at the time of leaving school; both exclude adulthood and a collective experience in the temporal and spatial dimensions represented. Strikingly, both narratives have circulated widely in the culture. If the Antin subject and the Rodriquez subject represent subjectivities that guarantee prevailing social relations, we can recognize an ideological pattern that crosses gendered and ethnic differences: both ethnicity and gendered subjectivity remain contained, temporally and spatially, in the schoolroom. Neither the Jewish immigrant woman nor the second-generation Chicano becomes adult. This containment further masks complex political and economic histories as individualism, upward mobility, and Anglo cultural superiority appear naturalized. In some ways the chronotopic image of the contained Other in ethnic autobiography remains more problematic than that found in canonical literature because such images seem to emerge from the alleged voice of the Other and so naturalize and legitimate dominant cultural images of the transformed American while containing the Other in preadult, childlike states—here, bounded by the schoolroom. Chronotopic analysis, therefore, becomes invaluable in examining subjectivities in ethnic autobiographies.

This raises again the question of the uses and purposes of autobiography. Because autobiographical subjects reproduce prevailing ideologies, the issues raised by autobiography are not simply literary or historical, but cultural ones. If we consider culture in the broadest sense to be what is prescribed and what is prohibited, then as autobiographies naturalize certain subject positions they serve to prescribe these positions and guarantee social relations implied by the subject. Thus, the Antin subject that identifies with dominant American institutions naturalizes that alliance for all immigrants. The question remains whether oppositional or resistant subject positions can also be represented in the autobiographical form. To borrow Bakhtin's metaphor, can we identify in autobiography the centrifugal forces, which move away from the center, as well as the centripedal forces, which move toward the center? We may agree that the Antin autobiographical subject represents the centripedal field of force, the Goldman subject represents centrifugal forces, and the Yezierska subject represents a position struggling with and against the center; however, we must avoid seeing these as positions emanating from essential selves. If we place these subjects chronotopically in the narrative and identify the discursive practices in which they are situated, we can trace the effect of discourses on subjects and identify multiple subjectivities in which they live. And as we begin to distinguish between narrator, historical subject, and autobiographical subject, we can avoid essentializing individuals, or the groups in which they live, and can associate subject patterns with discourses. Thus, whereas the Antin subject legitimates subject positions that guarantee prevailing social relations, Emma Goldman represents resisting positions and discourses, which might also hail the reader.

Finally, how do we read and understand the speaking subject of autobiography? Clearly, in the context of our postmodern world, we reside in multiple and contradictory discourses; the historical and economic conditions in which human beings live are also multiple and contradictory. To posit an essential self denies those contradictions and conditions. To imagine Mary Antin, for example, as an essentialist self, as the origin of her own meaning, speaking in an authentic voice, makes those dominant utterances, and the ideologies they mask, appear natural and legitimate—but it also denies her adult life and sexuality; it denies her gender and the multiple positions assumed as woman; it denies the traces of her ethnic past that remain after the transformation to American; and it denies the struggles in all these contradictions. When publishers anthologize these narratives and thus reproduce the subjectivities outside any historical contexts, these omissions become especially problematic for the readers. Furthermore, the desire to find a self in autobiography inevitably fails because of the impossibility of language to represent a whole. This search, however, led Patricia Spacks to claim that Goldman produces "an autobiography with no self at the center" (127). To make such an assertion denies the multiple subject positions that Goldman assumes throughout the autobiography; it also denies the reader the potential of being hailed by the resistant discourses the Goldman subject utters. To claim an essentialist self is to deny the way in which historical conditions, material forces, and cultural discourses shape articulations of the self. A theory of the subject in autobiography must posit the existence of multiple and contradictory subjectivities as the effect of multiple discourses at a particular historical moment.

Those threatened by postmodern theories of the subject seem to equate an attack on the coherent, autonomous self as an attack on human beings. Katherine Goodman in her volume on women's autobiography in Germany defends the "concept of self and the authenticity of experience" arguing that "conceptualizing a dispersed subject may be necessary for women—and genealogists who wish to avoid hierarchies—if they are to liberate the subject, any subject at any time, from universals. But the concept of the 'self' is essential if we are not to remain fatalistic and without a sense of choice" (xvi). Clearly, we must distinguish between the *humanist self* and *human beings* and rethink our notion of the human, rather than cling to a view of supposed choice deeply embedded in the ideology of the Enlightenment—which denies the lives of millions for whom "choice" remained nonexistent or severely circumscribed. Our notions of the humanist/essentialized self—naturalized in the last five hundred years in Europe as rational, coherent, unified, but also androcentric—is powerfully linked to American traditions of individualism. The humanist/essentialist view of the self tends to mask the way in which we are constituted in language and positioned differently there—depending on race, class, gender, or ethnicity. And because the humanist/essentialist model tends to universalize its view of the human being, it tends to dehistoricize individuals, to ignore the dialectic of the historical moment and ideological practices that shape subjectivities. When individuals do not conform to perceptions of what appears to constitute the human, individuals tend to blame themselves or to be blamed—rather than to acknowledge the ideologies, structures, economic and material conditions that produced less-than-human human beings. Further, making the humanist self seem natural tends to legitimate the violence done to the presumably less-than-human and is used as an explanation for poverty, degradation, and the multiple social and economic ills produced by systemic injustices.

Thus to cling to a notion of the meaning-making, coherent, unified individual—both generally and at the center of an autobiography—seems a travesty. The travesty is especially evident in the midst of a postmodern world—a world characterized by fragmentations, by multiple and contradictory narratives, by global struggles of the oppressed, and by a collapse of modern epistomologies and political systems. Because autobiography has acquired power in the culture to legitimate certain subject positions, autobiographical studies can be a site from which to not only challenge essentialist notions of the human being, but also to examine the effect of discourses on subjects, both those that seem to guarantee prevailing social relations and those that critique them. Autobiographical studies might also therefore provide a site for cultural critique and social change.

Notes

1   Mary Louise Briscoe, ed., *American Autobiography, 1945–1980*, ix. *Immigrant Women in the United States*, compiled by Donna Gabaccia, cites more than four hundred entries under "autobiographies." The proliferation of autobiographical studies focused on ethnic groups in the United States is reflected in current Modern Language Association's bibliographies. Recent conferences on autobiography (international, multicultural, and cross-disciplinary) suggest a broad interest, as well as the multiple perspectives employed in examining autobiography; for example, "Autobiography and Self-Representation," held 3–4 March 1990 at the University of California Humanities Research Institute, University of California, Irvine; "The Maine Autobiography Conference," from 29 September to 1 October 1989 in Portland, Maine; and "Autobiographies, Biographies and Life Histories of Women: Interdisciplinary Perspectives," 23–24 May 1986, at the University of Minnesota.

2   Henry Louis Gates, Jr., "James Gronnniosaw and the Trope of the Talking Book," 55. Gates takes the metaphor from Bakhtin and argues that the metaphor of double-voiced comes to bear in black texts on the trope of the Talking Book, the "ur-trope" of Anglo-African tradition.

3   Michael M. J. Fischer, "Ethnicity and the Post-Modern Arts of Memory," 195–96. Frances E. Mascia-Lees et al., "The Postmodernist Turn in Anthropology," argue persuasively that the volume omits women anthropologists and ignores the valuable contributions feminism can bring to anthropology. The writers argue that feminism and postmodernism remain dichotomous, that whereas feminism is a radical movement with a political agenda, postmodernism is not. Given these operating assumptions, the writers concede postmodernism to conservatives and ignore such writers as Chantal Mouffe and Julia Kristeva, certainly feminists *and* postmodern-

ists. For a powerful discussion of the political imperatives linking feminism and postmodernism and the importance of theorizing those relationships, see Teresa Ebert's *Patriarchal Narratives* and "The 'Difference' of Postmodern Feminism." See also *Feminism/Postmodernism,* edited by Linda J. Nicholson.

William Boelhower, another scholar whose work has focused on immigrant and ethnic autobiography, draws upon poststructuralist thinking, especially semiotics, to examine the constructions of identity in ethnic literature in the United States, especially in *Immigrant Autobiography* and *Through a Glass Darkly.* Like Fischer, however, Boelhower simply ignores the category of gender, as well as recent feminist scholarship.

4   Certainly, Richard Rodriquez's *Hunger of Memory: The Education of Richard Rodriquez* (Toronto, New York, Bantam Books: 1982), the autobiography of a second-generation Mexican-American speaks a dominant—meaning assimilationist— discourse in which American school experiences become an avenue for upward mobility and erase an ethnic past. Its wide circulation and support among Anglo-American readers suggests that the narrative serves to privilege certain Mexican-American subjectivities and so support prevailing social relations (see also notes 6 and 7 below).

5   Roland Barthes, *Roland Barthes,* 79, 167. Several discussions on the multiply positioned subject I find especially meaningful: Kaja Silverman's *Subject of Semiotics* is a particularly useful source; also meaningful is Terry Eagleton's discussion of Lacan and the distinctions among the "I's" of the speaking subject in *Literary Theory,* especially chapter five; and Julian Henriques, et al., *Changing the Subject,* has been invaluable in demonstrating the necessity of changing our notion of the essential self and the social consequences of not doing so.

6   Ramón Saldívar, "Ideologies of the Self," is the only study I am aware of that employs the chronotopic analysis of ethnic autobiography. The comparative study that focuses on Richard Rodriquez's *Hunger of Memory* and Ernesto Galarza's *Barrio Boy: The Story of a Boy's Acculturation* (1971; Notre Dame: U of Notre Dame P, 1980) emphasizes, however, the topos rather than the chronos. Briefly, Saldívar contrasts the private, school-focused, and individualized world of Rodriquez, with the public, integrated world of Galarza, evoked in the topos of the road and the barrio. He argues that Rodriquez's work masks its ideology, whereas Galarza's work affirms the conviction that the public is also private. He also contrasts the "exceptional time" of Rodriquez with the time of "dailiness" in Galarza, though less attention is given to the temporal dimensions. Saldívar's provocative analysis makes important contributions to our understanding of these autobiographies. (The essay is reprinted in Ramón Saldívar, *Chicano Narrative.*)

7   What is significant is that while the autobiographical Antin subject—the model— does not reach adulthood, neither do the two autobiographical subjects Saldívar contrasts in his chronotopic analysis that emphasizes topos. Neither autobiographical Rodriquez nor autobiographical Galarza reach adulthood. Although the Rodriquez autobiographical subject is roughly contemporaneous with the histor-

ical Rodriquez at the time of his writing, Galarza's autobiography was written when he was in his fifties and had already achieved a long record of labor organizing and radical politics, but this historical past is erased in the autobiography with focus on the barrio boy, as the title indicates. One could argue that the historical Galarza knows the political consequences of writing about his radical adult life, but what are the consequences for the reader—Chicano and Anglo-American—who never learns of Galarza's adult and political life and thus cannot imagine him outside adolescence, as an adult? (I am grateful to Genaro Padillo who pointed to Galarza's narrative time frame during a discussion at the Maine Autobiography Conference; Padillo noted that the chronotope of Antin's conclusion was similar to Galarza's.)

I suggest that Maxine Hong Kingston's *Woman Warrior* reflects a similar pattern. Although the autobiography includes multiple adult female figures, the "I" remains a child throughout the narrative. In the second story, "The White Tiger," the "I" becomes an adult warrior, but only in a vision, and then as a general. Thus only through dreaming can the narrator emerge as an adult, but there she must also mask femaleness as she becomes a (male) general. (I am grateful to Wendy Kozol for her observation about the imaginary and disguised figure in "The White Tiger.") Because *Woman Warrior* is so thoroughly appropriated in the academy (and, like the Antin and Rodriquez autobiographies, often serves to represent ethnic, in this case Chinese-American, autobiography) this chronotopic position of the auto-biographical "I" does not seem insignificant. One possible consequence of the institutional appropriation of ethnic autobiographies in which the speaking subject remains contained in time and space (as the school child) is that this image perpetuates a pattern of colonization, however subtle and invisible, by containing the gendered and ethnic Other in childhood.

References

Althusser, Louis. "Ideology and Ideological State Apparatuses (Notes Toward an Investigation)." *Lenin and Philosophy and Other Essays.* Trans. Ben Brewster. New York: Monthly Review, 1971.

Antin, Mary. *The Promised Land.* Boston: Houghton, 1912.

Bakhtin, M. M. *The Dialogic Imagination: Four Essays.* Trans. Caryl Emerson and Michael Holquist. Ed. Michael Holquist. Austin: U of Texas P, 1981.

Barthes, Roland. *Roland Barthes.* Trans. Richard Howard. New York: Noonday, 1977.

Baym, Nina. "Melodramas of Beset Manhood." *American Quarterly* 33 (1981): 123–39.

Benveniste, Emile. *Problems in General Linguistics.* Trans. Mary Elizabeth Meek. Coral Gables: U of Miami P, 1971.

Boelhower, William. *Immigrant Autobiography in the United States.* Venice: Essedue Edizion, 1982.

———. *Through a Glass Darkly: Ethnic Semiosis in American Literature.* Venice: Edizioni Helvetia, 1984.

Briscoe, Mary Louise, ed. *American Autobiography, 1945–1980: A Bibliography.* Madison: U of Wisconsin P, 1982.

Conn, Peter. *The Divided Mind: Ideology and Imagination in America, 1898–1917.* Cambridge: Cambridge UP, 1983.

Dearborn, Mary. "Anzia Yezierska and the Making of an Ethnic American Self." *The Invention of Ethnicity.* Ed. Werner Wollors. New York: Oxford UP, 1989.

———. *Pocahontas's Daughters: Gender and Ethnicity in American Culture.* New York: Oxford UP, 1986.

Drinnon, Richard. *Rebel in Paradise: A Biography of Emma Goldman.* Chicago: U of Chicago P, 1961.

Eagleton, Terry. *Literary Theory: Introduction.* Minneapolis: U of Minnesota P, 1983.

Ebert, Teresa. "The 'Difference' of Postmodern Feminism," *College English* 5.8 (December 1991): 886–904.

———. *Patriarchal Narratives: Toward a Postmodern Feminist Culture Critique.* (forthcoming).

Falk, Candace. *Love, Anarchy and Emma Goldman.* New York: Holt, 1984.

Fischer, Michael. "Ethnicity and the Postmodern Arts of Memory." *Writing Culture: The Poetics and Politics of Ethnography.* Ed. James Clifford and George E. Marcus. Berkeley: U of California P, 1986.

Foucault, Michel. *An Introduction.* Trans. Robert Hurley. New York: Random, 1978. Vol. 1 of *The History of Sexuality.* 3 vols. 1978–84.

Gabaccia, Donna, comp. *Immigrant Women in the United States: A Selectively Annotated Multidisciplinary Bibliography.* New York: Greenwood, 1989.

Gates, Henry Louis, Jr. "James Gronniosaw and the Trope of the Talking Book." *Studies in Autobiography.* Ed. James Olney. New York: Oxford UP, 1988.

Goldman, Emma. *Living My Life.* 1931. 2 vols. New York: Dover, 1970.

Goodman, Katherine. *Dis/Closures: Women's Autobiography in Germany Between 1790 and 1914.* New York: Lang, 1986.

Henriksen, Louise Levitas. *Anzia Yezierska: A Writer's Life.* [With assistance from Jo Ann Boydston]. New Brunswick: Rutgers UP, 1988.

Henriques, Julian, Wendy Holloway, Cathy Urwin, Couze Venn, and Valerie Walkerdine. *Changing the Subject: Psychology, Social Regulation and Subjectivity.* London: Methuen, 1984.

Holte, James Craig. *The Ethnic I: A Sourcebook for Ethnic-American Autobiography.* New York: Greenwood, 1988.

Jelinek, Estelle C. *The Tradition of Women's Autobiography: From Antiquity to the Present.* Boston: Twayne, 1986.

Kessler-Harris, Alice, ed. *The Open Cage: An Anzia Yezierska Collection.* New York: Persea, 1979.

Lyotard, Jean-Francois. *The Postmodern Condition: A Report on Knowledge.* Trans. Geoff Bennington and Brian Massumi. Minneapolis: U of Minnesota P, 1984.

Mascia-Lees, Frances E., Patricia Sharpe, and Colleen Ballerino Cohen. "The Postmodernist Turn in Anthropology: Cautions from a Feminist Perspective." *Signs* 15.1 (Autumn 1989): 7–33.

Mouffe, Chantal. "Radical Democracy: Modern or Postmodern." Trans. Paul Holdengraber. *Universal Abandon? The Politics of Postmodernism.* Ed. Andrew Ross. Minneapolis: U of Minnesota P, 1988.

Nicholson, Linda J., ed. *Feminism/Postmodernism.* New York: Routledge, 1990.

Saldívar, Ramón. *Chicano Narrative: The Dialectics of Difference.* Madison: U of Wisconsin P, 1990.

——. "Ideologies of the Self: Chicano Autobiography." *Diacritics* 15.3 (1985): 25–34.

Silverman, Kaja. *The Subject of Semiotics.* New York: Oxford UP, 1983.

Smith, Paul. *Discerning the Subject.* Minneapolis: U of Minnesota P, 1988.

Smith, Sidonie. *A Poetics of Women's Autobiography: Marginality and the Fictions of Self-Representation.* Bloomington: Indiana UP, 1987.

Sollors, Werner. *Beyond Ethnicity: Consent and Descent in American Culture.* New York: Oxford UP, 1986.

——, ed. *The Invention of Ethnicity.* New York: Oxford UP, 1989.

Spacks, Patricia. "Selves in Hiding." *Women's Autobiography: Essays in Criticism.* Ed. Estelle C. Jelineck. Bloomington: Indiana UP, 1980.

Stone, Albert E., ed. *The American Autobiography: A Collection of Critical Essays.* Englewood Cliffs, N.J.: Prentice, 1981.

Sundquist, Eric. *American Literature* 61.1 (1989): 120–21.

Wexler, Alice. *Emma Goldman in America.* Boston: Beacon, 1984.

——. *Emma Goldman in Exile: From the Russian Revolution to the Spanish Civil War.* Boston: Beacon, 1989.

Yezierska, Anzia. *Red Ribbon on a White Horse.* New York: Persea, 1950.

A Geography of Conversion: Dialogical
Boundaries of Self in Antin's
Promised Land

KIRSTEN WASSON

■

How long would you say, wise reader, it takes to make an American?
—*Mary Antin,* The Promised Land

In the introduction to her autobiography, Russian-born American immigrant Mary Antin writes:

> I was born, I have lived, and I have been made over. Is it not time to write my life's story? I am just as much out of the way as if I were dead, for I am absolutely other than the person whose story I have to tell. . . . I could speak in the third person and not feel that I was masquerading. . . . My life I have still to live; her life ended when mine began. (xix)

Antin's introduction to her life's story suggests that she modeled her narrative on a dominant American vision—one originated by seventeenth-century "confessors" proclaiming themselves new creatures, as a result of the transformative sea change. In this gesture of beginning again Antin mirrors the Puritan notion of a new life that overwhelms and erases the sins of an old self. Both Werner Sollors and Mary Dearborn have observed in the fiction and autobiographies of early twentieth-century Jewish-American writers a "familiar American typology of regeneration and rebirth" (Dearborn, 81). This adoption of biblical typology is not, of course, simply borrowed from the Puritans. As Sollors points out, Jews coming to America, with their connection to Israelite history, felt echoes of their ancestors' exodus and covenant with God: "the metaphor of the promised land was especially suited to Jewish immigrants" (650).[1]

Resonating with echoes of a cultural memory and with conventions of American aspiration, Antin's text tells more than one story of immigrating to the promised land. If one focuses only on the American aspiration, one might assume that her narrative tells the story of a life rejected. "Her life ended when mine began," she asserts. Indeed, *The Promised Land*'s statement of conversion is often cited in demonstrating Antin's "naivete," or "romantic" autobiographical characteristics. Most critics have read the book as a propagandistic testament to the wonders of the early twentieth-century Americanization process.[2] For example, Mary Dearborn, in an otherwise insightful discussion, makes the observation that Antin "thoroughly internalized the dominant culture's vision of the ethnic and the foreign. . . . *The Promised Land* seems to lack any alternative, protesting voice" (42). Although it is true that, as in the initial passage asserting conversion, such a voice is often unavailable, Antin's text is more complex than the monological pledge of allegiance some critics have considered it.

There is no denying that one voice in the autobiography retraces an outline of identity modeled on conversion rhetoric of American forefathers who rejected the Old World in celebrating the New. The autobiography's internalization of "the dominant culture's vision of the ethnic" is evident in Antin's borrowing from historically and literarily significant voices; she recognizes that the projection of her alien voice could threaten her legitimacy as an American.[3] Antin's outsider status as an Eastern European Jewish woman in the context of early twentieth-century nativism, eugenics, and social Darwinism virtually requires her adoption of this rhetoric; her way out of exclusion is to adopt the language of inclusion.

In *The Poetics of Women's Autobiography*, Sidonie Smith explains that "only in the fullness of membership can the fullness of rebellion unfold." For a woman writer "rebellious pursuit is potentially catastrophic; to call attention to her distinctiveness is to become 'unfeminine,'" and in Antin's case, un-American (Smith, 9). For Antin speaks from the melting pot, the prescribed location for transformation, where ideology dictates that identities of the past are dissolved and replaced by generic masks of faithfulness in America's democracy and hierarchies.[4] Aspiring to the privilege of membership, Antin pays homage to the notion of a converted identity in order to demonstrate the reverence of her candidacy, her willingness to obey the boundaries of gender and national identity.

However, Antin's "conversion" reveals an ambivalence toward adopting the word of the American fathers in order to be, in turn, adopted into the privileges of the dominant discourse. Antin voices a powerful protest against the indistinctness that androcentric traditions, rhetorical and otherwise, assign to the subjectivity of the Other. *The Promised Land* is interrupted in its telling of conversion-cum-legitimation when the auto-biographer calls attention to herself as an Eastern European Jewish woman who acquires from her past (and her re-creation of it) a sense of identity and specific forms of expression that are not easily rejected, nor easily translated into American ideals. Antin's protest is evident in two strains.

First, the descriptions of Antin's childhood in Russia focus on a community of female relatives that offers alternative interpretations of sacred male spiritual codes. The second example of a protesting voice is present in moments when Antin departs from conventions of autobiographical authorship. She drops her reverent tone and the impartiality asserted in her opening, and addresses the reader directly as "you," and accuses "you" of misreading her text and history. She points a finger at the Anglo-American reader who threatens to nullify the immigrant's past and discount as unauthentic her American present.[5] We may assume Antin's actual and implied reader is aligned with a paternal discourse of allegiance, adoption, and, ultimately, the power to erase the presence of the immigrant in the rhetoric of the melting pot.

My reading acknowledges that Antin's protest is unresolved in that her interruptions do not, finally, overwhelm the discourse of conversion with disruption nor ultimately prevent the containment of her exploration of self. Yet Antin does subvert Anglo-American expectations of the New World's promise negating and replacing the Old World's memory. In doing so, the text antagonizes the form of expression used to assert assimilation, the conversion narrative itself. In effect, the dialogue between the autobiography's "voice of allegiance" and "voice of protest" problematizes a paternalistic impulse to melt down, and thereby erase, the difference of the Other.

In addressing the linguistic tension in *The Promised Land*, I employ Bakhtinian theories of dialogic activity. Like other feminist critics, I have found Bakhtin's perspective useful for describing female strategies of resistance to dominant male discourse. Focusing on what Smith calls the "double-voiced structuring" in the text allows us to locate the subversive tension and uneasiness in Antin's response to the demands of the "sea change," the American code of transformation (51).

My discussion of the text's dialogized landscape begins with an analysis of Antin's childhood map, a geography of binary oppositions. I then read a number of scenes recounted from Antin's childhood that illustrate the creation of a sense of place and identity in sharp distinction from the American identity asserted elsewhere as her authentic self. In the third section I discuss Antin's self-reflexive interruptions of the conversion and its implied rejection of her origins, and finally I return to Antin's map of the world and examine the significance of the sea's symbolic role in this geography of conversion.

Bakhtin argues that "authoritative discourse," or "the word of the fathers," is "located in a distanced zone, organically connected with a past that is felt to be hierarchically higher" (342). As a woman moving between two cultures and their separate constructions of patriarchal memory, Mary Antin confronts more than one such nostalgic realm. Before her arrival in America, her childhood years are characterized by a keen awareness of divisions rooted in social hierarchy, a hierarchy that claims a historical right to power over the Jewish diaspora in Russia. The first half of the autobiography describes the world within the Pale, the region designated as the Jewish area of Russia where inhabitants were forced to obey czar-imposed regulations and restrictions on their cultural, religious, and economic lives. Jews were allowed to cross the borders of the Pale only with special permission or if they were drafted into the Russian army. They lived in fear of pogroms and riots that, often occurring on holy days, symbolically defiled Jewish history and identity. Antin describes her fear of physical assaults, but, interestingly, she remembers being more frightened of Gentile attempts to baptize her than other forms of harm (9).

"Within the Pale" is the title of her first chapter; it functions as an introduction to the narrative movement from captivity to exodus and promise. The chapter begins with the depiction of divisions between places and people, and the resulting geography created for Maryashe, Mary Antin's girlhood name. An early section of her narrative muses about where one town begins and another ends, where one sort of life is led and another sort is not, how far that which is familiar extends, and where the danger of being a foreign entity starts. For example, she recounts a trip to Vitebsk, a town much larger than her own Polotzk. She is surprised to discover in Vitebsk a continuation of the same river that runs through Polotsk: "It became clear to me that the Dvina [river] went on and on, like a railroad track, whereas I had always supposed that it stopped where Polotzk stopped. I had never seen the end of Polotzk. . . . But how could there be an end to Polotzk now?" (2). Antin's homeland is characterized by division; the separations between parts of the country mark the boundaries of familiarity and degrees of freedom. The river, on the other hand, connects the unknown to the familiar. For

Antin, it represents continuation, an organic process amidst foregone conclusions of the hierarchically structured landscape.

In Antin's geography Russia is the land of the authority that enforces oppression through violence and the denigration of Jewish traditions. Although this authority must be tolerated in order to survive, Maryashe's tolerance is subversive. She sees the Russian Gentiles "as a different species," reversing the normative standard by nominating the oppressors the "species" of difference. She describes the game she and her girlfriends play, which subverts the hierarchy of power. Along with such typical scenarios of "soldiers," and "house," "weddings and funerals," their games also include "playing Gentile," and "Gentile Funeral," in which Antin "plays" the corpse (106). Her mimicry of the opposite "species," in her dress-up game of Gentile death highlights an interest in role reversal as subversive performance and play. Conventional playacting becomes a moment of transfiguring identities; she and her friends temporarily become the other and denigrate the authority that, in their ordinary lives, defines their status as noncitizens. In assuming the privileged identity, she acts, however playfully, in defiance of cultural dichotomies and the marginalization of the Russian Jews.

Imitation is not always liberating, however. When it is an adult who "plays Gentile," a sin is committed against the laws of Judaism. "David the Substitute," is a man in Antin's community who commits such a sin. "For a sum of money" he temporarily adopts the identity of another man who has been drafted into the Russian army. Later he returns "aged and broken," and pays the penance for living with Gentiles and breaking Jewish law. Antin explains that "it was a sinful thing to do, to go as a soldier and be obliged to live like a Gentile, of his own free will" (15). She listens to David's voice as he performs his repentant sabbath duty:

> he forced himself to leave his bed before it was yet daylight, and go from street to street, all over Polotzk, calling on the people to wake and go to prayer. Many a Sabbath morning I awoke when David called, and lay listening to his voice as it passed and died out; and it was so sad that it hurt, as beautiful music hurts. I was glad to feel my sister lying beside me, for it was lonely in the gray dawn, with only David and me awake, and God waiting for the people's prayers. (16)

Maryashe's loneliness and "strange pain" at hearing David's voice reflect the poignancy of David's life as a "substitute" in which he is forced to imitate his own oppressors (17). At this point in her life, Antin's own instinct for imitation is precocious in its cognizance of what may be lost or gained in the adoption of another's identity, even temporarily. Thus we observe a certain resistance to the hierarchy inscribed in the borders separating Jews and Russian Catholics.

Antin's map of her early years includes another set of binary oppositions that she confronts from her position as a Jewish girl within the Pale. She is daily surrounded by the authority of the fathers of Judaism, the lawmakers and writers of the Talmud. In her second chapter, "Children of the Law," Antin explains that the Jews shielded themselves from dehumanizing national policies by maintaining their "religious integrity" through rigorous study of the Torah and "the minute observance of traditional rites" (29). Her earliest memories involve an awareness of the authority of the Talmud and the interpretation of its laws, which prescribe women's exclusive roles of wife and mother. Children in this environment are expected to feel the presence of the Talmud's laws and, by implication, the Hebraic forefathers' borders within the prescribed hierarchy of male and female realms. The morning prayer uttered by the boys includes thanking the Lord for "not having created me female" (33).

While boys her age learn Hebrew and study in the hope of becoming a Talmudic scholar, "a girl's real schoolroom was her mother's kitchen," where in Yiddish—the unscholarly and unsanctified *mama loshen* (mother tongue)—the girl is instructed in "the laws regulating a pious Jewish household and in the conduct proper for a Jewish wife" (34). Boys aspire to holiness through words and the acquisition of a language imbued with, as Bakhtin says, "a past that is felt to be hierarchically higher" (342). The tools of girls' spiritual dreams are a cook pot and the language of quotidian existence, business transactions, and gossip.

Although Antin recognizes the inequality within this picture, limitation is not the focus she presents to her audience, who expect their curiosities about the backward ways of Eastern Europe to be satisfied. Instead, her memories are filled with scenes of female spiritual strength and productivity that resist the Jewish woman's "inherited" limited subjectivity. Maryashe is nurtured by a group of women who implicitly encourage her urge to disrupt the authoritative discourse and to question the valorized past of forefathers whose words exclude women from the status of those who study the Talmud and learn Hebrew.

One of the first of a series of moments that addresses a female spiritual legacy is in the closing of "Children of the Law." We are presented with an image of Antin's mother who, significantly, has a great deal of economic power and community status in Polotsk. Hannah Hayye, manages her husband's store and has had an intensive education that included studying Hebrew, Russian, and German. Despite the secondary roles women customarily play in this world, she imparts to her daughter a sense of belonging and fluency within traditional religious history. Antin writes: "When I came to lie on my mother's breast, she sang me lullabies on lofty themes. I heard the names of Rebecca, Rachel, and Leah as early as the name of father, mother, nurse. My baby soul was enthralled by sad and noble cadences, as my mother sang of my ancient home in Palestine" (40). The mother's voice becomes an alternate source of identity wherein the maternal voice decenters and dialogizes the exclusive authority of patriarchal law. Hannah's spirituality is potent with powers of mystical meaning-making, the production of a sense of spiritual belonging.

Other descriptions of rituals similarly convey a feminine community and spiritual celebration that provides Maryashe with important elements of identity. For instance, the *mikweh*, the ritualized women's bathing, is characterized by the pleasure and sanctity of sensual experience outside the presence of men. An account of the purification ritual does not refer simply to cleansing the female body; in fact, upon returning home the women are treated by other female relatives "like heroes returned from victory . . . indulged with extra pieces of cake for tea," as they narrate anecdotes of their "expedition" (98). In Antin's memory female community takes precedence over a culturally inscribed sense of impurity associated with the *mikweh*, "the name of which it is indelicate to mention in the hearing of men" (97).

Another experience that the autobiographer's memory has an investment in is that of bathing nude in a river.

> Parties of women and girls went chattering and laughing down to the river bank. There was a particular spot that *belonged to the women*. Bathing costumes were simply absent, which caused the mermaids no embarrassment, for they were accustomed to see each other naked in the public hot baths. They had little fear of intrusion, for the spot was *sacred to them*. They splashed about and laughed and played tricks, with streaming hair and free gestures. (89; emphasis mine)

The female communal space here is sacred and sensual, despite the woman's twice-marginalized position within the Pale. As in Antin's early game of playing Gentile, forms of play, or tricks, may celebrate the very identities that are grounds for marginalization. This strategy responds to the erasure of women from sacred realms, and it recuperates female identity. Antin's party of women asserts female autonomy through physical expression; their free gesturing indicates a refuge from the male gaze and its language of desire. And it is not merely coincidental that two incidents of female expression are associated with bathing. Water figures large in Antin's map of divided spheres; water suggests a process at odds with the dominant culture's boundaries of privilege and marginalization.

Antin equates identity and expression with physical experience; this equation points to the literalness inherent in her definitions of place and belonging. In her sixth chapter, "The Tree of Knowledge," she makes explicit her direct form of interpretation: "It seems to me I do not know a single thing that I did not learn, more or less directly, through the corporeal senses. As long as I have my body, I need not despair of salvation" (136). Her salvation is the identity-building Antin does outside the law of the fathers, where she learns about the world through her senses—in the kitchen, at the *mikweh,* in the bathing pond. Within these boundaries, the knowledge of the body, expressed in the *mama loshen,* replaces the abstractions and symbols of Talmudic fathers' tools for understanding.

The oppressive dichotomies intrinsic in such androcentric structures are discussed by Margaret Homans in *Bearing the Word.* Homans explores woman's association with the literal in Western theories of language and social roles. She points to the inevitable objectifying of the female within such theories:

> Literal language together with the nature of matter to which it is epistomologically linked, is traditionally classified as feminine. . . .
> A dualism of presence and absence, of subject and object, structures everything our culture considers thinkable; yet a woman cannot participate in it as subject as easily as men because of the powerful, persuasive way in which the feminine is again and again said to be on the object side of the dyad. (4–5)

The word that women "bear" is marked by "absence." Although this absence has been conventionally figured as loss, women writers may recuperate and reinvest the word with meaning and subvert structures that contain and assign women to "the object side of the dyad." To this end Antin "embraces the connection to the literal," as Homans suggests, as a strategy to oppose androcentric metaphors of advantage and exclusion, possession and loss, and to revise the representation of the female as that which is always already absent.

Antin's descriptions of her childhood include several instances of direct defiance of androcentric codes and rituals. At one point she is gathered with other women to comply with an ordinance requiring women to weep for the fall of the temple, but instead of participating in the ritual that aligns women with a passive expression of loss, she finds herself laughing. She is observed by another lamenting woman who also giggles and finally all gathered there follow suit until "honest laughter snuffed out artificial grief" (128).

Another instance in which she defies the fathers' interpretations and their assignation of the female to a passive position occurs when she translates a passage of Genesis during a tutoring session with a *rebbe* (Hebrew instructor). Maryashe fails to show proper reverence for the dominant discourse and its past when she asks for a definition of "the beginning" and wants to know from what material God made the earth. "What sort of girl is this, that asks questions," the rebbe responds. Then she asks, "Who made God?" and the teacher leaves the room. "In his perturbation he even forgets to kiss the mezuzah on the door post" (115). Antin's questions lead the rebbe himself to forget prescribed reverence. In this revision of Eve's quest for knowledge, female curiosity and an instinct for a literal reading cause the temporary collapse of cultural codes governing sacred symbolic behavior.

In *Honey Mad Women: Emancipatory Strategies in Women's Writing* Patricia Yaeger explores the potential for a female "oral glee" that consumes and takes pleasure in language as it transgresses gendered boundaries of expression. Her theory employs a Bakhtinian perspective when she identifies "bilingual heroines" who, in their fluency in more than one language, experience a "subversive multi-voicedness" (37). Yaeger writes that "a second language can operate as a form of interruption, dispelling the power of the myth systems represented by the text's primary language" (37). In Antin's text the primary language is that of filiopiety; her life story is one governed by models of reverence for fathers whose own discourse excludes her. First the fathers of Talmud demand that she find spiritual expression only through the roles of mother and wife; then fathers of the American way demand a conversion that erases her past. To become the legitimate-voiced American Antin hopes to be, she is required to give up her strategies of transgression.

Yaeger's concept can be traced to Bakhtin's discussion of the problems experienced by an individual speaker of a foreign language. He writes: "It is not a free appropriation and assimilation of the word itself that authoritative discourse seeks to elicit from us; rather it demands our unconditional allegiance" (343). Antin's text imitates the sound of American allegiance with a good ear for the American melody; in the book's second half she reproduces New World nuances from both the revolutionary epoch and the era of literary transcendentalism. But Antin's fluency extends beyond the American voices she studies, and she does not neglect to remind her reader of her connection to an earlier tongue, a language of female community in which she was allowed to laugh and to apply literal interpretations to androcentric myths.

Antin is like one of Yaeger's bilingual heroines who "refuse to comply with critical ordinances which limit our understanding of women's relation to speech" (35–36). She uses her bilingualism to jar readers from the comfortable position of assuming they can guess her next assimilative move, that they can rest assured her past voices will be silenced in conversion. Antin's oral glee is evident in certain interruptive passages that disrupt the narrative's continuity as a before-and-after story. On these occasions the effect of recalling and explaining shifts; instead of playing the part of a confessor passively satisfying the reader's curiosity, the text aggressively addresses the audience's assumptions about the spectacle they behold. Her direct address demands recognition of the hierarchy within the geography of the confessor/confessee boundary; Antin points to the patronization inherent in the reader's interest.

Two narrative disruptions occur in middle chapters, describing periods before and after the Antin family exodus. The first disruption is inspired by the powerful memory of a literal taste of her past. Antin's glee is manifest in the invocation of Polotsk cheesecake, as the autobiographer celebrates her linguistic powers of defining an oral experience as well as an earlier self that the reader cannot possibly know.

> Do you think all your imported spices, all your scientific blending and manipulating, could produce so fragrant a morsel as that which I have on my tongue as I write? Glad am I that my mother, in her assiduous imitation of everything American, has forgotten the secrets of Polotzk cookery. At any rate, she does not practice it, and I am the richer in memories for her omissions. Polotzk cheese cake, as I now know it, has in it the flavor of daisies and clover picked on the Vall; the sweetness of Dvina water; the richness of newly turned

earth which I molded with bare feet and hands; the ripeness of red cherries bought by the dipperful in the marketplace; the fragrance of all my childhood's summers. (91)

The fragrant morsel carries the taste of her own ability to reproduce memories of a motherland where, during the baking of delicious cakes, the mother tongue imparted magical knowledge about the reproduction of her home's distinctness. That the past is recaptured on her tongue suggests Antin's faith in the body's form of knowing—reading the world through the senses, a mode of interpretation that depends on literal analysis.

Antin defines herself as a writer who uses the senses for re-creative memory that is more productive and meaningful than any recipe or scientific blending of the American aesthetic. She does not simply recount the cake-baking, she asserts it as a private taste her reader cannot share. In posing a question to her readers about their abilities to re-create a taste of her motherland, she demands that they become self-conscious of the readerly intent to erase the private value of her past. "You have nothing in your kitchen cupboard to give the pastry its notable flavor. It takes history to make such a cake" (90). Carrying her past on her tongue—an organ of speech—Antin is aware of a potential danger in making her "morsel" public; in this way, she attempts to control conversion of private material to public property. Ironically, this protest of her role as confessor is completed by her assertion that she is "an American among Americans" (93). Here Antin's desire for acceptance reappears in full force, contending with her protest.

A second interruptive passage is found in "The Promised Land," the chapter that falls in the middle of the autobiography; it is devoted to arrival in the New World. In "unravelling" the "tangle of events" that Antin says "made up the first breathless years of my American life," the autobiographer again briefly steps outside her conversion narrative to question the hierarchy of reader over writer, intrinsic in the conversion model. Describing the difficulties experienced by her father and other Jewish immigrants trying to start up a business in "the land of opportunity," she accusingly confronts the reader and the American gaze: "Dozens of these men pass under your eyes every day, my American friend, too absorbed in their honest affairs to notice the looks of suspicion which you cast at them, the repugnance with which you shrink from their touch" (182).

The passage continues, with Antin employing her strategy of direct address and questioning in order to force the reader out of the comfortable position of passive judgment.

> "The Jew Peddler!" you say, and dismiss him from your thoughts. . . . What if the creature with the untidy beard carries in his bosom his citizenship papers? What if the cross-legged tailor is supporting a boy in college who is one day going to mend your state constitution for you? What if the ragpicker's daughters are hastening over the ocean to teach your children in the public schools? Think, every time you pass the greasy alien on the street, that he was born thousands of years before the oldest native American; and he may have something to communicate to you, when you two shall have learned a common language. (182)

On one level this passage merely adheres to standard notions of American opportunity in the references to a second generation entering the work force as professionals and contributing to the nation's democratic institutions. But Antin is polemical about the rhetoric used to marginalize the first-generation immigrant who has difficulty partaking in America's abundance. In repeating the kind of slurs used against Jewish immigrants, she points to the abuse of power in the Anglo-American reading of the other. She goes further in her criticism when she reverses the hierarchy of pasts; she privileges the Jewish past instead of an American one. And her positing a common language invites the reader to imagine a form of communication that bridges difference instead of exploiting it. This language is one that the reader would have to learn, as the immigrant has had to learn the language of American opportunity.

In these interruptive passages Antin's protesting voice demands a dialogue with the rhetoric of Americanization-as-self-discovery. On the one hand Antin embraces this model in her celebration of the American education system and her intellectual growth within this institution. On the other, she is explicit in her criticism of the limitations placed on even so promising a pupil as herself, for the immigrant student suffers the frustration and pain of leading a double life. Antin's life in the promised land is not the unified forward motion a casual reading might suggest; she leads two lives in and out of the ghetto, and her narrative traverses back and forth over the line between poverty-stricken immigrant life and the world outside. At home she shares the struggle to pay for such essentials as rent and medicine for a cough that is never properly treated. At school she is a prodigy, and the author of a poem on George Washington published in the Boston *Herald* (237).

Her success provides some compensation for the family's sense of failure, but their position as tenants of the promised land is tenuous. Their apartments become increasingly more cramped, spare in furnishings, dark and dingy. In other words, their home of rebirth becomes less and less capable of renewing lives and fulfilling promises. And, significantly, the Antins' physical location during the dichotomous years of Mary's adolescence is liminal; as inhabitants of Boston, they are perched at the edge of the promised land.

This position, in which the proximity of the ocean is an obvious fact of life, allows Mary to confront its presence often and meaningfully. Antin's fascination with water's paradoxical powers of continuity and division point to the ocean's symbolic effect; water mirrors the defining of the self in that it is constantly evolving, contained and given coherence only by language that nominates it as existing within a single "body." This is important to the discussion of Antin's dialogic activity, for in writing an autobiography she creates a body of facts of her existence. In adopting the form of the conversion narrative she defines her self in terms of neat dichotomies that exist in one unified form, a body of binary oppositions—child/adult, Jew/American, dreamer of promise/inhabitant of promise. This pattern insists on America as the land of fulfillment, achievement, the definition of self.

This dangerously simplified geography maps out a symbolic order of identity that demands an individual to be all one thing or another; bounded continuity of self is a requirement. Linda Anderson writes that "it is more difficult for the [woman autobiographer] to believe in . . . a self that is unified" (60). Anderson locates the position that the woman autobiographer maintains as that of being on a "threshold":

> In writing herself the woman is also reaching into writing and her story will more obviously be informed by a dynamics of self-becoming. But there is no point of arrival; she can neither transcend herself nor attain to some authentic fullness of being. It is a dynamic which is shadowed by loss, which exists between loss, absence and what might be. As we have seen in psychoanalytic terms the woman's presence encircles an absence and her writing, too, exists at threshold, referring back in a constant process of coming into being. (60)

Such "dynamics of self-becoming" are in evidence in *The Promised Land*. Antin's identity is poised between separate horizons of potential definitions of self. Upon examining the text's involvement with sea imagery, one may say that Antin's position as a writer of her own story is, as Anderson describes it, on a threshold, a shore of arrival.

Antin narrates three significant events that paint her relationship to the sea. Her first is the literal sea change, the immigration from one shore to another. Interestingly, this event is described in a voice borrowed from her past. In fact most of the chapter entitled "The Exodus" is a compilation of passages from a long letter, originally written in Yiddish, to her uncle in the months after the family's arrival in America. The circumstances of her still having the letter involve the accidental spilling of a kerosene lamp on her writing: "I was obliged to make a fair copy for my uncle, and my father kept the oily, smelly original" (169). That her childhood letter is described with these adjectives implies an almost physical repulsion toward the expression of her younger self. Yet the fact that the chapter detailing the immigration process relies on this earlier perspective suggests a need to call upon her younger voice, to allow the original to speak.

One sensation of which this younger voice speaks is that of listening to the sea's "deep solemn groans," as "all of the voices of the world . . . turned into signs and then gathered into that one mournful sound" (179). The sound of the sea creates in her a powerful connective feeling: "And as I listened to its solemn voice, I felt as if I had found a friend, and knew that I loved the ocean. It seemed as if it were within as well as without, part of myself" (179). At this moment Maryashe experiences herself as a creature of physical, emotional, spiritual unbounded possibility; the "immeasurable distance from horizon to horizon" allows her to experience multivoiced expression. That the voice is "within as well as without, part of myself" underscores Antin's feeling of communion, which is associated here with the ocean. Because the narrator is speaking from an earlier stage of her life, before her conversion to an American childhood this communion resonates with the past, transcending the yet-to-be-fulfilled promise of the landing ahead.

Significantly, at the end of this fairly lengthy passage on the sea's power of connectiveness, Antin's mature voice returns to close the chapter with an abrupt shift in tone and message: "And so suffering, fearing, brooding, rejoicing, we crept nearer and nearer to the coveted shore, until on a glorious May morning, six weeks after our departure from Polotzk, our eyes beheld the Promised Land, and my father received us in his arms" (179). Antin is received by her father in the New World; her own role is suddenly passive, and her prose resonates with the language of Christian rebirth. The shift in Antin's voice makes explicit the re-placement of multivocality with a policy of bounded expression in the name of national unity. The crossing of the ocean represents Antin's acceptance of American boundaries around self and identity, for in turn-ing her back on the shores behind, she looks to the horizon of the New World. Yet this sea change is more than merely conversion. Maryashe's experience on the ocean privileges personal definitions of self and voice, and reminds her of internal resources, developed in the motherland, that empower her and provide her with understanding of, and faith in, her history.

A second moment in which Antin discusses her relationship to the symbol of her "crossing" occurs in the next chapter, "The Promised Land." Her father's first job includes working on the beach as a vendor, and so it is at the beach that the family spend much of their time. This time Antin approaches the ocean from the shore of the New World, and she is swimming instead of immigrating. She and a boy are caught in an undertow and are terrified to discover themselves suddenly struggling against the tide, far from the land. The experience is narrated in third person. As when she ambivalently employs her "smelly, oily" original letter in telling her story, Antin distances herself from her subject's vulnerability at the same time that she draws attention to the poignancy and drama of her experience: "Boy and girl turned without a word, four determined bare legs ploughing through the water, four scared eyes straining toward the land. Through an eternity of toil and fear they kept dumbly on, death at their heels, pride still in their hearts" (192). Once safe on shore the boy and girl have an exchange that demonstrates the vulnerable position of the female immigrant. The boy accuses her of being afraid and the girl replies that she, unlike he, does not know how to "schwimmen." The boy mimics her accent, responding that certainly he can "schwimmen." " 'An I can walk on my hands,' the tormentor calls after her. 'Say, you greenhorn, why don'tcher look?' " (193). The two children survive the sea's hidden powers together, but the boy translates the experience into an occasion for mockery and a demonstration of his prowess. Typically a symbolic location of transformation and death, the sea is, in male eyes, the ultimate conquest; to test the weight of his own bravery, the boy asserts the fear of his female companion.

During her crossing Antin identified the ocean as a place where one could hear "all the voices of the world." The anecdote about her con-frontation with one of America's native sons points to androcentric re-jection of multivocality; the sea is to be conquered and the immigrant girl's dialect to be mocked. This is how the narrator concludes the exchange: "The girl keeps straight on, vowing that she would never walk with that rude boy again, neither by land nor sea, not even though the waters should part at his bidding" (193). In ironically suggesting a connection between the boy and Moses, she mocks the boy's self-imposed authority and his tendency to figure the sea symbolically in terms of quests, power struggles, and mastery over the other.

In the last scene of the autobiography Antin makes most clear the geographical position she locates as her own in the narrative's topography of land, water, shore. After a number of chapters that outline Antin's hardships and joys as a student of American culture, the text's arrival at "The Burning Bush" announces what Antin calls the "second transformation of my life" (321). From the recounting of her first day of school to telling the story of being lauded, during her eighth-grade graduation ceremony, by a member of the school board as a paragon of American assimilation, Antin presents herself as an ever-curious, successful pupil, appreciated by her instructors. Her discovery of Hale House and its natural history club is the catalyst for the transformation of identity as a student of American culture to a student of the earth itself.[6] If her mind "stretches to embrace" the "idea of a great country when [she] exchanged Polotszk for America," it was "no such enlargement as [she] now experienced" (330). This enlargement seems to emphasize her place in the world as a creature of the earth rather than a citizen of any culturally defined region. Although the last three chapters contain many statements that glorify her second home ("the open workshop of America," is one example of her tribute to the melting pot [358]), her conclusion is far from a unified tribute to the nation and its provisions for the immigrant.

Antin's final self-portrait places her at the threshold of one of her favorite American institutions, the Boston Public Library, which she earlier characterizes in this way: "with a dignified granite front it was, flanked on all sides by noble old churches, museums, and school houses" (340). Clearly representative of the New World's argument for the dignity of institutionalized opportunity, this picture is a projection of Antin's voice of allegiance. At the same time however, Antin paints more than the homage this voice suggests. The book's final image depicts her on the granite bench in front of the library after a day's outing with the natural history club at the seashore. She holds a jar of seawater; her hair is damp with seaspray and the "roar of the tide" is still in her ears (363).

Antin stands on the land where promises of rebirth and conversion are fulfilled, but she carries along with her the sea and its connection to an earlier self and multivocality. Her rebirth is depicted as potentially an organic process occurring inside herself, rather than a charitable gift given to her (strings attached) from an adoptive father. She asks a question about her existence in this closing scene, and provides an answer that has little to do with national codes of self and success: "How shall I number the days of my life, except by the stars of the night, except by the salt drops of the sea?" (364). Taking on overtones of the prophets of the Hebrew Bible, the language points to a reading of experience in terms of the natural world, the concrete, visible world. The processes of a lifetime are perceived in terms of changes and continuities in the physical environment rather than culturally inscribed measurements of identity.

The image of the transportable seawater suggests defiance of authoritative discourse that defines lives in or out of bounds; her attachment to the shore, her effort to take the border with her—almost into the library—problematizes our reading of this life of assimilation. As when she remembers the taste of her mother's cake, Antin breaks a code of conversion in taking the sea with her—a gesture of recuperation—in her tale of beginning again. While she will surely enter the library before long, if not this day then the next, she does not, as one might expect, situate herself at the text's close in a position of heralding American institutions of learning from inside one. She is, instead, outside, but not looking in. She is busy valuing her identity as a creature of the world, aligned with the sea, amphibious in her tendency to cross borders as a way of life.

Antin concludes, perhaps necessarily for her reader's expectations, by nominating herself "the youngest of America's children." She has made herself over and deserves to belong here she assures those standing by the melting pot, waiting to see what will emerge. One cannot but be struck by the paradox of her simultaneous defiance of and desire for adoption. On one level, Antin has certainly been reborn. She has given birth to herself as a writer, the writer of a reproduction of her life. But the text threatens to contain her in its reproductive activity. For the immigrant's autobiography of conversion must pledge allegiance to early twentieth-century attitudes on immigration that define American traditions as hierarchically higher than others.

Just as the jar of seawater represents the containment of a number of forms of sea life, embodying, as it were, the ocean's multivocality, the text is a metaphor for the containment of Antin's identity. The jar's containment of the sea suggests the incompleteness of autobiography as self-definition. Dividing the ocean into separate pieces, the jar dissects the whole body of water. Antin's piece of sea is without one of its essential aspects, the movement that allows it to "speak" the "deep solemn groans" so meaningful to Antin. The attempt to conclude on an integration of past and future cannot be completely successful, for the boundaries of the textual contract require Antin's voice of allegiance to conclude the autobiography, potentially drowning out her voice of protest.

The tension between these two voices is evident even in Antin's introduction, to which I return by way of concluding. I began by observing that the introduction speaks beseechingly of conversion, of the desire to belong to America's family tree. Antin writes that she "long[s] to forget," and that "a long past vividly remembered is like a heavy garment that clings to your limbs when you would run" (xxii). Antin's ambivalence toward her past is distinctly articulated. But even in her opening statement she admits her past is not so easily discarded. She feels herself to be "consciously of two worlds" (xxii). The processes of "uprooting, transportation, replanting, acclimatization, and development," as she less than romantically lists them in the introduction, do not seem to have so effectively worked their magic that struggle is eliminated from her sense of identity. She longs to "shut the book" on her past, yet in so many ways the book—her autobiography—highlights her early years as a period of growth and understanding (xxii).

Those early years are lessons in surviving in the world as a Jewish woman. Given her gender and ethnicity it is unlikely that survival will ever be simple for her; even in this "new" world she cannot afford to forget those lessons in transgression, subversion, and the empowerment of female community. The inconsistencies in her approach to her past and her story reflect the paradox intrinsic to the "object" her conversion narrative attempts to gratefully create: the seamless Americanized immigrant, a species as vital as adopted seawater in a jar.

Mary Antin's autobiographical map focuses on a life that winds its way around inclusion and exclusion, never arriving at a location where it may accurately reflect itself. Like the river Dvina, the text's self-discovery is both continuous process and disunity. In his chapter of biography on Mary Antin, Sam Bass Warner, Jr., tells us that Antin had a five-year stint on the lecture circuit as a result of the dramatic success of her autobiography. But after those five years, the "instant celebrity" suffered a nervous breakdown, "no longer willing to accept Mary Antin the performer as her authentic self" (31). Antin wrote of this experience: "I was a success. But applause and fat fees and return engagements were unconvincing in the absence of a sense of vocation. I got out of the business as soon as I could, by the back door of a nervous breakdown, but glad of any exit from what I considered a false position. I felt I had not earned the authority the public allowed me" (Warner 31). This self-reflection, written several decades after the publication of *The Promised Land*, reveals a lifelong hunger for the acquisition of a voice unified by authority and authenticity. Antin's theme must continue to be examined in terms of a dialogical performance of the search for identity, the auto-biography's address to its audience, and most important, its "speaking engagement" with itself.

Notes

1   For the approximately 2.5 million Jews emigrating from Czarist Russia between 1882 and 1924, there was hope that God's promise to Abraham could be fulfilled in their turn-of-the-century passage to America. Irving Howe explains that "the masses of [Eastern European] Jews, those both a little Orthodox and a little agnostic, acted out of a deep common impulse: America was different from all other countries, America meant . . . the sons could find a path such as Jews had never before been able to discover" (253). According to Richard Tuerk, in embracing the American promise of a home governed on the principle of equal rights, Mary Antin employs the story of the Exodus from Egypt "explicitly" (30). This modeling is evident in the titles of chapters and the form of the narration, which is centered around a structure of captivity and freedom.

2   Richard Tuerk refers to "the naivete of the acceptance of the child protagonist as well as the adult narrator of the view that America is the Promised Land" (33). Evelyn Avery calls *The Promised Land* a "romantic immigrant view of America" (53). Allen Guttmann chides the book's "considerable underestimation of the difficulties faced by less gifted immigrants" (28), and Sarah Blacher Cohen reprimands Antin for her "eagerness to become assimilated" (34). Steven Rubin, however, provides an alternative reading; he concludes that the narrator has not "truly abandoned her religious and cultural past without a trace of remorse" (41). He points out that "instead of affirming Mary Antin's eagerness to forsake the values and manners of the old world, the tone, style, and specific language of much of the book—especially that which describes her former life—reveal an uncertain relationship between the author's present identity and her past self" (41).

3   At the turn of the century in the United States, the connotations of Jewish identity were such that Antin and other Jewish immigrants had to confront a stereotype of the single-mindedly manipulative intruder. In *Becoming American* Thomas J. Archdeacon demonstrates the pervasiveness of the problem: "In the more credulous backwaters of the nation, men and women associated Jews with the faraway cities and half-understood market systems that kept them on the margin of economic ruin. The Jews, whom they rarely met and whom they never saw in the sweatshops

and slums, became international financiers, producing nothing themselves but capable of manipulating the world's economy for their own ends. Even sophisticated conservatives of refined social backgrounds were wont to exploit the Jews' supposedly complete involvement in the pursuit of money as an explanation for the apparent victory of crass materialism in late Victorian society. More portentous, the detractors of the Jews spread in the United States poisonous lore of the Hebrews' heathenism and their supported enmity, even to the point of blood-letting, toward Christians" (158–59). As the context in which Antin's story is written, the popularity of such anti-Semitism makes a nonthreatening profile the highest priority for the immigrant autobiographer attempting to "inoffensively" model herself after her audience's image.

4   Archdeacon demonstrates that the position allotted to the American Jew within these hierarchies was prescribed by the contemporary anthropological theories of race. He writes that "according to popular understanding, at the apex of the white race were the Nordics, or Teutons, who represented the highest grades of intelligence, initiative, and leadership among humans; in the middle were the Alpines, who were described as the prototypical peasants; and at the bottom were the Mediterraneans, along with the Jews, who constituted something of a Hybrid race" (161–62).

5   Quite possibly one such reader was Barrett Wendell, one of the men of letters who served as a mentor during her education in "the American way." Wendell's attitude toward Antin's identity is clear in a letter: "[Antin] has developed an irritating habit of describing herself and her people as Americans, in distinction from such folks as Edith and me, who have been here for three hundred years" (282). That Antin's desire to nominate herself American is threatening to Wendell is underscored by his use of the term for "authentic" Americans—"folks," a word he says is "old Yankee English," as opposed to Antin's "people," a term that implies they are "the other" to Wendell (282). [Mary Dearborn deserves the credit for discovering this letter of Wendell's; she quotes it in *Pocahontas's Daughters* (222).]

6   Antin's relationship to her discoveries in the Hale House natural history club seem complicated by her idealization of the club's founder, Edward Everett Hale, "The Grand Old Man of Boston," (344,). It is troubling that her caption under a picture of his office reads "The Famous Study, That Was Fit To Have Been Preserved As A Shrine," and that Hale's wife reminds her of Martha Washington (348). It is also troubling that Hale's daughter, a painter, offers Antin money to pose as a model, a gesture that Antin herself suggests is a form of charity. A patronizing impulse is present in this old American family's attitude toward her; this makes Antin's connection to the Hale House fit the mold of a "typical" relationship between an "authentic" American and a grateful immigrant. Nevertheless, it is interesting that Hale is reported as asking her "a great many questions about Russia, in a manner that made me feel I was an authority on the subject" (345). That this very authentic (surely Barrett Wendell would agree) Yankee values Antin's Old World experience suggests that her attachment to him is motivated by more than a simple, slavish

devotion to his embodiment of American identity. Hale grants Antin a degree of authority, not the kind she has to earn, but one into which she was born.

References

Anderson, Linda. "At the Threshold of the Self: Women and Autobiography." *Women's Writing: A Challenge to Theory.* Ed. Moira Monteith. New York: St. Martin's, 1986.

Antin, Mary. *The Promised Land.* Princeton: Princeton UP, 1985.

Archdeacon, Thomas J. *Becoming American: An Ethnic History.* New York: Free Press–Macmillan, 1983.

Avery, Evelyn. "Oh My Mishpocha: Some Jewish Women Writers from Antin to Kaplan View the Family." *Studies in American Jewish Literature* 5 (1986): 44–53.

Bakhtin, Mikhail. "Discourse in the Novel." *The Dialogic Imagination: Four Essays.* Trans. Caryl Emerson and Michael Holquist. Ed. Michael Holquist. Austin: U of Texas P, 1981.

Cohen, Sarah Blacher. "Mary Antin's *The Promised Land:* A Breach of Promise." *Studies in American Jewish Literature* 3 (Fall 1977): 28–35.

Dearborn, Mary. *Pocahontas's Daughters: Gender and Ethnicity in American Culture.* New York: Oxford UP, 1986.

Guttmann, Allen. *The Jewish Writer in America: Assimilation and the Crisis of Identity.* New York: Oxford UP, 1971.

Homans, Margaret. *Bearing the Word: Representation, Reproduction, and Women's Place in Language.* Chicago: U of Chicago P, 1986.

Howe, Irving. *World of Our Fathers.* New York: Harcourt, 1976.

Rubin, Steven J. "Style and Meaning in Mary Antin's *The Promised Land:* A Reevaluation." *Studies in American Jewish Literature* 5 (1986): 35–43.

Smith, Sidonie. *A Poetics of Women's Autobiography: Marginality and the Fictions of Self-Representation.* Bloomington: Indiana UP, 1987.

Sollors, Werner. "Literature and Ethnicity." *Harvard Encyclopedia of American Ethnic Groups.* Cambridge: Harvard UP, 1980. 647–65.

Tuerk, Richard. "The Youngest of America's Children in Mary Antin's *The Promised Land.*" *Studies in American Jewish Literature* 5 (1986): 29–34.

Warner, Sam Bass, Jr. *Province of Reason.* Cambridge: Belknap–Harvard UP, 1984.

Wendell, Barrett. *Barrett Wendell and His Letters.* Ed. M. A. DeWolfe Howe. Boston: Atlantic Monthly, 1928.

Yaeger, Patricia. *Honey-Mad Women: Emancipatory Strategies in Women's Writing.* New York: Columbia UP, 1988.

PART IV

"I am truly becoming a specter"

Posing: Autobiography and the

Subject of Photography

PAUL JAY

∎

When we think of autobiography, we usually think of a narrative, or story, that recounts events or experiences in the life of the writer. Such narratives may be fictionalized, they may be poems, or ostensibly straightforward and honest accounts of a life. In whatever form, they depend heavily on the memory of experiences that have occurred sequentially in time (though these experiences may be represented in the text in nonchronological, or even fragmented, ways). Whatever concept writers have of their identity, or self, it is usually tied in an intimate way to those events, to the shaping impact they seem to have had. We assume, in short, that the subject of an autobiography is the product of moment upon moment, experience upon experience.

My aim is not to question the defining role that what I call "historical memory" has in autobiographical writing. What I want to do is examine the important, though sometimes overlooked, role of "visual memory" both in autobiographical writing and in the conceptions of self-identity it embodies.[1] I want to do this by focusing in particular on the photograph—both the photograph as a subject *in* autobiography, and the subject as he or she comes to be defined *by* a photograph reproduced (or alluded to) in an autobiography. These two topics are, of course, intimately related, as specific photographs are often used in autobiography precisely because they have come to represent forces that have helped define the identity of the writer. But beyond this, a creative, constitutive relationship exists between image and identity in autobiographical writing. Visual memory, the "reading" of images from the past—be they fixed in a photograph or fluid in the mind's eye—can often be integral to the construction of identity in autobiographical works.

I discuss three very different texts, related only in their various preoccupations with images and photographs: Roland Barthes's *La Chambre Clair* (Camera Lucida), Marguerite Duras's *L'amant* (The Lover), and

N. Scott Momaday's *The Names: A Memoir*. In addition, I touch briefly on the work of the photographer Cindy Sherman. Barthes's book and Sherman's photographs can be construed as "autobiographical" in only the loosest sense of the word. However, I'm less interested in making a case for their being autobiographies than I am in examining what they have to say about the relationship between the cultural production of images and the conceptions of identity, subjectivity, and self-representation. What they have to say, I maintain, bears directly on the theoretical question of who is speaking in an autobiography.

Duras's and Momaday's books—as memoirs—fit more comfortably our conventional conceptions of what constitutes an autobiographical text. The authors share with Barthes and Sherman, however, a fascination with the image and its relationship to concepts of identity and subjectivity. Duras's fictionalized memoir of two years of her youth in Indochina doesn't contain a single photograph (with the important exception of the portrait on the cover), but it is literally fixated on a specific image she describes as a "photograph [that] might have been taken" (10). This fixation unfolds in a series of readings of that image—readings that structure her text because the image has come to structure her self-identity. Momaday's *Memoir*, on the other hand, which is about his ancestry as well as his own childhood and adolescence, contains twenty-five portraits of members of his family (four of Momaday himself as a child), each with a handwritten comment by the author. In this text, so preoccupied with *naming*, images have an important role as well. There are no discussions of photographs in Momaday's book, but there are a number of suggestive meditations on the relationship between visual memory and identity that I examine. Like Duras, he is concerned less with the relationship between subjectivity and posing than with the act of reading images, the act of interpreting visual memories in a way that becomes integral to the very construction of identity.

Early in his analysis of the "central features" of photography Barthes tells us that because he is unable to write from the point of view of a photographer he will make himself "the measure of photographic knowledge": "I decided to take myself as mediator for all Photography. Starting from a few personal impulses, I would try to formulate the fundamental feature, the universal without which there would be no Photography" (8–9). This shift leads Barthes to conflate cultural analysis with autobiographical inquiry, for these "personal impulses" lead to an increasing preoccupation with the significance of a photograph of his recently deceased mother. Making himself the mediator of his work leads more immediately, however, to a rich and somewhat paradoxical meditation on posing for his own portrait. Making himself the measure of photographic knowledge in this way, Barthes enters into a series of observations about the relationship between posing, the photographic image, and self-identity.

No doubt it is metaphorically that I derive my existence from the photographer. But though this dependence is an imaginary one . . . I experience it with the anguish of an uncertain filiation: an image— my image—will be generated. . . . If only I could "come out" on paper as on a classical canvas, endowed with a noble expression— thoughtful, intelligent, etc.! . . . But since what I want to have captured is a delicate moral texture and not a mimicry, and since Photography is anything but subtle except in the hands of the very greatest portraitists, I don't know how to work upon my skin from within. I decide to "let drift" over my lips and in my eyes a faint smile which I mean to be "indefinable," in which I might suggest, along with the qualities of my nature, my amused consciousness of the whole photographic ritual: I lend myself to the social game, I pose, I know I am posing, I want you to know that I am posing, but (to square the circle) this additional message must in no way alter the precious essence of my individuality: what I am, apart from any effigy. What I want, in short, is that my (mobile) image, buffeted among a thousand shifting photographs, altering with situation and age, should always coincide with my (profound) "self"; but it is the contrary that must be said: "myself" never coincides with my image; for it is the image which is heavy, motionless, stubborn (which is why society sustains it), and "myself" which is light, divided, dispersed. . . . Alas, I am doomed by (well-meaning) Photography always to have an expression: my body never finds its zero degree. . . .

In front of the lens, I am at the same time: the one I think I am, the one I want others to think I am, the one the photographer thinks I am, and the one he makes use of to exhibit his art. In other words, a strange action: I do not stop imitating myself, and because of this, each time I am (or let myself be) photographed, I invariably suffer from a sensation of inauthenticity, sometimes of imposture . . . the Photograph represents the very subtle moment when, to tell the truth, I am neither subject nor object but a subject who feels he is becoming an object: I then experience a micro-version of death. . . . I am truly becoming a specter. (11–14)

In this passage Barthes draws our attention to how posing is a form of self-representation, and I suggest that it is therefore linked to the question of self-representation in autobiography. Indeed, the whole passage reads as a kind of miniature allegory of the autobiographical act.[2] For Barthes, posing embodies an existential drama of nearly operatic proportions. It constitutes a form of self-representation at once conscious and unconscious, fraught with anguish, uncertainty, suffering, and doom. Posing involves a dramatic struggle for control and authenticity, a struggle between intentionality and convention, the essential and the objectified. Posing, for Barthes, is a site, or theater, of self-creation in which the subject desires to project something delicate and moral, to literally work upon the "skin from within," to "let drift," to "mean" and be his profound, essential self. But it is also a theater of conventions and rituals working to appropriate that self for its own ends. Thus the central and impossible need: "I lend myself to the social game, I pose, I know I am posing, I want you to know that I am posing, but . . . this . . . must in no way alter the precious essence of my individuality: what I am, apart from any effigy." The inevitable tension between self and effigy is linked to the subject's desire to find in its photographed body a "zero degree" of selfhood, a pure rendering of the absolutely "me." On the one hand, there is the pressing of this desire for authentic self-expression, on the other, the appropriating desire of the photographer, the ritual of posing, the camera. The result, the source of the subject's anguish and suffering, is a dispersed self: "In front of the lens" he is at once "the one I think I am, the one I want others to think I am, the one the photographer thinks I am, and the one he makes use of to exhibit his art."

The specter raised at the end of this passage is a twin one: "inauthenticity" and "objectification." The very assumption that there even exists a "profound self" separable from "mobile images," a "precious essence of . . . individuality" existing "apart from any effigy," is put in question, for the self seems never to coincide with its image. Barthes's treatment of posing is really about the impossibility of not posing. It questions the very concept of authenticity and turns it into a kind of simulacrum in which the subject cannot stop "imitating" himself. "All I look *like*," Barthes writes later, "is other photographs of myself, and this to infinity: no one is ever anything but the copy of a copy" (102). But worse than the specter of inauthenticity is the specter of objectification, the fear that the always-inauthentic image does in fact constitute the objectified self. The problem Barthes's remarks on posing reveals is that the so-called profound or essential self can never be represented as such. Indeed the very nature of this essential self becomes paradoxical: its subjectivity is linked to a notion of authenticity, yet any image of that self is a sign of its objectification, and hence, its inauthenticity. The authentic self, in Barthes's terms, is finally an impossibility, for it would be a self freed from the process of becoming an object.

The experience of becoming an object is "a micro-version of death," then, not in any literal sense. It is the specter of the death of the subject as a concept comprehended by phrases like "profound self" and "precious essence of my individuality." The suffering and anguish here are linked specifically to the possibility that authenticity—defined as the self's freedom from being constituted as an object—is illusory. If there is a sense of horror here, it is horror at the concept of self, or identity, stripped of its illusory foundations in some immaterial essence or spirit, and of its autonomy as "subject" in the grammatical sense of the word— that which acts as opposed to that which is acted upon.

The specific death of the subject Barthes glimpses here is dramatized in the work of the photographer Cindy Sherman. Her self portraits—or self-dramatizations—taken over a ten-year period and gathered together for a retrospective at the Whitney Museum of Art in 1987, explicitly question the Barthesian desire for an essential or authentic subjectivity free from the process of objectification. Sherman's work, like Barthes's essay, is about posing, about the relationship between poses, images, and identity. However, it explicitly questions the concept of authenticity Barthes's remarks only worry over, and it does so by playing out a kind of drama in which the clean lines between the posed and the authentic, the object and the subject, culture and self—those Barthes longs to keep somehow intact—are deconstructed.[3]

Figures 1 through 3 are representative of the photographs Sherman presents in the first part of her series. Usually based on the imagery of movie stills and fashion shots (figure 1), and dramatizing popular images of cool eroticism (figure 2) or stereotypical situations filtered through male fantasies of female desire (figure 3), they present the viewer with Sherman posed in a repetoire of images familiar from popular culture. Each pose confronts the viewer with banal forms of subjectivity utterly familiar from a mass culture in which not only dress and gesture but personality itself is constructed out of a social nexus of commodified images and ideal types. There is, of course, something grotesque about these images, and in the second part of her series the self-portraits turn decidedly macabre (figure 4). In the first series the underlying sense that her subjects are dominated by subtle and not-so-subtle forms of social and cultural discipline—which erases any trace of "individual" subjectivity—surfaces in the second series in an explicit way as Sherman poses herself as women who seem profoundly disturbed, disoriented, and defeated. In the final series, the image of the individual or coherent subject is literally exploded in a series of images (figure 5) in which body parts are strewn like detritus across a microcosmic wasteland. The self starts out

Figures 1 and 2 Cindy Sherman, Untitled, #74, 1980, and Untitled #113, 1982. Courtesy of Metro Pictures, New York

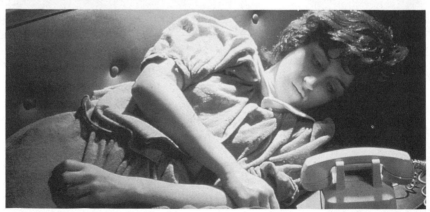

Figures 3 and 4   Cindy Sherman, Untitled, #90, 1981, and Untitled #137, 1984.
Courtesy of Metro Pictures, New York

in these photographs as a wholly commodified object, descends into
images that bespeak the eventual horror such a situation can lead to, and
finally explodes the individual amidst a pile of rubble.

The narrative these photographs evoke ends with the subject's emergence as a grotesque version of the Barthesian specter, a microversion of
death in which identity is submitted first to the process of objectification, then to dispersal, and finally to obliteration—a last gesture that
seems to renounce once and for all the authenticity of Barthes's profound
self and Sherman's own project of recording the course of its demise. Are
these self-portraits? Or are they dramatic enactments that reproduce
cultural types? It is the point of Sherman's project to make the answer to
these questions irrelevant, for her work suggests that the so-called self-
portrait may always be in part the portrait of a cultural type, the image of
a subject whose identity has been objectified by social forces. What
Barthes calls the profound self is collapsed in these photographs into the
mobile image—the two become indistinguishable. Identity here is indeed caught in a kind of simulacrum, so that Barthes's lament that no
one in a photograph "is ever anything but the copy of a copy" becomes a
kind of gloss on the point of Sherman's project.

Figure 5   Cindy Sherman, Untitled #167, 1986. Courtesy of Metro Pictures, New York

Sherman's work is clearly meant to dramatize the way in which identity is caught up in the process of objectification that Barthes writes about (and laments). As the critic Peter Schjeldahl writes about Sherman's work, it "leads out into semiotic mazes of the popular culture and simultaneously inward, to confused and confusing recesses of the self," so that her images seem to "spark across the gap . . . between self and culture" (7). I would go even further and insist that in her work the "recesses of the self" are treated as a semiotic maze. Barthes's fear that posing captures an essential kind of inauthenticity is mirrored in Sherman's ability to represent the self as a subject of and in that maze. However, her self-portraits work to collapse the very distinction between outer and inner, between pop culture and authentic subjectivity. They replace the viewer's need to recognize likeness with the necessity of deciphering semiotic codes. The steady demise toward the grotesque in her work also seems to virtually enact the horror and anguish Barthes experiences as he comes face-to-face with the specter of objectification and inauthenticity. However, the emergence of the grotesque and the inexorable slide toward dispersal and obliteration that Sherman's photographs recount seem less a Barthesian lament than the double gesture of renunciation I referred to above: both an affirmation of the subject's inescapable nature as an object and the achievement of a kind of narrative closure for her inquiry.

Though they respond differently to the fact of objectification they investigate, both Barthes and Sherman force us to turn our attention to its processes, to focus on the production and reproduction of images churned out by a complex cultural machinery that continually mediates what we like to call personal identity. Indeed their work insists on our seeing how the very concept of identity has been in part determined by that machinery. The critic Lisa Philips has written of Sherman that her photographs "project a . . . mixture of desire, anticipation, victimization, and suffering," and as a photographer she "deflects the gaze of" the viewer away from her subject and "toward reproduction itself, forcing the viewers to recognize their own conditioning" (15). Both Barthes and Sherman in their treatment of the subject of identity (and the identity of the subject) share this fascination with conditioning and reproduction, with charting, in their own way, how the images and gestures that have come to constitute the semiotic maze of popular culture reproduce themselves in the pose of the subject, whose authenticity is in turn conditioned by that maze. While Barthes's desire is to defend his essential self from this conditioning, Sherman dramatizes its inevitability.

I am not, of course, trying to make the case that Sherman's photographs actually constitute autobiography, although they can, no doubt, be construed as recording her "life," even her experience and her likeness. What I am claiming, however, is that her portraits examine the cultural conditions in which identity is fashioned, and as selected and shown by Sherman they are given the shape of a narrative about that investigation. Seen from this perspective, her self-portraits take the shape of something like an autobiographical metanarrative about the course of one artist's investigation of subjectivity, scrutinizing the very concepts of identity and subjectivity in a way that turns that act into a memoir of itself.

Marguerite Duras's *Lover* shares with Cindy Sherman's work a fascination with image, specifically, a fascination with the relationship between image and identity. Like the collection of images in Sherman's project, the image that fascinates Duras is a kind of composite that, to recall Lisa Phillips's observation, "project[s] a mixture of desire, anticipation, victimization, and suffering" and that forces the attention of the reader on the processes that condition and lead to the reproduction of that image. The image I have in mind here is that of a fifteen-and-a-half-year-old

Figure 6 Cover, *The Lover*

Duras crossing the Mekong River on a ferryboat on the day she meets her Chinese lover. Both her sense of self-identity and the narrative she recounts about the formation of that identity are evoked in repeated and extended attempts to fix and understand that image from her past, which expands and shifts as she returns again and again to read its significance.

Two images confront us before we encounter the description of the Mekong river crossing. The first is the photograph of Duras in her youth reproduced on the cover (figure 6); the second is the opening description of her aged, "ravaged" face (in a sense, the book will be written to explain the change registered by this juxtaposition of faces, as if the ravaged face had its origin in the ravishment *The Lover* recounts). "One day," the book begins, "I was already old, in the entrance of a public place, a man came up to me. He introduced himself and said, 'I've known you for years. Everyone says you were beautiful when you were young, but I want to tell you I think you're more beautiful now than then. Rather than your face as a young woman, I prefer your face as it is now. Ravaged'" (3). Duras immediately juxtaposes this image with the one on the cover of the book—her teenage face—an image that will quickly merge with that of her crossing the Mekong River. Of that image she writes "I often think of the image only I can see now, and of which I've never spoken.

It's always there, in the same silence, amazing. It's the only image of myself I like, the only one in which I recognize myself" (3–4).

The image unfolds before the reader in fits and starts, simply at first, then with increasing complexity and force until the entire narrative evolves out of her attempts to fill in and read it. First: "So, I'm fifteen and a half. It's on a ferry crossing the Mekong River. The image lasts all the way across" (5). Then, later: "On the ferry, look, I've still got my hair. Fifteen and a half. I'm using make-up already. I use Creme Tokalon, and try to camouflage the freckles on my cheeks, under the eyes. On top of the Creme Tokalon I put natural-color powder-Houbigant. The powder is my mother's, she wears it to go to government receptions. That day I've got lipstick on too, dark red, cherry, as the fashion was then" (16). And still later: "Fifteen and a half. The body is thin, undersized almost, childish breasts still, red and pale-pink make-up. And the clothes, the clothes that might make people laugh, but don't. I can see it's all there. All there, but nothing yet done. I can see it in the eyes, all there already in the eyes. I want to write. I've already told my mother: That's what I want to do—write" (20–21).

This last image, with its emphasis on the eyes, recalls the portrait of Duras reproduced on the cover of *The Lover*. Indeed its identity unfolds in the book in a series of retrospective readings of its formation. The face on the cover foretells the aged, ravaged one ("now I see that when I was very young . . . fifteen, I already had a face that foretold the one I acquired through drink in middle age" [8–9]). Reading the image here is a process of recognizing the prophecy of a later identity in the face of her youth or, as she puts it, seeing how "the space" for writing, desire and pleasure existed in her then: "I had the face of pleasure, and yet I had no knowledge of pleasure. There was no mistaking that face. . . . That was how everything started for me—with that flagrant, exhausted face, those rings around the eyes, in advance of time and experience" (9).

These passages, linked as they are with the photograph on the book's cover, underscore how reading her visual memory becomes integral to the formation of her identity as she writes. Both the subject in her book and her own subjectivity seem embodied in this image. "It's all there" before anything has been done, and what is required of her now in the autobiographical act is to retrospectively read the significance of this visual memory, to read into this image a meaning and an identity. This is why the recognition that her identity is "all there" in the image is linked to her desire to be a writer, for she has come to recognize the explicit link between language, writing, and subjectivity.

Duras orients her book around an image because what that image evokes can say more about her life than any conventional autobiographical narrative might. Near the beginning of her book she insists that "the story of my life doesn't exist. Does not exist. There's never any center to it. No path, no line" (8). What's being set aside here is the story as narrative progression, as a path or line that leads to a center. The way in is through the image, or rather the story evolves out of the image that is its center. Event and identity unfold in a fragmented, nonchronological way as evocations born of an image, residing in a face, the result of a "crossing."

This image of herself has become detached from all the other images she has of herself:

> I think it was during this journey that the image became detached, removed from all the rest. It might have existed, a photograph might have been taken, just like any other, somewhere else, in other circumstances. But it wasn't. . . . The photograph could only have been taken if someone could have known in advance how important it was to be in my life, that event, that crossing of the river. But while it was happening, no one even knew of its existence. Except God. And that's why—it couldn't have been otherwise—the image doesn't exist. It was omitted. Forgotten. It never was detached or removed from all the rest. And it's to this, this failure to have been created, that the image owes its virtue: the virtue of representing, of being the creator of, an absolute. (10)

Here, paradoxically, the "photograph" exists as an immaterial thing, created retrospectively in the subject's reading of an image. This crossing in Duras's life could not have been recorded when it happened because no one could know how important it would be. For Duras, the photograph not taken exists in her unconscious, and part of the autobiographical act involves tracking her identity through a reading of its significance. Self-representation here becomes a form of self-analysis, which turns on the retrospectively constructed meaning of an image. This process is in fact not unlike what happens in psychoanalysis, especially in terms of the way Lacan has characterized it: "What we teach the subject to recognize as his unconscious is his history—that is to say, we help him to perfect the contemporary historization of the facts which have already determined a certain number of the historical 'turning points' in his existence" (23). *The Lover* is a contemporary historization of such facts, but particularly the contemporary reading of an image in Duras's visual memory, the image of a literal crossing that subsequently became a turning point in her life. In her book, autobiography is literally a function of this visual memory; narrative unfolds as the reading of an image, and the text stands in for a photograph that was never taken.

Duras's preoccupation with visual memory, her privileging of image over narrative is mirrored in Momaday's *The Names: A Memoir*. In the following passage he writes about how images have for him an importance transcending that of "moments or events":

> Memory begins to qualify the imagination, to give it another formation, one that is peculiar to the self. I remember isolated, yet fragmented and confused, images—and images, shifting, enlarging, is the word, rather than moments or events—[images] which are mine alone and which are especially vivid to me. They involve me wholly and immediately. . . . They call for a certain attitude of belief on my part now; that is, they must mean something, but their best reality does not consist in meaning. They are not stories in that sense, but they are storylike, mythic, never evolved but evolving ever. . . . If I were to remember other things, I should be someone else. (61–63)

Memory here is specifically visual, and it is the remembered image that works on the imagination, rather than vice versa. Imagination is contained in—and contained by—the remembered image, which lends to the imagination its very form and makes it peculiar, or specific, to the self. Those images are "fragmented and confused," yet they take precedence in the memory over temporal moments and events. The teleological unfolding of events in a story is contrasted here with the more fantastical, ever evolving, shifting and enlarging of images from Momaday's past, images that involve him wholly and immediately and that have their best reality in something beyond meaning. They specifically are *not* stories, but they *are* storylike, even mythic. This shifting and enlarging of images from the past until their best reality becomes mythic is similar to the process observed in Duras's extended meditations on her crossing of the Mekong River, a crossing whose meaning was less tied to its status as an event than to its status as a shifting and enlarging image. Momaday's remarks here serve as a gloss on the function of the image for Duras in *The Lover*, not least in the assertion on his part that "if I were to remember other things, I should be someone else."

This assertion of the primary role of images in the construction of identity helps explain the presence in Momaday's book of so many photographs, for each represents a mythic aspect of his own identity. It might seem somewhat paradoxical that a memoir called *The Names* turns so importantly on images. In Momaday's text, however, a clear relationship exists between naming and images. The mythic, storylike aspect of past images for Momaday suggests that autobiography involves an extended kind of naming of those images and that this naming is integral to the construction of identity. Kenneth Burke has written about the relationship between writing and naming in a way that suggests something about its function in Momaday's book. In Burke's essay "Literature as Equipment for Living" he says that literary writing is a form of naming: "A work like *Madame Bovary* . . . is the strategic naming of a situation. It singles out a pattern of experience that is sufficiently representative of our social structure, that recurs sufficiently often *mutandis mutatis,* for people to 'need a word for it' and to adopt an attitude towards it" (300). For Burke, naming involves using language to give shape, scope, and significance to some observed or perceived image, act, or event. It suggests that naming is in fact a form of writing and that writing is an extended act of naming. The names in *The Names* are interpretive readings that conjure up identity and as such are linked to the images identity contains.

A passage in Momaday's book that describes the experience of viewing his own image reflected in a kerosense lamp dramatizes in a particularly striking way the creative relationship between image and identity:

> I can almost see into the summer of a year in my childhood. I am again in my grandmother's house, where I have come to stay for a month. . . . I am thoughtful. I see into the green, transparent base of a kerosene lamp; there is a still circle within it, the surface of a deeper transparency. . . . Something of me has just now moved upon the metal throat of the lamp, some distortion of myself, nonetheless recognizable, and I am distracted. I look for my image then in the globe, rising a little in my chair, but I see nothing but my ghost, another transparency, glass upon glass. . . . I take up a pencil and set the point against a sheet of paper and define the head of a boy, bowed slightly, facing right. I fill in quickly only a few details, the line of the eye, the curve of the mouth, the ear, the hair . . . there is life and expression in the face, a conjugation that I could not have imagined in these markings. . . . The boy looks down at something. . . . He is contained in his expression—and fixed, as if

the foundation upon which his flesh and bones are set cannot be shaken . . . he is the inscrutable reflection of my own vague certainty. And then I write, in my child's hand, beneath the drawing, "This is someone. Maybe this is Mammedaty. This is Mammedaty when he was a boy." And I wonder at the words. *What are they? . . .* The page bears the likeness of a boy . . . and his name consists in the letters there, the words, the other likeness . . . the legend of the boy's having been, of his going on. I have said it, I have set it down. I trace the words; I touch myself to the words, and they stand for me. (92–93)

This passage dramatically renders the shifting and enlarging of images Momaday wrote about in the earlier passage. It is a kind of extended metaphor of how his identity is autobiographically fashioned in the struggle to name the self reflected in the images reproduced in his book. Here an isolated, fragmented, confused image shifts and enlarges until it becomes mythic, demanding from him a certain attitude or belief. Seeing into deep transparencies suggests the creative acts of reading and naming. The layering of meaning and significance here is so complex that the described scene can finally be seen to stand for—or represent— the very act of autobiography that contains it. Just as in the recollected moment Momaday could "see into" the base of the lamp, so as he writes he can "almost see into the summer" of his childhood when this event took place, as if the past itself now exists as a transparency, glass upon glass, within which his identity is being forged. The act of looking for his image *then* in the globe is duplicated by his extended effort in the *Memoir* to look for himself in his globe of remembered images. The sequence of events in this scene suggests (or mimics) the sequence of events in the autobiographical act Momaday has been performing; in this scene he shifts from fixing on an image, to naming, and then writing. First the image, "and then I write," then the wonder that "his name consists in the letters there." The act of drawing, which occurs between perception and writing, is a mediating one, the pencil linking the image with writing. Taking up the pencil he attempts to define a life and an expression that in the reflection seem a recognizable yet ghostly distortion of himself. (Of course there are two kinds of reflection at work here, one constituted by his image in the glass, the other by his attempt to see into it, to reflect on it.) Momaday adds meaning to this ghostly transparency first by drawing it, then by naming it ("Maybe this is Mammedaty . . . when he was a boy"), then by writing.

This scene dramatizes an extended moment of self-definition that in every detail prefigures the one embodied in the act of writing *The Names*. The passage lays equal stress on the importance of the image (the boy's reflection in the lamp), its ghostly and distorted, yet recognizable, nature, the struggle to fix and name its expression, to write out its identity, and to trace the words in a way that finally makes them stand for him.

It is important to note that the book's preoccupation with identity and naming unfolds in the wider context of Momaday's story about his struggle with the process of assimilation, one in which the desire to blend in and be a part of the dominant, Anglo culture is continually at odds with his desire to connect with and deepen his identity as an Indian. For that identity is in part a function of specifiable political and social forces beyond his personal control. (Just as Duras's identity in *The Lover* is formed in the contexts of racism, colonialism, and sexism.) In this struggle Momaday's mother represents for him a fascinating, even paradoxical, model. Mayme Natchee Scott was born in Kentucky with only a small trace of Indian blood (figures 7 and 8). But out of her slight Indian heritage she literally imagined an identity for herself. Momaday writes that

> in 1929 my mother was a Southern Belle; she was about to embark upon an extraordinary life. It was about this time that she began to

Figures 7–10   From N. Scott Momady, *The Names: A Memoir* (Tucson: University of Arizona Press, 1976).

ly mother. (Perhaps the doll's name was 'Natachee, too.)

My mother. There is something Russian or Asian about her here. She has become a beautiful woman.

Figure 8

see herself as an Indian. That dim native heritage became a fascination and a cause for her, inasmuch, perhaps, as it enabled her to assume an attitude of defiance, an attitude which she assumed with particular style and satisfaction; it became her. She imagined who she was. This act of the imagination was, I believe, among the most important events of my mother's early life, as later the same essential act was to be among the most important of my own. (24–25)

Here again Momaday stresses the constitutive relationship between image and identity. What differentiates that relationship from the ones represented by Barthes, Sherman, and Duras is that Momaday's mother's choice is just that, a choice that is willful and direct. She fashions her identity in response to an image, realizes herself as a subject in an act of naming that is both defiant and stylish. Unlike Duras, whose identity is retrospectively read out of an image from her past, Momaday's mother siezes on an image that will be prospective, out of which she will fashion an identity for the future. There is something Shermanesque about the photographs of her in headdress, which Momaday reproduces; they seem to parody the very heritage she adopts (figures 9 and 10). They recall Barthes's remarks about posing, with his emphasis on how the conventions of the pose signify an identity beyond the control of the subject. They seem to embody that specter of objectification Barthes associates with a microversion of death. Indeed, "identity" in these photographs is on the verge of being subsumed by the dominant culture's debased objectification of it.

But for Momaday, his mother's willful decision to "imagine who she was," the conscious act of seeing herself as an Indian, confronts the effects of that objectification by incorporating it. For Momaday, his mother's identity has a kind of authenticity that lies not in a romantic notion of self-discovery, nor in the idea that she somehow intuited an essential self, but in the fact that she willfully and imaginatively constructed it. That the identity she chose had already been objectified by American culture—a fact underscored by the photographs in headress— seems to be overcome in Momaday's mind by the willful choice his mother made to identify herself as Indian, an essential act of ironic incorporation that became a model for his own struggle to name an identity for himself out of the disparate images in his book.

The ironic quality in these photographs of Momaday's mother has the effect of muting the element of parody they seem on the surface to embody. Although there is something potentially pathetic about them, that pathos is undermined by the very incorporation of their triviality in the image repertoire that constitutes his mother's identity, for her culture has made that triviality—as an already coded sign—nearly inescapable. The photographs suggest that in imagining her Indian identity she must incorporate the burden of having to assume the trivialized, objectified quality of that identity—that in so doing, she also can move beyond it. So she puts on the knowledge that her identity has already been appropriated and objectified with its power. The pictures of Mayme Scott dramatize the objectification of the self discussed by Barthes and captured in Sherman's photographs. At the same time, however, they represent the incorporation of that objectified image in an identity whose authenticity, nevertheless, cannot be canceled out by *in*authenticity. The private image she has of herself, evoked by what Momaday calls her dim Indian heritage, assimilates the objectified parody of itself embodied in these images and therefore works to neutralize the very inauthenticity they seem to signify.

Both Momaday and Duras represent identity in their texts as something that can be chosen or constructed, but, at the same time, as something that cannot escape the process of objectification Barthes writes about. (For Duras, of course, that process of objectification is rooted in the ideology of a patriarchal culture at once sexist, colonialist, and racist; whereas for Mayme Scott it is rooted in white American culture's coloni-

My mother called herself "Little Moon"

My parents about the time of their marriage

Figures 9 and 10

zation and objectification of the Native American.) Both Barthes and Sherman, however, emphasize the extent to which such objectification is in part the function of a kind of cultural machinery of image production and reproduction that always threatens the self's sense of autonomy and authenticity.

Together, these texts evoke a dynamic process always at work in the construction—and transformation—of identity. On the one hand, Duras's story and Sherman's photographs emphasize the determinism of cultural forces; on the other, Mayme Scott's story emphasizes the possibility of imagining an identity, an act that, in incorporating the culturally conditioned one, somehow transforms or personalizes it. Identity, then, is always the result of a complex interaction between cultural forces and what we call the private imagination, but the line between the two seems impossible to draw. There surely is a real sense in which we choose or imagine our identities, but those choices are always mediated by culturally conditioned possibilities that work to circumscribe what we can imagine for ourselves and to question the very categories of the chosen and the conditional.

For Barthes this produces the kind of existential anxiety dramatized in his passage about the subject becoming an object. It is a process that introduces the seemingly inauthentic and reproduced into a self he wants to keep essential and authentic. Driven by a romantic nostalgia for a concept of self free from objectification, Barthes's remarks about posing seek to hold to an absolute distinction between the essential and the objectified that would preclude the process I'm referring to.

Cindy Sherman, on the other hand, collapses the distinctions controlling Barthes's discourse: for her, there is no essential self that is not in part the product of objectifying cultural forces. Her photographs end up dramatizing the kind of dialectical tension I've been referring to. There is, to be sure, a sense of horror and anguish in her work, but it has its source in an increasingly intense response to a form of victimization specific to patriarchal culture, rather than in a lament over the loss of a concept of selfhood.

Part of what is foregrounded in the texts of Duras and Momaday is the important role that reading visual images has in the dialectical process I've been speaking of. Whether retrospective or visionary, this act of reading involves choice and is an effort at overcoming. This suggests, finally, that the central image of crossing in Duras's book links it to Momaday's remarks about his mother. Crossing can stand as a kind of emblem of the transformation of identity enacted both by Duras in writing her text and by Mayme Scott in seeing or imagining herself an Indian. Duras's retrospective writing crosses back over and reads an image crucial to her identity, and in so doing she takes a measure of control over it. Mayme Scott's crossing involves a willful self-transformation that takes her from southern belle to Native American. That crossing is the result of a prospective vision that attempts to choose, and thus control, identity. Crossing paths in my analysis of posing, they underscore each in their own way the role of the image in the construction of what we call identity.

Notes

1   Of course the distinction between "historical" and "visual" memory is somewhat overschematic, for there is a visual quality to our recollections about the past, and we tend to experience images from our past in a historical context. Although this is the case, distinguishing between the two is a necessary step in analyzing the neglected role of the visual image in autobiographical writing.

2   Compare this passage, for example, with the following oft-quoted observation of Paul DeMan's: "We assume that life *produces* the autobiography as an act produces its consequences, but can we not suggest, with equal justice, that the autobiographical project may itself produce and determine the life and that whatever the writer

does is in fact governed by the technical demands of self-portraiture and thus determined, in all its aspects, by the resources of his medium?" (919). What DeMan says here about "the technical demands of self-portraiture" parallels exactly what Barthes is saying about how the technical demands of photographic portraiture— the resources of its medium—determine the subject who is represented.

3 The same process seems at work toward essentially the same end in Sandra Bernhard's performance film *Without You I'm Nothing* (1990). Bernhard's impersonations of female performers from Barbra Striesand to Patti Smith are wound around a loosely autobiographical narrative about her own identity as a performer. The impersonations, an uncanny blend of parody and homage, serve to dramatize the extent to which her own identity is inseparable from the cultural roles that determine her performances.

References

Barthes, Roland. *Camera Lucida: Reflections on Photography.* Trans. Richard Howard. New York: Hill and Wang, 1981.

Burke, Kenneth. "Literature as Equipment for Living." *The Philosophy of Literary Form.* Berkeley: U of California P, 1973. 293–304.

DeMan, Paul. "Autobiography as De-facement." *MLN* 94 (1979): 919–30.

Duras, Marguerite. *The Lover.* New York: Pantheon, 1985.

Lacan, Jacques. *The Language of the Self: The Function of Language in Psychoanalysis.* Trans. Anthony Wilden. Baltimore: Johns Hopkins UP, 1968.

Momaday, N. Scott. *The Names: A Memoir.* Tucson: U of Arizona P, 1976.

Philips, Lisa. "Cindy Sherman's Cindy Shermans." *Cindy Sherman.* New York: Whitney Museum of American Art, 1987. 13–16.

Sherman, Cindy. *Cindy Sherman.* New York: Whitney Museum of American Art, 1987.

Schjedahl, Peter. "The Oracle of Images." *Cindy Sherman.* New York: Whitney Museum of American Art, 1987.

Plains Indian Names and "the Autobiographical Act"

HERTHA D. WONG

■

Names and Autobiography

The passion for the name . . . expresses the cry for existence of personal identity itself. The deep subject of autobiography is the proper name.—Philippe Lejeune, "The Autobiographical Contract"

Despite our postmodern skepticism about the representability of the self, regardless of whether "announcements of the death of the unified self are premature" (Eakin, "Narrative and Chronology," 38), we stubbornly persist in believing in, speaking of, and writing about ourselves.[1] Any representation of self is a linguistic, cultural, and historical construction as well as a social and personal one. "Everyone is . . . aware of this indeterminacy of the first person," says Philippe Lejeune, "and it is not an accident that we attempt to resolve the indeterminacy by anchoring it to the proper name" (210). In fact, Lejeune asserts "the passion for the name . . . expresses the cry for existence of personal identity itself. The deep subject of autobiography is the proper name" (209). As problem-ridden as it may be, the proper name highlights both a unified self (a conflation of speaker/author and narrator) and a multiple self (a contiguity of the many voices embedded in language). Our names, then, reflect a personal and a social identity and serve at least two semantic functions: referential and expressive.[2] "Most of the thinking done by philosophers and linguists about the nature of proper names," says linguist Marianne Mithun, "has been limited to Indo-European names, especially English, or to philosophical constructs based on English names" (40). My interest here is in nineteenth-century Plains Indian names as they have been translated into English. This is not a linguistic analysis, but a theoretical consideration of the autobiographical dimensions of serial naming as practiced by nineteenth-century

Plains Indian males and recorded by European American authorities, and its subsequent treatment by twentieth-century Kiowa autobiographer N. Scott Momaday. I focus on men's names for two reasons. First, men, rather than women, generally acquired numerous names over a lifetime, each name reflecting a character trait, accomplishment, or life transition. Second, when officials of the United States government (with the assistance of some assimilated Native Americans) compiled the tribal enrollment lists in the late nineteenth century, they routinely insisted that males be listed as heads of households. Just as early ethnographers concentrated their attention on men and their activities, census takers focused on men and their names. As a result there is a more substantial record of men's names than women's.

Like many other indigenous peoples, nineteenth-century Plains Indians shared a sense of a collective identity, what Arnold Krupat has referred to as a "dialogic" self (*The Voice in the Margin* 133). Such a "relational self" reflected deep connections, not only to one's people, but to the land and its natural cycles as well.[3] Nineteenth-century Plains Indian males, however, displayed a particularly lively sense of individuality within this communal context. Whereas Plains Indian women were encouraged to be the educators and tradition bearers, ensuring the continuance of the nation by teaching the young people, men were expected to provide for the well being of the people by hunting, warring, and obtaining spiritual visions. Demonstrating excellence in these martial and spiritual practices was a way to earn individual prestige and community affirmation. Men were encouraged to perform such exploits and were often expected to narrate them afterward. Oral and pictographic autobiographical accounts of brave deeds, known as coup tales, were common, and a man's names were often determined by his accomplishments and the community's affirmation of them. Although a man's proper names were not designed as autobiography (that is, as a self-consciously constructed, chronological narrative of the physical and spiritual events of his life), they reveal a great deal about his character and accomplishments and narrate key transformations in his life. A proper name, and naming practices in general, can be examined as one (of many) fundamental type(s) of self-narration, similar to what Elizabeth Bruss has called an "autobiographical act"—an illocutionary act that constructs and narrates personal identity. This is not to assert that names and naming practices are autobiography (or even necessarily always autobiographical), but to suggest, as Paul Jay says of the relationship between "image and identity" elsewhere in this volume, that "there is a creative, constitutive relationship" between, in this case, names and identity. Serial naming might be seen as a narrative production and performance of identity.

Scholars of Native American autobiography generally have focused on oral life histories solicited, translated, and edited by European American amanuenses. Because Western definitions of autobiography have been applied to the study of indigenous personal narratives, some scholars have concluded that Indian autobiography did not exist prior to what Krupat, in *For Those Who Come After*, labels "bicultural composite compositions" of the nineteenth century (xi). But early Native American self-narrations were not based on European American notions of self, life, or writing. Prior to the arrival of Europeans, indigenous people had numerous oral and pictographic forms in which to share their personal narratives. H. David Brumble, one of the earliest advocates for precontact indigenous autobiography, recognizes at least "six fairly distinct kinds of preliterate autobiographical narratives" (22). Certainly these autobiographical modes do not conform to most European American notions of autobiography, which emphasize autonomous individuality and insist that autobiography is the story of one's life written by oneself. Plains Indian autobiographical forms emphasize a communal as well as an individual self; they often narrate a series of anecdotal moments rather than a unified, chronological life story; and they may be spoken, performed, painted, or otherwise crafted, rather than written. Storytelling performances and pictographic self-narrations challenge interpretive approaches based on assumptions about alphabetic literacy.

Considering nineteenth-century Plains Indian names as serial, but nonlinear, autobiographical acts raises a number of issues. Certainly, Native notions of the metonymic function of the proper name challenge the postmodern insistence on language as an arbitrary set of signs. For many Native Americans, there is, indeed, an intimate connection between the word and the world, a link further enlivened in ritual where language is thought not merely to describe but to reconfigure reality. Also, examining names in light of autobiography confounds the early Eurocentric insistence in autobiography studies that "genuine" autobiography should present a developed and unified story narrated by an older person who reviews an important life in its entirety. In contrast, nineteenth-century Plains Indian proper names can be more aptly likened to the seemingly discontinuous autobiographical narratives of Western diaries and journals, which narrate the immediacy of discrete moments in the present rather than reflections about the past, taking place in the present, shaped into a unified and chronological narrative. Because a name is often conferred by others, rather than taken by oneself, the very process of identity construction agitates European-American ideas about self-invention, self-representation, and self-narration. If names are bestowed by someone else, how can they be *auto-biographical*? A relational identity, though, depends for its existence, and to a certain extent for its expression, on others. In fact, Howard Gardner suggests that for people in a communal society "one's self *is* other people" (272). When this is so, being given a name by one's community constructs and reflects an identity just as accurately as inventing one's own name might in individualist societies. Besides, if what Bakhtin suggests is true, the "I" in any culture is inherently polyvocal and the construction of an individual subject is always a collaborative social activity.

In nineteenth-century Plains Indian practices, the proper name might reflect accomplishments of the past, aspirations for the future, or connections to geography, family, clan, or the spiritual world in the present. Proper names might embody personal anecdotes, family stories, and tribal myths, as well as the dynamic relationship among them. Names, then, could be profoundly narrative as well as descriptive. Finally, among Plains tribes, individuals, particularly men, were often given (or sometimes took for themselves) several names over a lifetime, revising and updating their life narratives as they lived them. Generally, men acquired many more names than women, reflecting their secular and spiritual accomplishments. Women, on the other hand, sometimes took new names at transitional moments such as puberty or marriage. Pretty-shield, a Crow Indian woman, was given her name by her paternal grandfather—the owner of a particularly handsome painted war-shield. According to Crow custom, explains Pretty-shield, "a woman's name never changed unless, when she was very young, she did not grow strong" (19). In that case, parents "sometimes asked one of [the child's] grandfathers to change her name to help her" (19). The idea is that altering a young girl's name (her fundamental self-representation) reshapes her life. Such differences in the naming practices for men and women suggest clearly defined gender roles. Whereas changing male names reflect men's protean activities, relatively stable female names mirror women's roles in preserving tribal traditions. By the time some of these (mostly male) names were recorded by U.S. officials in the late nineteenth century, English appellations were added to each person's constellation of Native names, reflecting bicultural identities imposed by colonialism.

Nineteenth- and Early Twentieth-Century Plains Indian Names

I name him Aleek-chea-ahoosh [Many Achievements] because in my dream I saw him count many coups.—*Grandfather to Plenty-coups' mother,* Plenty-coups: Chief of the Crow

Categorizing, Conferring, Keeping Secret, and Acquiring Names

Using Red Cloud's 1884 pictorial census, the 1884 Oglala Roster, and pictographic names from "winter counts [that is, tribal histories] of The-Flame, The-Swan, American-Horse, and Cloud-Shield" as sources, nineteenth-century ethnologist Garrick Mallery divides Plains Indian personal names into four categories: objective, metaphoric, animal, and vegetable (445–59). Objective names might also be called descriptive names. They include such straightforward appellations as Long-Hair, High-Back-Bone, Left-Handed-Big-Nose, or Squint Eyes. With such names as The Stabber, Licks-with-his-Tongue, or Knock-a-hole-in-the-head, there is an implicit narrative as well as an embedded description. We wonder, for instance, about the story of how Licks-with-his-Tongue got his name. A man's name seems to present one key event in the plot of a segment of his life rather than the fully developed story of his entire life. Certainly in a small and tightly knit community where everyone knows each other's personal stories, an elaborated autobiographical narrative is not needed. People can fill in the details for themselves.

Metaphoric names, Mallery's second category, are also descriptive, of course, but indirectly—by comparing the person to someone or something else—rather than directly. "Wolf-Ear," according to Mallery, "probably refers to size, and is substantially the same as big-ear" (453). Similarly, the name Tongue is not strictly descriptive, but is a derisive or humorous metonym for someone who "mouths off." Although Mallery makes them distinct categories, animal and vegetable names are certainly metaphoric. Mouse, Badger, and Spotted-Elk may refer to the characteristics of the animal that the person has acquired or aspires to acquire—diligence, prowess, or swiftness, for example—or the name may refer to some spirit animal seen in a vision. The name Badger, for instance, may belong to someone who fights like that feisty beast. Some animal names borrow characteristics from objective names, such as "Bear-Looks-Back," which is a bear-in-action, a metaphoric personal narrative. Though less common, vegetable names do occur. The name Tree-in-the-Face sounds as if it might present an exciting story of a tree climber or a falling tree, but Mallery says it simply describes the painted face of the person. Here Mallery suggests a static description rather than a narrative moment frozen in paint. The tree-painted face itself, however, might be read as the man's spiritual symbolism.

Colors added to names, for example, Black Elk or Red Cloud, sometimes are based on "a mythical or symbolic significance attributed to colors" (Mallery 446). Such names are often earned or received because of an individual's spiritual aspirations or accomplishments, rather than his worldly achievements. The symbolic significance of color may differ from nation to nation, even, sometimes, from person to person. The Lakota holy man Black Elk provides a detailed explanation of the color symbolism of his vision, whereas Lame Deer describes in his autobiography a slightly variant version of the symbolism of Lakota colors. Both Black Elk and Lame Deer agree, however, that certain colors are associated with specific cardinal points, which, in turn, are associated with certain characteristics. Thus Black Elk, whose power is from the Thunder-Beings in the West, has an appropriate name (passed down to him from his father) because, as he explains, black is the color of the West—the place of introspection and the origin of storm clouds.

Charles Alexander Eastman, a Santee Sioux who earned a degree in science from Dartmouth College and in 1890 a medical degree from Boston University, wrote numerous books to educate European Americans about Indian life and beliefs. In *The Soul of the Indian* he categorizes Indian names as nicknames, deed names, birth names, or names with "a religious and symbolic meaning" (43). A name reflects the nature of the individual. For example, a "man of forcible character" would usually have "the name of the buffalo or bear, lightning or some dread natural force," whereas a more peaceful man "may be called Swift Bird or Blue Sky" (44). Women's names were often associated with "the home" and included adjectives like "pretty" or "good" (44). "Names of any dignity or importance," notes Eastman, "must be conferred by the old men," particularly if the names have "spiritual significance" (44). A spiritual name, he adds, was "sometimes borne by three generations, but each individual must prove that he is worthy of it" (45).

A proper name, a reflection of a person's individual characteristics and the community's aspirations for and judgments of that person, can reveal a great deal about his or her traits, achievements, and goals. This and the belief in the sacred nature of language may be part of the reason many indigenous people traditionally do not address others by their personal names, but rather by kinship terms or family endearments. Many have noted the reticence, if not outright refusal, of many indigenous people to speak their personal names. In his 1902 autobiography, *Indian Boyhood,* Charles Eastman explains that "Indian etiquette" requires "avoiding the direct address" (55). Instead of a personal name, a "term of relationship or some title of courtesy was commonly used . . . by those who wished to show respect" (55). Although Everard Thurn studied the Indians of Guiana, Mallery believes that what he says about a person's name given at birth is true of the indigenous people of North America as well: "But these names seem of little use, in that owners have a very strong objection to telling or using them, apparently on the ground that the name is part of the man, and that he who knows the name has part of the owner of that name in his power" (Mallery 444–45). For many traditional indigenous people, an individual's first given name is never spoken, as it is considered a sacred connection to the spirit world. Such a name is a gift of essential being whose privacy must be protected.

Because of this traditional reticence to speak (or write) about oneself, talking about oneself unduly or speaking one's name is considered bad manners or, at the very least, inappropriate behavior. Eastman makes this clear in his second autobiography, *From the Deep Woods to Civilization,* when he describes his first day at school. When the European-American teacher asks him what his name is, Eastman does not respond. "Evidently [the instructor] had not been among the Indians long," reasons the young Eastman, "or he would not have asked that question. It takes a tactician and a diplomat to get an Indian to tell his name!" (22). The teacher gives up his attempt in the face of such adamant resistance.[4] Only when people have earned a status acknowledged by the community can they speak of themselves without being severely criticized as egotistical (or ignored altogether).

Even more important than categories of names or the secrecy of first names, is the fact that nineteenth-century Plains Indian names *changed* throughout life to reflect an individual's spiritual and worldly accomplishments. Among the Kiowa, for instance, three names were given: at birth, adolescence, and adulthood. For the Mandans, "until the child received a name, it was not considered a part of the . . . village but of the 'baby home' from whence it had come" (Bowers, as quoted in Beck and Walters 201). A name, then, conferred status as a community member. New names were given or acknowledged "at first menstruation for girls, initiation into a solidarity for boys, success in hunting and war for boys, and the acquisition of supernatural power in the vision quest for both sexes" (Driver 390). Plains Indian men might acquire "a dozen or more names in a lifetime by performing as many successive deeds of distinction" (Driver 390).

Plenty-coups, a Crow warrior, and Charles Eastman, a Sioux physician, provide sound examples of the ways such names can function. Plenty-coups is a name that sounds as if it could only have been earned after a long and successful career fighting, raiding, and counting coup (to count coup was "to touch a live enemy with the hand or with a special coup stick and get away without being harmed" [Josephy 114])—all socially sanctioned means to earn status for a warrior and his people.[5] But Plenty-coups explains that his name was given to him by his grandfather. "I name him Aleek-chea-ahoosh [Many Achievements]," the grandfather announced to the boy's mother, "because in my dream I saw him count many coups" (27). Since "all the people knew this," Plenty-coups felt "obliged to excel" (27). "I must live up to my name, you see," explains Plenty-coups (28). Such a promissory name serves to inspire the child to fulfill the vision of his name (and of his family's aspirations for him).

In *Indian Boyhood* Charles Eastman explains how he had "to bear the humiliating name Hakadah, "the pitiful last" (a name given to him when his mother died shortly after his birth), "until [he] should earn a more dignified and appropriate name" (21). Several years later, after a victory in a lacrosse game, the medicine man Chankpee-yuhah conferred a new name on Hakadah. "Ohiyesa (or Winner) shall be thy name henceforth," he announced. "Be brave, be patient, and thou shalt always win. Thy name is Ohiyesa" (47–48). It is important that the gathered people witness and approve his new appellation, given "in memory of this victory" (47). Eastman's first name, Hakadah, records the unfortunate circumstances of his birth and his place within his family structure. Ohiyesa, his second name "earned" for him from communal accomplishment, reflects the band's lacrosse victory, but more importantly his community's belief in his future potential. The "Pitiful Last" becomes the "Winner." Still later, he became Dr. Charles Alexander Eastman, taking on a white man's name to reflect what he describes as his transition from "the deep woods to civilization."

Plains Indian Pictographic Autographs

Writing in 1888 for the Bureau of American Ethnology, Garrick Mallery stated that Indian personal names "were generally connative," and because of their "sometimes objective and sometimes ideographic nature," they can be "expressed in sign language" and "portrayed in pictographs" (442–45). It is revealing to consider the manner in which a name was portrayed, or signed. The Plains Indian way to "write" a name pictographically was to draw a head with a line coming from the head or mouth, connecting the body and the pictured object which signified the name (known as a name-symbol). Similarly, in sign language, after the sign for the object had been gestured, the person passed "the index finger forward from the mouth in a direct line" (Mallery 442–43). Signifying one's name, whether in pictograph or sign language (both pantribal languages to a degree), required a link between an individual (quite literally a head or mouth) and the objectified personal name, paralleling the process of the speaker speaking his or her name (the breath, then, takes the place of the line, connecting person to name). As well as emphasizing the physical connection between the individual and the name, between self and self-referent, the pictographic autograph suggests that the name emanates from the self. The Cheyenne Wuxpais (Daniel Littlechief) displayed this autograph convention for Albert Gatschet when he drew twenty-nine examples (labeled *a* through *cc*) of Cheyenne autographs (figure 1).

Illustrations *a* through *o* show a variety of free-floating heads, each with a line connecting head and name-symbol. In figures *p* through *cc*, on the other hand, Wuxpais has omitted the heads and simply drawn the name-symbols. Notice how the name-symbol in figure *a* is a man with a head that is too large in relation to his body, indicating his name: Big Head (Makstsiyá). Similarly, the second autograph (*b*) highlights a belted tunic to convey the name Tied with Belt (Ákutsi). Sometimes action is indicated, as in the name-symbols *h* and *i:* Woman Walking About (Ámixtsi) and Woman Walking at Night (Ta-éwiuxtsi). Note the tracks indicating movement behind the woman in name-symbol *h* and the darkened sky surrounding the walking woman signifying night in *i*. The bottom row of autographs (*p* through *cc*) illustrates an assortment of bird and bear names, each associated with certain characteristics. Autograph *q* is Spotted Eagle (Nitchxü-immāsts) and *u* is Yellow Hawk (Hihúwe-i ánu), for instance; *w* is a half-bird, half-bear illustrating the name of Bird Bear (Wíksihi náxku). Figures *x* through *bb* display an assortment of bear names (*x* is the name-symbol for White Bear, or Wúxpi náxku; *z* is the autograph of Red Bear, or Náxk ma-āsts); *cc* is Star (Hutúxk). Often the name-symbol is synecdochic, like Roman Nose (Wō x̄ini in figure *e*) in which the pronounced profile stands for the entire person, or Black Elk in which the elk head stands for the whole elk. Such pictographic names recall John Sturrock's early description of "the new model autobiographer" who writes associative autobiography that presents a spatial "diagram of the autobiographer" rather than a linear narrative description (61).

It is not surprising that, after European American subjugation of Plains Indian people, the pictographic signature changed and finally all but disappeared. Such effacement of Native names and autographs reflects the United States government's intent to erase Indian identity altogether. When the last Plains Indian warriors to resist U.S. invasion of Indian land were defeated, many were sent east and imprisoned in Fort Marion at Saint Augustine, Florida, (1875–78). These prisoners of war were provided drawing materials and encouraged to depict their former lives. Autographed pictographic ledger books drawn at this time reveal something of the transformation of Plains Indian pictographic self-representation. At times, the name-symbol dominates, with no obvious relation to the head (that is, it is not connected by a line). In Howling Wolf's 1877 sketch book, for instance, his autograph (figure 2) is a drawing of a seated howling wolf. The wolf's head is thrown back; the lines emanating from the wolf's snout indicate howling. This detailed drawing of a wolf replaces earlier less realistic depictions. Tangible changes in the materials and circumstances of pictographic production (such as colored pencils and paper in place of vegetable dyes and tanned animal hides, as well as ample time due to imprisonment) led to more realism in name-symbols and pictography overall.

At times the name-symbol is accompanied by the name written in English or syllabary. Sometimes the writing was added by a European American sponsor or friend, as in the case of Howling Wolf. Beneath Howling Wolf's name-symbol, Eva Scott, the woman who provided the sketchbook and drawing materials, wrote his name: "Honennisto—Cheyenne for Howling Wolf." Sometimes, though, the writing was done by the artist himself (especially in the Fort Marion pictographic sketchbooks, because the prisoners were taught to write). This was the case with Packer who provided what we could call a double or triple signature (figure 3). To the right of his head, Packer drew his name-symbol—an outline of a man with a pronounced back, probably indicating a pack. In addition, to assist European American readers unfamiliar with Plains Indian pictographic conventions, he wrote "Packer" in English. He wrote his name in English a second time directly above his head.

At other times, the autograph was translated entirely from pictogra-

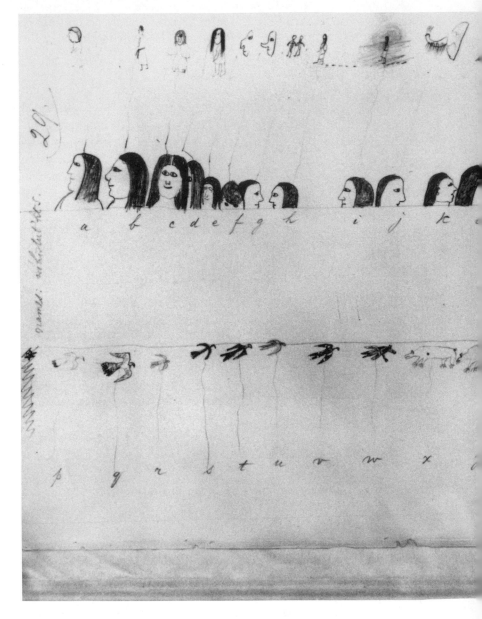

phy to writing. Zo-Tom, for example (figure 4), wrote his name in the English alphabet, but still used the pictographic convention of drawing a line to connect the written name to the depiction of himself. Finally, at least among the Fort Marion prisoners, the name-symbol disappeared altogether (Petersen 53), perhaps indicating the Native artists' lack of

Figure 1 Cheyenne Autographs from "Cheyenne Drawings" by Wuxpais (Daniel Littlechief), 1891. (Courtesy of the Newberry Library, Chicago). Wuxpais illustrates a variety of Cheyenne autographs and interprets them for Albert Gatschet. For the top row (illustrations *a–o*), a line drawn from the top of the head is connected to a name-symbol above. The oversized head on the human figure in example *a*, for instance, translates as Big Head (Makstsiyá); *c* is Red Eye Woman (Ma-eyúkini-i) (note the enlarged and darkened left eye); *e* is Roman Nose (Wóxini) with its obvious proboscis; *j* represents the warrior Hair-Arm (Mámishiaxts) (although it resembles the trunk of an elephant, this is the arm of a hair-fringed shirt); and *m* is Kills Across the River (Húxu wina-án) (note the victim has fallen on the far side of the small squiggly line that represents a river). For the bottom row (illustrations *p–cc*), Wuxpais omits the heads and simply illustrates the name-symbols. In these examples, names are derived from the natural world, especially birds (*p–v*) and bears (*x–bb*). Illustration *w* is half-bird, half-bear indicating the name Bird Bear (Wíksihi náxku); *q* is Spotted Eagle (Nitchxúimmāsts); *y* is Yellow Bear (Náxkwi húwāsts); and *cc* is Star (Hutúxk). During the imprisonment of the Plains warriors such name-symbols were replaced by costume-symbols or writing in syllabary or English.

European American expectations of individual authorship, a transition to writing, or a degree of acculturation to the use of European American drawing materials and conventions. Perhaps also, with prolonged imprisonment and abundant drawing materials, these men had the time to identify themselves by drawing detailed depictions of their individual

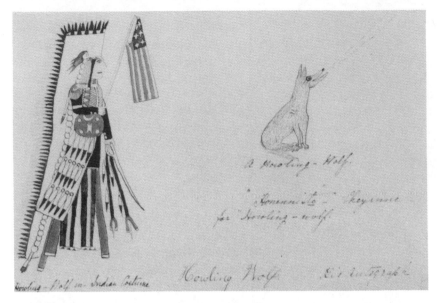

Figure 2   "Howling Wolf in Indian Costume" by Howling Wolf, Cheyenne, 1877. (Courtesy of the Southwest Museum, Los Angeles, California. Neg. No. 34,653). Howling Wolf drew this while he was imprisoned at Fort Marion in Saint Augustine, Florida. Rather than the traditional pictographic narrative action moving from right to left, this picture is read from left to right. On the left is Howling Wolf, wearing a feathered bonnet, a bird amulet, and a breastplate. He carries his feathered and painted hide shield (for spiritual protection), a sword, and the U.S. flag. On the right is his name-symbol: a seated howling wolf. With head thrown back, the wolf howls (indicated by the lines emanating from the wolf's snout). There is no line connecting the name-symbol to the figure on the left, but beneath the pictographic autograph is Howling Wolf's name written in Cheyenne and English (by Miss Eva Scott, the artist who encouraged Howling Wolf and Zo-Tom to draw and supplied them with art materials during their imprisonment).

dress, ornamentation, and martial accouterments.[6] Such details, known as costume-symbols, served as identifying markers for each warrior and sometimes replaced name-symbols.[7]

The Kiowa chief White Horse, known to whites as "a murderer, ravisher, and . . . general scoundrel" (*Catholic World* as quoted in Petersen 118) and to Indians as a heroic warrior and defender of his people, used a variety of autographs in his collaborative drawings. His pictographic autographs provide a clear example of the transition from using a name-symbol to using a costume-symbol during a time of violent transition. In one drawing (executed sometime between May 1875 and November 1876 in prison at Fort Marion), he depicted himself on horseback (figure 5). His wife rides on a horse behind, carrying his battle gear. He identified himself most obviously using the traditional name-symbol: a line connects his head with the outline of a white horse above him. In the same drawing, however, he used his costume-symbol with which he identified himself by depicting details of his dress and adornment. In this case, his costume-symbol consists of "his blue shield with its distinctive pattern and his blue face paint with a white disk" (Petersen 54). In another sketch (figure 6), drawn sometime between May 1875 and April 1878, White Horse pictorially narrated his feat of roping a buffalo. This time his signature was written in English above his head but with no connecting line. It is difficult to determine whether the variety of White Horse's signatures reveals the influence of imposed European American literacy or the considerable flexibility in the conventions of Plains Indian autographs.

Multiple Names in Transition

Ironically, government records provide much of the available information about the multiple names of Plains Indian warriors in the late nineteenth century. Since "the Crow Indians," anthropologists claim, "are the only Plains tribe with matrilineal descent" (Driver 37), the imposition of a European American patriarchal naming system on Plains people by United States officials may not have been entirely alien to all Native practices. But tribal enrollment lists—catalogs of tribal members compiled in the late nineteenth and early twentieth centuries—did not accurately record serial names. Officials routinely listed only one of a man's several names. Prison records, however, noted what officials referred to as the "aliases" of Indian prisoners of war. The Cheyenne and Kiowa men described below were all labeled "ringleaders" for fighting against United States encroachment on Indian land; all were imprisoned at Fort Marion as a result. Each of them had a variety of names, both Native American and European American. The Cheyenne Cohoe's name, for instance, was derived from "the Spanish 'cojo,' meaning lame" (Hoebel and Petersen 6). This is the name with which he autographed his pictographs. But Cohoe was also known as Mapera-mohe (Water Elk or Moose) or Mohe (Elk) (Hoebel and Petersen 4). Lt. Richard H. Pratt, commonly referred to as Captain Pratt, listed Cohoe's name on the Fort Marion prison records as "Broken Leg." In 1879, after

Figure 3 "Packer's Triple Signature" by Packer and White Bear, Arapahoes, May 1875 to April 1878. (Courtesy of Hampton University Archives). Unlike Howling Wolf (figure 2), who drew his name-symbol and left it to his Euro-American sponsor to translate it for a non-Indian audience, Packer provided three distinct autographs. Just to the right of his head is his name-symbol: an outline of a man with a pronounced back, probably representing a pack. In addition, to assist those unfamiliar with Plains Indian autograph conventions, he wrote his name in English to the right of his name-symbol. He added a second signature in English just above his head. Similarly, White Bear identified himself by writing his name in English above his picture. For those familiar with pictography and with Packer, the shield he carries (a type of costume-symbol) might be enough to identify him.

he was freed from prison, Cohoe went to Hampton Normal and Agricultural Institute, the school for free black students that opened its doors to Indians in 1878. There he was baptized Cohoe, but "acquired a dignified Cheyenne equivalent" of the name as well: "Nohnicas" or "Cripple" (Hoebel and Petersen 6). After he returned to his reservation, he added yet another name. Probably because of his European American contact, he became known as William Cohoe, taking on an English first name and using the Spanish version of his Cheyenne name as a surname.

Other Plains Indian prisoners of war, such as Bears Heart, Making Medicine, and Oheltoint, followed a similar pattern. Like Cohoe, Bears Heart (a translation of the Cheyenne Nockkoist) was imprisoned for three years at Fort Marion. In 1878 he attended Hampton Institute where he was baptized Bear's Heart. Both Captain Pratt and the clergy recorders were careful to add the apostrophe. By 1880 Bears Heart "first signed his names with the prefix 'James,'" which Petersen suggests was a "compliment to Hampton's 'oldest trustee'" (102), James A. Garfield,

whose presidential inauguration, Bears Heart attended. A third Cheyenne, Making Medicine (a translation of the Cheyenne Okuhhatuh) had
at least two aliases: Bear Going Straight and Noksowist. However, he
was baptized David Pendleton, taking the surname of his clergyman
"benefactor." According to Petersen, "Oakerhater" (which sounds like an
Anglicization of Okuhhatuh) was sometimes added to his new surname.

Similarly, Kiowa warrior Ohettoint's names included High Forehead,
Charley Buffalo, and Padai (Twin). (He had a twin brother named
White Buffalo.) He was baptized Ohettoint in 1879, but he "was enrolled in the police under an Irish-Kiowa version": Charles O'Hetowit
(Petersen 169). After several variations of this name, he became "Oheltoint in 1894, and the name stuck" (Petersen 169). He was still known
also as Charley Buffalo. What is evident here is the traditional multiplicity of Plains Indian proper names, the European American lack of
understanding of such protean naming practices, and (despite the move
of the owner of the names toward adopting a single Christian name) the

Figure 4   "A Class of Indians in Fort Marion with Their Teacher, Mrs. Gibbs" by Zo-Tom, Kiowa, 1877. (Courtesy of the Southwest Museum, Los Angeles, California. Neg. No. 34,649). Zo-Tom drew this classroom scene while imprisoned at Fort Marion in Florida. His sketchbook was supplied by Miss Eva Scott. Instead of the long-haired, ornamented Kiowa warriors of his earlier drawings, Zo-Tom drew seven short-haired Indian students wearing Western clothing, sitting neatly in a row, studying English. The teacher stands primly before them. Although Zo-Tom wrote his name using the English alphabet, he still drew a line from his head (he is the second man from the left) to the written autograph. He also identified Making Medicine (second man from the right) in the same fashion. Among the drawings by Fort Marion prisoners the name-symbol almost disappeared, replaced by the costume-symbol or the written signature.

persistent vitality of many names. For such men, their new white men's names did not necessarily erase their Indian names. Instead of transforming Cohoe, Bears Heart, Making Medicine, and Oheltoint into white men (or assimilated Native Americans), their European American names (William Cohoe, James Bear's Heart, David Pendleton, and Charley Oheltoint) were absorbed into the dynamic identities reflected in their existing configuration of names. Thus their names directly reflect a historical crisis more than, as Lejeune suggests, an identity crisis. Nonetheless, this historical upheaval challenged the very conditions of personal identity as configured by Plains people.

Clearly, nineteenth-century Plains Indian naming customs differed markedly from European American naming traditions, in which children receive a given name, a middle name, and a surname (usually identifying the father's family), which will be theirs throughout life. Taking a husband's name or acquiring a title such as MD indicates a change of social, economic, or legal status. In some nineteenth-century Plains Indian cultures, a child received a secret or war name at birth, a given name (perhaps to reflect a family or clan name, embody the family's wish for the child's future, or describe the child's physical appearance) (Mallery 442–45). Then throughout life, the individual acquired new names to document personal achievements and transitions. Although the nineteenth-century Plains Indian practice of serial naming contrasts with European American formal naming traditions (except, as Leigh

Figure 5 "Cheyenne or Kiowa Indian while at Ft. Marion in St. Augustine, Florida," from "Drawing Book" by White Horse, Kiowa, ca. 1876. (Courtesy of Joslyn Art Museum, Omaha, Nebraska, Gift of Mrs. J. Barlow Reynolds, 1949). The Kiowa chief, White Horse, also imprisoned in Fort Marion, used a variety of autographs in this picture, providing a good example of both a name-symbol and a costume-symbol. On the top left of the page, his name-symbol—an outline of a white horse—is connected by a short line to the top of his head. A costume-symbol identifies him in a second way. The distinctive pattern on his blue shield (carried by his wife on the right) identifies him as White Horse.

Figure 6 "Lariating a Buffalo" by White Horse, Kiowa, May 1875–April 1878. (Courtesy of the Yale Collection of Western Americana, Beinecke Rare Book and Manuscript Library). Rather than the convention of right-to-left flow-of-action, this drawing is symmetrical. On the right is an enormous buffalo. On the left, having tied the rope to a tree, White Horse runs toward the buffalo which he has lariated. His flowing, unbound hair and arched legs indicate fast motion. In contrast to his name-symbol and costume-symbol in figure 5, White Horse wrote his name in English above his head, but with no connecting line to his figure.

Gilmore suggests, in the case of women who remarry periodically and take on sequentially each new husband's name), it is similar, in some ways, to the more informal and flexible European American practice of taking and conferring nicknames. Like European American nicknames, Plains Indian names change several times throughout a person's life, reflecting notable characteristics, events, and achievements. Similarly, like nicknames, Plains Indian names are generally given by family and community members. Plains Indian serial names and European American nicknames alike do not function in a rigid linear chronology. Just because Little Susie grows up to become Susan, for instance, does not necessarily mean that family and friends replace the childhood cognomen with the more adult name. It is more likely that both names commingle (at least in memory) as part of a multifaceted sense of identity. Unlike nicknames, however, some Plains Indian names, particularly spiritual names, are conferred in much more serious circumstances. Naming ceremonies, on such occasions, provide community affirmation of an individual's new identity, a type of secular and spiritual transformation.

A name, then, may be an oral or artistic symbol of the individual, a representation that can be modified to reflect the changes a person has undergone. The Plains Indian process of recurrent naming suggests an

Lariating a Buffalo

acknowledgment and affirmation of an ever-changing self and history. As individuals traveled through life, they received new names, recording the important deeds and events of that life and reflecting and shaping an identity that, like Coyote, the trickster culture hero, is continually moving about. In his autobiography, *The Names*, N. Scott Momaday tells us that the Kiowa storyteller Pohd-lohk "believed that a man's life proceeds from his name, in the way a river proceeds from its source" (n.p.). We might amend Momaday's sentence to say that for a nineteenth-century Plains Indian male, life proceeded from his names, each new name joining the others before it, creating a changing, but continuous personal history—a palimpsestic configuration of the self. It is important to keep in mind that such recurrent naming was not a linear process of a new name replacing the one before it. Rather, all the names existed in dynamic relation to one another.

Nineteenth-century Plains Indian names, considered individually, are similar to diary entries recording the discrete events and exploits of a day. Just as the Western forms of diaries and journals reflect the daily cycles of an individual's life over an extended period, the Plains Indian autobiographical form of serial naming provides continual updates on a person's life. According to Felicity Nussbaum the form of the "diary works against a fixed identity" by allowing one to record the minute fluctuations of the self in the process of daily living (137). In the same manner, although not a daily record of personal experience, progressive naming, by oneself and others, highlights and transcribes individual achievements in the context of community. Taken collectively, such serial names are like miniature autobiographies, organizing an individual's life story by documenting the pattern of physical and spiritual events that shape that life. A person's collection of names is not a linear, chronological account of his life, however. A birth name may represent a private identity, a spiritual substratum of the self, that is not spoken by even the most intimate family members. New names do not replace earlier names, but assimilate new interpretations of earlier identities, altering the onomastic configuration of identity.

Such progressive naming reflects a fluid rather than a frozen sense of identity. This perplexed already suspicious U.S. authorities who throughout the latter part of the nineteenth century were trying to remove, round up, and restrain Native peoples. The General Allotment Act (also known as the Dawes Act) of 1887 provided for the allotment of reservation land to individual Indians. This was an attempt, once and for all, to force Indians into farming and ranching, to instill in them a sense of property ownership (and, consequently, to eliminate the reservation and encourage assimilation into the European American population) and, ultimately, to free reservation land for takeover by whites. To accomplish this, an accurate list of names of Native Americans was necessary. European American officials, of course, were leery of such changing, not to mention unspellable, names. Often Indians took a white name for official business with the Bureau of Indian Affairs. Fixing a name, an often alien one at that, on the page, reflects the predominant nineteenth-century European American impulse to freeze, in print if not in fact, Native peoples. Imposing a relatively unchanging naming system on more dynamic naming systems was one strategy to accomplish this.

N. Scott Momaday's *Names*

A man's life proceeds from his name, in the way a river proceeds from its source.
—*N. Scott Momaday,* The Names

A century later, N. Scott Momaday affirms the importance of names for Plains Indian identity. In a 1981 interview Momaday had this to say about names:

I believe that a man is his name. The name and the existence are indivisible. One has to live up to his name. . . . Somewhere in the Indian mentality there is that idea that when someone is given a name—and, by the way, it transcends Indian cultures certainly— when a man is given a name, existence is given to him, too. And what could be worse than not having a name. (Momaday as quoted in Schubnell 49–50)

Unpopular as Momaday's notion of names may be with postmodern scholars who find no inherent connection between words and things, Momaday insists that, for him, one's name and one's existence are indivisible. Such a notion aligns Momaday with those autobiography theorists who prefer "to conceptualize the relation between the self and language as a mutually constituting interdependency" (Eakin, *Fictions in Autobiography* 8), rather than to think of the self as some pure essence preceding language.

Momaday's second autobiography, *The Names*, emphasizes his belief not only in the referentiality of names, but in their creative possibilities. The book's title, the acknowledgment ("in devotion to those whose names I bear and to those who bear my names"), and the genealogical chart (with the name of each relative handwritten by Momaday) all testify to Momaday's belief in the intimate relationship between proper names and personal identity. In fact, Momaday explains that "the great principle of selection in the book is the principle of naming . . . a very complicated and a sacred business" (Quoted in Woodward 88). The first words of the brief section preceding the prologue announce: "My name is Tsoai-talee. I am, therefore, Tsoai-talee, therefore I am. The storyteller Pohd-lohk gave me the name Tsoai-talee. He believed that a man's life proceeds from his name, in the way a river proceeds from its source" (n.p.). In essence, the first two sentences may be translated: I have a name, therefore I am that name, therefore I am. For Momaday and, he would have us believe, for his people, a name precedes one's existence, not vice versa. It is worth noting that Pohd-lohk is a storyteller, one who shapes language into meaning and delight. In naming Momaday (Tsoai-talee) Pohd-lohk creates him, just as in naming his relatives, Momaday fashions them for the reader. The name Tsoai-talee also embodies a story, is itself a story—the story of the tree-stump-turned-giant-rock and the seven sisters who, chased by their brother-turned-bear, are lifted into the sky by the tree and transformed into the Big Dipper. As the tree elevates the girls to safety, the bear-brother reaches his huge paws up to snatch them, scoring the growing tree with his great claws. The tree, now scratched all around by the bear, becomes Devils Tower and the seven sisters are transformed into the seven stars of the Big Dipper. This story explains the origin of Tsoai: "the great black igneous monolith that rises out of the Black Hills of Wyoming" (Momaday 55) known today as Devils Tower. Thus the name (Tsoai-talee, or Rock-Tree Boy), like the story, links Momaday and his people to the past, to a specific geographical location, and to the heavens.

Just as names are crucial in the prefatory materials, names are important in the first chapter. Momaday begins the first paragraph with a list of generic names: "animals," "birds," "objects," "forms," and "sounds"; and he ends the paragraph with the names of his distant Kiowa relatives: "Pohd-lohk, Keahdinekeah, Aho" (3). The very next paragraph continues Momaday's recitation of the names of the dead, this time the European American relatives on his mother's side: "Galyen, Scott, McMillan" (3). This generations-old coalition of names leads inevitably to his own. The Kiowa names—Kau-au-ointy, Keahdinekeah, and Mammedaty—move alongside the European American names—I. J. Galyen, Nancy Scott, and Theodore Ellis—before they mingle in his parents (who have both Native American and European American names): Huan-toa (Alfred) and Natachee (Mayme). Just as Mammedaty, Momaday's paternal grandfather, "persists in his name," so do all his ancestors who, according to Momaday, have "invested the shadow of [their] presence in . . . [their] name[s]" (26). Like a Kiowa Adam, Momaday delights in creating catalogs of names—of things, events, stories, and people. The names throughout *The Names* are certainly "interpretive readings that conjure up identity," as Paul Jay has said, but, I would add, for Momaday, names construct identity as well. By beginning and ending his autobiography with the names of his ancestors, those whose names he claims as part of himself, Momaday self-consciously reconstructs a Kiowa identity—an identity threatened, ravaged, and often destroyed by the dominant society—in the late twentieth century.

In sections three and four of part one, Momaday brings these names to life by describing their histories. The third section is devoted primarily to his European American ancestors—Theodore Scott and Anne Ellis, Momaday's maternal grandparents, and to his part-Indian mother, Natachee, "the namesake of that dark mystery," her Cherokee grandmother, Natachee Galyen (Momaday 20). Again emphasizing the constitutive interrelationship between name and identity, Momaday claims that his mother's name alone was reason enough for her to begin "to see herself as an Indian" (25). Such a view recalls the practice of conferring promissory names into which the nameholder must grow. It also raises controversial questions about the highly contested subject of Native identity, a key focus of Momaday's autobiography.[8]

Section four, focusing on Momaday's Kiowa relatives, opens with yet another name: Mammedaty, Momaday's paternal grandfather. Momaday writes: "Mammedaty was my grandfather, whom I never knew. Yet he came to be imagined posthumously in the going on of the blood, having invested the shadow of his presence in an object or a word, in his name above all. He enters into my dreams; he persists in his name" (26). From the name Mammedaty, the linguistic trace of the grandfather he never knew, Momaday imagines the man himself. As well as his grandfather, Momaday introduces his grandmother, Aho, and his great-great-grandmother, Kau-au-ointy.

Similarly, section five deals with Momaday's father, Huan-toa, who was renamed Alfred Morris after a white friend of the family (a common Plains Indian practice of serial naming, but also an indication of changing times). In sections six and seven, Momaday describes his parents' courtship and marriage and his own birth. He gives special attention to his name on the standard certificate of birth: Navarro Scotte Mammedaty. As we might expect, the "first notable event" in his life was his family's journey to Devils Tower, the place from which his Kiowa name is derived. He ends this brief section by stating his intention to "imagine a day in the life of a man, Pohd-lohk, who gave [him] a name" (42). These seven sections name and describe Momaday's relatives.

Not surprisingly, the lengthy section eight is devoted to Pohd-lohk (which in Kiowa means Old Wolf): the name-giver. Momaday tells a story about "a young man" who "heard in a high wind the whimper of young wolves," and "had known at once, instinctively, where and what they were, and he went to them quietly, directly" (46). The young man sang softly to the wolves as they "lay huddled among the rocks" (46). The next paragraph consists of only three italicized words: *"Pohd-lohk, old wolf"* (46). Momaday asserts that the relation between a self and a name is mysterious and powerful. Because of his name, suggests Momaday, Pohd-lohk knows instinctively where and what the wolves were and how to respond to them. With such a personal understanding of the magic of names, Pohd-lohk is an especially powerful bestower of names.

The name Tsoai-talee was given to the boy Momaday by the storyteller Pohd-lohk who, not coincidentally, relates to him the origin, history, and stories of the Kiowa. Momaday explains: "Pohd-lohk spoke, as if telling a story, of the coming-out people, of their long journey. He spoke of how it was that everything began, of Tsoai, and of the stars falling or holding fast in strange patterns in the sky. And in this, at last, Pohd-lohk affirmed the whole life of the child in a name, saying: Now you are, Tsoai-talee" (57). The origin of the Kiowa, their history, and their relation to the universe are all essential aspects of Kiowa identity that converge in the child's name. The name, then, embodies these mythical and historical mysteries. The punctuation of the last line is crucial. It is not "Now you are Tsoai-talee," a simple announcement. The comma makes all the difference in meaning: "Now you are, Tsoai-talee" is a proclamation of existence itself. In fact, as Momaday would have it, through him (his name), the stories and lives of his people live on.

Suggestive of nineteenth-century Plains Indian naming practices, Momaday himself has several names: Navarro Scotte Mammedaty (recorded on his birth certificate), Tsoai-talee (Rock-Tree Boy), Tsotohah (Red Bluff), and N. Scott Momaday. Momaday emphasizes his "first Indian name," Tsoai-talee; he also has a "second Indian name"—Tsotohah (Red Bluff)—which he downplays (170). Since Tsotohah does not lend itself to as many mythical, historical, or geographic resonances as Tsoai-talee, Momaday mentions it only twice and relegates it to his glossary of Indian terms, an alternative identity lurking among the untold stories beyond this text. In an interview with Charles L. Woodard, Momaday mentions yet another of his Indian names—Wanbli Wanjila (Eagle Alone)—given to him by a Lakota elder (90). Momaday does not emphasize the dynamic aspect of Plains Indian naming. However, he shows how Kiowa names have changed historically (his earlier Kiowa relatives have only Kiowa names, for instance, while his more recent Kiowa relatives have both Kiowa and non-Kiowa names). He illustrates also how an intimate connection to a landscape and an entire history of a people may be crucial ingredients of a name. He does not, however, emphasize the sense of possibility of earning ever new names (reflecting current achievements and new identities) throughout his life. Instead, Momaday treats names, especially his first Indian name, as preservers of tribal identity. Perhaps this explains why he is willing to reveal some of his names. Like others before him, Momaday wishes to preserve something of the Kiowa past in writing for future generations—even if it means unprecedented personal revelation.

Nineteenth-century (and to varying degrees twentieth-century) Plains Indian serial naming is an autobiographical act, a language act that creates and narrates personal identity. Considering a person's current name allows others to learn about a specific event, exploit, or relationship; reading a person's accumulated names, like reading a collection of letters or a set of diary entries, reveals a more detailed personal narrative than any one name, letter, or diary entry can provide. Like diaries, journals, or letters, such a configuration of names allows for "articulating a multiplicity of contestatory selves" (Nussbaum 132), for documenting the transformative moments of one's life, for narrating one's community-endorsed accomplishments, or for giving voice to a polyphonous *I*. Such names might be spoken or depicted in pictographs, providing a multidimensional self-narration that reflects both individual and community, worldly and spiritual, and past and present possibilities. For Momaday, names give existence and reflect individual and community, as well as contemporary and historical, realities. They also preserve a tribal affiliation and tradition. Plains Indian names, then, function not merely as labels, but as compact personal and tribal histories. In addition, names are profoundly narrative; stories nestle within stories—personal, historical, and mythical. A proper name (or constellation of names) evokes a connection to community, place (in time and space), and universe—all of which create and narrate a vital sense of self that struggles against indeterminacy.

Notes

1 The term "the Autobiographical Act" is from Elizabeth Bruss's book, *Autobiographical Acts: The Changing Situation of a Literary Genre* (Baltimore: Johns Hopkins UP, 1976).

2 For a feminist discussion of the "semantic duplicity of the proper name" as it relates to European American women, see Donna Perreault, "On Women's Strategies Against Their Im/Proper Names," p. 1.

3 Susan Stanford Friedman uses the term "relational self" to describe how diverse American women describe their notions of themselves as related to, rather than separate from, others.

4 For a discussion of how "focusing so intently on oneself . . . blithering on about your own life and thoughts is very bad form for Indians," see Brian Swann and Arnold Krupat, *I Tell You Now*, p. xii.

5 Although such deeds were generally performed by men, there are some examples of women warriors. See Pretty-shield for accounts of Strikes-two, a sixty-year-old woman who defends her camp with a root digger (202–3) and Finds-them-and-kills-them and The-other-magpie, two Crow women who "fought with Three-stars [General Crook] on the Rosebud" (227–31).

6   The fact that women were not routinely imprisoned is not the only reason they did not display these types of autographs. Apparently Plains Indian women did not produce realistic representations like the men, but rather geometric designs, usually on such items as parfleches.

7   For an account of how a costume-symbol (details of dress and adornment) replaced the name-symbol in the drawings of Fort Marion prisoners, see Petersen.

8   For a discussion of authenticity, objectification, and Natachee Momaday as Momaday presents her in *The Names,* see Paul Jay's essay in this volume.

References

Beck, Peggy V., and Anna L. Walters. *The Sacred: Ways of Knowledge, Sources of Life.* Tsaile, Ariz.: Navajo Community Coll. P, 1977.

Brumble, H. David. *American Indian Autobiography.* Berkeley: U of California P, 1988.

Bruss, Elizabeth. *Autobiographical Acts: The Changing Situation of a Literary Genre.* Baltimore: Johns Hopkins UP, 1976.

Driver, Harold E. *Indians of North America.* 2d. ed. 1961. Chicago: U of Chicago P, 1969.

Eakin, Paul John. *Fictions in Autobiography: Studies in the Art of Self-Invention.* Princeton: Princeton UP, 1985.

——. "Narrative and Chronology as Structures of Reference and the New Model Autobiographer." *Studies in Autobiography.* Ed. James Olney. New York: Oxford UP, 1988. 32–41.

Eastman, Charles Alexander. *From the Deep Woods to Civilization: Chapters in the Autobiography of an Indian.* 1916. Lincoln: U of Nebraska P, 1977.

——. *Indian Boyhood.* 1902. Greenwich, Conn.: Fawcett, 1972.

——. *The Soul of the Indian: An Interpretation.* 1911. Lincoln: U of Nebraska P, 1980.

Friedman, Susan Stanford. "Women's Autobiographical Selves: Theory and Practice." *The Private Self: Theory and Practice of Women's Autobiographical Writings.* Ed. Shari Benstock. Chapel Hill: U of North Carolina P, 1988. 34–62.

Gardner, Howard. *Frames of Mind: The Theory of Multiple Intelligences.* New York: Basic, 1983.

Hoebel, E. Adamson, and Karen Daniels Petersen, eds. *A Cheyenne Sketchbook.* By Cohoe. Norman: U of Oklahoma P, 1964.

Jay, Paul. "Posing: Autobiography and the Subject of Photography." *Autobiography and Postmodernism.* Ed. Kathleen Ashley, Leigh Gilmore, and Gerald Peters. Amherst: U of Massachusetts P, 1994.

Joseph, Alvin M., Jr. *The Indian Heritage of America.* New York: Bantam, 1968.

Krupat, Arnold. *For Those Who Come After: A Study of Native American Autobiography.* Berkeley: U of California P, 1985.

——. *The Voice in the Margin: Native American Literature and the Canon.* Berkeley: U of California P, 1989.

Lejeune, Philippe. "The Autobiographical Contract." *French Literary Theory Today: A Reader.* Ed. Tzvetan Todorov. New York: Cambridge UP, 1982. 192–222.

Mallery, Garrick. "Picture-Writing of the American Indians." *Tenth Annual Report of the Bureau of Ethnology* to the Secretary of the Smithsonian Institution, 1888–89. Ed. J. Powell. Washington, D.C.: GPO, 1892. New York: Dover, 1972.

Mithun, Marianne. "Principles of Naming in Mohawk." *Naming Systems.* 1980 Proceedings of the American Ethnological Society. Ed. Elisabeth Tooker. Washington, D.C.: American Ethnological Society, 1984. 40–54.

Momaday, N. Scott. *The Names: A Memoir.* New York: Harper, 1976.

Nussbaum, Felicity. "Toward Conceptualizing Diary." *Studies in Autobiography.* Ed. James Olney. New York: Oxford UP, 1988. 128–40.

Perreault, Donna. "On Women's Strategies Against Their Im/Proper Names: A Psychoanalytic Meditation." Unpublished ms. 1986.

Petersen, Karen Daniels. *Plains Indian Art from Fort Marion.* Norman: U of Oklahoma P, 1971.

Plenty-coups. *Plenty-coups: Chief of the Crows.* 1930. Ed. Frank B. Linderman. Lincoln: U of Nebraska P, 1972.

Pretty-shield. *Pretty-shield: Medicine Woman of the Crows.* 1932. Ed. Frank B. Linderman. Lincoln: U of Nebraska P, 1972.

Schubnell, Matthias. *N. Scott Momaday: The Cultural and Literary Background.* Norman: U of Oklahoma P, 1985.

Sturrock, John. "The New Model Autobiographer." *New Literary History* 9 (Autumn 1977): 51–63.

Swann, Brian, and Arnold Krupat, eds. *I Tell You Now: Autobiographical Essays by Native American Writers.* Lincoln: U of Nebraska P, 1987.

Woodard, Charles L. *Ancestral Voice: Conversations with N. Scott Momaday.* Lincoln: U of Nebraska P, 1989.

Nuptial Interruptions: Autobiographical Boundaries
in Wordsworth's "Farewell"

DAVID P. HANEY

∎

Autobiographical Boundaries

A poem that proclaims itself to be autobiographical calls special attention to its boundaries. "A Farewell" is Wordsworth's 1802 meditation on the boundaries of his "little Nook of mountain ground" in Grasmere, boundaries that not only enclose an important geographical space, but also mark an important autobiographical transition: the poem previews the crossing and recrossing of these boundaries on the poet's journey to visit his former lover, Annette Vallon, in France and then to wed Mary Hutchinson, who will join William and his sister, Dorothy, in the enclosed world of their Grasmere home. This strange piece of prospective autobiography offers us an occasion to meditate more generally on the insistent but indeterminate boundaries of the autobiographical genre.

Several important textual boundaries are, from the perspective of autobiography, versions of the one that defines a work as autobiographical. The expressive boundary between a poem and its origin, the mimetic boundary between a poem and its referent, the discursive boundary between speaker and audience, and the textual boundary between an individual poem and the whole of a poet's work all echo the complex boundary between the autobiographical text and the life in and about which it is written. The insistent presence of that boundary—the force with which poetic structures and other events in life establish themselves within the divided structure of a binary relationship—provides a provisional figural support for a shifting relationship that is only superficially binary. Autobiographical texts such as Wordsworth's *Prelude* are as busy producing a new self as they are representing an old one. Thus the material on the "life" side of the boundary is an unstable mixture, certainly not reducible to a linear narrative, of the child who is father of the man, the man writing the poem, and the future poet to be enabled by this act of writing. This triple relationship between life and text is also thematized within the autobiographical text, on the "poem" side of the boundary: the story of *The Prelude* becomes the constantly revised story of the painful struggle and hopeful blending of these three selves, a series of rhetorical moves back and forth across what little is left of the initial demarcation of autobiography from life.

For us, much more so than for Wordsworth, one manifestation of this boundary is the named genre autobiography, a recognizable set of literary conventions that separates autobiography from other genres as well as from the life outside an autobiography.[1] As Wordsworth's embarrassment about *The Prelude* shows, self-writing was for him still only justifiable in the service of a larger purpose, such as *The Recluse*. In that sense the tentative generic boundary of *The Prelude*—marking off its independent existence as autobiography—existed only so that it could be effaced as *The Prelude* was taken up into a larger work. However, that boundary was strong enough to keep Wordsworth's poem on his own life from entering the public realm while its author was still alive. Perhaps, as in Borges's "Parable of the Palace," this reflects the inability of the poem and its autobiographical referent—the living person—to occupy the same space in the world. However, that very taboo separating the poem from life outside the poem is also an enabling boundary: it is precisely the complex oppositions between the autobiographical text and the life it both reflects and reshapes that generate the peculiar power of *The Prelude*.

Two radically different views of interpretive boundaries will help us to understand the autobiographical boundaries set up by "A Farewell." The first is what Derrida calls "the law of genre." That which identifies a genre by marking its borders—the designation "novel," in Derrida's example, or the designation "autobiography" here—is paradoxically included and excluded from the genre itself, "generating" and "degenerating" the genre:

> This inclusion and this exclusion do not remain exterior to one another; they do not exclude each other. But neither are they immanent or identical to each other. They are neither one nor two. They form what I shall call the *genre-clause*, a clause stating at once the juridical utterance, the precedent-making designation and the law-text, but also the closure, the closing that excludes itself from what it includes (one could also speak of a floodgate [*écluse*] of

genre). The clause or floodgate of genre declasses what it allows to be classed. It tolls the knell of genealogy or of genericity, which it however also brings forth to the light of day. Putting to death the very thing that it engenders, it cuts a strange figure; a formless form, it remains nearly invisible, it neither sees the day nor brings itself to light. Without it, neither genre nor literature come to light, but as soon as there is this blinking of an eye, this clause or this floodgate of genre, at the very moment that a genre or a literature is broached, at that very moment, degenerescence has begun, the end begins. (Derrida 61–62)

The very boundary that engenders the genre also destroys it, because the act of engendering is also the act of limiting and because that boundary is exactly what cannot be included within the bounded area, though it is also exactly what makes the bounded area exist. This incommensurability results in violence; the legislative act of boundary-creation invades the bounded area, and "with the inevitable dividing of the trait that marks membership, the boundary of the set comes to form, by invagination, an internal pocket larger than the whole" (Derrida 55).[2] In autobiography this process is simply demonstrated by the fact that the boundary of the narrative—the line separating text from life—is turned in on the autobiography itself and forms "an internal pocket larger than the whole" by becoming a potentially overwhelming, uncontainable concern of the autobiography, precisely because that line cannot be contained *within* the autobiography. Thus *The Prelude* is both engendered and interrupted by the problematic boundary between the written life and the writing life that surrounds it.

The sudden appearance of "Imagination" in book 6 is perhaps the most dramatic example of this interruption and invagination of the autobiography by its own boundary:

> Imagination!—lifting up itself
> Before the eye and progress of my song
> Like an unfathered vapour, here that power,
> In all the might of its endowments, came
> Athwart me. (*The Prelude* [1805] 6.525–29)

The autobiography is interrupted and temporarily brought to a halt by the appearance of "Imagination," the very force that generates autobiographical (and all other) poetry. This interruption is also an invagination: the imagination, which is the boundary between the poem and the poet's life in the sense that it is the power that effects the transformation of life to poetry, enters the space of the poem, turning the imaginative boundary of the poem inward to such an extent that the imagination moves from its position outside the poem as a generating force to an anomalous position within the poem as an event. But it is an event that cannot really be contained within the poem, because it is a force ontologically prior to the poem itself and, as a force more powerful than any individual poetic manifestation, it is "larger" than the "whole" of the poem it enters.

This boundary can also be read as a horizon, the term Hans-Georg Gadamer inherits from Nietzsche and Husserl to designate "the range of vision that includes everything that can be seen from a particular vantage point" (Gadamer 302). "The closed horizon that is supposed to enclose a culture is an abstraction. The historical movement of human life consists in the fact that it is never absolutely bound to any one standpoint, and hence can never have a truly closed horizon. The horizon is, rather, something into which we move and that moves with us. Horizons change for a person who is moving" (Gadamer 304).[3]

Both Derrida's closure-marking "genre-clause" and Gadamer's historical horizon can be thought of as enclosing the same autobiographical area—Derrida's by legislating and demarcating the genre of autobiography, Gadamer's by staking out that which can be viewed from the autobiographical perspective. For Gadamer the boundary's deadly closure is defused because it is recognized from the start as an abstraction; its provisionality allows the boundary to be successively trespassed by the forward movement of interpretation. These two interpretations of the boundary enclosing an autobiographical text are of course in many ways incompatible: Derrida's boundary is a law of textuality, whereas Gadamer's horizon limits and enables an interpretive activity that refuses to see the mechanisms of semiology or textuality as paradigmatic.[4] However, the two concepts enclose and expose the same spaces within an autobiographical text, bringing to consciousness the provisional limits of understanding in one case and generic textual boundaries in another. That is, a term such as autobiography (or "the poem on my own life") establishes a moving horizon of interpretation and legislates the birth and death of the text bounded by such a term. Insofar as it can be seen as a moving interpretive horizon it is productive of meaning; insofar as the energy of that movement is turned inward in a process by which "the boundary of the set comes to form, by invagination, an internal pocket larger than the whole," the engendering of meaning and the creation of a genre are accompanied by the opposite movement of "degenerescence."

Both concepts can be traced back—if only indirectly—to Kant's insight that to limit the field of understanding is to be able to think of that which is beyond the horizon only—but positively—in terms of the boundary itself, which means that relationships, not positive essences, are the stuff of thought: "But the setting of a boundary to the field of the understanding by something, which is otherwise unknown to it, is still a cognition which belongs to reason even at this standpoint, and by which it is neither confined within the sensible, nor straying without it, but only refers, as befits the knowledge of a boundary, to the relation between that which lies without it, and that which is contained within it" (Kant 133–34). The Gadamerian and Derridean concepts illuminate each other as they pull the Kantian boundary in opposite directions; neither Gadamer nor Derrida will succumb to the compromise of a stable boundary isolating the thereby identifiable "phenomenal" from the "noumenal." Derrida shows us the violence involved in the boundary's relationship to that which it bounds, and Gadamer offers us the possibility of seeing life on that unstable boundary as productive of meaning. The autobiographical self is positively constituted by its shifting horizons, the horizons of, for example, its relationship to the life after the poem and to its constitutive web of language and other selves. These horizons also name the autobiographical self and intrude their boundary-status into that which they name; they partake of the invagination described by Derrida, a process that destroys the very inside/ outside relationship the boundary has established.

But most importantly, these horizons, even if construed negatively, are a location from which it is possible to write. As Lacoue-Labarthe and Nancy say (in a passage from *The Literary Absolute* cited approvingly by Derrida) of the Schlegels' Romantic poetics, "generation is dissolution, *Auflösung.* . . . Not only dissolution as decomposition or resolution but, beyond simple chemism . . . organicity itself or the process of auto-formation. Actually, this is far from able to delimit a genre, but it equates Genre with totality (with the absolute) in the dissolution of all limits and the absolutization of all particularity" (91). Wordsworth's ambivalent respect for generic boundaries—as evidenced by his careful but confusing classification, from 1815 on, of his poems according to asymmetrical criteria of genre, occasion, topic, and (most prominently) psychological faculty—would never have allowed him to assent to such a complete absolutization-through-dissolution of genre. However, the creative dissolution of boundaries is an important part of his autobiographical rhetoric, as well as a cornerstone of his well-known arguments against the artificial divisions instituted by neoclassical poetic diction. The dissolution of boundaries in Wordsworthian autobiography shows up most clearly in the rhetoric of *The Prelude,* which is energized by the dissolution of the poem's own figural structures. The figure of childhood autonomy in book 1, the mother-child relationship in book 2, and the French Revolution in the later books (to name only a few) all function as temporarily adequate figures that get the story told, but that are "outgrown" by the progress of the text as quickly as the events they contextualize supersede each other: childhood autonomy enters a world of temporal connections; the Blest Babe episode modulates into the death of the poet's mother; and of course French freedom becomes tyranny. The autobiographical narrative proceeds by establishing figures for the self from the "inside," then stepping "outside" of those figures as they collapse, entering still other figures that are erected to enclose the collapsed ones, and repeating the process, which occurs in (as well as between) the narrative "life" and the discursive dialogue with Coleridge "about" that life. Such a narrative must confront at every turn the paradoxical relationship between figural boundaries and that which is bounded, but must continue with the faith that all is "gratulant if rightly understood" (*The Prelude* [1805] 13.385).[5] The paradoxes in the "law of the genre" are precisely the forces that generate life, that incarnate spirit into life, thought into language. For Derrida to say that the generic boundary generates both genre and degenerescence is to say that it creates a life, but a life whose mortality is in constant view, a life "travelling towards the grave" (*The Prelude* [1805] 1.269), profitably or unprofitably as the case may be.

Going for Mary

Thomas De Quincey, defending Wordsworth against Hazlitt's complaint that the poet never wrote about events such as marriage, suggests why Wordsworth's treatment of a wedding must in any case be indirect:

> Whoever looks searchingly into the characteristic genius of Wordsworth will see that he does not willingly deal with a passion in its direct aspect, or presenting an unmodified contour, but in forms more complex and oblique, and when passing under the shadow of

some secondary passion. . . . A wedding-day is, in many a life, the sunniest of its days. But, unless it is overcast with some event more tragic than could be wished, its uniformity of blaze, without shade or relief, makes it insipid to the mere bystander. ("On Wordsworth's Poetry," *Collected Writings* 11:301–3)

In "A Farewell," one of whose topics is the most directly experienced wedding day that can be imagined, the poet's own, the requisite obliqueness and complexity are provided by the many boundaries that lie between the poet and the wedding. This poem, written in the spring of 1802, looks forward to William and Dorothy's prospective departure from Grasmere on a journey that would include both their visit to William's former lover, Annette Vallon, in France and William's marriage to Mary Hutchinson. A highly condensed meditation on the problems of autobiographical boundaries, "A Farewell" is unusual in that the main autobiographical referent—Wordsworth's marriage—is in the unknown future instead of the experienced past; this adds a new uncertainty to an already complex set of autobiographical boundaries.

The crossing of several overlapping boundaries is anticipated: the temporary departure from the all-important domestic enclosure of Dove Cottage, the transition from life with Dorothy to marriage with Mary, and the crossing of the English Channel to visit his former lover and his illegitimate daughter. However, the poet writes from the perspective of one very specific boundary, on one side of which is the enclosed "little Nook of mountain ground," and on the other side of which is the journey to Mary and to Annette:

> Farewell, thou little Nook of mountain ground,
> Thou rocky corner in the lowest stair
> Of Fairfield's mighty Temple that doth bound
> One side of our whole vale with grandeur rare,
> Sweet Garden-orchard! of all spots that are
> The loveliest surely man hath ever found,
> Farewell! we leave thee to heaven's peaceful care
> Thee and the Cottage which thou dost surround. (1–8)

The near side is the enclosed, protected space surrounding Dove Cottage, brother and sister, poetry—the horizon of a poetic, literary vision whose interior can easily function as the personified addressee of the poem. In this picturesque framing of the Nook, the potentially sublime or disjunctive relation of Dove Cottage to the surrounding mountains is harmonized into the relation between "stair" and "temple," all under "heaven's peaceful care."[6] The implied far side of this protective boundary is the open world of the relation to Annette, William's peripheral involvement in the French Revolution, and the wedding to Mary, which, from this interior perspective, can only be indicated by an empty temporality characterized as inaccessible—"For two months now in vain we shall be sought" (18)—or, later, as "burning": "Two burning months let summer overleap" (62).[7] This protective poetic circle drawn around Dove Cottage clearly outlines the personified Nook, creating a horizon that domesticates the relation to the unknown region beyond with the promise that its only explicit representative—Mary Hutchinson (who is also already an insider[8])—will soon be safely within the magic circle.

The problem of the poem's title, however, begins to suggest that the boundary between the poetic interior and the worldly exterior—ultimately, the boundary that both separates and links literary genres and other processes of life—is itself a deeply historical creation that begins as a fluid horizon and only years later acquires a generic determinacy adequate to the thematic boundary established in the opening lines. Dorothy refers to this poem in her 1802 journal on 29 May as William's "poem on Going for Mary" (129), on 31 May as "the poem on 'Our Departure'" (129), and on 17 June as "the poem on our going for Mary" (137). The repeated references suggest Dorothy's understandable preoccupation with this poem about her brother's marriage; it is mentioned more often than the "Immortality" ode, which was under way at the same time. She always refers to the poem by privileging its referent—a poem "on" something—but the differences in her designations suggest her vacillation in thinking of the poem as a somewhat autonomous poetic text titled "Our Departure," bounded by the words she was lovingly transcribing, or as the indicator of a trip connected to her life by the first-person possessive plural pronoun—"our going for Mary." Her first mention of the poem as "on Going for Mary" lies somewhere between these extremes: the capitalization of "Going" and the absence of "our" suggest a title, but the wording and the absence of quotation marks parallel the 17 June emphasis on the poem's occasion rather than its textual constitution. Like many of Wordsworth's poems, it was untitled in manuscript (that is, without the clear generic boundary that a title can impose), and was finally published in 1815 as "A Farewell," having made the full journey from the event of a "departure" to a generically identifiable linguistic narrative: a "farewell" appropriately included under "Poems Founded on the Affections."[9]

The rhetoric by means of which this boundary enclosing the "little Nook of mountain ground" is established—a boundary that is both a scene of interruption or invagination and a horizon of interpretation— depends at the simplest level on the ability of marriage simultaneously to be a trope of interruption and a trope of fusion. Any marriage, of course, is a Saidian "beginning" in the sense that it establishes a new continuity (a double one in the sense of a new temporality *and* a new intersubjectivity) in an act of discontinuity, the interruption of a previous continuity. For Wordsworth, however, the situation is special and complex, partly because the shift is not between two discrete states—bachelor to husband—but rather involves, as Albert Cook notes, the complex overlaying of one "family" (William, Mary, and their future children) on another (William, Dorothy, and Basil Montague), with the acknowledgment of the relation to Annette Vallon and his illegitimate daughter, Caroline, as an essential part of the transition from one state to another (*Cook* 8–9). (William, or at least his friends and family, saw the closure of his affair with Annette, newly enabled by the Peace of Amiens, as an important prerequisite for his marriage to Mary.)

This bounding circle is both established and problematized by the displacement of the courtship ritual from Mary to the "little Nook." The gesture of "farewell" establishes a defamiliarizing distance from the domestic Grasmere, allowing for it to be courted as that which can appear as a coquettish, unpredictable other—"O most constant and most fickle place!" (41)—(in a way that the familiar though absent Mary perhaps cannot be) and to be pictured as pining for the absent inhabitants who are represented only by gifts:

> For two months now in vain we shall be sought:
> We leave you here in solitude to dwell
> With these our latest gifts of tender thought. (18–20)

This personifying differentiation based on gender is of course the same differentiation between speaker and beloved that helps to define various genres of love-poetry and that informs the entire speaker-addressee relationship in this poem. Stuart Curran points out the close etymological association of "genre" and "gender" (9), an association exploited by Derrida (70) and Lacoue-Labarthe and Nancy (91). Here, as the Nook is courted as an other and a woman, it also implicitly switches gender and becomes a displaced version of himself, for Mary will "wed" the place as well as the man: "She'll come to you; to you herself will wed" (31).[10] Mary Jacobus, using Derrida's essay to read the "Vadracour and Julia" episode in *The Prelude*, argues that Wordsworth's reading of the French Revolution in terms of romance—putting "a woman's face on the Revolution" (52)—uses gender difference to establish the generic identity of the autobiographer, and then excises that difference in the "man-to-man" (53) figure of *The Prelude* as a letter to Coleridge. Wordsworth performs a similar operation in "A Farewell" by conflating the Nook's role as a love object with its role as a surrogate husband, thus effacing the gender difference even as that very difference helps constitute the poem generically as a kind of love-poem. Not only is the gender difference established and effaced, but also the very boundary between speaker and beloved: the Nook is both an other to be courted and William himself as Mary's intended. The figural structure of courtship remains, but the content of the poles changes: William's relation to the Nook as a figure for Mary becomes Mary's relation to the Nook as a figure for William.

Thus the *structure* of the differential courtship ritual is established at the expense of its specific "props of affection" (*The Prelude* [1805] 2.294) or actual life-content. In a move familiar from contemporary passages in *The Prelude*, a kind of figural scaffolding is set up that holds contradictions apart so that we can see them, but reveals its own provisionality as it questions the very oppositions it erects. Thus courtship ritual is the figure within which the complexities of the poem can be worked out. But it becomes clear, as the poles of the figure switch around and if the story of Annette (just on the other side of this poem's boundary, as it is just on the other side of the Vadracour and Julia story in *The Prelude*) is taken into account, that this figure masks a promiscuous, incestuous, and even extrahuman range of possible pairs:[11] William–Mary, William–Dorothy, William–Annette, Mary–Nook, William–Nook, etc. In other words, the boundary drawn around the Nook is figurally the relationship of courtship and marriage, providing a horizon that, recognizing its own provisionality, enables the play of a variety of relationships, a play that would be much more threatening were it not for this figural mask and support.

Any generic or thematic boundary must be supported by a sense of legality that separates the legitimate from the illegitimate, and William was certainly concerned with seeing his illegitimate relationship with Annette resolved and superseded by the legitimate relationship with Mary. But the courtship of the Nook, an act involved in the separation of future legitimacy from past illegitimacy, mixes these very categories, as does the invagination described by Derrida, which both legitimates and negates the boundary's relationship to what it bounds. Put otherwise, to court a Nook is generically legitimate according to a variety of literary traditions in which a landscape can be personified, but that very generic legitimacy provides the occasion for and the horizon of a play that forces us to rethink the binary categories of legitimacy and illegitimacy—a play that is not outside the law, but that forces the law to accommodate the outside.

This courtship figure is supported and complicated by the figural relationship of gift exchange and the poem's uncertain vacillation between the worlds of gifts and commodities. Wordsworth begins the relationship with deceptive simplicity by stating that the thoughts constituting this poem will function as ritual substitutes for his and Dorothy's absent selves: "We leave you here in solitude to dwell / With these our latest gifts of tender thought" (19–20). However, the logic of gift exchange is both a support for the poem's figural structure and an indication of a problem. As Lewis Hyde points out, a gift-economy (as opposed to a commodity-economy) operates on a principle of unity rather than alienation: "A gift, when it moves across the boundary, either stops being a gift or else abolishes the boundary. A commodity can cross the line without any change in its nature; moreover, its exchange will often establish a boundary where none previously existed (as, for example, in the sale of a necessity to a friend). *Logos*-trade draws the boundary, *eros*-trade erases it" (61).[12] Thus the asymmetrical movement of gifts among the three players (Nook, William, Mary) establishes a unity that is precisely not dependent on a binary reciprocal relationship of the kind that a boundary entails. As Hyde points out, gift-economies work best in an asymmetrical relationship of three (1 gives to 2, 2 gives to 3, 3 gives to 1), because an exchange between a pair can tend toward a rational ascertainment of value (rather than undefinable worth), which leads to the hoarding of property rather than the giving of gifts (16). Clearly Wordsworth is describing a gift cycle here by his very emphasis on the unnecessary nature of the gift exchange; he says to the Nook, "Thou . . . Hast taken gifts which thou dost little need" (38–40). The gift does not have an economic value that can supply a need according to a set of reciprocal and bounded relationships. On the contrary, its worth is a function of its status as an economically superfluous gesture that establishes connections by effacing the kinds of boundaries set up by reciprocal relationships.

Thus the cycle of gift-exchange joins the multivalent image of courtship in order to support the principle of a connection—an effacement of bounds—that can accommodate the asymmetrical grouping of William,

Mary, and the Nook (and, of course, Dorothy, always implied by the plural first person pronoun). This is the sense in which the Nook's love is boundless, a boundlessness misinterpreted by those outside the boundary of the Nook as waywardness:

> And, O most constant and most fickle place!
> That hath a wayward heart, as thou dost shew
> To them who look not daily on thy face,
> Who being lov'd in love no bounds dost know. (41–44)

That boundlessness, however, is precisely a combination of "constant" and "fickle." A constant boundlessness must allow for a constant crossing of boundaries; "fickle" is one way to describe someone who shifts from one set of boundaries to another, thus effacing the boundaries. This is a problem in a poem that has established itself upon the drawing of a generic and thematic boundary around the "little Nook of mountain ground." The Nook is "fair in [it]self and beautiful alone," that is autonomous and separate, and at the same time boundless in love.

Two kinds of boundaries are at stake here: the boundaries between individuals within the Wordsworth circle, and the boundary drawn around that circle. If, as Hyde says is sometimes possible (80–81), those two sets could be kept apart, there would be no problem: a gift-economy could operate within the circle, maintaining its unity, while an alienating economy, setting up difference, could protect it from the outside. However, those boundaries are by no means separate sets. In "A Farewell" this is illustrated by the controlling motif of departure, which on the one hand establishes the line around Dove Cottage as one that will ultimately enclose and protect the unifying gift-economy among individuals, but on the other hand establishes that line as one that currently divides individuals—Mary on one side and William on the other—and that must therefore be effaced.[13] Thus the Nook, which "being lov'd in love no bounds dost know" in the sixth stanza, exhibits the boundlessness appropriate to the Dove Cottage gift-economy that must extend to the absent Mary, but the Nook must also maintain the protective and constitutive bounds that characterized it in the first two stanzas.

This is an image of a larger problem in Wordsworth's poetry. Because the personal circle is the stuff of public poetry for him, the very act of writing and publishing necessitates both the establishment and the effacement of the line: the protective line drawn around Grasmere is part of the appealing thematic material, but it is precisely the line that must be crossed every time a poem is published. In a simple sense this is exactly the combination of an internal community of bonding gift-exchange, the Grasmere circle, and an external relation of alienating commodity-exchange, the public marketing of that circle, that Hyde describes as operating in guilds of artisans and scientific communities (81).[14] Charles J. Rzepka examines the intertwining of gift and commodity relationships in "Resolution and Independence," another poem from the spring of 1802. He argues that, as Wordsworth suffered the stress of increasing financial burdens, including his approaching marriage and his responsibility to Annette, he was forced to confront the idea of poetry as both gift and commodity, and that the Leech-Gatherer provided a model for the resolution of the conflict: "Income earner and gift giver, the Leech-Gatherer as poet is both an agent of the marketplace and an agent of divine grace, persevering at the two tasks that Wordsworth faces as a poet in 1802 and showing them to be compatible" (243). "A Farewell" reveals the difficulty of maintaining the gift-commodity distinction when the gift relationship cannot be contained within the circle (Mary, part of the gift-economy, is still outside), and when the commodity relationship is precisely the marketing of a gift-economy.

The problematic relationship between gift and commodity is suggested by the poem's own language of gifts. The line naming the poet's farewell thoughts as "these our latest gifts of tender thought" (20) is immediately followed by an image of taking from, not giving to, the addressed Nook; he bids farewell to the "Bright Gowan" and "marsh-marygold" "whom from the borders of the lake we brought / And placed together near our rocky well" (23–24). This is a removal of the flowers from their liminal position near natural water (on the lake's border) to a position near the "rocky well," a water source that has been appropriated for human use: the flowers' naturally indeterminate existence on the threshold is violated as they are brought within the domestic circle. However, neither taking nor giving seems to affect the autonomy of the Nook, independent as it appears to be of human processes. After describing the transplantation of "chosen plants and blossoms blown / Among the distant mountains" (34–35), the poet admits to the Nook that

> Thou for our sakes, though Nature's Child indeed,
> Fair in thyself and beautiful alone,
> Hast taken gifts which thou dost little need. (38–40)

That independence and autonomy, which grounds the noneconomic giving of unneeded gifts, depends on the establishment of a careful boundary between the human scene ("for our sakes") and the Nook's natural heritage ("though Nature's Child indeed"). However, that difference implicitly contradicts the boundary that earlier fenced off the Nook as a repository for human private property: "this is the place which holds our private store / Of things earth makes and sun doth shine upon" (14–15).

At the moment the Nook is granted the boundlessness that so complicates the clear boundary that encircled it earlier—a complication reflected in the interpenetration of incompatible gift- and commodity-systems—it becomes a speaking voice within the poem, closely connected to the very poetic voice that must engage this problem of boundaries, both thematically and professionally. In a complex play between the poet's voice and an image of that voice granted to the Nook, the autobiographical poetic voice speaks from the boundary that, in Derrida's terms, both generates the space within it and entails a process of degenerescence, because the boundary can be neither included in nor excluded from the space it "encloses": the Nook must be an enclosed protective world and at the same time a source of bound*less* love. But this boundary, now articulated as a voice shared by the narrator and the hitherto "other" Nook, is at the same time a Gadamerian horizon: it is the provisional boundary enabling speech in this poem, the peculiarly Wordsworthian speech—partly borrowed from a natural other, as is often the case—that establishes and crosses the line drawn around the self in Romantic autobiographical writing.[15]

The Nook's first statement is a command, "Let them go!" (45) This expresses the unrestricted nature of its love in a gesture of unrestrictiveness, invoking the two senses in which love can know "no bounds" (in the first sense it is the self that is unbounded; the second sense implies a promise not to bind others). This is imputed to the Nook without a specific time; it seems to be merely what the Nook says whenever its inhabitants "forsake" it. Soon, however, the Nook becomes a temporally specific co-narrator. The Nook is asked, during the poet's absence, to "be slow / And travel with the year at a soft pace" (47–48), and then to aid in narrating William and Dorothy's shared past to Mary: "Help us to tell her of years gone by / And this sweet spring the best-belov'd and best" (49–50). This aid is necessary because "Joy will be gone in its mortality, / Something must stay to tell us of the rest" (51–52). Two ideas are presented in this gradually more concrete personification, and they are not quite distinguished: (1) both the Nook and the poet are necessary narrators because the joy of this spring will pass and must be preserved in narrative, and (2) the Nook will be an important narrator because it will stay and be able to "tell" of what happened while the inhabitants were gone, of "the rest," which presumably refers to the memorial remainder left behind after the departure of mortal joy. In the first sense, the poet is a co-narrator ("Help us to tell") and in the second sense he is an auditor ("tell us"). Thus, through this voice that repeats the Nook's problematic boundary situation, the poet is both joined with the Nook and separated from the Nook in what is (almost) the same narrative act.

This progress of the voice partakes of the invagination Derrida describes. The poetic voice is, in a very important sense, the boundary of the text: that which articulates the poem, and that which is by convention the link between poet and reader. At this point in the poem, that boundary-voice is reduplicated in an echo as the Nook gains its own narrative voice. The echoing poetic voices, calling attention to themselves as voices, become more and more insistent: the boundary, theoretically uncontainable within the boundary area, intrudes itself more and more. It has not yet formed "an internal pocket larger than the whole," but the poet's own voice clearly has competition.[16] That competition comes to an end, however, with the song about the sparrow's nest, which concludes the penultimate stanza: "And in this bush our sparrow built its nest, / Of which I sung one song that will not die" (55–56). The construction of the sparrow's nest at first seems merely reminiscent of the playful domestic construction of the "Indian shed, / Our own contrivance, building without peer" (26–27) which was part of the Nook back in the early stanzas when it was being "courted." Suddenly, however, this image leads to an assertion of the poet's immortal authority over a sparrow in a "song that will not die"; this bird is not only an example or analogue of the poet's own domestic nesting activity, as was the Indian shed, but is now part of the private property in the poet's own nest; it is *our* sparrow. This immortal song adds another boundary voice to the growing chorus, but the process of the boundary entering the bounded is here turned into an assertion of poetic authority; the law of genre by which the boundary invades the bounded area is manipulated into a kind of poetic martial law by which the poet gains control over this textual process. The interpretive play around boundary-crossing comes to a halt in this assertion of an absolute line of narrative authority, and with the exclamation "O happy Garden!" (57) the final stanza of the poem reasserts a relatively unquestioned boundary of thematic and generic convention.

This closure can only be accomplished by means of another poetic text. The "one song that will not die" is the poem "The Sparrow's Nest," also composed in the spring of 1802. The forceful intrusion of this poem into "A Farewell" suggests that, in order to end the poem, which means to put a stop to the voice that has been generated by the problematic tension between boundaries and boundlessness, a boundary needs to be applied that is truly different from that which it bounds, and that therefore will not partake of the invasion of boundaries described by Derrida. This new boundary is a poetic voice. But because it is the voice of a different poem, it escapes the problematic status of a voice that, like the narrative voice of "A Farewell" and its echo in the Nook, comes into being as a boundary for this poem. That textual logic tells only half the story, however, because of course the "other" poem is not at all isolated from the matters at hand. The poem invoked as an emblem of the poet's bounding authority is less about a sparrow's nest than it is about a source of authority implicit throughout the entire network of relationships underlying "A Farewell": William's sister and cottage-mate Dorothy. "The Sparrow's Nest" ends with this praise of Dorothy as William's vehicle of perception:

> The Blessing of my later years
> Was with me when a Boy;
> She gave me eyes, she gave me ears;
> And humble cares, and delicate fears;
> A heart, the fountain of sweet tears;
> And love, and thought, and joy. (15–20)

Thus, Dorothy's central role in the complex relations set up by this poem, implicit all along, is here asserted explicitly (though still at a distance) in the poem's most authoritative gesture. Her relationship to William represents what may be the most problematic mixing of legitimate and illegitimate categories in all of the poem's relationships,[17] but here she is invoked to resolve the indeterminacy of the boundaries, which has been an issue on so many levels of the poem. One poem halts another poem, and one indeterminacy provides the authority to circumscribe another.

That gesture enables the closing stanza, which legislates the boundaries of the poem into a conventional, legitimate paean to the Garden. With language that Keats might have noted with pleasure, this final stanza displaces the problems of boundaries to the border between sleep and waking, and eventually to dream flowers rather than real flowers, in a gesture that makes the Nook an unquestionably interiorized space: the garden is

> lov'd for waking hours,
> For soft half-slumbers that did gently steep
> Our spirits, carrying with them dreams of flowers,
> Belov'd for days of rest in fruit-tree bowers! (58–61)

The boundary between inside the Nook and outside is clearly set; the time outside the Nook will be "burning months," and the return will be a reentry into a safe maternal space: "Into thy bosom we again shall creep." The potentially illegitimate invagination suggested by the generic, sexual, and geographic boundary-crossing in the poem is translated into a legitimate, if regressive, return to the safe boundaries set by the image of the mother. Dorothy's specific though hidden presence in "The Sparrow's Nest" indirectly provides the authority by which the boundaries are put back in place, and both the violence suggested by Derrida and the possibilities suggested by Gadamer are closed off. The poet's authority is, on the one hand, asserted as he claims the immortality of his poetry and, on the other hand, effaced as he posits that authority as beginning with Dorothy and ending in the bosom of the Nook.

Forms of Acknowledgment

The intensity of this poem's rhetorical effort has a clear biographical correlative in the spring of 1802, as William was struggling with the complex boundaries of the three relationships that pose these issues of boundaries and legitimacy: the legitimate relationship to Mary, the illegitimate relation to Annette, and the most important relation to Dorothy, which confounds categories of legitimacy as it forms a kind of fulcrum for both the legitimate and the illegitimate relationships. It was Dorothy, after all, who seems to have been writing the letters to both Annette and Mary that established their relation to William. No wonder William sought a rhetoric that would, on the one hand, contain and express the violence inherent in establishing an autobiographical generic boundary, and, at the same time, generate a narrative life—or at least a poem—out of the confounding of the opposition between legitimacy and illegitimacy, boundaries and boundlessness. Though this may be going too far, we could even speculate that this confounding of boundaries expresses William's ambivalence in the face of pressure to sort out his relationships to Dorothy, Annette, and Mary as his wedding approached.

The way in which Wordsworth has faced this set of rhetorical problems can be usefully placed into the context of another modern thinker who, along with Derrida and Gadamer, may help us understand the broader significance of the autobiographer's dilemma as represented by Wordsworth's strangely convoluted epithalamium. In *In Quest of the Ordinary* and other works, Stanley Cavell's version of postanalytic philosophy rests on his discovery that "the argument between the skeptic and the antiskeptic had no satisfactory conclusion" (5); neither the adoption of skepticism as a full-fledged program nor the resolution of skepticism into knowledge is philosophically tenable. For Cavell, "skepticism is a place, perhaps the central secular place, in which the human wish to deny the condition of human existence is expressed; and so long as the denial is essential to what we think of as the human, skepticism cannot, or must not, be denied" (5). Cavell shows skepticism becoming animism; suspicion of the world's unknowability is translated into the kind of murderous suspicion we have of another person, in "the thought that skeptical doubt is to be interpreted as jealousy and that our relation to the world that remains is as to something that has died at our hands" (55). He reads Romanticism as an attempt to work out a way to live with this fundamental fact of human finitude and the otherness of the world, and Wordsworth's attempt in "A Farewell" to negotiate the relationship between the inside and the outside of the boundary around the Nook—fundamentally a problem of how to know what is beyond the boundary—can be seen as part of this project.

Cavell sees two approaches to this boundary. One is to appropriate the other who is to be known in a misguided attempt, ultimately suicidal, to achieve a "knowledge" that denies skepticism, what, in *The Claim of Reason*, he calls "some picture of what knowing another, or being known by another, would really come to—a harmony, a concord, a union, a transparence, a governance, a power—against which our actual successes at knowing, and being known, are poor things" (440). According to Cavell, this is what Coleridge's Ancient Mariner attempts in killing the albatross: the Mariner "finds that he has murdered to connect, to stuff nature into his words, to make poems of it, which no further power can overcome." His acts "are self-absorbed, narcissistic, as if to parody that supposed self-reflection that some philosophers take to constitute one's possession of a mind" (*In Quest of the Ordinary* 60). The more intelligible and powerful concept is "acknowledgment," whose relationship to knowledge is described as follows in a much earlier essay, "Knowing and Acknowledging":

It isn't as if being in a position to acknowledge something is *weaker* than being in a position to know it. On the contrary: from my acknowledging that I am late it follows that I know I'm late . . . but from my knowing I am late, it does not follow that I acknowledge I'm late. . . . One could say: acknowledgment goes beyond knowledge. (Goes beyond not, so to speak, in the order of knowledge, but in its requirement that I *do* something or reveal something on the basis of that knowledge.) (*Must We Mean What We Say* 256–57)

As this concept is developed in *The Claim of Reason* and *In Quest of the Ordinary*, it becomes even more forcefully an acknowledgment of otherness and loss: "*The Claim of Reason* suggests the moral of skepticism to be that the existence of the world and others in it is not a matter to be known, but one to be acknowledged. And now what emerges is that what is to be acknowledged is this existence as separate from me, as gone from me. . . . The world must be regained every day, in repetition, regained as gone" (*In Quest of the Ordinary* 172).

In "A Farewell" Wordsworth presents the autobiographer's attempt to connect a private world (represented by the Nook) with one outside (represented by the journey to Annette and to Mary) in terms of the figural strategies I have outlined above, and like Cavell he recognizes through these figures (which include a strange substitution of the Nook for Mary) that the relation to Mary cannot be contained within the traditional skeptic's alternatives of certain knowledge or its impossibility. "Her pleasures are in wild fields gathered" (29), and thus like William and Dorothy who have brought the Nook "plants and blossoms blown / Among the distant mountains" (34–35), she is already an insider in Dove Cottage's world of gift-exchange, and thus can in some sense be "known" by the other insiders. On the other hand, the poem is built upon a boundary set up between the present world of Grasmere and the absent worlds of both Mary and Annette: a recognition of the skeptical distance placed between the poet and the object of knowledge. The poet's relationship to the Nook presents the courtship as a paradoxical combination of boundaries and boundlessness, and as a relationship that moves from the poet's playful and partly dismissive accusation of irrational coquetry ("O most constant and most fickle place!") to an important granting of a narrative voice to the Nook. This granting of voice is as close as the poem will come to a Cavellian "acknowledgment." The Nook is momentarily engaged as a conversational partner, recognized as an other in a relationship that entails action, rather than the passive knowledge of certainty or uncertainty. The Nook is also a voice that can only be "regained as gone"; it gains its own voice to be acknowledged and listened to—not "known"—even as, "stay[ing] to tell us of the rest," it will be lost to the departing William and Dorothy.[18] It is almost as if we are on the road to what Cavell, in reference to the 1942 movie *Woman of the Year*, identifies as a good marriage: "a scene in which the chance for happiness is shown as the mutual acknowledgment of separateness" (*In Quest of the Ordinary* 178).

However, just as this voice gains autonomy (moving from one that will "help us to tell" to one that will "tell us"), it is displaced by the speaker, and the penultimate stanza ends with one voice—Wordsworth's poem about Dorothy. By the final stanza, Mary is "[she] who will be ours" (63), with whom William will "creep" inside the boundaries of the maternal bosom. This is clearly a retreat from a relationship of "acknowledgment" into what is, in Cavell's terms, the worst possible state, combining both the extremes of skepticism and false knowledge that Cavell is trying to avoid. Mary is the victim of a bad-faith attempt at "knowledge" rather than "acknowledgment" in that she has been reduced to the property of William and Dorothy (she will be "ours"), but a despairing negative skepticism is also suggested: the retreat into the maternal bosom is a refusal even to face the world outside the boundary, a refusal to confront the problems posed by skepticism. The poet's final assertion of authority over the Nook and Mary is not unlike the Mariner's shooting of the albatross as read by Cavell: an attempt at knowledge that avoids the fuller step of acknowledgment.

I end with this discussion of Stanley Cavell and Mary Hutchinson not for the sake of a reading that will demonstrate Mary's suppression (this reading imputes to William a much more complex set of anxieties about his impending marriage), but because the questions raised by Cavell, put alongside those raised by Derrida and Gadamer, are the important questions raised by Romantic autobiography. Cavell's notion of acknowledgment, which is far more complex than my summary suggests, can help move the theoretical discussion of autobiography beyond the now tired questions of representational adequacy. The primary autobiographical question for Wordsworth is not whether the self can be known or accurately represented; the writing of autobiography is too heavily involved with negotiating the construction of various selves and preparing for the future to exhibit more than a passing interest in the question of self-representation. When, for example, in "Tintern Abbey" the poet says "I cannot paint / What then I was," he is less interested in the representability of the past than in the inexpressibility of a literally "thought-less" youthful relation to the world. For Wordsworth, the boundary between autobiography and life does not depend on an absolute distinction between literary language and ordinary language, between auto-biographical text and a separate life-referent; the autobiography is not a signifier for a signified concept of life. For Wordsworth, literary language and ordinary language merged, not only because he "proposed to [him]self to imitate, and, as far as is possible, to adopt the very language of men" (W. Wordsworth, *Prose Works* 1.130), but also because, as Doro-thy's journal shows, the language of poetry was an intimate part of the ordinary language of the Wordsworths' lives.

The important question, as I have tried to show in my reading of "A Farewell," is how an autobiographically constructed self can negotiate a boundary that will acknowledge the otherness of that which is uncontainable within the boundary of knowledge (Cavell), confront the dangerous implications of the law of genre (Derrida), but operate with the enabling flexibility of a provisional horizon (Gadamer). The boundary around (and necessarily within) the autobiographical text can be coextensive with the boundary between ideology and history or the boundary established by gender construction, boundaries that have been exhaustively studied by much recent criticism. For the autobiographer, however, it is most importantly a mortal, fragile, overpowering, and changing boundary provisionally enclosing a space in which—and an energy by which—the relationship between legitimacy and illegitimacy, boundaries and boundlessness, can be acknowledged, negotiated, and written.[19]

Notes

1   For Wordsworth, of course, this was only beginning to become a convention on its own, separate from biography; see Cockshut (3).

2   Invagination, in the sense Derrida uses it, means, in both English and French, to form a pocket in something by turning it in on itself. The association with "vagina," which Derrida certainly intends in his link between invagination and generation, comes from both words' common source in the Latin word for "sheath."

3   This notion of "horizon" perhaps enters contemporary critical discourse more often via Bakhtin and Medvedev's notion of "ideological horizon" than by way of Gadamer's usage, though Bakhtin and Medvedev's use of the term also appears to come from the Husserlian tradition. Both senses of "horizon" substitute the notion of a moving horizon for a mimetic and reified relation between concepts and cultures: Bakhtin and Medvedev attack the Russian literary history of the 1920s that

saw literature as simply representing fully formed ideologies and thus mistakenly ignored its "ideological independence and originality"; literature should be seen, they argue, as reflecting "the living process of the generation of" a contradictory and developing "ideological horizon" (18–19). Gadamer attacks a historical naivete that would see cultures as closed structures susceptible to objective representation. The contexts within which they apply this concept are of course very different: Gadamer starts from individuals' attempts to understand each other with the goal of fusing horizons in a higher understanding, whereas Bakhtin and Medvedev start from the foundational cultural function of ideology and use the phenomenological notion of the "horizon" to deepen literature's ideological role as an "independent superstructure" reflecting "the economic base that is common to all ideologies" (18).

4 For a survey of the wide range of possibilities for connecting and opposing the thought of Gadamer and Derrida, see Michelfelder and Palmer's *Dialogue and Deconstruction*. My argument does not depend on a resolution to the complex question of their agreement or disagreement; I see them as providing useful complementary approaches to the same network of problems.

5 I have examined this construction and dissolution of figural structures in "The Emergence of the Autobiographical Figure" and "Incarnation and the Autobiographical Exit."

6 Janet Varner Gunn discusses the autobiographical implications of the boundary between "the topos of the picturesque" and "hermeneutic of landscape." The former, of which the Nook seems to be a good example, is the idealized perspective of the Claude-glass's reorganized reflection, and the latter is the more authentically integrated "temporalized and oriented space which is *place*" (83). Though her phenomenological premises enable the discovery of an "authentic" Wordsworthian temporality, which obscures some significant problems posed by language, Gunn's discussion of the relation between self and world as "a creative dialectic between participation and distantiation" (59) that does not aim for a simple transcendence of the boundary between inside and outside is relevant to the present argument. See also Angus Fletcher's discussion of the boundary between "temple" and "labyrinth" in "'Positive Negation.'"

7 The relationship between event and poem is of course a complex one for Wordsworth; Alan Liu has exhaustively studied the way in which the poems from this period—the sonnet on Westminster Bridge in particular—repress and recall history across the poems' boundaries. My interest is much more local: I am less concerned with the return of the repressed, or even the mechanism of that process, than I am with determining how the various boundaries of the poem—as "laws" or "horizons"—function in the production of poetic meaning or knowledge.

8 Not only is this factually true, in that Mary was a long-time acquaintance, but Mary was also publicly perceived this way—see De Quincey, *Recollections of the Lake Poets*, 129: "This was Mrs. Wordsworth, cousin of the poet; and, for the last five years or more, his wife." To De Quincey she was clearly an "insider" cousin first, and only secondarily and recently an imported outsider.

9 As Jared Curtis, the editor of the authoritative Cornell edition of Wordsworth's 1800–1807 poems, points out, there is no clear reason for the exclusion of "A Farewell" from the 1807 *Poems, in Two Volumes* (559), and the poem was on an early list of poems for that project (20); this further reinforces the poem's generic indeterminacy. Other revisions between 1802 and 1815, not surprisingly, delete some specific personal references and generalize the tone of the poem.

10 In his discussion of "A Farewell," Kurt Heinzelman notes that in the tribute to Dorothy at the end of the 1805 *Prelude*, William's "physiology or outward aspect becomes metaphorically transformed into an interiorized space . . . an enclosure like the Grasmere orchard"; see Heinzelman's "Cult of Domesticity" 66–67 and the 1805 *Prelude* 13.224–36.

11 "Possible pairs" within the Wordsworth circle were problematic in life as well as poetry, including not only William's relationships with Annette, Mary, and Dorothy, but also Coleridge's failing marriage to Sara Fricker and his attraction (beginning in November 1799) to Sara Hutchinson, William's future sister-in-law. On the blotting-paper opposite Dorothy's 15 May 1802 journal entry (the day after she wrote to Annette, the day she received "a melancholy letter from Coleridge," and two weeks before Wordsworth finished "A Farewell") is a cryptic arrangement of the names of Coleridge, Dorothy, William, John Wordsworth, Mary, and Sara that suggests a variety of possible pairings. Kurt Heinzelman discusses this entry as part of his demonstration of how Dorothy manages the various pairings and triplings in the Grasmere household in order to "keep the household as a unit of work-engendering value intact" ("The Cult of Domesticity" 7).

12 For an interesting application of Hyde's idea to Coleridge's relationship with Wordsworth, see Modiano's essay.

13 De Quincey, who had been both inside and outside the Wordsworth circle, provides in *Recollections of the Lakes and the Lake Poets* his view of boundaries being manifested and crossed in this description of his first entrance into the circle of Dove Cottage in 1807: "*Through the little gate* I pressed forward; ten steps beyond it lay *the principal door of the house.* . . . A *little semi-vestibule between two doors* prefaced the *entrance* into what might be considered the principal room of the cottage. . . . I saw sufficiently to be aware of two ladies just *entering the room, from a doorway opening upon a little staircase*" (128–29; emphasis mine).

14 See Kurt Heinzelman's analysis of Wordsworth's attempt to confront the difficulties of the modern poet by setting up an economic relationship with his readers: the poet "turn[s] the new economics of capitalism into a labor theory of poetic value in which the labor bestowed by the poet may be directly exchanged through the auxiliary and cooperating labor of the reader" (*Economics of the Imagination* 221). For Heinzelman, the culmination of this process is precisely the "marketing" of "Home at Grasmere" (both the place and the poem) in an economy that posits the reader as a productive consumer: "the poem seems purposefully, determinedly, to 'commercialize' Wordsworth's 'real' property at Grasmere so as to contract it into

an imaginative form—'Home at Grasmere'—which the sympathetic reader may appropriate as he will" (231).

15 See for example, *The Prelude,* book 1: "With what strange utterance did the loud dry wind / Blow through my ears" (348–49), and "The sands of Westmoreland, the creeks and bays / Of Cumbria's rocky limits, they can tell" (594–95). As Geoffrey Hartman says, "Wordsworth projects nature as something that . . . textualizes a phantom voice" (194).

16 This competition is perhaps a consequence of the risk taken by the Wordsworthian poet who, in Heinzelman's view, institutes an economy that depends equally on the "labor" of poet and reader. The poet is put in the powerful but (at least in "A Farewell") unstable position of acting as his own reader. As Heinzelman says of "Resolution and Independence," "Wordsworth himself, as a 'reader' in the poem, acts out the exchanges which he hopes the poem might perpetuate in contracting the labor of *its* reader(s)" (*Economics of the Imagination* 215).

17 See Gill's balanced commentary on the sexual but nonexclusive nature of William and Dorothy's relationship (202–3). Perhaps the most striking example of how the categories of "sister" and "wife" were mixed in this relationship is Dorothy's journal description of a private "wedding" ritual between William and Dorothy on the day of his actual wedding ceremony (which Dorothy did not attend): "I gave him the wedding ring—with how deep a blessing! I took it from my forefinger where I had worn it the whole of the night before—he slipped it again onto my finger and blessed me fervently" (154).

18 The hermeneutically paradigmatic act of conversation is for Gadamer a similarly laudable and life-promoting recognition of otherness: "To reach an understanding in a dialogue is not merely a matter of putting oneself forward and successfully asserting one's point of view, but being transformed into a communion in which we do not remain what we were" (379). Cavell would not give the notion of "communion" such status, of course, but both are otherwise describing a similar gesture.

19 I am grateful to Kurt Heinzelman for his detailed reading of an earlier version of this essay and for his many useful comments.

References

Bakhtin, M. M., and P. N. Medvedev. *The Formal Method in Literary Scholarship.* Trans. Albert J. Wehrle. Cambridge: Harvard UP, 1985.

Borges, Jorge Luis. "The Parable of the Palace." *A Personal Anthology.* Ed. Anthony Kerrigan. New York: Grove, 1967.

Cavell, Stanley. *The Claim of Reason: Wittgenstein, Skepticism, Morality, and Tragedy.* Oxford: Oxford UP, 1979.

——. *Must We Mean What We Say? A Book of Essays.* New York: Scribners, 1969.

——. *In Quest of the Ordinary: Lines of Skepticism and Romanticism.* Chicago: U of Chicago P, 1988.

Cockshut, A.O.J. *The Art of Autobiography in 19th and 20th Century England.* New Haven: Yale UP, 1984.

Cook, Albert S. *Thresholds: Studies in the Romantic Experience.* Madison: U of Wisconsin P, 1985.

Curran, Stuart. *Poetic Form and British Romanticism.* New York: Oxford UP 1986.

De Quincey, Thomas. *Recollections of the Lakes and the Lake Poets.* Ed. David Wright. New York: Penguin, 1970.

——. *De Quincey's Collected Writings.* Ed. David Masson. 14 vols. London: Black, 1896–97.

Derrida, Jacques. "The Law of Genre." Trans. Avital Ronell. *On Narrative.* Ed. W.J.T. Mitchell. Chicago: U of Chicago P, 1981. 51–77.

Fletcher, Angus. "'Positive Negation': Threshold, Sequence, and Personification in Coleridge." *New Perspectives on Coleridge and Wordsworth: Selected Papers from the English Institute.* Ed. Geoffrey Hartman. New York: Columbia UP, 1972.

Gadamer, Hans-Georg. *Truth and Method.* 2d ed. Trans. Joel Weinsheimer and Donald G. Marshall. New York: Crossroad, 1989.

Gill, Stephen. *William Wordsworth: A Life.* Oxford: Oxford UP, 1989.

Gunn, Janet Varner. *Autobiography: Toward a Poetics of Experience.* Philadelphia: U of Pennsylvania P, 1982.

Haney, David P. "The Emergence of the Autobiographical Figure in *The Prelude,* Book I." *Studies in Romanticism* 20 (1981): 33–63.

——. "Incarnation and the Autobiographical Exit: Wordsworth's *Prelude,* Books 9–13 (1805)." *Studies in Romanticism* 29 (1990): 523–54.

Hartman, Geoffrey. "Words, Wish, Wordsworth." *Deconstruction and Criticism.* Ed. Harold Bloom et al. New York: Seabury, 1979. 177–216.

Heinzelman, Kurt. "The Cult of Domesticity: Dorothy and William Wordsworth at Grasmere." *Romanticism and Feminism.* Ed. Anne K. Mellor. Bloomington: Indiana UP, 1988. 52–78.

——. *The Economics of the Imagination.* Amherst: U of Massachusetts P, 1980.

Hyde, W. Lewis. *The Gift: Imagination and the Erotic Life of Property.* New York: Random, 1983.

Jacobus, Mary. "The Law of/and Gender: Genre Theory and *The Prelude.*" *Diacritics* 14 (Winter 1984): 47–57.

Kant, Immanuel. *Prolegomena to Any Future Metaphysics That Can Qualify as a Science.* Trans. Paul Carus. Lasalle, Ill.: Open Court, 1902.

Lacoue-Labarthe, Philippe, and Jean-Luc Nancy. *The Literary Absolute: The Theory of Literature in German Romanticism.* Trans. Philip Barnard and Cheryl Lester. Albany: State U of New York P, 1988.

Liu, Alan. *Wordsworth: The Sense of History.* Stanford: Stanford UP, 1988.

Michelfelder, Diane P., and Richard E. Palmer, eds. *Dialogue and Deconstruction: The Gadamer-Derrida Encounter.* Albany: State U of New York P, 1989.

Modiano, Raimonda. "Coleridge and Wordsworth: The Ethics of Gift Exchange and Literary Ownership." *Wordsworth Circle* 20 (1989): 113–20.

Rzepka, Charles J. "A Gift that Complicates Employ: Poetry and Poverty in 'Resolution and Independence.'" *Studies in Romanticism* 28 (1989): 225–47.

Said, Edward W. *Beginnings: Intention and Method.* New York: Basic Books, 1975.

Wordsworth, Dorothy. *The Journals of Dorothy Wordsworth.* Ed. Mary Moorman. New York: Oxford UP, 1971.

Wordsworth, William. *Poems, in Two Volumes, and Other Poems, 1800–1807.* Ed. Jared Curtis. Ithaca: Cornell UP, 1983.

——. *The Prelude: 1799, 1805, 1850.* Ed. Jonathan Wordsworth et al. New York: Norton, 1979.

——. *The Prose Works of William Wordsworth.* Ed. W.J.B. Owen and Jane Worthington Smyther. 3 vols. Oxford: Oxford UP, 1974.

Identity's Body

SIDONIE SMITH

■

If the body is not a "being," but a variable boundary, a surface whose permeability is politically regulated, a signifying practice within a cultural field of gender hierarchy and compulsory heterosexuality, then what language is left for understanding this corporeal enactment, gender, that constitutes its "interior" signification on its surface?—Judith Butler, GENDER TROUBLE

Woman lives her body as object as well as subject.—Iris Marion Young, "Throwing Like a Girl"

The body has been made so problematic for women that it has often seemed easier to shrug it off and travel as a disembodied spirit.—Adrienne Rich, OF WOMAN BORN

What might skin have to do with autobiographical writing and autobiographical writing with skin? Certainly discursive capillaries circulate one's "flesh and blood" through the textual body of self-writing, wrapped up as it is in the anatomy of origins and genealogies. Filiations are forged back through forerunners, sometimes forward toward offspring. But flesh and blood also move through other capillary actions since skin is the literal and metaphorical borderland between the materiality of the autobiographical "I" and the contextual surround of the world. It functions simultaneously as a personal and political, a psychological and ideological boundary of meaning, a contested border of restraint and of transgression through which subjectivity emerges and over which plays what Nancy Fraser via Michel Foucault calls "the 'capillary' character of modern power" (Fraser 3).

For subjectivity is not, after all, an out-of-body experience. The "autobiographical subject" of bourgeois humanism may have emerged as a unitary, essentialized "self," somehow locally and universally operative irrespective of or despite the bodily surround; and the body and its desires might have been banished to the borders of consciousness through the ideological enshrinement of what M. M. Bakhtin called the "classi-cal," or classicized, body and the redeployment of its other, the grotesque body (Bakhtin; Stallybrass and White 1–26); but current notions of the constitution of the subject anchor subjectivity very much in the body. And so skin is the "in" surround. We may even speculate that subjectivity is the elaborate residue of the border politics of the body since bodies locate us topographically, temporally, socioculturally as well as linguis-tically in a series of transcodings alongs multiple axes of meaning. And so, to ask once again, What does skin have to do with autobiography and autobiography with skin? Much I think—as the body of the text, the body of the narrator, the body of the narrated I, the cultural body, and the body politic all merge in skins and skeins of meaning. I want to explore the politics of autobiographical skins.

Bodies seem to position us as demarcated subjects separate from oth-ers and to locate us in bounded temporalities and trajectories of identi-fication. Thus the body seems to be the nearest, most central home we know, the very ground upon which a "notion of a coherent, historically continuous, stable identity" can be founded (Martin and Mohanty 195). Residence in bodies also encourages us to sustain the illusion of an indisputable continuity between biology and certain social and cultural phenomena such as gender and race. But the body only seems to anchor us in a finite, discrete, unified surround—a private surround, temptingly stable and impermeable. There is only apparent continuity since, para-doxically, bodies, at once so close to us as to seem indissoluble from any notion of "me" or "I," can also disrupt the too-easy stability of singular identities (Martin 81). The bodily home can be an illusive terrain, per-haps the home of a stranger. If it is only apparently continuous with our identity or identification as an individual, then the politics of the body can open up a space of contradiction, drift, homelessness, a gap through which a complex heterogeneity destabilizes our sense of any stable iden-tification. Thus we might, after Biddy Martin and Chandra Talpade Mohanty, find that we are not "at home" in our bodies: "'Being home' refers to the place where one lives within familiar, safe, protected bound-aries; 'not being home' is a matter of realizing that home was an illusion of coherence and safety based on the exclusion of specific histories of oppression and resistance, the repression of differences even within one-self" (196). The body is our most material site of potential homelessness.

The palpable play of discomforts, of an experience of homelessness inside the body, forces us to ask about the relationship of the body to culture's body and the body politic. Although bodies provide us, as individuals, the boundaries of our isolated being, they are obviously and critically communal and discursive bodies; and community creates a superfluity of "body" that marks us in practices, discourses, and temporalities. For communities surrounding us normalize certain bodies and render abnormal or grotesque other bodies, thereby situating our body somewhere in the field of bodies. To invoke Denise Riley, communities determine how often and for how long we are located "in the body" culturally (103–4). They determine in good part when the actual and the discursive bodies can fall away from consciousness and when they cannot, when they are invoked and for what purposes. Communal discourses and practices also determine how the material body is called together as a unified or coherent material reality with specific identity contents. For instance, separate parts of the body are brought together and assigned meaning through the nominative identification of the "female" or "male" body. According to Judith Butler "these numerous features gain social meaning and unification through their articulation within the category of sex" (*Gender Trouble* 114). But Butler goes on to suggest, by way of explicating Monique Wittig's theorizing of "sex," that "the 'integrity' and 'unity' of the body, often thought to be positive ideals, serve the purposes of fragmentation, restriction, and domination" since only certain parts of the body are aligned in the consolidation of sexual identification and since those body parts must fulfill certain specific functions and be positioned in appropriate places to be considered normal (*Gender Trouble* 115).[1]

Paradoxically a unified body is only consolidated on the ground of the fragmented body. Some fragments align into gender identification, others into racial or ethnic identifications. Moreover, while there are unlimited material differences from one body to another, only certain body parts make up the "meaningful" cultural and social differences. And culturally only certain bodies are experienced as different. The body is thus parceled out and policed through discursive systems that establish identities through differences, that normalize certain bodies and render other bodies culturally abnormal, even grotesque. The fragmented materiality of bodies helps sustain the illusion of indisputable continuity between biology and culturally constructed identities, the illusion of stable categorizations.

One effect of consolidating identity through bodily coherence, unification, and demarcation is the establishment of order amid chaos, and the establishment of the subject amid "abject" others. Since the body is what Butler describes as "a region of *cultural* unruliness and disorder," since the life of the body is multiple and unpredictable, the body is subjected to delimitation by the "socially hegemonic" (*Gender Trouble* 131). Reinvested in limits and impermeabilities, it serves as the margin joining and separating the subject and the other, the inner and the outer, the male and the female, one race and another. It is this politics of the body's borders that determines the complex relationship of individuals to their bodies, to the bodies of others, to fantasies of the founding subject, and to the body politics. Drawing all these alignments together in her reworking of Julia Kristeva's notion of the abject and Iris Marion Young's analysis of the micropolitics of racism, sexism, and homophobia, Butler argues that "the repudiation of bodies for their sex, sexuality, and/or color is an 'expulsion' followed by a 'repulsion' that founds and consolidates culturally hegemonic identities along sex/race/sexuality axes of differentiation" (*Gender Trouble* 133; see also Young, *Justice* 141–48).[2] Consolidation of hegemonic identities requires the consolidation of the essentialized identities of the others, of all the abject, with the effect that "the body rendered as Other—the body repressed or denied and, then, projected reemerges for this [hegemonic] 'I' as the view of others as essentially body" (Butler, "Variations" 133). Thus certain people, those positioned off-center from the dominant group, those claiming or assigned nonhegemonic identities, find themselves partitioned in their bodies, culturally embodied. But this essentialized body and stable identity are compelling fabrications whose regulation may be only partially effective.[3] Such bodies are always a fascinating object of desire, an invitation to the gaze.

A final introductory suggestion about bodies: The body functions as a powerful source of metaphors for the social. It offers itself up, in bits and pieces, in its blood, immune system, organs, in its topography and pathology, for use in constructing the social environment and assigning persons their places in that environment. This facile movement from the body to the body politic makes the invocation of the body for the purposes of the social a discursive commonplace. Mary Douglas suggests in *Danger and Purity* that "the body is a model that can stand for any bounded system. Its boundaries can represent any boundaries which are threatened or precarious" (115). Drawn to the cultural meanings of the body and its borders and drawing on the work of Bakhtin, Peter Stallybrass and Allon White elegantly elaborate, in *The Politics and Poetics of Transgression*, how "the body cannot be thought separately from the social formation, symbolic topography and the constitution of the subject. The body is neither a purely natural given nor is it merely a textual metaphor, it is a privileged operator for the transcoding of these other areas. Thinking the body is thinking social topography and vice versa" (192). Thus they trace the implications of transcodings between four symbolic domains—"psychic forms, the human body, geographical space and the social order"—as a way of understanding ordering principles of modern western cultures: "Divisions and discriminations in one domain are continually structured, legitimated and dissolved by reference to the vertical symbolic hierarchy which operates in the other three domains" (3). This metaphoric use of the body has consequences for what Fraser calls "the social meanings of our bodies" (136). For any specific body may be overwritten by this social inscription. The body categorized as abnormal, for instance, becomes associated with those forces threatening the stability of the body politic. It becomes a pollutant.

Autobiographical Bodies

But what of autobiographical writing, a writing practice in the West complicit in the consolidation of the bourgeois subject. Is the autobiographical body "identity's body"? Yes and no, or rather, provisionally so. More than identity's body, that is, gender's body or race's body or sexuality's body or ethnicity's body, the body is subjectivity's body. " 'The body' is not, for all its corporeality," suggests Riley, "an originating point nor yet a terminus; it is a result or an effect" (102). Thus identity's body is not the alpha and omega of subjectivity. If offers, rather, one possible "point of departure of the process of self-consciousness, a process by which one begins to know that and how the personal is political, that and how the subject is specifically and materially en-gendered in its social conditions and possibilities of existence" (De Lauretis, "Feminist Studies" 9). Identities may be points of departure. They are simultaneously fabrications, amalgams of fantasies of stable positionings. As fabrications they are "subject to change" (Miller 114), though not to the inevitability of change. And the changes are brought about through the very "practices of self-representation which illuminate the contradictory, multiple construction of subjectivity at the intersections, but also in the interstices of ideologies of gender, race, and sexuality" (Martin 82). The body cannot be sought in essentialized identifications. In fact, identity may be the bane of subjectivity's existence. Thus we have to look at the cultural practices that surface on the body and through the body to get at the emergence of the autobiographical subject.

The autobiographer's specific body is the site of multiple solicitations, multiple markings, multiple invocations of subject positions. It is not one culturally charged body, unified, stable, finite, or final. Nor can it be identified along one consuming and unchanging axis. It is the site of heterogeneous axes of signification that become constitutive of the subject of autobiography. Bearing multiple marks of location, bodies position the autobiographical subject at the nexus of culturally specific experiences, of health, gender, race, sexual orientation, and at the nexus of what Teresa de Lauretis terms "micropolitical practices" (*Technologies of Gender* 9–10), which derive from the cultural meaning of those points of identification. The very complexity of this experientially based history can be used to challenge, disturb, and displace the neat categorizations (and fragmentation or unification) of bodies.

Moreover there are multiple bodies in the autobiographical text that coalesce in complex autobiographical alignments. There is the "specific body" of the autobiographical speaker/narrator. Then there is the "subject body" of the autobiographical I. There is the "cultural body" somewhere out there soliciting specific autobiographical orientations to the body. And there is, as Carroll Smith-Rosenberg notes, "the body politic whose materiality the physical body symbolically represents" (102), whose metaphorical capacities impinge on the deployment of specific bodies, determine the narrative itineraries of both the privatized and the publicized body, and determine the linguistic components of the culture's imaginary repertoire of representations. The orientation of self-representational practices to these bodies, and the deployment of the body in these practices, reveal the political erotics of autobiographical subjectivity. Thus we can look to autobiographical practices to see the effects of the body's representations, how the deployment of the body invites certain consolidations of subjectivity.

Autobiographical practice, then, is one of those cultural occasions when the history of the body intersects with the deployment of female subjectivity as the woman writer struggles with multivalent embodiment. And so some kind of history of the body is always inscribed in women's autobiographical texts—muted or loud, mimetically recapitulative or subversive. We might therefore ask of each autobiographical text a series of interrelated questions. Whose body is speaking? What specific body does the autobiographical subject claim in her text? Where is the body narratively to be found and how does it circulate through the text? Does the body drop away as a location of autobiographical identity or does the speaker insist on its founding identification? What are the implications for subjectivity of the body's positioning? What is the body's autobiographical lexicon? How is the body the performative boundary between inner and outer, the subject and the world? What kind of performance is the body allowed to give? What policing actions impinge on the circulation of the body? What are the strategic purposes and uses around which the body has been autobiographically mobilized? Is the body a source of subversive autobiographical practice, a potential emancipatory vehicle for autobiographical practice? What is the relationship of autobiographical body politics to the body politic, of individual anatomy to cultural anatomy? How are other bodies arranged in the text? Are these bodies exoticized, eroticized, dominated, colonized? Before whom is the autobiographical speaker revealing or concealing (or both) her body? Is the autobiographical body being given to the reader, or withheld? Whose history of the body is being written?

Before looking at these ideas about the autobiographical body through two twentieth-century texts, I want to comment briefly on the complex body politics of women's autobiographical writing up to the twentieth century. With the caveat that I am making a vast generalization here, one that invites argument, I suggest that until recently women who wrote autobiographically, at least within the context of traditional Western autobiographical practices, had to make sure that their body had been neutralized before, in both senses of the word, their text. Women had to discursively consolidate themselves as subjects through pursuit of an out-of-body experience precisely because their bodies were heavily and inescapably gendered, intensely fabricated. Thus they had to write out of their bodies or write off their bodies to gain an audience at all. Moreover, the universalization of the white male body as the normative source of sexual knowledge, meaning, and identification effectively mobilized the objectification of the female body and its occlusion. As the gaze of Western autobiographical discourses fastened itself on the female body, it positioned the woman writer in a particular body. Although the nature of that particular body might have altered historically, as Riley has argued, the woman autobiographer always remained self-consciously in her body even as she erased the body from her text. Thus the autobiographical mode solicited the identification of a woman with and against her body. She had to turn down the level of the body and assume the subject position of "man" while simultaneously turning up the level of the body to assure her reader that her body was aligned as a "woman's" body should be aligned socially within the matrices of reproduction and nurturing. To choose neither of these modes was to write something "scandalous," to write the "grotesque."[4]

Perhaps Harriet Jacobs's slave narrative reveals most dramatically the body politics of women's autobiographical practice. In Jacob's text the female body troubles the generic edges of the male slave narrative and the tropes of white womanhood. Already violated, used for clandestine sexual purposes, her body is the very ground upon which the subsequent narrative is written. For the history of her body founds the rhetorical strategies of the text. The subject of the autobiography is the subjected body of the autobiographer. And the complex narrative postures of the autobiographer are required because of the specific history of the violated body. Jacob's struggle with the politicized body in an overtly hostile and oppressive body politic, her literal struggle with homelessness (of the body), provoke certain elasticities of self-representation that point toward the self-conscious struggles of the twentieth-century autobiographer with the politics of female embodiment, toward the interesting eruptions of the body in women's recent autobiographical practices.

Maxine Hong Kingston, for instance, opens her much-commented-on memoir *The Woman Warrior* with the cautionary tale her mother told her when she began menstruating. This tale inaugurates a series of five narratives assembled on the bodies of women. There is the body of "no-name aunt" that plugs up the town's water supply. There is Fa Mu Lan's body with words carved on its back. There are the bodies of girl-babies floating down the river of the Chinese sayings. There is the stoned body of the madwoman. There is the narrator's cut frenum. Bodies are everywhere. The onset of menstruation begins Kingston's memoir; it brings the opening chronology of Lillian Hellman's *An Unfinished Woman* to a close. It is as if the narrative cannot keep its chronological line going once Hellman remembers hitting puberty. There is the body of the African girl Jebbta in Beryl Markham's *West with the Night*, the female body onto which Markham has focused any female identification. There is the omnipresent body of the great goddess in Isak Dinesen's *Out of Africa*, a sensual surround that invites Dinesen to identification in her racial difference. There is the out-of-body narrative device of Gertrude Stein's *Autobiography of Alice B. Toklas*, the forced and imaginative non-identification between autobiographer and autobiographical narrator. There is the metaphorics of skin that drives Annie Dillard's *American Childhood*. But for the purposes of this discussion I want to focus now on two disparate texts: Virginia Woolf's "Sketch of the Past" written from 1939 to 1941 and Cherríe Moraga's *Loving in the War Years*, published in the early 1980s.

The Grape Eyeball and the Bourgeois Body

These were two of the adventures of my professional life. The first—killing the Angel in the House—I think I solved. She died. But the second, telling the truth about my own experiences as a body, I do not think I solved.—Virginia Woolf, "Professions for Women"

To inaugurate her narrative, Woolf opens her unfinished "Sketch" not with historical details of family lineage, not with paternal and maternal origins, but with the fragments of her earliest memories, those pre-linguistic moments of sensual pleasure and receptivity before the infant body has been unhinged from mind and imagination. Two moments in particular capture her memory: Sitting on her mother's lap, she is enveloped by the large "passion" flowers on her mother's dress. Lying in her crib at St. Ives, she feels the wind, listens to the sounds of water, wind, and window covering, sees the light play through space. These privileged moments of preindividualized being she associates with ecstasy—with the semiotic pleasure of pure sensation and experiential wholeness, with instinct and passion. Here is the moment before repression has begun its work.[5] "If life has a base that it stands upon," she claims, "if it is a bowl that one fills and fills and fills—then my bowl without a doubt stands upon this memory" ("Sketch" 64).

To the experience of pre-Oedipal bondedness and boundlessness in which her body and her mother's body are the sources of ecstasy, Woolf juxtaposes several horrifyingly vivid memories that signify for the older narrator the transition from the childhood of nondifferentiation to the young womanhood of overdetermined sexual identification. The memory of standing before a mirror, ashamed of the figure she sees projected in the glass, marks a radical change. In trying to understand the significance of this memory, she concludes: "I must have been ashamed or afraid of my own body" ("Sketch" 68). In the mirror she sees reflected a demarked, bounded, totalized body, a body captured in the gaze. Hard-edged, impermeable, confined, that body lacks the fluidity, the openness, the permeability identified with her earliest memories, ones that she says provided her with rapture and ecstasy. Here, body and background, ground and figure are dramatically separated from one another.

Woolf follows this memory with her dramatic revelation of childhood sexual abuse:

> There was a slab outside the dining room door for standing dishes upon. Once when I was very small Gerald Duckworth lifted me

onto this, and as I sat there he began to explore my body. I can remember the feel of his hand going under my clothes; going firmly and steadily lower and lower. I remember how I hoped that he would stop; how I stiffened and wriggled as his hand approached my private parts. But it did not stop. His hand explored my private parts too. I remember resenting, disliking it—what is the word for so dumb and mixed a feeling? It must have been strong, since I still recall it. This seems to show that a feeling about certain parts of the body; how they must not be touched; how it is wrong to allow them to be touched; must be instinctive. It proves that Virginia Stephen was not born on the 25th January 1882, but was born many thousands of years ago; and had from the very first to encounter instincts already acquired by thousands of ancestresses in the past. ("Sketch" 69)

Then directly after this revelation, she remembers a (perhaps) oneiric vision in which she catches a glimpse of herself in a mirror, only now there is an animal visible behind her. In the latter vision, the specular conjunction of body and animal graphically identifies her body with the animal world, with the irrational, the contaminating and unruly, thus with the grotesque or carnivalesque. Graphically, Woolf renders her body as source of lowliness and animality, of disgust and shame, and reveals the motivations for her inhibitions, her repressions.

Several aspects of this succession of memories command the reader's attention. First, with the revelation of sexual abuse Woolf introduces a liminal scene in which the young girl experiences the loss of her own body to the sexual domination and exploitation of a patriarch, an older brother and putative protector. Her body is literally taken away from her. With the intrusion of Gerald Duckworth's hand, the child experiences the painful recognition that her body is not hers to control, that it is there for others to handle. If that handling is physically invasive, it is also culturally pervasive. For Woolf interjects here her memory of childhood injunctions against bodies being touched (Spilka 31). Therefore it is not only Gerald Duckworth's sexual abuse but bourgeois Victorian taboos surrounding the body that effectively remove the feeling subject from her own body, from that specific source of ecstasy.

Second, the feeling of horror she recalls derives from her knowledge, however conscious or unconscious, of that specular self that encloses her in identity's body. That very body defines and delimits her as female subject, tying her to her destiny as woman. In the mirror she sees what

Hélène Cixous has called "the uncanny stranger on display—the ailing or dead figure, which so often turns out to be the nasty companion, the cause and location of inhibitions" (250). But something more happens here. If, as John Berger has argued in considering the relationship of women to the mirror, "the surveyor of woman in herself is male: the surveyed female" (47), then the recollection of uneasiness is a recollection of a shift in the subject's position. As the "I" who looks at that body becomes the observer, the body the observed, that "I" assumes the place of the male subject. Looking in the mirror, the young Virginia gazes at her body as men will later do. Thus the act of looking in the mirror implicates her in the very practice that she will later so vigorously abjure, the experience of her stepbrother's creation of her as the object of the public gaze, as a woman in the heterosexual economy.

These memories reveal the symbolic and imaginary processes whereby the female subject is consolidated in ways that support the privileges of male-bourgeois subject, the "coding of his repulsion in relation to the other in order to autonomize himself" (Kristeva 82), and the consequent coding of the self-revulsion of the female subject. The young Virginia is positioned in a body that she experiences as a source of shame and of alienation. The regulatory processes brought to bear on the imagination render the female body other, animal, therefore abject, and exclude that body and its unruliness from the domain of the "higher" subject. Woolf's oneiric vision signals the internalization of this symbolic consolidation. Simultaneously, bourgeois culture locates women in their bodies, imposes the total identification of woman with her body. A woman becomes the cultural abject, identified in her difference, solidified in her very embodiment. Woolf's specular "moments of being," or rather, moments of splitting, reveal how as a woman she is doubly indemnified. She is the cultural abject: she abjects her own body.

The degree of abjection is revealed in the subtle movement of narrative voice in the passage about Gerald's invasive hand. Woolf shifts the narrative voice away from the "I" of the narrating subject by invoking the distancing device of third-person narrative, referring to herself as the object "Virginia Stephen." Moreover, she increasingly distances her responses from their immediate source in the subsequent analysis of motive. First she suggests the shame might have derived from her fear of being caught looking at herself since to do so would violate her childhood identification with a "tomboy code" ("Sketch" 67). But she proceeds to trace the shame back further to ancestral predispositions over which she has no control. Recalling that "femininity was strong in our family," she suggests that the Stephen women "were famous for our beauty," a beauty she finds gives her "pride and pleasure"; but she also notes that "[her] natural love for beauty was checked by some ancestral dread" ("Sketch" 68). This dread may reach back only two generations to a "spartan, ascetic, puritanical" grandfather from whom she inherited "some opposite instinct." Or it may go further back to prehistory, to the ancestresses of the race to whom she traces discomfort with invasions of her body. She displaces the source of bodily disgust from her experiential history to the instinctual life of the human species. She cannot, as Sue Roe notes, even describe the sensations in this passage as she could in describing her earliest memories; she seems to have no words for talking about her own sexualized body and no personal narratives for conveying her response (Roe 49).[6]

These moments of being separate Woolf's narrative of childhood from her narrative of young adulthood and signify for the older narrator the transition from the childhood of sexual nondifferentiation to the young Victorian womanhood of overdetermined sexual identification. For the older writer, the figure in the glass is a representation of female selfhood shackled to the female body and engendered through specific social, cultural, historical conditions. What shocks the young girl does not shock the older woman, who recognizes too clearly the ways in which the fabricated body and the female subject in that body are constituted out of the "invisible presences" of patriarchal ideology: "Consider what immense forces society brings to play upon each of us," writes Woolf, "how that society changes from decade to decade; and also from class to class; well, if we cannot analyze these invisible presences, we know very little of the subject of the memoir" ("Sketch" 80). The autobiographer thus proceeds to track, if sketchily, the social construction of sexual difference within the bourgeois Victorian household.

First she describes the centrality of the mother in her childhood (a great cathedral space) and the shock of her mother's death. It is as if symbolically the death of her mother is the final taking of the body from the young girl, a grand anesthesia. Then she tracks the next phase of her grand anesthesia through her subsequent relationship to mothering. In a series of inhabitations of identity, the young Stella replaces the dead mother, Vanessa replaces the dead Stella, and Virginia joins Vanessa in assuming the cultural place of dutiful daughterhood.[7] Against their wills, the daughters/sisters are fashioned into models of nurturant femininity. The connection between the mirror scene and this narrative of displacements is joined in the female body. If the earlier reflection in the mirror confronts her with her own abjection, a sense of bodily dispossession, the subsequent filling-in-the-place-of-the-mother forces her back to total embodiment.[8] In the gaze of the men around here she is possessed entirely by the body of woman. The latter part of the "Sketch" thus focuses on the sociofamilial regulation of her body.

Because bourgeois gender ideologies spatialized the separate spheres through the physical division of the house into study and drawing room, her body determines her assignment to certain household spaces. It also locates her in certain clothes, the "habits" about which the older narrator remembers feeling so much discomfort. Woolf recognized how effectively clothes, external signs of sexual difference, influenced hearts, brains, and language. And in "Sketch" she suggests how social life becomes synonymous with female bodily display as she remembers the distress she felt when her brothers introduced her into society. In one more way, they "handled" her by turning her into an object of the male gaze, by turning her body into a source of male pleasure.

Spatial assignments and clothes are components in the regulation of her body; so too are manners, those sets of behaviors associated with space and dress. Stallybrass and White point out that, as "regulations of the body," manners "become the site of a profound interconnection of ideology and subjectivity, a zone of transcoding at once astonishingly trivial and microscopically important. Traversed by regulative forces quite beyond its conscious control, the body is territorialized in accordance with hierarchies and topographical rules which it enacts automatically, which come from elsewhere and which make it a point of intersection and flow within the elaborate symbolic systems of the socius" (90). Ultimately, Woolf's body becomes a commodified body, designed, produced, and consumed, a process Woolf acknowledges in her imagery of the machine (Albright 11): "And so, while father preserved the framework of 1860, George filled in the framework with all kinds of minutely teethed saws; and the machine into which we were inserted in 1900 therefore held us tight; and brought innumerable teeth into play" ("Sketch" 131). Those teeth are so many sets of manners, gearing her up for the finished product, a young lady.

The source of oppressive assignments of gendered characteristics, the body is glimpsed momentarily, in the mirror, and then erased, withheld from the reader. While it continues to haunt the narrative as the uncanny stranger, another material figure displaces the narrator's body. In fact the body is fragmented into a writerly metaphor, or rather the materiality of the body is concentrated into a metaphorical orb, a kind of transparent eyeball. Her resistance to her own body (and her early memory of being positioned in her mother's lap as a sensate being) sends her vision toward the transparent eyeball, away from the solid individuality of embodied subjects.

In "Street Haunting" Woolf describes leaving the narrow, Clarissa-esque room of self to become absorbed in the street where "the shell-like covering which our souls have excreted to house themselves, to make for themselves a shape distinct from others, is broken, and there is left of all these wrinkles and roughnesses a central oyster of perceptiveness, an enormous eye" (156). Only too aware of the constrictions, foreclosures, stillnesses, and narrowing rigidities of the totalized "shape distinct from others," the individual subject determined by identity politics, this modernist writer bemoans the unitary, metaphysical self's tendency to foreclose, to silence, the potential and heterogeneous lives and selves every human being has in the beginning of life, "those embryo lives which attend about us in early youth until 'I' suppress[es] them" ("Ill" 199). Woolf understood how one by one these possible trajectories of self are foreclosed by identity, left behind in the wake of the powerful, the totalizing "I." Taking trips—geographical, cultural, psychological—enables the individual to "penetrate a little way, far enough to give oneself the illusion that one is not tethered to a single mind, but can put on briefly for a few minutes the bodies and minds of others" ("Street Haunting" 165), that one can escape identity. An alternative self to this hard (male) nut is "something so varied and wandering that it is only when we give the rein to its wishes and let it take its way unimpeded that we are indeed ourselves" ("Street Haunting" 161). Positioning herself in the transparent eyeball Woolf takes the opportunity to perform beyond constraining identities, especially sexual identities. She also escapes the confining boundaries of one body, the boundaries of identity's body.

Significantly, she returns to this figure in "Sketch" as she identifies her infant self with a transparent eyeball, although the exact image is one of fruit. She has "the feeling, as I describe it sometimes to myself, of lying in a grape and seeing through a film of semi-transparent yellow" (65). This great, grape eyeball is sense itself, open to impressions, absorbing color, sound, smell, rhythm: "I am hardly aware of myself, but only of the sensation. I am only the container of the feeling of ecstasy, of the feeling of rapture" ("Sketch" 67). "Grape" selfhood is a place of fluidity, of openness to the multiplicity of sensations, to the indivisible interactions between the child and the mother. Always permeable, this pre-Oedipal subjectivity immerses itself in the "cotton wool" of daily life, situates itself as an invitation to exchange. The time of the great, grape eyeball is the moment before the "I" intrudes, before interpretation disrupts the sense of unity, that seamless exchange between the experiencing self and the experienced world, before entry into the symbolic realm marks the difference of subject and other, before the mirror presents the girl with the image of her body, locus of sexual difference and discomfort, locus of identity and of homelessness. This is the time before sexual division, before the hard mirror edges of male and female selfhoods intrude, before the performances of gender are invoked.

This figure of the transparent grape, described in "Street Haunting" as "a central oyster of perceptiveness, an enormous eye," is critical to Woolf's critique of metaphysical selfhood and its regulation of the body. For the transparent eyeball combines both matter and spirit, contains opposites. A material entity, a sensual organ, it takes in, imbibes the external world, acting as conduit for external experience. Yet it is simultaneously a metaphorical locus of spirit, vision, illumination, interpretation. Conjoining both matter and spirit, external reality and internal vision, the transparent eyeball lies on the border between inside and outside, mind and matter, subject and other. Disembodied, the transparent eyeball as locus of ecstasy is not tied to a finite body, but functions as an experiencing point of contact between inner and outer. The older woman's metaphor of the transparent eyeball effectively connects her to the grape-infant Virginia who experienced the pure ecstasy of semiotic union, the commingling of self and other, the seamless transition between inside and outside she identifies with her earliest memories. Signifying the desire of the self to traverse permeable ego boundaries, to float with facility between past and present, self and other, being and nonbeing, the metaphor, in linking her to that earlier moment of erotic/semiotic pleasure, posits a diffusive and absorptive, rather than appropriative, subjectivity. The metaphor provides a way for the older writer to elaborate another kind of subjectivity than that of the universal human subject. In addition, it allows her to displace, to deconstruct that pervasive phallocentric trope of vision, the one Luce Irigaray describes as "man's eye—understood as substitute for the penis" (145). Finally, the metaphor allows her to transform the shamefilled and alienating homelessness she feels as she confronts her body to a visionary homelessness that signals release from the social fabrication of female embodiment. The baseness (lowness) of the body is transformed into the disembodied vision (highness) of the transparent eyeball. This eyeball can metaphorically leave the individual body. And "Virginia" can escape the abject body, gender hierarchy, and disgust.

Woolf's narrative reveals how various technologies of self-representation call the early twentieth-century middle-class body and its female bourgeois subject into being. The narrative simultaneously charts an imaginary route by which the alienated subject tries to escape identity's body in a gesture of sublimation that extrudes a nonbodied, higher vision from the grotesque body. Here the need to escape the female body effectively joins the need to resist the isolating individuality of the masculine "I." Resistance to one kind of carnivalesque image, the animal in the glass, leads to another variation of the carnivalesque image, the boundless eye. But the contradictions of the boundless "I" are inescapable in Woolf's narrative. As it seeks to escape bounded identifications, the floating eyeball functions as a locus of resistance to stable topographies of class and gender relationships. It cannot be kept in its place/space/singular identity. And yet, the elevation of the disembodied eyeball also supports the very baseness of the body, the very repression of the female body that anchors the bourgeois subject and the practices of traditional autobiography.

Warring over and with the Body

What I never quite understood until this writing is that to be without a sex—to be bodiless—as I sought to be to escape the burgeoning sexuality of my adolescence, my confused early days of active heterosexuality, and later my panicked lesbianism, means also to be without a race. I never attributed my removal from physicality to have anything to do with race, only sex, only desire for women. And yet, as I grew up sexually, it was my race, along with my sex, that was being denied me at every turn.—Cherríe Moraga, Loving in the War Years

Unlike Woolf, whose repression of the body erases a contaminating desire through sublimation and who thus writes herself out of her body, Cherríe Moraga brings the autobiographical body out from under the processes of erasure, assuming her body as narrative point of departure: she discovers that the body functions as a lens through which she comes to see her complex cultural positioning as woman, lesbian, light-skinned Chicana. Her title signals directly the interrelationship of the body and the body politic, the forced juncture of the personal and the political. "War years" are the most exigently political years, or perhaps they are the years when politics has failed. They invoke the battleground upon which the struggle for cultural meaning is waged, for Moraga, the culturally censored and the self-censoring body of the Chicana. And "loving in the war years" is a kind of revolutionary gesture, calling as it does "for this kind of risking/without a home to call our own" (Moraga 30). War years are years of homelessness in and out of the body.

Throughout the poems and the prose narratives that make up the text, the narrator insists on being in the body, on the being of bodies. Bodies surround the text, move in and through it. They are eaten, for instance: in the memory of her grandmother who gestures love as edible consumption; in the poem "An Open Invitation to a Meal" in which the "I"/lover figures as a "piece of cake" to be consumed (22). The knees of religious women grind against the floor of churches (18). The body of the suicide falls through air. Lips, breasts, thighs, legs, knees, eyes, cunts, backs, skin. Parts of the body are named, colorfully described. Movements of the body are mapped. Poetry keeps the emotional pulse of the body's experience beating alongside, not subordinated to, the prose critique. The prose analysis keeps positioning the body in its specific discursive domains of meaning, keeps attending to the mediations enacted on the body by the body politic. Inscribing embodiedness everywhere, the narrator challenges the notion of an individuality, an autobiographer distinct from a specific body. Ultimately this new kind of history of the body motivates an alternative autobiographical practice through which, as Lourdes Torres notes, Moraga "explores how women are denied a right to their bodies through the repression of their sexuality, the lifelong threat of sexual violence, and the denial of reproductive rights" (278).

Thus Moraga writes her body in order to break the circuit of control over representations of female sexuality that "are designed to accommodate and normalize masculine preferences and patterns of gratification" (Singer, 139) in both the dominant Anglo culture and what Mae Gwendolyn Henderson terms the "ambiguously (non)hegemonic" culture (120), here Chicano culture. But Moraga writes a specific body, and its specific history of practices. She does not write the body of a homogenized woman; that universalized body, suggests Naomi Schor, "conspires in the denial of the very real lived differences—sexual, ethnic, racial, national, cultural, economic, generational—that divide women from each other and from themselves" (42). Moraga's specific body is "female" and "lesbian" and "colored" and "working class/poor." It is positioned in and out of Chicano culture, in and out of Anglo culture. And compounding the various specificities of cultural placement, Moraga's body can "pass" back and forth between two cultures, the Anglo and Chicano, the straight and the lesbian. This body founds the narrator's double move: she not only writes the body, but critiques the social meaning of that body by elaborating her relationship to the nexus of oppression inscribed on it: "In this country, lesbianism is a poverty—as is being brown, as is being a woman, as is being just plain poor. The danger lies in ranking the oppressions. *The danger lies in failing to acknowledge the specificity of the oppression*" (52).

The narrator's engagement with her specific body forces her to confront the palpability of color and the politics of chromatism. Anglo culture renders the Chicano body as one of the abject; but the shade of the body determines the relative degree of abjection within both dominant and marginal cultures and the degree of fluidity in both the self-assignment and communal assignment of racial identity. Moraga confronts this chromatism as she considers her positioning in the skin of "la guerra": "I was 'la guera'—fair-skinned. Born with the features of my Chicana mother, but the skin of my Anglo father, I had it made. . . . In fact, everything about my upbringing (at least what occurred on a conscious level) attempted to bleach me of what color I did have" (51). Fair skin allows her to escape the culturally abnormative, or abject, body of the Chicana figured by her mother and to pass for white, to assume the normatively white body of the dominant culture and its identity structures. This ability to assume the dominant identity sustains the illusion that she can, paradoxically, escape identity's body, can exist without being called to her body culturally.

But in one of the narratives, she describes how, when Cecelia, her autobiographical protagonist, lives with a black lover, "color move[s] in with her" (36). Discovering that skin color "makes all the difference in the world" (36), she finds her skin to be no longer the secure anchorage it had seemed to be. New knowledge changes inescapably the feel of skin: "Soon her body began to change with this way of seeing. She felt her skin, like a casing, a beige bag into which the guts of her life were poured. And inside it, she swam through her day. Upstream. Downtown. Underground. Always, the shell of this skin, leading her around" (36). And this psychological homelessness inside her own skin leads to her recognition of cultural homelessness as she comes to understand the ways in which her ability to assume the identity of an Anglo separates her from her family and her community: "I feel at times I am trying to bulldoze my way back into a people who force me to leave them in the first place, who taught me to take my whiteness and run with it. Run with it. Who want nothing to do with me, the likes of me, the white of me—in them" (95). Her very skin sets her loose into anxious homelessness.

The narrator considers this instability of identification an oppressive rather than liberatory condition: "You call this a choice! To constantly push up against a wall of resistance from your own people or to fall away nameless into the mainstream of this country, running with our common blood?" (97). The surface/color of the skin permits her to change cultural identities, to move noiselessly between two cultures; but under the skin she turns against the skin in her, turns against her heritage and thus the source of her subjectivity. She thereby participates in the abjection of her own body. "But at the age of twenty-seven," she writes, "it is frightening to acknowledge that I have internalized a racism and classism, where the object of oppression is not only someone *outside* my skin, but the someone *inside* my skin. In fact, to a large degree, the real battle with such oppression, for all of us, begins under the skin" (54).

Moraga's narrative reveals that because of the color of a particular part of her body she could choose to resist identity's body, the cultural consolidation of her body parts into a unified identity as Chicana. But the price of passing was racial disidentification. The operations of sexual disidentification are equally complex and are inextricable from those of racial disidentification. Within Chicano culture the female-in-sex is *la chingada*, "the fucked-one." Her very sexuality as expressed in the sexual act becomes grotesque, contaminated, unclean, "base" (119). With this ideology of female sexuality the Chicana is alienated from her bodily home: "If the simple act of sex then—the penetration itself—implies the female's filthiness, non-humanness, it is no wonder Chicanas often divorce ourselves from the conscious recognition of our own sexuality" (119). Denied a pleasurable body, the Chicana is assigned instead another kind of body—the compulsory heterosexual body, even more specifically the repressed heterosexual body.[9]

In the midst of this cultural surround, Moraga recalls how her body moved her in different directions, moved her away from an anchorage in heterosexuality: "I have always known too much. It was too clear to me— too tangible—too alive in the breath of my nose, the pulse in my thighs, the deep exhales that flowed from my chest when I moved into a woman's arms" (116). And so she describes how the disjunction between the cultural expectation of her identification as "heterosexual woman" and her own bodily knowledge led her to a state of physical and emotional homelessness, toward yet another kind of grotesquerie: "And if we have lesbian feelings—want not only to be penetrated, but to penetrate—what perverse kind of monstrosities we must indeed be" (119). In yet another powerful technology of (hetero)sexuality, the young girl is driven by the fragmentation of her body toward a reified disembodiment: "I see now that in order not to embody the chingada, not the femalized, and therefore perverse version of the chingon, I became pure spirit—bodiless. For what, indeed, must my body look like if I were both the chingada and the chingon" (120).

The abject female body is not only a personal body, however. It is the community's body, one which threatens to contaminate the body politic, to destroy the very fabric of cultural identity and nationalism. Within Chicano culture the elaborate and compelling myth of Malinche operates to police the female body and to keep identity fixed in a repressed body whose very erasure consolidates "la familia" and male privilege. Identifying woman's body as the site of cultural betrayal, the myth operates as "the public regulation of fantasy through the surface politics of the body" (Butler, *Gender Trouble* 136). "This myth of the inherent unreliability of women, our natural propensity for treachery," writes Moraga, "has been carved into the very bone of Mexican/Chicano collective psychology" (101). It effectively disjoins the Chicana from her own body, from what Susan Rubin Suleiman refers to as the "wildness of the unconscious" (16), and weds her to her subordinate position in marriage and to all men.

Malinche's myth assigns the Chicana to this specific kind of sexuality; it also scripts the effects of her refusal to accept this assignment as it scripts the effects of Moraga's refusing the gender assignments of compulsory heterosexuality: "The woman who defies her role as subservient to her husband, father, brother, or son by taking control of her own sexual destiny is purported to be a 'traitor to her race' by contributing to the 'genocide' of her people—whether or not she has children. In short, even if the defiant woman is not a lesbian, she is purported to be one; for, like the lesbian in the Chicano imagination, she is *una Malinchista*. Like the Malinche of Mexican history, she is corrupted by foreign influences which threaten to destroy her people" (113). The female body opens up to foreign influences, foreign infiltration, foreign insemination, to foreign meaning and control. It is the breached boundary that destabilizes inner and outer, that invites further penetration by the dominant order, the very source of oppression. It is the opening through which leaks out the (endogamous) life of the people. The body politic thus takes up the female body in its war with the dominant culture, making the female body the contestatory middle term between the male/dominant culture of the

Anglos and the male/subdominant culture of the Chicanos. In the body politic female sexuality metaphorically and literally saps the male of his privileges, as it threatens to erase his original identity.

Insisting on her body as an excluded term in the constitution of dominant identities, Moraga ultimately places the body of the Chicana lesbian before the reader in all its materiality, offering a destabilizing cultural performance. Now the "grotesque" body speaks back, "defiantly displaying" in the words of Carroll Smith-Rosenberg, its "own sexuality as a symbol of social resistance" (103) and thus of various kinds of empowerment.[10] First, Moraga rewrites the history of Malinche, complicating the act of treachery by introducing a family tragedy in which the daughter Malinche is rejected by her mother in favor of the son who will inherit power. The daughter locates the treachery elsewhere than in Malinche's cooperation with Cortez. She locates it in "la familia." For it is a treachery Moraga herself experiences at the hands of her own mother. Moreover, in historicizing Malinche, Moraga recovers the body of Malinche and of the Chicana from the legend, and in so doing gives her body autobiographically as a gift and as a source of liberation.[11]

Second, Moraga figures the lesbian as an empowered figure of desire: "In stepping outside the confines of the institution of heterosexuality, I was indeed *choosing* sex freely. *The lesbian as institutionalized outcast*" (124–25). "The most visible manifestation of a woman taking control of her own sexual identity and destiny" (112), she is the revolutionary figure whose very relationship to her body inaugurates cultural critique. And cultural critique, as Linda Singer suggests, is critical to liberation: "Women who do not know or are incapable of representing what they want are that much less likely to demand or pursue it. The absence of a female-identified discourse adequate to representing women's sexuality in its difference is both a symptom of and instrumental to the continued subjugation of women within the patriarchal order" (139).

Third, Moraga makes explicit the connection between the discourse invoked by the body and the acquisition of new knowledge: "It wasn't until I acknowledged and confronted my own lesbianism in the flesh, that my heartfelt identification with and empathy for my mother's oppression—due to being poor, uneducated, and Chicana—was realized. My lesbianism is the avenue through which I have learned the most about silence and oppression, and it continues to be the most tactile reminder to me that we are not free human beings" (52). In scripting a positive, empowered, pleasurable body, Moraga disturbs dominant systems of knowledge that have normalized the female body, either as "male/the same" or as "grotesque." Autobiographical writing thus compels the subject toward a new knowledge, a new way of interpreting the practices of the body politic through the material body and its desires.

Fourth, Moraga effectively releases the lesbian body from the pornographic gaze of (male) discourses by writing for an audience she constitutes as sympathetic rather than voyeuristic. Although she cannot control what kind of readings her autobiographical text will receive, although she cannot filter out all voyeuristic gazes, she can interrupt the specular scenes of lesbian desire with a clearheaded and full-bodied critique of compulsory heterosexuality and its political and institutional implications. And since the body politic of both Chicano and Anglo cultures is founded on the heterosexual construction of men and women, Moraga's empowerment of the lesbian body serves to unsettle normative practices of sexuality that consolidate identity through the fragmentation (the putative unification) of the body.

And finally, instead of parceling out the body, sending various parts toward specific experiences of oppression (skin color toward race, breasts toward gender), Moraga surveys the meanings written all over the body in an attempt to make her meaning out of multiplicity: "Sexuality, race, and sex have usually been presented in contradiction to each other, rather than as part and parcel of a complex web of personal and political identity and oppression" (109). And yet, simultaneously, she resists the colonizing gesture of a false universalization of experience: "As a Chicana lesbian, I write of the connection my own feminism has had with my sexual desire for women. This is my story. I can tell no other than the one I understand" (139). By keeping the carnivalesque body of the lesbian woman of color always in the fore, by incorporating fragments of that body throughout, Moraga insists on the material specificity of the body that speaks and on the specific discourses, practices, and contexts that inscribe the cultural meaning of that body. In effect, Moraga's text/body enacts the return of the political unconscious (in both cultures that she straddles), interrupts a complacent self-identity founded on the abjection of the lesbian woman of color. Pursuing a sexual discourse adequate to the task of describing and creating knowledge about her specific libidinal economy (Singer 137), Moraga politically realigns the lesbian body and dismembers a stifling identity politics, dismembers, that is, identity's body and the bodiliness of the universal subject.

Attending to the body that speaks in "A Sketch of the Past" and *Loving in the War Years* allows us to consider the political and aesthetic implications of identity's body. Woolf's narrative reveals a nostalgia for the body before the cultural construction of identity (and the very real trauma of sexual abuse that testifies to the politics of gender) intrudes and partitions her off in identity's body. To escape the grotesque body, she imagines herself a disembodied spirit, the transparent eyeball. While the metaphor enables certain aesthetic practices, such as the pursuit of narrative anonymity through which Woolf contests the cultural consolidation of male identity, it also, through its contradictions, sustains the troubled relationship between autobiography and the female body. Speaking colored lesbian sexuality, Moraga choreographs an alternative history of the body. Body and mind, sexual desire and political critique, the body's anatomy and the anatomy of the body politic, the material and discursive, poetry and prose weave in and out of one another. The ideological marking of boundaries separating the body from the body politic, those boundaries through which the white/male/bourgeois subject and the textual politics of traditional Western autobiography ensure one another (Stallybrass and White 193), are here transgressed by the very body whose positioning as grotesque has underwritten those boundaries. Moraga's interrogation of identity politics through the theorizing of the very body's flesh reveals how efficiently the specificities of the body have been erased through Woolf's comfortably middle-class escape from embodiment. After all, Woolf never mentions the color of the skin that needs escaping.

What does skin have to do with autobiography?

Notes

1 "That penis, vagina, breasts, and so forth, are named sexual parts," argues Butler, "is both a restriction of the erogenous body to those parts and a fragmentation of the body as a whole. Indeed, the 'unity' imposed upon the body by the category of sex is a 'disunity,' a fragmentation and compartmentalization, and a reduction of erotogeneity" (*Gender Trouble* 114).

2 Butler provides the following summary of Julia Kristeva's notion of the abject: "The 'abject' designates that which has been expelled from the body, discharged as excrement, literally rendered 'Other.' This appears as an expulsion of alien elements, but the alien is effectively established through this expulsion. The construction of the 'not-me' as the abject establishes the boundaries of the body which are also the first contours of the subject. . . . The boundary of the body as well as the distinction between internal and external is established through the ejection and transvaluation of something originally part of identity into a defiling otherness" (*Gender Trouble* 133).

3 In developing her theory of gender performance Butler argues: "that the gendered body is performative suggests that it has no ontological status apart from the various acts which constitute its reality. This also suggests that if that reality is fabricated as an interior essence, that very interiority is an effect and function of a decidedly public and social discourse, the public regulation of fantasy through the surface politics of the body, the gender border control that differentiates inner from outer, and so institutes the 'integrity' of the subject. In other words, acts and gestures, articulated and enacted desires create the illusion of an interior and organizing gender core, an illusion discursively maintained for the purposes of the regulation of sexuality within the obligatory frame of reproductive heterosexuality" (*Gender Trouble* 136).

4 For a provocative discussion of the contours of scandal and the body of woman, see Felicity A. Nussbaum, chapter 8.

5 Woolf began to read Freud seriously as she revised the biography of Roger Fry. For a discussion of the significance of her reading of Freud, see Broughton.

6 For a related analysis of Woolf's relationship to sensuality, see Phyllis Rose, who argues that Woolf erases sexuality from the text, even though the opening richly elaborates moments of sensual ecstasy. For Rose the memoirs exude a "well-bred, repressed, but unmistakable eroticism." Despite this "unmistakable" marking of the body, Rose concludes that "Woolf goes out of her way in 'A Sketch of the Past' to prove that she was frigid from birth, telling about Gerald Duckworth's exploration of her and her response to it to assert the myth of her congenital asexuality. She protests, one feels, rather too strongly, and the sensual texture of her recollections belies her point. This was not an anesthetic childhood" (17–18).

7 For a comparative discussion of this process in Woolf's "Reminiscences" and "Sketch," see McCracken.

8 See Rose for another structural understanding of "Sketch." Rose argues that the structure is tripartite. The first act takes up the maternal story; the second act the two deaths, of her mother and Stella, and what Rose calls the fatality of mothering; the third act takes up the male ego and egotism and the relationship of the daughter to the father and to the larger social arena.

9 The phrase "compulsory heterosexual" is used by Adrienne Rich in her essay "Compulsory Heterosexuality" and taken up by Butler in *Gender Trouble*.

10 "The extent to which our sexuality and identity as Chicanas have been distorted both within our culture and by the dominant culture is the measure of how great a source of our potential power it holds" (Moraga 136).

11 For a discussion of the gift and its potentially anarchic meanings, see Mary Ann Caws on Lewis Hyde's recent theorizing of the gift: "To the theories of Mauss, Hyde adds emotion in the place of economics: what cannot be given does not exist as a gift. . . . A gift, he says, is anarchist property, 'because both anarchism and gift exchange share the assumption that it is not when a part of the self is inhibited and restrained, but when a part of the self is given away, that community appears.' The fragmented self—even a part of us—thus given away uninhibitedly, after Manner-

ism into Surrealism, and to all observers equally, may redeem—should we acquiesce in it—the sort of communal vision that a more classic holistic tradition was not able to save" (285).

References

Albright, Daniel. "Virginia Woolf as Autobiographer." *Kenyon Review* 6 (Fall 1984): 1–17.

Bakhtin, M. M. *Rabelais and his World.* Trans. H. Iswolsky. Cambridge: MIT P, 1968.

Berger, John. *Ways of Seeing.* New York: Viking, 1973.

Broughton, Panthea Reid. " 'Virginia is Anal': Speculations on Virginia Woolf's Writing *Roger Fry* and Reading Sigmund Freud." *Journal of Modern Literature* 14 (1987): 151–57.

Butler, Judith. *Gender Trouble: Feminism and the Subversion of Identity.* New York: Routledge, 1990.

——. "Variations on Sex and Gender: Beauvoir, Wittig and Foucault." *Feminism as Critique: On the Politics of Gender.* Ed. Seyla Benhabib and Drucilla Cornell. Minneapolis: U of Minnesota P, 1987.

Caws, Mary Ann. "Ladies Shot and Painted: Female Embodiment in Surrealist Art." *The Female Body in Western Culture: Contemporary Perspectives.* Ed. Susan Rubin Suleiman. Cambridge: Harvard UP, 1986. 262–87.

Cixous, Hélène. "The Laugh of the Medusa." *New French Feminisms.* Ed. Elaine Marks and Isabelle de Courtivron. New York: Schocken, 1981. 245–64.

De Lauretis, Teresa. "Feminist Studies/Critical Studies: Issues, Terms, and Contexts." *Feminist Studies/Critical Studies.* Ed. Teresa de Lauretis. Bloomington: Indiana UP, 1986. 1–19.

——. *Technologies of Gender: Essays on Feminism, Film, and Fiction.* Bloomington: Indiana UP, 1987.

Dillard, Annie. *An American Childhood.* New York: Harper, 1987.

Dinesen, Isak. *Out of Africa.* New York: Random, 1965.

Douglas, Mary. *Purity and Danger.* London: Routledge, 1969.

Fraser, Nancy. *Unruly Practices: Power, Discourse and Gender in Contemporary Social Theory.* Minneapolis: U of Minnesota P, 1989.

Hellman, Lillian. *An Unfinished Woman.* Boston: Little, 1969.

Henderson, Mae Gwendolyn. "Speaking in Tongues: Dialogics, Dialectics, and the Black Woman Writer's Literary Tradition." *Reading Black, Reading Feminist: A Critical Anthology.* Ed. Henry Louis Gates, Jr. New York: Meridian, 1990. 116–42.

Irigaray, Luce. *Speculum of the Other Woman.* Trans. Gillian C. Gill. Ithaca: Cornell UP, 1985.

Jacobs, Harriet. *Incidents in the Life of a Slave Girl.* Ed. Jean Fagan Yellin. Cambridge: Harvard UP, 1987.

Kingston, Maxine Hong. *The Woman Warrior: Memoirs of a Girlhood among Ghosts.* New York: Vintage, 1975.

Kristeva, Julia. *Powers of Horror: An Essay in Abjection.* Trans. L. S. Roudiez. New York: Columbia UP, 1982.

McCracken, LuAnn. "'The synthesis of my being': Autobiography and the Reproduction of Identity in Virginia Woolf." *Tulsa Studies in Women's Literature* 9 (1990): 61–67.

Markham, Beryl. *West with the Night.* San Francisco: North Point, 1983.

Martin, Biddy. "Lesbian Identity and Autobiographical Difference[s]." *Life/Lines: Theorizing Women's Autobiography.* Ed. Bella Brodzki and Celeste Schenck. Ithaca: Cornell UP, 1988. 77–103.

Martin, Biddy, and Chandra Talpade Mohanty. "Feminist Politics: What's Home Got to Do with It?" *Feminist Studies/Critical Studies.* Ed. Teresa de Lauretis. Bloomington: Indiana UP, 1986. 191–212.

Miller, Nancy K. "Changing the Subject: Authorship, Writing, and the Reader." *Feminist Studies/Critical Studies.* Ed. Teresa de Lauretis. Bloomington: Indiana UP, 1986. 102–20.

Moraga, Cherríe. *Loving in the War Years.* Boston: South End, 1983.

Nussbaum, Felicity A. *The Autobiographical Subject: Gender and Ideology in Eighteenth-Century England.* Baltimore: Johns Hopkins UP, 1989.

Rich, Adrienne. "Compulsory Heterosexuality and Lesbian Experience." *Signs* 5 (1980): 631–60.

——. *Of Woman Born: Motherhood as Experience and Institution.* New York: Norton, 1986.

Riley, Denise. *"Am I That Name?": Feminism and the Category of 'Women' in History.* Minneapolis: U of Minnesota P, 1988.

Roe, Sue. *Writing and Gender: Virginia Woolf's Writing Practice.* New York: St. Martin's, 1990.

Rose, Phyllis. *Woman of Letters: A Life of Virginia Woolf.* New York: Oxford UP, 1978.

Schor, Naomi. "This Essentialism Which Is Not One: Coming to Grips with Irigaray." *Differences: A Journal of Feminist Cultural Studies* 1 (1989): 38–58.

Singer, Linda. "True Confessions: Cixous and Foucault on Sexuality and Power." *The*

Thinking Muse: Feminism and Modern French Philosophy. Ed. Jeffner Allen and Iris Marion Young. Bloomington: Indiana UP, 1989. 136–55.

Smith-Rosenberg, Carroll. "The Body Politic." *Coming to Terms: Feminism, Theory, Politics.* Ed. Elizabeth Weed. New York: Routledge, 1989. 101–21.

Spilka, Mark. *Virginia Woolf's Quarrel with Grieving.* Lincoln: U of Nebraska P, 1980.

Stallybrass, Peter, and Allon White. *The Politics and Poetics of Transgression.* Ithaca: Cornell UP, 1986.

Stein, Gertrude. *The Autobiography of Alice B. Toklas.* New York: Random, 1933.

Suleiman, Susan Rubin. "Re/Writing the Body: The Politics and Poetics of Female Eroticism." *The Female Body in Western Culture: Contemporary Perspectives.* Ed. Susan Rubin Suleiman. Cambridge: Harvard UP, 1986. 7–29.

Torres, Lourdes. "The Construction of the Self in U.S. Latina Autobiographies." *Third World Women and the Politics of Feminism.* Ed. Chandra Talpade Mohanty, Ann Russo, and Lourdes Torres. Bloomington: Indiana UP, 1991. 271–87.

Woolf, Virginia. "On Being Ill." *Collected Essays.* Vol. 4. London: Hogarth, 1967. 193–203.

——. "Professions for Women." *Collected Essays.* Vol. 2. London: Hogarth, 1967. 284–89.

——. "Sketch of the Past." *Moments of Being.* New York: Harcourt, 1976. 64–137.

——. "Street Haunting: A London Adventure." *Collected Essays.* Vol. 4. London: Hogarth, 1967. 155–66.

Young, Iris Marion. *Justice and the Politics of Difference.* Princeton: Princeton UP, 1990.

——. "Throwing Like a Girl: A Phenomenology of Feminine Body Comportment, Motility, and Spatiality." *The Thinking Muse: Feminism and Modern French Philosophy.* Bloomington: Indiana UP, 1989. 51–70.

"An appearance walking in a forest the sexes burn":

Autobiography and the Construction

of the Feminine Body

SHIRLEY NEUMAN

■

Absent Bodies

Bodies rarely figure in autobiography. Even movie stars—those icons of an ideal body and of the material, emotional, and sexual sustenance it can earn its keeper—tend in their autobiographies to minimize the significance of their bodies to their personal and professional lives. Once surgeons, cosmeticians, hairdressers, and fashion designers have reinscribed an idealized body on the matter these actress-autobiographers provide, they—or their ghostwriters—generally strive above all to demonstrate the spiritual quest behind their culturally produced and idealized bodies. The histories of autobiography and of its criticism construe the self as individuated and coherent rather than as the product of social construction and as a subject-in-process and work consistently toward repression of the representation of bodies in autobiography. Such representation, when present at all, is to be found almost entirely in narratives of childhood, where supposedly untempered bodies are (mis)represented with Rousseauistic rather than Hollywood idealism, as uninscribed by culture.

We can cite many reasons for this near effacement of bodies in autobiography, chief among them a Platonic tradition that opposes the spiritual to the corporeal, and then identifies "self" with the spiritual. The same opposition informs the elevation of soul over body in Christian theology as it does the Enlightenment definition of "man" as "a thing or substance whose whole essence or nature is only to think, and which, to exist, has no need of space nor of any material thing or body" (Descartes 25). The corporeal functions as the binary opposite by which the spiritual is understood; the corporeal remains necessary to the spiritual at the same time that it must necessarily be transcended in philosophy and repressed in representation. Within this paradigm, the tradition of autobiography, like many narratives of western cultures, has established access to public discourse about the self as synonymous with spiritual quest and has consequently repressed representations of bodies within the genre. Where women's autobiography is concerned, this synonymity functions as a double handicap. As Sidonie Smith points out, to write autobiography a woman must enter the arena of public, intellectual/ spiritual discourse, which is to say that, historically, she has had to transgress the cultural norms that defined her womanhood in terms of the private sphere (44–62).[1] Moreover, in a set of equivalences that the Greek philosophers protested too much, and feminist philosophers and theorists have very often protested against, soul or intellect has more particularly been ascribed to men, matter or body ascribed to women.[2] A literary-philosophic tradition that identifies women as corporeal leaves the woman autobiographer in the position of identifying her self with her body, of creating herself through technologies of the body.[3] Contradictorily, a tradition of autobiography that identifies the genre with spirituality leaves the potential woman autobiographer in the position of either not writing at all, or of having to invent a self that is female and noncorporeal, which is to say, in the impossible position of inventing a self outside western cultures' inscriptions of femininity on and through her body.

Here I focus on two anomalous moments in contemporary autobiographies by women, moments when the genre's discursive repression of bodies is ruptured or exceeded; when a socially inscribed feminine body becomes both the subject of and the process in the text. I take my conception of a feminine body from Elizabeth Grosz who dismantles the distinction between biologically sexed bodies and social gender:

> It is . . . a matter of . . . a *social mapping* of the body tracing its anatomical and physiological details by social representations. The procedures which mark male and female bodies ensure that the biological capacities of bodies are always socially coded into sexually distinct categories. It is the *social inscription of sexed bodies*, . . . that is significant for feminist purposes" ("Inscriptions"; her emphasis).[4]

Although the biological, material characteristics of sexed bodies exist on a broad continuum, their social coding into the categories of male and female has the effect of polarizing differences at the expense of the many possible positions along the continuum and of constructing gender relations in terms of heterosexual relations.[5]

Feminine bodies, then, are constituted in the social mapping of female bodies which are *"always already cultural."* Such a body, like all bodies, is a "threshold term between nature and culture, being both natural and cultural" ("Notes" 7; her emphasis).[6] It is what Grosz, refashioning Foucault to serve what she names "corporeal feminism,"[7] calls a *"textualised* body" ("Inscriptions" 62), one in which diet, adornment, exercise, surgery, gesture, pleasures, performances, idealizations all produce or inscribe it in such a way that it is not only controlled but is also made into "an *interface* between 'privatised' experience and signifying culture" ("Notes" 10). These inscriptions of a body, Grosz argues, are "directed towards the acquisition of appropriate cultural attitudes, beliefs and values," that is, toward the production of a body's "interiority" ("Notes" 10). These socially inscribed bodies stand where the subject of autobiography has always stood: as Stephen Spender put it: "An autobiographer is really writing a story of two lives: his life as it appears to himself, . . . when he looks out at the world from behind his eye-sockets; and his life as it appears from outside in the minds of others; a view which tends to become in part his own view of himself also, since he is influenced by the opinions of these others" (viii).

But where Foucault sees bodies as sites of ideological codification, Grosz would take us one step further and see bodies as produced by and productive of ideology and social power, as both "the means by which power is disseminated and a potential object of resistance to power" ("Notes" 12). Such bodies are not, of course, inscribed by and resistant to ideologies of gender alone; rather, their inscriptions produce and are produced by any number of intersections between gender and other ideologies, such as those of class and race.[8]

By addressing two anomalous moments when self-representations of a feminine body rupture and exceed the spiritual discourse of autobiography, I not only demonstrate the ways in which women autobiographers' representations of their bodies and of the "interiority," or psychic effects, of those bodies are produced by ideology, but also ask about the extent to which they are productive of ideology. My first instance, the conclusion of Kate Simon's *Bronx Primitive*, records a decisive moment in the girl-child's inscription by femininity. My second anomalous moment is provided by Violette Leduc. In three volumes—*La Bâtarde, La Folie en tête*, and *La chasse à l'amour*—she displays more extensively, and with greater awareness than any other autobiographer I know of, the effects on her creation of a self of the social inscription of her body as feminine.

"Lolita, my twin"

An account of growing up in a neighborhood of Jewish, Italian, and Polish immigrants, *Bronx Primitive* has much in common with both the bildungsroman and with a dominant tradition of male autobiography that we might label preludes, or narratives of "the growth of the auto-biographer's mind": it chronicles first influences, the realization of the capacity for self-determination in the repudiation of a parentally chosen vocation, and an emergent sexual awareness. Men's preludes most often represent the adolescent's relation to his body as an unresolved oscilla-tion between carnal longing and romantic yearnings, which are confused and commingled with artistic aspirations. *Bronx Primitive,* however, gives us a much more physically terrifying view of the girl's development. The immigrant niece of Kate's father masturbates by rubbing herself against Kate's legs in bed at night; his immigrant nephew makes "night raids" (123) on her in which he stops just short of penetration; her breasts are "felt up" (158) by the barber; she is taken to the movies by a family friend and feels his hand trying to creep into her bloomers. Kate the child is clearheaded and resourceful in the face of these attacks. She recognizes (perhaps with some help from the mature narrator of this autobiography) that her father knows about at least some of these as-saults and is complicit in making her "a thing that had no feelings, no thoughts, no choices . . . a 'street girl' for anyone in the Family" (173). She resists the nephew, refuses the invitations to the movies, defies her fa-ther's quasi-incestuous expectation that she become a concert pianist under his management. She also resists the feminization of her flesh. In a move that one feminist critic has identified as the will among certain women artists to destroy the female body rather than "destroy her Self" by identifying with "birth, belly, and body—all these synecdoches of femininity" (Export 7), she binds her breasts "tighter and still tighter" until she has "dug long cuts under [her] arms, the blood staining the ribbon" (Simon 145).

But all this clearheaded awareness about what is being done to her, all this resistance in both its resourceful and self-mutilating aspects, is transmogrified on the day that Kate can claim a more socially legitimat-ing blood, the day "I had *achieved* my first menstrual period" (177; my emphasis). On that day, her mother bestows a gift with decidedly social meanings. She gives Kate her first "woman's dress," one of "thin voile . . . no collar . . . shaped, pinched in under my breasts, narrowing down to a waist, billowing out in a gathered skirt, covering my knees" (177–78).

This "woman's dress" immediately overwrites the physiological fact of first menstruation by the social construction of femininity. In the passage that follows, that femininity produces Kate's pleasure in her own body and her identification of herself with it, it gives her a sense of power, and it idealizes her in a wide range of sexual and erotic encounters. She wears the dress to walk in the park the next afternoon:

> I heard little and saw less; aware only of the tucks on my ribs, the sloping seams at the sides, the swing of the skirt as it brushed my knees. I held my naked, collarless neck stiff and high. . . . My waist was a golden ring, my sides as I stroked them had the curved perfection of antelope's horns. . . . I approved of the taste of all the strokers and pinchers. I understood what they felt, felt it myself as I continued to stroke my superb sides. . . . There was a boundless world of choices opening around me. . . . The next time Mr. Silverberg offered to take me to the movies I would suggest that we go to [a restaurant] first, like a real date, and push his hand away firmly when it began to crawl. Or let it crawl while I laughed at him. . . . The next time I went to Helen Roth's house, her high-school brother would kneel and lay at my feet a sheaf of long-stemmed red roses. . . .
>
> I was ready for all of them and for Rudolph Valentino; to play, to tease, to amorously accept, to confidently reject. Lolita, my twin, was born decades later, yet a twin of the thirteen-and-a-half-year-old striding through Crotona Park, passing the spiky red flowers toward a kingdom of mesmerized men—young, old, skinny, fat, good-looking, ugly, well dressed, shabby, bachelors, fathers—all her subjects. As desirable as Gloria Swanson, as steely as Nita Naldi, as winsome as Marion Davies, she was, like them, invincible and immortal. (178–79)

Kate Simon was in her sixties when she published *Bronx Primitive* and it is difficult to miss the irony half a century's vantage has introduced into this passage. But that irony, partly because it is so affectionate, does not hamper the identification that many women readers in western cultures will experience with the thirteen-year-old learning to identify her pleasure, her self, and her power in terms of her feminine body. Many of us will at some point have approved the taste of the strokers and pinchers even as we failed to relish and actively resisted the stroking and pinching. Many of us will have desired the tribute of some more or less sentimental, culturally approved symbol of love. And many of us will have identified with Hollywood's rhetoric of femininity as invincible and immortal, while resisting the recognition that Hollywood cinema humiliates, subdues through marriage, or kills, with remarkable frequency, heroines who aspire to invincibility. In this we have only read in accord with the cultural codes of femininity, which we have interiorized through their inscription on our own bodies.

Simon's irony never *forces* our reading beyond an affectionate amusement for Kate; however, a quality of indeterminacy in it does *allow* the feminist reader to intimate that to hear little and see less is *not* enabling. This reader will recognize that to tease, to accept or to mock the crawling hands—or, for that matter, the red roses—is not boundless choice, but merely making the best of a cultural construction of femininity that demands that women await overtures, whether they come from the boy next door, Valentino, or Humbert Humbert. And no feminist reader will fail to recall that Lolita spends more time crying or nearly catatonic with despair than she does reading comics, chewing gum, or painting her toenails. Nor are we apt to forget our last sight of this nymphet as a bedraggled, debt-ridden, pregnant seventeen-year-old.

Still, however ironic a feminist reading we give this passage, two facts resist that reading. We cannot ignore the *lightness* of Simon's irony, which is to say we cannot be certain how far her irony transforms the feminine fantasy of the young Kate into the feminist recognitions I have sketched here, an uncertainty that proves particularly unsettling given that the evocation of Lolita as Kate's twin is grounded on the narrator's identification with the point of view of Humbert Humbert, her molester. Nor can we escape the fact that, by convention, the conclusions of bildungsromans and preludes intimate that the protagonist has achieved a sense of self and vocation. Simon leaves her Kate initiated into femininity, imagining herself and pleasuring herself through identification with her body as it is inscribed and conscripted by the ideology of femininity, an identification that is both self-creation and discovery of her vocation.

"An appearance walking in a forest the sexes burn"

The structure of Simon's autobiography leaves her readers free, if they wish, to imagine that Kate goes on to exercise the power through and over men granted, within very precise constraints, to some women within an ideology of femininity; it leaves us free, too, to imagine that this concluding scene marks the end of young Kate's resistance to that ideology. In women's autobiography, as in their lives, the process of the inscription of the body as feminine, the resistance and unease femininity generates, is sometimes particularly evident when an autobiographer's body has been judged, by herself or others, as ugly, or when there is residual conflict about the assumptions of heterosexuality on which the ideology of femininity is founded.[9] The remainder of my discussion here focuses on one such "ugly" body in autobiography, that is, on its cultural inscription as ugly; on the autobiographer's attempts to produce it as feminine and, finally, as heterosexual; and on the ways in which this textualization of the exteriority of her body produces her interiority as subject. The body is Violette Leduc's.[10]

In a history of representations of ideologically produced bodies, Leduc's autobiographies would stand at an instructive juncture. They are the product, at least in part, of modernists' concerns with masculinity, femininity, and sexuality, concerns stimulated by the women's movement of the late nineteenth and early twentieth centuries and by psychoanalysis. As Isabelle de Courtivron has pointed out, Leduc also stands between a "generation of French women writers who . . . had succeeded in conforming to established notions of 'masculine' and 'feminine' literary styles—while disguising their own voices in ways that are only now being uncovered" and "post-1968 feminist writers" (57). Most of her writing was done as a protégé of Simone de Beauvoir, her staunchest supporter and most loved and admired friend, for whose sake Leduc claimed to have gone on writing (*Mad* 45). De Beauvoir's trenchant analysis of how "one is not born, but rather becomes, a woman" (301) had been published in 1949, a time at which Leduc had published her first two novels but had not yet moved from autobiographical fiction to autobiography. The most intense and deliberative phase of Leduc's own becoming a woman, as it is recorded in the autobiography, was enacted in the late 1920s and early 1930s, at the time when such arbiters of the beautiful as *Vogue* were shifting from portraits of society beauties to "how-to" articles and an image of "ready-to-wear beauty" (Lakoff and Scherr 82). This new direction formulated beauty as the means to wealth and status rather than as the effect of wealth (80). The fashion magazines' mixture of "lives of the beautiful and famous" with self-help-to-beauty articles promised "the reader the *possibility* of beauty" (81). That promised possibility, however, lays the ground for self-loathing: *not* to be beautiful is to fail to take advantage of possibilities, and is, therefore, a woman's own fault. In short, for a woman writing at Violette Leduc's historical juncture, the representation of her body is, more than usually, ambiguous and shifting ground.

Leduc's self-representation dwells on her ugliness: she is thin, bony, flat-chested; her nose is too long, her mouth too wide, her eyes too small, and her hair too fine. She sees hers as a "thankless face" (*La Bâtarde* 41), a judgment frequently offered and corroborated by those around her.[11] In the three volumes of Leduc's autobiography, the inscription of Violette's body as feminine, because female, but as not-feminine, because punishingly ugly, produces her self-loathing and her self-fragmentaton. Virulent self-mutilating reactions to rejection—"If I were to mince my sex, if I were to serve it stuffed in an eggplant" (*Chasse* 61)—are commonplace in this autobiography. Her efforts to produce her body consistently with cultural norms of femininity both obsess and disable her.

Birth, for Violette Leduc, marks the beginning of the sociolegal textualization of her body at the intersection of gender, class, and legitimacy. The title of the first volume of her autobiography announces this: she is *La Bâtarde*, "the unrecognized daughter of a son of good family" and the maid whom he seduced and then persuaded to leave without making her condition known. Throughout the three volumes that follow, variations on this sociolegal definition of Violette and ugliness are linked and mutually reinforcing, decisively so in the associative chronology that provides the context for Violette's mother Berthe's marriage. That chronology brings into implicit relationship three events: Violette's understanding that her stepfather wishes "in a vague way" that she did not exist as the visible sign of "the weight of a great love" (*La Bâtarde* 56); her first menstruation (*La Bâtarde* 57); and the knowledge that she "was ugly, that [her classmates] found it amusing" (*La Bâtarde* 58). Over and over again in this autobiography, what bastardy and the failure to meet the standards of feminine beauty have in common is a failure to be legitimate and a concomitant déclassement. That femininity might, to all social intents and purposes, wipe out the illegitimacy of Violette's birth is the hope with which her mother and grandmother present her body as a sign of the social class of the father whose name unfortunately does not stand behind this façade:

> I am the unrecognized daughter of a son of good family. Therefore I must wear a medallion on a fine gold chain, embroidered dresses and long pantalettes, I must have a fair skin and silky hair in order to compete with the rich children in the town when my grand-

mother takes me out into the park . . . in public: the façade. . . . My
mother and my grandmother . . . are attempting to ward off ill luck
with talismans when they tie ribbons on their little girl. The park is
the arena, I am their little torero, I must vanquish every well-fed
infant in the town. (*La Bâtarde* 27)

Standing in for the legitimacy of the father's name, the insignia of femininity in this passage serve to make the absent father present. They also
construct Violette's body as a site of class and gender ambivalence. Femi-
nized, she is also a "torero" sent forth to "vanquish" the class from which
the presence of her father's absence excludes her.

The extent of the psychic ravage inflicted in the inscription of Violette's body as feminine and her internalization of that inscription is
indexed by the distance gone between her first and last erotic relationships. The first occurs when she is a schoolgirl of seventeen; the last
when she is a woman of fifty-one. The first affair is with her schoolmate
Isabelle and its description is characterized by an explicit lyricism. Secreted in Isabelle's cubicle, they are surrounded by the socializing agency
of the school, but unseen by it. Indeed, their desire cannot be seen within
a sex-gender system indifferent to sexualities functioning outside the
male-female opposition that grounds heterosexuality.[12] In their lovemaking it is as if their bodies had been—utopianly—uninscribed by gender. Violette's actions as she first prepares to cross the corridor to Isabelle's bed specifically attempt to repudiate inscriptions of femininity on
her body. While thinking that "one's personality could be changed by
wearing expensive clothes," she chooses to remove her silk nightgown
bought in "a lingerie boutique" and with it the culture's injunctions to
feminine self-improvement; she chooses, when crossing the aisle to Isabelle's cubicle, to wear the "regulation nightgown" of the school, which
Isabelle also wears (82). Outside the representations of gender, these two
are briefly free to invent their sexuality on reciprocal and new terms.

The distance the body inscribed by femininity must go from the
lyricism, the reciprocity, and the pleasure that Leduc re-creates in her
description of Violette making love with Isabelle is measured by its
contrast with the autobiography's concluding representation of eroticism, Violette's affair with René in *La Chasse à l'amour*. Here a woman
waits. She obsessively keeps her hair and her makeup in order. When he
comes, she cooks, wearing a "little apron" like her mother the maid did
before her; although now she is the intellectual, he the workingman,
still, "you, my mother, and your little white apron, you suffocate me" (*La*

Bâtarde 24). She is careful to maintain a certain psychological space for him between her writing table and her bed all the while he folds his clothes on the chair she sits at to write. She interprets his behavior in terms of what "a man" does. She caresses him with what she describes as an Oriental subtlety, identifying herself with the feminine as exotic Other. She feels "warmed and beautiful" (*La Chasse* 180). She is more than fifty; she comes. The "ice" of the "more than thirty years" since she first associated her stepfather's discomfort about her illegitimacy with her ugliness melts (*La Bâtarde* 56). When René stays away, she trembles behind her door, counting the minutes, hours, days, weeks; she seeks him without shame only to be turned out into the rain; she cannot write; she clutches the "altar" of the chair on which he laid his clothes and stains the parquet beneath it with her tears (*La Chasse* 291). She is ugly, she is old. When he returns, she allows him to come upon her "in flagrant délit of desolation" (287); she accuses; she demands explanations; she weeps; she clutches his feet: she makes a spectacle of her age, her ugliness, her grief, its excess. Her body—its sobs, its gestures, its very fluids—is on display, part of a performance demanding the catharsis of pity, love. She speaks of loyalty, friendship; she accedes when he asks, "What is this, your stories of friendship, of comraderie? A man goes with a woman, it's simple. Now let's go to bed" (270). She revenges herself for his failure to take her out in public—is he ashamed of her figure? her face? her age?—by staging herself as sexual prey over whom he and his brother "fight to the death" (288); he tells her not to worry about it. He has already told her that she "no longer has a human face" (287). She is a woman in love. She is "resigned" to losing him: she can keep him for "some hours" only so long as she gives him her "velvet fingers, her satin womb. It's rush hour, woman" (288). She becomes a spectacle to herself: "Two acrobats rolled on the bed" (290). He does not return.

From the adolescent's jouissance to the middle-aged woman's experience of her sexuality as a loss foretold in an enactment of feminine abjection, Violette traverses this distance in a series of invitations and of losses, each of which stages her body as spectacle. *La Bâtarde* is clear that a body socially constructed as the object of another's gaze is a body without freedom. When Isabelle visits Violette in her home, Violette exults in their "freedom" from the fear of detection by school monitors, but Isabelle knows that this is precisely the moment at which they "aren't free" (104), that in the bourgeois home and their planned excursions into the public world of fairs they are already constructed as gendered, embodied subjects. Violette's mother, Berthe, furthers that gendered social inscription. In a ploy that claims Violette for femininity, Berthe insists that Violette model a new dress, "encouraging [her] coquetry" so that she is "aflame" for the dress, for their "evening out" and "drawn closer and closer" to her mother and farther and farther from Isabelle (107). That the rivalry between Berthe and Isabelle is a struggle over the inscription of femininity on the daughter/lover's body becomes explicit in the merry-go-round scene that ends the affair. Isabelle registers her recognition that she has lost Violette to her mother's injunctions in the name of femininity by forcing her to take up the feminine position of specular object: "she helped me into my seat on the outside horse—the outside one so that I could see, so that I could be seen." Where Isabelle avoids, rejects the streamers both men and women are throwing at her, Violette becomes "entangled, enmeshed" in those thrown by one young man and directs back at him the streamers Isabelle commands her to throw (108). Violette has made one more decisive turn on the merry-go-round of the ideology of femininity/heterosexuality and the ways in which it inscribes her body and more often than not is interiorized as self-loathing.

The rivalry between Berthe and Isabelle over whether their daughter/lover's body will be inscribed as feminine tempts one to posit an unresolved Oedipal conflict as productive of Violette's ambivalence about femininity and heterosexuality.[13] In the autobiography, Violette undergoes psychoanalytic treatment and she herself provides fragments of a conventional psychoanalytic narrative of pre-Oedipal childhood, asserting that she wants to be her father rather than have her father. "I want to heal your wound, mother. Impossible. It will never close. He is your wound, and I am the picture of him" (*La Bâtarde* 24). The wound here is richly suggestive of exploitation of servant by master, of sexual violation, and of the tearing of tissue in birth, as well as of grief, none of which precludes its also standing as an image of the mother's "castration."

Three circumstances, however, prevent what the psychoanalytic narrative terms a "normal" shift in the erotic object from mother to father. First, Violette lives in a world bounded by her mother and grandmother, sharing her mother's bed until she is thirteen. There is no father figure whom Violette can take as erotic object, and the pre-Oedipal phase of erotic pleasure derived from contact with the mother's body is prolonged into pubescence. Second, Violette sees her mother as taking on, through the process of mourning and remembrance as well as through the dynamics of the single-parent household, the attributes of Violette's father. "My mother is my father," she several times insists (*La Bâtarde* 51).

Third, Violette is ambivalent about her expulsion from her mother's bed upon Berthe's marriage. On the one hand, she feels it as a failure of femininity: "I thought . . . that I had ceased to be her daughter because I wasn't attractive" (54). On the other hand, she reenacts the process of mourning outlined by Freud, by which the individual preserves the love of someone she has lost by identifying with the lost other so completely that her attributes become part of the ego structure.[14] At the onset of menstruation, and displaced by Berthe's new husband, she appropriates her mother's "wound" and birthing; she creates herself by embodying her mother's visible and particularly feminine "shame": "My wound reopened. My wound: where you were torn out of me" (57).

The dynamic of sex-gender identification here is quite opposite, how-ever, to that described by Freudian and neo-Freudian theories of psycho-sexual development. Jacques Lacan, for example, posits that a woman "finds the signifier of her own desire in the body of the one to whom she addresses her demand for love" (84). Since Lacan has already hypothe-sized the phallus as the "privileged signifier" of all desire (82), he is necessarily suggesting that a woman will find the signifier of her desire in the phallus and will therefore address her "demand for love" to one who "has" the phallus. The entire explanation assumes heterosexuality and, when Lacan goes on to hypothesize lesbianism as follow[ing] "from a disappointment which reinforces . . . the demand for love" (85), he again assumes heterosexuality as the prior and disappointing relationship. That is, he posits lesbianism as following from heterosexual disappoint-ment.[15] This is precisely what Leduc does *not* outline as the process of her own gendered and sexualized subject formation. Violette is disap-pointed first in her mother, then in Isabelle. That disappointment issues in her first tentative and ambivalent heterosexual relationship. It also is-sues in a renunciation of the (impossible) attempt to create and embody the self otherwise than within the representations of femininity, a renun-ciation that is played out in the text of Violette's body itself "between the interlocking teeth of [the] double self-abnegation" (*La Bâtarde* 159) of her last lesbian lover, Hermine, and her first heterosexual lover, Gabriel.

For Gabriel, she *performs* masculinity, dressing like a man, playing "little fellow." "I was his man, he was my woman" (188).[16] But because gender is "always already" inscribed on sexed bodies, Violette's perfor-mance of masculinity signifies differently from the masculinely inscribed male body's. Nor can it play out on heterosexual terrain the sexual poli-tics of butch-femme roles, even if Gabriel does cooperate by wanting to wear a lily in his fly when they go out together (*La Bâtarde* 155). In this relationship Violette is not the butch who, as Sue-Ellen Case puts it, "proudly displays the possession of the penis" even though "there is no referent in sight." She neither passes as a man nor, like a butch, plays "on the phallic economy rather than to it" ("Towards a Butch-Femme Aesthetic" 64). Rather, Leduc writes:

> I wanted to be the hard focus of attention for the customers in a café . . . , because I was ashamed of my face and because I wanted to force it upon them at the same time. I admit it: I wanted to be attractive to Gabriel. The necktie I wore: my sex for Gabriel; the carnation in my buttonhole . . . : my sex for Gabriel. . . . It was with a kind of fever that I bought : . . . a pair of man's shorts, for a day's boating. . . . Ten years later he told me: "Your shorts were too big. I was rowing. I could see." (167)

Far from suppressing femininity, Violette's masculine masquerade only makes the corporeal inscription of femininity more visible for it is motivated by her failure to meet the standards of the "beauty system," which is such a significant ideology of control in femininity.[17] Moreover it functions by an opposition in which, seeming to be a man, she displays herself the more obviously as not-male to a male gaze. Violette's specular position in relation to Gabriel, like her socioeconomic one, is part of the process and the result of her inscription as a feminine subject. She needs Gabriel to construct her as feminine by being "there to look at me, to plead with his eyes. . . . No questions. Just the gaze" (159). So constructed, she is enrolled as "a member of that great band of women who were bought things by men" (126).[18]

With Hermine, Violette agrees that she "will be her baby, yes" (155). From the beginning of the relationship, Hermine requires from Violette the kind of femininity through which her mother had earlier reclaimed her from Isabelle. Visiting Hermine, Violette feels that "I *had* to get into bed, I had to powder my face, I had to wear a luxurious nightgown" (155; my emphasis). In Hermine's embrace and under her sponsorship, the "beauty system" takes over Violette's self-conception: "I wanted the impossible: the eyes, the complexion, the hair, the nose, above all the nose, as well as the self-assurance, the arrogance of the mannequins" of *Vogue* magazine (166). Here there is nothing of the "ironized and 'camped up'" performance of butch-femme roles (Case 64). Hermine does not play butch and Violette's inscription by femininity operates at a level of the real in which personal, social, sexual, and economic independence are all finally forfeit.

The cultural script of femininity for which Hermine acts as producer is staged with particular virulence in two sequences—in each of which Violette becomes the object of a masculine gaze, in each of which she is the consumer who is consumed. In the first sequence, she enters a department store, hearing in her head the voices of her mother and Hermine enjoining her to "be a woman," to wear "a hat, with longer hair, a cloche hat" (178). In a violent rejection of femininity that is also a capitulation to it, she steals knickers, powderpuffs, compacts, trinkets. She steals out of anger at femininity and out of anger at her unfeminine ugliness, steals not only to "be a woman" but "in order to rob the other women of the things that made them feminine. Rape performed in a private darkness, for the others couldn't see me" (179). Women, however, are by definition seen; caught by the store detective and thoroughly frightened she succumbs to Hermine's desire to buy her "heaps of things"—powderpuffs, underwear in every color in satin, silk, and voile. "She wants a woman, she shall have a woman and I shall have no reason to steal, I said to myself" (182). That this decision enrolls Violette in a whole new sociosexual economy becomes apparent shortly after, when Violette first allows a man to pick her up. Femininity entails specularity, a fact Leduc here registers by again shifting into the third person; specularity entails a conscription into a social-political position that is a kind of prostitution, a fact she registers in Violette's disappointment: "She left him empty-handed. All she had wanted from him was a bundle of franc notes" (183).

In the second sequence, Violette is completely complicit in the production of her feminine body. Wanting "to be rejuvenated at the age of twenty-four" (*La Bâtarde* 190), she exercises to prevent a double chin and begins frequenting designer sales. Her skin is no longer hers since she has taken "the veil of coquetry," but is instead engraved with the insignia of that coquetry: "Speak, mirror, say you're tired of copying me, say it's not . . . really a pretty sight to see a thigh in the grip of a suspender, squeezed by a stocking top. . . . If I could only sew my stockings with a running stitch into my flesh" (201). What takes over is what Elizabeth Dempster calls the "economy of shame," by which even those who strive hardest for beauty must always fail before the idealized feminine body of cultural production. Violette's private mirror is "nice. . . . It takes, it gives back, love, always love" (204). In women's self-creation through the mirror, however, the mirror doubles as self and audience (La Belle 62). Thus, for Violette, the fashion designer Schiaparelli's public mirror, reflecting the judgment of the saleswoman, is "a vampire. I look terrible. . . . I feel the pain of it in the entrails of my great mouth, my big nose, my little eyes. Pleasing others, pleasing oneself. Twofold bondage" (203). Caught in the double bind of self-love and self-loathing she has her hair dressed, at far too great a cost, like Joan Crawford's and imagines herself "delivered" from ugliness, "reborn free" (215). "Here I am," she tells us, "being born in Paris" at the precise moment that a passing woman, one "all hips, with a face neither beautiful nor homely," turns and shouts words like "blows striking all over my body" (217–18). The words: "If I had a face like that I'd kill myself" (222).

In this economy of shame in which a Violette has become a trolloping "Lolette" and still can't please (204), it is not primarily significant that Violette's erotic attachment is to another woman or that she is judged a failure by other women. They mediate and help enforce the inscription of femininity, but Violette's feminine body is not constituted in relation to them. The economy of shame is one in which the feminine body is constituted as presented to a male gaze. Violette's existence as feminine depends on the gaze of men and on their economic power. She knows herself as "feminine" when she walks, her limbs oiled by exercise, her hairdo, her hat, her high heels, her designer dress, her makeup, on the streets and is accosted by men. In the culmination of this sequence, Violette simultaneously apotheosizes herself as feminine body and prostitutes herself while a man watches her and her many reflections. She makes love to Hermine, for money with which she plans to buy a table, in a roomful of mirrors, before a man who has picked her up when she has been promenading her feminine goods. This set scene from pornography makes several points. In it Violette punishes Hermine by inscribing her body within the circle of that male gaze with which Hermine has helped so thoroughly to construct Violette's body. As revenge, it effectively signals Violette's "disappointment" in the lesbian love of Hermine, which has conscripted her for femininity; from now on, she takes men as erotic objects. The distance between the two women and the man, whose reflection Violette sees as he watches them, but who never touches them, re-presents the feminine body as not-male and as specular construction. It enacts what Isabelle knew years before, that two women, their bodies brought within the purview of a man's gaze or the social order structured by that gaze "aren't free." The sum paid, which enables Violette as a consumer, designates her as consumed.

It also completes Violette's interiorization of the ideology of femininity/heterosexuality inscribed externally on her body. From now on, she will, however despairingly, however hopelessly, take as erotic objects men, however inappropriate they prove to be for her own needs. From now on, she must be seen to know she is loved. And if a male gaze should fail her, as it emphatically does in the case of the homosexual Jacques, whom she adores but who neither encourages nor gratifies her, she will imagine it into being in a paranoid fantasy of his setting spies on her every movement, leaving signs in every discarded cigarette pack in her path, taking time himself to peep at her most intimate life through holes in her ceiling. From now on, she *will* be seen.

And yet: the lovers are unsuitably chosen, and Violette loves them in self-damaging ways. Her femininity serves her poorly and seems, at best, an ill-fitting costume. Wishing to please others, she seems not unlike the woman in Joan Riviere's 1929 case study who "assumed" femininity and wore it "as a mask, both to hide the possession of masculinity and to divert the reprisals expected if she was found to possess it" (38). That it is in fact two women who enjoin Violette to adopt the mask of womanliness does not change this: rather it returns us to the fact that gender relations in western cultures are constructed in terms of heterosexual relations and that, in heterosexuality, femininity is understood by contrast and analogy with masculinity. Short of reinventing heterosexuality, or of finding means of representing other sexualities, the injunction to "be a woman," no matter who utters it, is an injunction to please men.

But if we step back from Violette's deflected lesbianism and recall the technologies by which she inscribes femininity on her body and internalizes it in her psyche, we realize, as did Joan Riviere, that there is no difference between femininity as a more or less conscious masquerade and what Riviere terms "genuine womanliness," by which I take it she means femininity that represents a woman's "main development" rather than a compensatory strategy (38). As Stephen Heath so succinctly puts it in his rereading of Riviere, femininity is itself a "representation, the representation of the woman" in "subjection to men" (53–54). Because femininity is a representation, we are not, as later commentators from Lacan to Mary Ann Doane ("Masquerade Reconsidered" 47–48) have made clear, dealing with "real" femininity but with a representation that has real effects. In a social and political order in which women *are* subject to men—and we must remember the period in which Violette Leduc wrote, as well as her class, education, and femaleness—the only identity available to women, as Heath argues, is this masquerade (55). For Violette, alienation—I quote Heath—"becomes a *structural* condition of being a woman. . . . Alienation is playing the game which is the act of womanliness and the act is her identity. . . . She *sticks* to it" (54; his emphasis). Hence the specularity that characterizes so much of Violette's self-representation as she watches herself being watched (and judged) in the performance of femininity.[19] Caught up in the mirror game, Violette is a woman and is not a woman. She cannot carry off the masquerade, but she cannot give it up. For when the masquerade is so inscribed, sewn into the flesh as it were, no matter how obvious or crooked the seams, it cannot be unstitched.

Except, perhaps, by autobiography?

I began by setting the mind/body distinction, which has dominated thinking about the self in western cultures, against the concept of a "textualised body," which cannot exist prior to culture and culture's representations of it and which, therefore, cannot be distinct from the mind in self-representation. I made reference to Elizabeth Grosz's suggestion that this culturally inscribed body is the site not only of the inscription of social power, which the subject internalizes as experience, but also of possible resistance to that power and of counterideological inscriptions. And I went on to read moments when two autobiographers' bodies, conscripted into femininity, became recognizable as representations in a genre that, at least as it has been used by women, has traditionally not seen the feminine body. In *Bronx Primitive*, Simon does represent the feminine body, but she also seems to subscribe to a notion of the "natural" child's body as preceding its cultural inscription as feminine. The encoding of Kate's body as feminine marks a definitive stage in her maturity, her discovery of a vocation, and her entry into culture rather than a process always already begun and continuing. If, as feminist subjects, we choose to read from both within and without the discursive space of the femininity within which young Kate comes to understand her world, the structure of Simon's narrative, and perhaps even a certain complacency in her irony, do not allow us the certainty that she too is representing herself as both within and without the constructions of femininity.[20]

Because Leduc's autobiography represents Violette's body as textualized from birth in terms of multiple ideologies, and because that textualization produces the gaps, as it were, between the corporeal inscription and its reception by those for whose gaze it is embodied, we can push our questions further where her autobiography is concerned. Does Leduc, by writing autobiography, take Violette's body, written by cultural signification and medium for its internalization, and make it *produce* different cultural significations? Put another way, does this textualized body assume agency in the act of Leduc's writing autobiography? What does the act of writing over this already written body perform? The answer, I think, is as shifting and multiple and uncertain as Violette's feminine subjectivity itself.

Leduc does, of course, assume agency by daring to write about the body in a way that denies the mind/body distinction common in public and autobiographical discourse. More importantly, she does so by using the specularity that underlies the social construction of heterosexuality and femininity in order to rethink and make homologous the display of the self that informs autobiography and the display of the body that informs femininity. Like femininity, Leduc's autobiography begins and is sustained as an act of pleasing others: Violette begins writing fiction at the exasperated order of Maurice Sachs and continues with fiction and then autobiography under Simone de Beauvoir's never-failing question, Are you writing? (and with the assurance that de Beauvoir will read Violette's pages). In this her autobiography is a *dédoublement* with a difference of the process of the construction of Violette's body as feminine in the text. The feminine body and the text perform, Leduc hopes, to the same end—in the "present" of her writing, "May 15, 1961," she tells us, "I haven't changed; I still haven't overcome my desire to juggle with words so that people will notice me" (*La Bâtarde* 317). At the level of the representation of femininity in the text, noticing her, we readers become complicit in the specularization that constructs her feminine, textualized body in the text. Noticing or not noticing her, we become complicit in the economy of shame by which the feminine, textualized body in the text fails before the social construction of an ideal body.

Leduc, however, takes advantage of the gaps between the subject position of the autobiographer writing in the present and the subject position of Violette in the past, about whom she writes. She is careful to foreground the contemporary Leduc, engaged in the act of writing her autobiography, several times in the course of the three volumes. This Leduc is conspicuously present in the opening passages of *La Bâtarde* and in the closing of *La Chasse à l'amour*, both of which represent her as alone, sitting out of doors on an "uncorruptible" schedule each day, with "iron discipline" writing the books we are reading (*La Chasse* 401). The economic independence that has made it possible by the end of the third volume to spend solitary summers in the rural village of Faucon is the direct result of the writing of the first volume. That is, Leduc the-subject-writing-an-autobiography is not self-identical with Violette-the-subject-of-her-autobiography. Leduc displays the inscription of

Violette's body by femininity and, in the ambivalences, griefs, conflicts, and masquerade with which Violette surrounds that inscription, displays the points of resistance to it. Violette is *within* femininity, but even there, in the anger with which vulgarity so often disrupts sentimentality and abjection in the narrative (recall that aside, "It's rush hour, woman") and in the narrative display of the production of Violette's body as feminine, Leduc performs much more than the masquerade of her femininity. Standing within gender ideology, she also stands outside it, making visible the repressions, displacements, submissions, self-loathings, self-abnegations, and abjections that are among its effects and that it represses. Writing autobiography, Leduc undertakes to understand femininity with a double vision that lets her represent her entanglement and the net that entangles her. Both aspects of that doubled self-representation beckon the reader to gaze at the repressions that sustain the nonrepresentation of bodies in autobiography and to recognize the ways in which many autobiographers may be "an appearance walking in a forest the sexes burn."

Notes

1 Carolyn Heilbrun has also addressed "the degree to which women [have] internalized the 'facts' dictated to them by male psychology" and the extent to which this has prevented their writing "successful" autobiography (19). She also considers the forms of women's autobiography, emergent in the last few years, that have allowed women to articulate their sense of their selves.

2 See Spelman for a feminist analysis of the implications of Greek thought for the construction of femininity. Grosz discusses its implications for our understanding of bodies ("Notes" 4–6).

3 On women's self-creation through identification with technologies of the body and with their mirror-images, see, respectively, Valie Export and Jenijoy La Belle.

4 More recently, Judith Butler has argued from the same premises. "To what extent does the body *come into being* in and through the mark(s) of gender?" she asks (8; her emphasis); "to what extent do *regulatory practices* of gender formation and division constitute identity, the internal coherence of the subject, indeed, the self-identical status of the person?" (16; her emphasis). Butler describes gender as "performative—that is, constituting the identity it is purported to be. . . . We might state as a corollary: There is no gender identity behind the expressions of gender; that identity is performatively constituted by the very 'expressions' that are said to be its results" (25).

5 Wendy Hollway, "Gender Difference and the Production of Subjectivity," in Henriques et al., discusses gender relations as founded on heterosexual relations. For

discussion of her argument, see Teresa de Lauretis, "The Technology of Gender" (15–17).

6 Butler comes to the same conclusion: "This very concept of sex-as-matter, sex-as-instrument-of-cultural-signification, however, is a discursive formation that acts as a naturalized foundation for the nature/culture distinction and the strategies of domination that that distinction supports" (37).

7 Corporeal feminism: "an understanding of corporeality that is compatible with feminist struggles to undermine patriarchal structures and to form self-defined terms and representations" (Grosz, "Notes" 3).

8 See De Lauretis's reference in "The Technology of Gender" to "a subject engendered in the experiencing of race and class, as well as sexual, relations; a subject, therefore, not unified but rather multiple, and not so much divided as contradicted" (2). On the subject of the self in autobiography as created at multiple, different, and specific intersections of gender, race, class, age, nationality, etc., see Neuman, "Autobiography: From Different Poetics to a Poetics of Difference."

9 For a reading of the ways in which the accounts of female psychosexual development proffered by Freud, Riviere, and Lacan are founded on an assumption of heterosexuality that serves to mask a primary homosexuality, see Butler 43–65.

10 "An appearance walking in a forest the sexes burn" is Violette's description of herself at the moment when she enters the department store and begins stealing feminine "fripperies" (*La Bâtarde* 178).

11 One of many examples the autobiography offers occurs shortly after Violette has her nose shortened. She goes to a bar with a friend where they see Jacques Prévert, whose comment to a friend, as he looks at Violette, they overhear: "It's her mouth, her eyes, her cheekbones they should have fixed" (*La Bâtarde* 460).

12 On the question of western culture's "indifference" to lesbian sexualities, which "are not recognizable as representation" by these cultures (De Lauretis, "The Technology of Gender" 25), that is, which cannot be seen within the processes by which these cultures produce gender, see De Lauretis, "Sexual Indifference and Lesbian Representation" and "The Female Body and Heterosexual Presumption." That Violette's next affair with Hermine *is* seen does not change the fact that lesbian sexualities are among those that cannot be seen. *What* is seen is the transgression of heterosexual codes, not the representation of sexuality that Hermine and Violette invent. Furthermore, Hermine is fired and Violette expelled from the school; that is, the school, as a social organization whose functions include the inscription of gendering, acts so as to make even the transgressive aspect of lesbian sexuality once again invisible to itself.

13 Leduc's first novel, *L'Affamée*, about her relationship with her mother, has in fact received an extended psychoanalytic reading by Pièr Girard.

14 Freud elaborates the concepts of mourning and melancholia in relation to the development of the ego in "Mourning and Melancholia" (1917) and in "The Ego and the Super-Ego (Ego-Ideal)" (1923). For an excellent summary, to which I am indebted, see Butler (57–65).

15   For a more extended discussion of Lacan's arguments about female hetero- and homosexuality, see Butler 43–50. I am particularly indebted to her trenchant question, "could it not be equally clear . . . that heterosexuality issues from a disappointed homosexuality?" (49).

16   All her heterosexual attractions are marked by such gender ambivalence. In these loves, however, Violette no longer displays masculinity; rather she projects femininity onto the lover, whether the homosexual Jacques Guérin or the unambiguously heterosexual René, whom she feminizes, in order to "reassure" herself, by dwelling on his lowered eyes, long lashes, contralto voice, and "weakness" compared to her "strength" (*La Chasse* 160–61).

17   I take the term "beauty system" from Dean MacCannell and Juliet Flower MacCannell's essay "The Beauty System" in which they analyze beauty as a system of culture determining the relationship between the sexes.

18   The need to be bought things figures as an aspect of Violette's femininity throughout most of her adult life. It is central in the relation with Hermine. From the wealthy Jacques, Violette extracts purchases as testimony to the love he denies her.

19   Butler (47–57) discusses the psychoanalytic interpretations of femininity as performance offered by Riviere, Lacan, and Heath. The criticism of western philosophical traditions that construct femininity as a specular image of masculinity has been most fully elaborated by Luce Irigaray in *Speculum of the Other Woman*. In film theory, a consideration of femininity has been a major link between the instability of the subject positions of women and the problems that arise around women as spectators; see, particularly, the work of Mary Ann Doane. Two critics read femininity as capable of producing ideology: Mary Russo, who sees it as a strategy of Bakhtinian "dialogical laughter" (226) and Sue-Ellen Case, who interprets it in the context of butch-femme relationships as a send-up of heterosexuality. These last two readings, while enabling, are difficult to sustain before the obsessive self-loathing of Leduc's representation.

20   Teresa de Lauretis defines "the subject of feminism" as characterized by "a movement back and forth between the representation of gender (in its male-centered frame of reference) and what that representation leaves out or, more pointedly, makes unrepresentable" ("The Technology of Gender" 26).

References

Butler, Judith. *Gender Trouble: Feminism and the Subversion of Identity*. New York: Routledge, 1990.

Case, Sue Ellen. "Towards a Butch-Femme Aesthetic." *Body//Masquerade*. Special issue of *Discourse* 11.1 (1988–89): 55–73.

Courtivron, Isabelle de. *Violette Leduc*. Boston: Twayne, 1985.

De Beauvoir, Simone. *The Second Sex.* 1949. Trans. and ed. H. M. Parshley. New York: Vintage, 1952.

De Lauretis, Teresa. "The Female Body and Heterosexual Presumption." *Semiotica* 67.3/4 (1987): 259–79.

——. "Sexual Indifference and Lesbian Representation." *Theatre Journal* 40.2 (1988): 155–77.

——. "The Technology of Gender." *Technologies of Gender: Essays on Theory, Film, and Fiction.* Bloomington: Indiana UP, 1987. 1–30.

Dempster, Elizabeth. "Women Writing the Body: Let's Watch a Little How She Dances." *Grafts: Feminist Cultural Criticism.* Ed. Susan Sheridan. London: Verso, 1988. 35–54.

Descartes, René. *Discourse on Method and Meditations.* Trans. Laurence J. Lafleur. Indianapolis: Bobbs-Merrill, 1960.

Doane, Mary Ann. *The Desire to Desire: The Woman's Film of the 1940s.* Bloomington: Indiana UP, 1987.

——. "Film and Masquerade: Theorizing the Female Spectator." *Screen* 23.3/4 (1982): 74–87.

——. "Masquerade Reconsidered: Further Thoughts on the Female Spectator." *Body//Masquerade.* Special issue of *Discourse* 11.1 (1988–89): 42–54.

——. "Woman's Stake: Filming the Female Body." *Feminism and Film Theory.* Ed. Constance Penley. New York: Routledge, 1988. 216–28.

Export, Valie. "The Real and Its Double: The Body." *Body//Masquerade.* Special issue of *Discourse* 11.1 (1988–89): 3–27.

Foucault, Michel. *The History of Sexuality.* 3 vols. Trans. Robert Hurley. New York: Vintage, 1980–88.

Freud, Sigmund. "The Ego and the Super-Ego (Ego-Ideal)." *The Ego and the Id.* Ed. James Strachey. Trans. Joan Riviere. New York: Norton, 1960.

——. "Mourning and Melancholia." *General Psychological Theory.* Ed. Philip Rieff. New York: Macmillan, 1976.

Girard, Pièr. *Oedipe masqué: Une lecture psychanalytique de* L'Affamée *de Violette Leduc.* Paris: Éditions des femmes, 1986.

Grosz, Elizabeth. "Inscriptions and Body Maps: Representations and the Corporeal." *Feminine, Masculine and Representation.* Ed. Terry Threadgold and Anne Cranny-Francis. Sydney: Allen and Unwin, 1990. 62–74.

——. "Notes Towards a Corporeal Feminism." *Feminism and the Body.* Ed. Judith Allen and Elizabeth Grosz. Special issue of *Australian Feminist Studies* 5 (1987): 1–16.

Heath, Stephen. "Joan Riviere and the Masquerade." *Formations of Fantasy.* Ed. Victor Burgin, James Donald, and Cora Kaplan. London: Methuen, 1986. 45–61.

Heilbrun, Carolyn G. "Woman's Autobiographical Writings: New Forms." *Modern Selves: Essays on Modern British and American Autobiography.* Ed. Philip Dodd. London: Frank Cass, 1986.

Henriques, Julian, Wendy Hollway, Cathy Urwin, Couze Venn, and Valerie Walkerdine, eds. *Changing the Subject: Psychology, Social Regulation and Subjectivity.* London: Methuen, 1984.

Irigaray, Luce. *Speculum of the Other Woman.* Trans. Gillian C. Gill. Ithaca: Cornell UP, 1985.

La Belle, Jenijoy. *Herself Beheld: The Literature of the Looking Glass.* Ithaca: Cornell UP, 1988.

Lacan, Jacques. "The Meaning of the Phallus." *Feminine Sexuality: Jacques Lacan and the "école freudienne."* Ed. Juliet Mitchell and Jacqueline Rose. Trans. Jacqueline Rose. New York: Norton, 1982. 74–85.

Lakoff, Robin Tolmach, and Raquel L. Scherr. *Face Value: The Politics of Beauty.* Boston: Routledge, 1984.

Leduc, Violette. *La Bâtarde: An Autobiography.* 1964. Trans. Derek Coltman. London: Virago, 1985.

——. *La Chasse à l'amour.* Paris: Éditions Gallimard, 1973. Quotations in English are my translations.

——. *Mad in Pursuit.* 1970. Trans. Derek Coltman. London: Hart-Davis, 1971.

MacCannell, Dean, and Juliet Flower MacCannell. "The Beauty System." *The Ideology of Conduct: Essays on Literature and the History of Sexuality.* Ed. Nancy Armstrong and Leonard Tennenhouse. New York: Methuen, 1987. 206–38.

Riviere, Joan. "Womanliness as a Masquerade." 1929. *Formations of Fantasy.* Ed. Victor Burgin, James Donald, and Cora Kaplan. London: Methuen, 1986. 35–44.

Russo, Mary. "Female Grotesques: Carnival and Theory." *Feminist Studies/Critical Studies.* Ed. Teresa de Lauretis. Bloomington: Indiana UP, 1986. 213–29.

Simon, Kate. *Bronx Primitive: Portraits in a Childhood.* New York: Viking, 1982.

Smith, Sidonie. *A Poetics of Women's Autobiography: Marginality and the Fictions of Self-Representation.* Bloomington: Indiana UP, 1987.

Spelman, Elizabeth V. "Woman as Body: Ancient and Contemporary Views." *Feminist Studies* 8.1 (Spring 1982): 109–31.

Spender, Stephen. *World Within World: The Autobiography of Stephen Spender.* London: Hamish Hamilton, 1951.

Notes on Contributors

■

KATHLEEN ASHLEY is professor of English at the University of Southern Maine. She has edited *Victor Turner and the Construction of Cultural Criticism: Between Literature and Anthropology* and edited, with Pamela Sheingorn, *Interpreting Cultural Symbols: St. Anne and Late Medieval Society.* She is completing a book on medieval cultural performance.

BETTY BERGLAND is assistant professor of history at the University of Wisconsin, River Falls. Her book, *Reading the Autobiographical Subject: Gender and Ethnicity in the "New World" Patriarchy* is being considered for publication.

ANDREI CODRESCU is Writer-in-Residence at Louisiana State University, where he edits the journal *Exquisite Corpse.* He is author of numerous books of poetry and autobiographies as well as a recent book on the Romanian revolution. He is also a frequent commentator on National Public Radio.

MICHAEL M. J. FISCHER has taught at Chicago, Harvard, and Rice, and currently teaches at M.I.T. in the Program in Science, Technology and Society and the Department of Anthropology. He is author, with George Marcus, of *Anthropology as Cultural Critique* and, with Mehdi Abedi, of *Debating Muslims: Cultural Dialogues in Postmodernity and Tradition.*

LEIGH GILMORE is associate professor of English at the University of Southern Maine. She is the author of *Autobiographics: A Feminist Theory of Women's Self-Representation.* Currently, she is writing on obscenity law, modernism, and sexuality.

DAVID P. HANEY is associate professor of English at Auburn University in Auburn, Alabama. He is the author of *William Wordsworth and the Hermeneutics of Incarnation* as well as several articles on Wordsworth and Keats.

PAUL JAY is associate professor of English and graduate programs director at Loyola University of Chicago. He is the author of *Being in the Text: Self-Representation from Wordsworth to Roland Barthes.* He has published essays on critical theory, architecture, and photography, and has just completed a book on American cultural criticism and the problem of modernity.

SHIRLEY NEUMAN, professor and chair of English at the University of Alberta, has written numerous essays on autobiography, women's writing, and Canadian literature, as well as monographs on the autobiographies of W. B. Yeats and Gertrude Stein. She is editor of *Autobiography and Questions of Gender,* and editor, with Smaro Kamboureli, of *A Mazing Space: Writing Canadian Women Writing* and (with Glennis Stephenson) of *Reimagining Women: Representations of Women in Culture.*

CHRISTOPHER ORTIZ is a doctoral student in the critical studies program of the Department of Film and Television at the University of California, Los Angeles.

GERALD PETERS is associate professor of English at the University of Southern Maine. He has edited and translated *Diary of Anna Baerg 1916–1924,* a journal written in the Ukraine during the Russian revolution and civil war. He is the author of *The Mutilating God: Authorship and Authority in the Narrative of Conversion.*

SIDONIE SMITH is professor of English at Binghamton University. She is the author of *Where I'm Bound: Patterns of Slavery and Freedom in Black American Autobiography; A Poetics of Women's Autobiography: Marginality and the Fictions of Self-Representation; Subjectivity, Identity, and the Body: Women's Autobiographical Practices in the Twentieth Century;* author, with Julia Watson, of *De/Colonizing the Subject: The Politics of Gender in Women's Autobiography;* and, with Gisela Brinker-Gabler, of *Writing New Identities: Gender, Nationalism, and Immigration in New European Subjects.* She is currently completing a book on women's travel narratives.

KIRSTEN WASSON is assistant professor of English at Hobart and William Smith Colleges and is working on a book-length study of Mary Antin, Elizabeth Stern, and Anzia Yezierska. Her discussion of Antin is included in *The Anthology of American Jewish Women Writers.*

HERTHA D. WONG is associate professor of English at the University of California at Berkeley. She has published several articles on Native American literatures and is the author of *Sending My Heart Back Across the Years: Tradition and Innovation in Native American Autobiography.*